Using Internet Primary Sources to Teach Critical Thinking Skills in the Visual Arts

Pamela J. Eyerdam

LIBRARIES
U N L I M I T E D
A Member of the Greenwood Publishing Group

Westport, Connecticut • London

Copyright © 2003 Pamela J. Eyerdam
All Rights Reserved
Printed in the United States of America

LIBRARIES UNLIMITED
A Member of Greenwood Publishing Group, Inc.
88 Post Road West
Westport, CT 06881
1-800-225-5800
www.lu.com/tip

Library of Congress Cataloging-in-Publication Data

Eyerdam, Pamela J.
    Using Internet primary sources to teach critical thinking skills in the visual arts / by Pamela J. Eyerdam.
        p. cm. — (Libraries Unlimited professional guides in school librarianship series)
Includes bibliographical references and index.
    ISBN 0–313–31555–8 (pbk.)
    1. Art history—Study and teaching. 2. Art—Computer network resources. I. Title. II. Series.
    N380 .E95 2003
    707'.8'5—dc21
                                                2002007891

Contents

Part II
Applying Critical Thinking Skills
in the Visual Arts

Acknowledgments

I would like to thank several people who supported my efforts. Thanks to Gail Junion-Metz, who referred my name to the publisher. To my editors: Debby Adams, Erin Sprague, and Carmel Huestis. To several student assistants who helped me find and verify web sites: Julie Brown, Opapun (Lex) Pumacheep, Eranka Weerasuriya, and a special thanks to Tara Carr. To my colleagues at the library, who were understanding and supportive. To my family, last but not least to my husband Bryan, who was there when I needed him most and his constant support.

I would also like to acknowledge the Cleveland State University Library. The library provided me with the electronic access and online resources that I needed to produce this text. I also want to commend the online version of *The Grove Dictionary of Art* and many of the online exhibition galleries that museums have produced.

Frequently Referred to Web Sites of Associations, Art Education Programs, and Resources

Alacritude. *Elibrary: Research Without Legwork.*
http://ask.elibrary.com/index.asp
[5 October 2002]

American Libraries Association. *The Voice of America's Libraries: ALA: American Libraries Association Home Page.*
http://www.ala.org/
[5 October 2002]

Art Institute of Chicago. *Art Institute of Chicago: Student and Teacher Programs.*
http://www.artic.edu/aic/students/index.html

Art Institute of Chicago. *Art Institute of Chicago: Student and Teacher Programs: ArtAccess.*
http://www.artic.edu/artaccess/

Art Institute of Chicago. *Art Institute of Chicago: Student and Teacher Programs: Cleopatra: A Multimedia Guide to Art of the Ancient World.*
http://www.artic.edu/cleo/
[5 October 2002]

Art Teacher on the Net. *Art Teacher on the Net Home Page.*
http://www.artmuseums.com/
[5 October 2002]

Artcyclopedia. *Artcyclopedia: The Fine Art Search Engine.*
http://www.artcyclopedia.com/
[5 October 2002]

ArtEduTech, Mount Mary College, Milwaukee, WI. *ArtEduTech: Welcome to ArtEduTech!*
http://www.mtmary.edu/artedutech/artedutech
_MAIN.html
[5 October 2002]

Artists' Rights Society. *ARS: Artists' Rights Society Home Page.*
http://www.arsny.com/
[5 October 2002]

ArtMagick. *Welcome to ArtMagick.*
http://www.artmagick.com/
[5 October 2002]

ArtsConnectEd. *ArtsConnectEd: Walker Art Center: Minneapolis Institute of Arts.*
http://www.artsconnected.org/
[5 October 2002]

Association for the Advancement of Arts Education. *Association for the Advancement of Arts Education Home Page.*
http://www.aaae.org/
[5 October 2002]

Cleveland Museum of Art. *Cleveland Museum of Art: Explore: Education and Research: For Schools and Teachers: Teachers Resource Center.*
http://www.clevelandart.org/educatn/trc-news
/index.html
[5 October 2002]

Columbia Electronic Encyclopedia (1994, 2000). *Infoplease.com: All the Information You Need.*
http://www.infoplease.com/
[5 October 2002]

Crayola. *Crayola: Educators.*
http://www.crayola.com/educators/
[5 October 2002]

Delahunt, Michael. *ArtLex Art Dictionary.*
http://www.artlex.com/
[5 October 2002]

Detroit Institute of Arts, Detroit, MI. *Detroit Institute of Arts: Education: Lesson Plans.*
http://www.dia.org/education/lesson.html
[5 October 2002]

Elliot, Roger. *Original ArtSchool OnLine.*
http://www.angelfire.com/ar/rogerart/
[5 October 2002]

Emory University, Atlanta, GA. *Michael C. Carlos Museum of Emory University: Programs for Schools and Teachers: Odyssey Online.*
http://carlos.emory.edu/ODYSSEY/MidElem _Home.html
[15 October 2002]

ERIC Clearinghouse on Information & Technology. *AskERIC: Lesson Plans: Arts.*
http://www.askeric.org/cgi-bin/lessons.cgi/Arts
[5 October 2002]

Fleischer Museum of American and Russian Impressionism, Scottsdale, Arizona. *Welcome to the Fleischer Museum.*
http://www.fleischer.org/intro.html
[5 October 2002]

Georgia O'Keeffe Museum, Santa Fe, NM. *Georgia O'Keeffe Museum: Education and Programs.*
http://www.okeeffemuseum.org/programs/index.html
[5 October 2002]

Gerten-Jackson, Carol. *CGFA: A Virtual Art Museum: Alphabetical Index.*
http://sunsite.dk/cgfa/fineart.htm
[5 October 2002]

J. Paul Getty Trust. *ArtsEdNet: The Getty's Art Education Web Site Home Page.*
http://www.getty.edu/artsednet/
[5 October 2002]

Harden Mark. *Artchive.*
http://www.artchive.com/ftp_site.htm
[5 October 2002]

Hood Museum of Art. Dartmouth College, Hanover, NH. *Hood Museum of Art: Faculty and Student Resources.*
http://www.dartmouth.edu/~hood/cap /facultystudentre.html
[5 October 2002]

Idaho 4-H, University of Idaho. *Kidspace Art.*
http://www.ets.uidaho.edu/4-H/kidspace/
[5 October 2002]

Interactive Learning Paradigms Inc. *ArtSource: Table of Contents.*
http://www.ilpi.com/artsource/welcome.html#toc
[5 October 2002]

Kelsey Museum of Archeology, University of Michigan, Ann Arbor, MI. *Kelsey Museum of Archeology: Educational Programs.*
http://www.lsa.umich.edu/kelsey/educational.html
[5 October 2002]

Kennedy Center. *Kennedy Center ArtsEdge.*
http://artsedge.kennedy-center.org/
[5 October 2002]

Kimbell Art Museum, Fort Worth, TX. *Kimbell Art Museum: Education and Events: Programs for Educators and School Groups.*
http://www.kimbellart.org/education/educators.cfm ?id=18
[5 October 2002]

Knight, Kevin. *Catholic Encyclopedia Online Edition (2002).*
http://www.newadvent.org/cathen/
[5 October 2002]

Krannert Art Museum, University of Illinois at Urbana-Champaign. *Krannert Art Museum and Kinkead Pavilion: Education and Resources.*
http://www.art.uiuc.edu/galleries/kam/index.html
[5 October 2002]

Kren, Emil and Daniel Marx. *Web Gallery of Art: Introduction.*
http://gallery.euroweb.hu/welcome.html (no frames)
http://gallery.euroweb.hu/index1.html (frames)
http://www.kfki.hu/~arthp/index1.html (mirror site —frames)
[5 October 2002]

Library of Congress. *The Learning Page: Lesson Plans: Using Primary Sources in the Classroom.*
http://memory.loc.gov/ammem/ndlpedu/lessons /primary.html
[5 October 2002]

Macmillan Publishers Limited. *The Grove Dictionary of Art Online: Free Trials and Sample Searches.*
http://www.grovereference.com/TDA/online/freetrials.htm
[5 October 2002]

Merriam-Webster, Inc. *Merriam-Webster Online: The Language Center.*
http://www.m-w.com/netdict.htm
[5 October 2002]

Metropolitan Museum of Art, New York. *Metropolitan Museum of Art: Educational Resources.*
http://www.metmuseum.org/education/index.asp
[5 October 2002]

Minneapolis Institute of Arts, MN. *Minneapolis Institute of Arts: Education: Interactive Programs for Teachers & Students.*
http://www.artsmia.org/interactive-media/teachers-students.cfm
[5 October 2002]

Musée d'Orsay, Paris. *Musée d'Orsay: Students/ Education: Online Resources.*
http://www.musee-orsay.fr:8081/ORSAY/orsaygb/PROGRAM.NSF/6757ef6dee474116802563cd004f90ca/1f3324d799074722c1256ba40046bb7f?OpenDocument
[5 October 2002]

El Museo del Barrio, New York, NY. *El Museo del Barrio: Educational Programs.*
http://www.elmuseo.org/edu.html
[15 October 2002]

Museum of Antiquities, University of Saskatchewan. *Museum of Antiquities: Educational Programming and Summer Children's Workshops.*
http://www.usask.ca/antiquities/Educational_Programming.html
[15 October 2002]

Museum of Fine Arts, Boston. *Museum of Fine Arts, Boston: Museum Learning and Public Programs: Teachers.*
http://www.mfa.org/education/teachersandstudents.htm
[15 October 2002]

Museum of Spanish Colonial Arts, Santa Fe, NM. *Museum of Spanish Colonial Art: Education Programs of the Museum of Spanish Colonial Art.*
http://www.spanishcolonial.org/schedule.shtml
[15 October 2002]

MuseumSpot. *MuseumSpot Home Page.*
http://www.museumspot.com/
[5 October 2002]

National Art Education Association. *NAEA: National Art Education Association Home Page.*
http://www.naea-reston.org/
[5 October 2002]

National Gallery of Art, Washington, D.C. *National Gallery of Art: Education.*
http://www.nga.gov/education/education.htm
[5 October 2002]

National Museum of Women in the Arts: Resources for Educators.
http://www.nmwa.org/resources/edu_workshop.asp
[28 September 2002]

National PTA. *National PTA Home Page.*
http://www.pta.org/index.asp
[5 October 2002]

North Carolina Museum of Art Foundation, Raleigh, NC. *North Carolina Museum of Art: Education and Museum Services: Teacher Resources.*
http://ncartmuseum.org/education/teacher.shtml
[5 October 2002]

Olga's Gallery. *Olga's Gallery Home Page.*
http://www.abcgallery.com/
[5 October 2002]

Pacific Bell. *Eyes on Art.*
http://www.kn.pacbell.com/wired/art2/index.html
[5 October 2002]

Pacific Bell. *Eyes on Art: ArtSpeak 101.*
http://www.kn.pacbell.com/wired/art2/artspeak/artspeak.html

Pacific Bell. *Eyes on Art: ArtSpeak 101: Visual Glossary: Defining the Elements of Artistic Design.*
http://www.kn.pacbell.com/wired/art2/artspeak/visual_terms.html
[5 October 2002]

Pacific Bell. *Eyes on Art: No Fear o' Eras*
http://www.kn.pacbell.com/wired/art2/eras/index.html
[5 October 2002]

Philadelphia Museum of Art, Philadelphia, PA. *Philadelphia Museum of Art: Education: Teaching Resources.*
http://www.philamuseum.org/education/resources.shtml
[5 October 2002]

Pioch, Nicolas. *WebMuseum, Paris: Famous Artworks Exhibition.*
http://www.ibiblio.org/wm/paint/
[5 October 2002]

Portland Museum of Art, Portland, ME. *Portland Museum of Art: Education Programs.*
http://www.portlandmuseum.org/educ.html
[5 October 2002]

Roland, Craig. University of Florida, Gainesville, FL. *@rt room Home Page.*
http://www.arts.ufl.edu/art/rt_room/
[5 October 2002]

San Francisco Museum of Modern Art, CA. *San Francisco Museum of Modern Art: Education: e.school: Content and Curriculum.*
http://www.sfmoma.org/eschool/curriculum.html
[5 October 2002]

Sanford. *Educational Web Adventures.*
http://www.sanford-artedventures.com/
[5 October 2002]

Smithsonian Institution. *National Museum of African Art: Education Programs.*
http://www.nmafa.si.edu/educ/educprog.htm
[5 October 2002]

Smithsonian Institution. *Smithsonian American Art Museum: Education.*
http://nmaa-ryder.si.edu/education/main.html
[5 October 2002]

Smithsonian Institution. *Smithsonian Magazine: Explore.*
http://www.smithsonianmag.com/smithsonian/
[5 October 2002]

Tate Gallery, London. *Tate: E-Learning.*
http://www.tate.org.uk/elearning/default.htm
[5 October 2002]

Tigertail Associates. *Tigertail Virtual Art Museum.*
http://tvm.tigtail.org/TVM/M_View/E/Efp.html
[5 October 2002]

University of Michigan School of Art and Design, Ann Arbor, MI. *Mother of All Art and Art History Links.*
http://www.art-design.umich.edu/mother/
[5 October 2002]

University of Pennsylvania Museum of Archaeology and Anthropology, Philadelphia, PA. *University of Pennsylvania Museum of Archaeology and Anthropology: Educational Services.*
http://www.upenn.edu/museum/PublicServices/edservices.html
[5 October 2002]

University of Rochester Department of Art and Art History, Rochester, NY. *Tools and Resources Writing Guide.*
http://www.rochester.edu/college/AAH/tools/writingguide.htm
[5 October 2002]

Utah Museum of Fine Arts, Salt Lake City, UT. *Utah Museum of Fine Arts: Educational Services.*
http://www.utah.edu/umfa/edprograms.html
[5 October 2002]

VSA arts. *VSA (Very Special Arts for People with Disabilities) Arts Home Page.*
http://www.vsarts.org/
[5 October 2002]

Witcombe, Chris. *Art History Resources on the Web.*
http://witcombe.sbc.edu/ARTHLinks.html
[5 October 2002]

World Wide Arts Resources Corp. *World Wide Art Resources Home Page.*
http://wwar.com/
[5 October 2002]

Xrefer. *Xrefer, The Web's Reference Engine.*
http://www.xrefer.com/
[5 October 2002]

Young Audiences, Inc. *Young Audiences: A Bright Idea in Education Home Page.*
http://www.youngaudiences.org/
[5 October 2002]

Introduction

One may wonder why critical thinking skills need to be developed for the subject of the visual arts. Students often feel that they have to be a talented artist in order to take art classes. The goal of modern art education encompasses a different approach to teaching art. Based on the program of Discipline-Based Art Education (DBAE), a more comprehensive approach includes learning the creative process, art history, criticism, and aesthetics. All these elements involve teaching students how to think in order to solve problems. This is a lifelong skill that needs to be developed and that the visual arts can foster. Each of us has a creative side that needs to be nurtured and appreciated. Not everyone is born with a natural artistic talent, but with proper instruction, one can learn, appreciate, and disseminate information through the creative process.

Since the 1980s, it has become the goal of art educators to develop and provide stimulating multimedia instructional materials to enhance learning. The Internet is the latest development that exceeds the boundaries of access, time, space, and language. Online image galleries, museums, lesson plans, publications, dictionaries, and encyclopedias are now available from anywhere in the world through the Internet. Teachers, librarians, and students can have these resources at their fingertips in minutes, if not seconds.

This text focuses mainly on Western art history and particularly painting. There are examples of other media as well, such as sculpture, drawings, prints, and architecture. Because of the comprehensive nature of art history, it was difficult to include non-Western examples. The last chapter introduces the importance of including diverse subjects to students in an art lesson.

The first chapter provides a brief history of art education. Chapter 2 reviews design elements and principles and ways to develop critical thinking skills with art history, criticism, and aesthetics. Chapter 3 discusses the Internet as a primary source for the visual arts and explains how to evaluate web sites. It also includes technical information about how to make the Internet work for you and your students. Finally, the rest of the chapters are designed to help you and your students understand elements and principles of design using Internet sites and then to apply those elements and principles to the chronological study of art history. The "Site Summary" sections briefly explain time periods and styles, introduce artists, and pose intriguing questions based on the cited Internet web sites. Some questions refer to more than one web site. Students will learn how to minimize a screen to view images alternately and compare images. Identifying credible and interesting web sites is time consuming but worth the effort in order to enhance learning using an alternate medium such as the Internet.

This book is a guide to those web sites that offer great information about the visual arts and art history. It can be used as a web-based course, a tutorial, or extra credit, or it can supplement a traditional classroom format. Most important, it can introduce you and your students to the different ideas, societies, religions, histories, and cultures that can be experienced through the understanding and appreciation of the visual arts.

PART I

History, Critical Thinking, and Using the Internet

CHAPTER 1

A Brief History of the Developments in Art Education

Perhaps the earliest known form of art instruction appeared on the walls of ancient caves. Humans taught one another the simple techniques of drawing as an act of performing rituals and preserving spirituality. Other crafts were created for ritual purposes as well as functionality. Often they would teach these crafts to other family members in order to carry on traditions. Eventually, master craftsmen, who taught those outside the family unit, developed schools. This is evidenced by the techniques or styles associated with a master and seen on fragments traced from Egyptian workshops of the Amarna period (fourteenth century B.C.) and from the classical Greek workshops of the fifth and fourth centuries B.C.

By the early medieval period beginning in the eighth century A.D., formal training known as the guild system was developed. The guild system was a form of apprenticeship in which a master craftsman trained a young student for several years. The guild wardens evaluated the student's work, and, if they approved it, the student advanced to journeyman level. A journeyman worked in the field as a form of internship. Again, after a period of time, the journeyman submitted his work (this time called a "masterpiece") to the guild members for appraisal. If they accepted it, he was qualified as a master and was allowed to set up a shop of his own. The only other recognized formal training was that received in the workshops of the monasteries.

The guild system was a social structure created to recognize craftsmen and create a level of professionalism, similar to that of our modern-day unions. The Renaissance of the fifteenth century created a new status for artists. An artist with formal training beyond the elements of drawing, geometry, and proportion attained a higher position in society. Those who had knowledge of the classics, literature, music, science, and anatomy were considered more aesthetically trained and were recognized as artists. The Medici family was instrumental in attracting artists to teach others from their private collection of classical art.

By the sixteenth century, this concept developed into what is known as the art academy. The academy formulated an actual curriculum that consisted of lectures about culture and aesthetics and copying from the masters. The Royal Academy of Painting and Sculpture was established in Paris in 1648 and became a national institution. Again, the curriculum focused on drawing and lectures, and students studied from printed sources available in the reference library. Drawing was the foundation for learning, and aspects of painting and sculpting were controlled and approved according to the academy's rules. The academy structure was not only rigorous but also strict and elite. This elitism excluded women from attending the academy, with few exceptions. By the eighteenth century, the guild system had, for the most part, disappeared, and academies were flourishing. Students who wanted to be trained but were rejected from the academy sought out individual artists. These artists charged a fee, included no formal curriculum, had the students copy from their work, and then critiqued the students' work. This arrangement gave women an opportunity to receive artistic training. Classes consisted of copying drawings and paintings of the masters. An important transition occurred during the eighteenth century, when artists reacted against the academy. This became particularly evident during the Romantic era, when artists preferred a more natural and realistic depiction of landscapes and genre scenes. By the mid–nineteenth century, some academies were incorporating landscape classes while still adhering to their formal curriculum. Academies also began to admit women into segregated classes, yet they were still excluded from attending life-drawing sessions.

By the late nineteenth century, other developments in art education included the incorporation of psychological studies related to art. Several psychologists recognized that art and expression are important to a child's development. James Sully of London's University College and other psychologists recognized that the type of drawings a child produced at different ages indicated the child's development. There was a connection between their drawings and their inner feelings that presented an opportunity to teach and nurture creativity and emotional development. Art academies began to expand their programs to include professional training for art educators. Walter Smith, founder of the first professional training academy for art educators in Massachusetts, established his curriculum during the 1870s.

By the first quarter of the twentieth century, John Dewey and other educators had introduced the idea of incorporating play and creativity into the classroom to stimulate learning. Thus, teachers could use art in the curriculum as an important tool to develop a child's creative and critical thinking skills. They encouraged students to draw, learn design principles, appreciate natural elements, and study color. Another educator, Arthur Wesley Dow from Columbia University, taught a more systematic approach to design principles. The concepts of composition, line, color, and shape helped students not only to create but also to understand how these elements are important to the process of creation. This approach became the premise of the art curriculum of appreciation, aesthetics, and criticism. The maturation of twentieth-century modern art was nurtured by these new curriculum concepts. Teaching students how to appreciate works of art and artifacts by using critical thinking skills and aesthetics became the trademark for modern art education. When presented in the classroom, a discussion and a written analysis reinforced these aesthetic components and other social and moral values associated with artwork. However, the depression of 1929 and the following years prevented most schools from introducing an art curriculum. Not many people could afford to become teachers, much less art teachers, during the depression. Depression-era programs of the 1930s helped boost the economy and encouraged people to become teachers. Teacher certification became a four-year program, and art educators, such as Viktor Lowenfeld and Victor D'Amico, introduced ideas that encouraged children to express themselves freely (Corwin 2001, 2). D'Amico was instrumental to the movement and educated the public about modern art. He worked with the New York Museum of Modern Art and other art organizations that denounced politicians who attacked and tried to ban the teaching of modern art in schools. D'Amico felt that modern abstract art promoted creativity, which is vital for a healthy, progressive society. Another pioneer, Edwin Ziegfeld, conducted studies to see whether an art program in schools would enhance the quality of life. Ziegfeld, who taught regularly in schools, felt that art should be part of daily life and that it was not just for the social or intellectual elite. He believed that art education could help build a strong and healthy democratic society.

During the 1940s and 1950s, several psychologists felt that art could teach students about social and moral issues. The United States opened its doors to scholars, psychologists, and artists who fled the Nazis in Europe during and after World War II. Many of them joined American universities and developed advanced art programs such as the one Lowenfeld established at Pennsylvania State University. Lowenfeld believed that the goal of art education was "not the art itself, or the aesthetic product, or the aesthetic experience, but rather the child who grows up more creatively and sensitively and applies his experience in the arts to whatever life situations may be applicable" (Michael 1982). Lowenfeld trained art teachers to teach social and moral issues through the visual arts. Others scholars attempted to explain a child's development from a psychological perspective. The British scholar Herbert Read felt that creativity could be a vehicle to form international unity and promote peace and harmony among cultures. Rudolf Arnheim applied theories of cognitive psychology to explain the creative process. Arnheim described how the mind visually organizes things that one sees according to what one perceives. In 1947 the National Art Education Association (NAEA) was established by merging four regional art education associations and became the largest such professional association in the United States. The NAEA's mission is "to advance art education through professional development, service, advancement of knowledge, and leadership. To that end, the Association will: promote quality instruction in visual arts education conducted by certified teachers of art; encourage research in art education; hold public discussions; sponsor institutes, conferences, and programs; publish articles, reports, and surveys; and work with other related agencies in support of visual arts education" (Corwin 2001, ii).

By the late 1950s and early 1960s, the arts curriculum had become too generalized and stagnant due to insufficient time for instruction and a shortage of stimulating instructional materials. Not until the 1980s did audiovisual materials become a vital means of stimulating instruction and learning. Teachers introduced their students to art, literature, and the sciences by using films, videos, posters, slides, television, and sound recordings. Later in the 1980s, the personal computer became another source to enrich learning. During the 1990s, the library media center became a resource center equipped with computers that offered Internet access to teachers and students. The Internet's value has earned it a valid place within the classroom for instructional purposes. Internet access is no longer limited to the school library media center but is now incorporated into classrooms themselves. The Internet is becoming a common instructional tool, but like any tool, one needs to learn how to use it properly. This is the goal of web-based learning for the twenty-first century.

A 1961 report, *Art Education in the Secondary School,* by the National Association of Secondary Principals, examined the role of visual arts education in schools. The association recognized the need to improve arts education because it can teach values and aesthetics and improve one's quality of life. The curriculum should be designed for students who vary in abilities, interests, and level of curiosity. Educator Jerome Bruner established a curriculum that promoted the development of critical thinking skills in a given subject. This inspired Manuel Barkan of Ohio State University to develop a curriculum that teaches basic design principles in studio classes, promoting a discussion that critiques a work of art and then points out elements to assess and appreciate that work. Schools that were identified as "culturally disadvantaged" received federal funds during the Johnson and Nixon administrations of the late 1960s and early 1970s. The money was used to develop art programs that promoted cultural diversity, developed communication and critical thinking skills, and gave children a learning option that was not limited to the traditional classroom setting. Federal money also supported programs that took children to visit various art museums and galleries and conducted research to design new instructional materials that included multimedia materials. But cohesiveness was lacking between these efforts that would establish a national standard. There was a need to restructure the general education curriculum that would focus on a comprehensive approach to art. The National Art Education Association endorsed ideas for a written art curriculum that would provide teacher training, develop and acquire instructional materials, create a budget, and consider other alternatives to assist art teachers.

State departments of education and local school districts decide how a subject is taught in the classroom. In the mid-1980s, Dwaine Greer wrote an article describing a comprehensive approach to art that he termed "discipline-based art education" (DBAE). Although the concept was not new, his approach was. DBAE would include advanced training for teachers and access to a variety of curriculum resources, provide opportunities for funding, and create networks for teachers to expand and share ideas on a national level. One of the major resources that developed in the early 1980s was the Getty Center for Education in the Arts (now called the Getty Education Institute for the Arts). Entrepreneur J. Paul Getty set up a trust program in California that supported and funded efforts to develop and teach comprehensive approaches to art.

The Getty Education Institute for the Arts has formed partnerships with scholars, schools, teachers, professional organizations, government (federal, state, regional, and local), commercial ventures, and other funding opportunities to create a network of support for arts education. Their commitment is "to sustain a discipline-based approach, supported by the movement to create national standards for art education" (J. Paul Getty Trust 2001, 16). The program is primarily for grades K–12 but also promotes lifelong learning skills that can be utilized in adult education as well. DBAE is based on the foundation of four disciplines: creating art, art criticism, art history, and aesthetics.

- **Creating Art:** This involves learning, understanding, and enjoying the process of creation, working with specific tools, and learning techniques of the medium.

- **Art Criticism:** Understanding the elements of design, learning how to describe objects, and developing thinking skills that can apply different aspects of life to an object will help one to develop constructive criticism skills.

- **Art History:** Acquiring knowledge about an object placed in its context of history, culture, place, and style will frame a better understanding of why such a piece was made and what its function and purpose are.

- **Aesthetics:** An understanding of why viewers consider a piece beautiful, fascinating, curious, and intriguing is important.

These four disciplines can assist us in learning about each other so we can live, respect, and appreciate one another despite our differences. The classroom can set the stage for discussion, writing, and conducting research. The program consists of a written art curriculum, a unit of lesson plans, classes taught by certified art teachers, access to school- and community-based art programs, an assessment study report, the integration of art into other subject areas, an art program designed for all students, support for the program by the appropriate school boards and education administrators, and the use of technology and other types of multimedia that enhance learning options and promote creativity.

Since then, other core organizations have lobbied for arts education to become a central part of the general education program. In 1988 the National Endowment for the Arts (NEA) issued a report titled *Towards Civilization: A Report on Arts Education,* which states that fostering creativity and critical thinking skills will produce students who will be assets to society. The United States Congress and former President Clinton adopted recommendations from the report *Goals 2000: Educate America Act* that would create standards for teaching art as a core subject. This mandate became federal law and stimulated education reform for the twenty-first century. Such standards will provide all students the opportunity to a high-quality education in the arts. This legislation recognizes the need for humans to connect with one another in a way that transcends traditional learning methods. Arts education can be an element to enhance interaction in various cultures, societies, genders, and ages.

In 1994, a report titled *National Standards for Arts Education: What Every Young American Should Know and Be Able to Do in the Arts* introduced curriculum guidelines to reform and improve arts education in the United States. The goal was to set standards that all fifty states would follow. Opponents of such a program argued that too much time would be spent on "analyzing and talking about art" rather than producing it. The Getty Education Institute became the leader in promoting DBAE. Today the four basic foundations of DBAE (art making, art criticism, art history, and aesthetics) are taught in most schools across the country. Students improve their critical thinking and written- and spoken-language skills by simply analyzing and communicating about what they see in an artwork. The Internet is a resource for teaching art in new ways that reach out globally. Its potential grows daily, and teachers are able to communicate easily with each other and share ideas. Any student can "visit" a museum collection located in another country. The knowledge they gain about the world and other cultures is a tremendous asset. Most of all, learning to value these things makes their lives more pleasurable.

Suggested Web Sites About Art Education and DBAE

J. Paul Getty Trust. *ArtsEdNet: The Getty's Art Education Web Site: Explore Art: Visitor Guide: Learning and Teaching for Teachers.*
http://www.getty.edu/visit/learning/teachers.html
[5 October 2002]

J. Paul Getty Trust. *ArtsEdNet: The Getty's Art Education Web Site Home.*
http://www.getty.edu/artsednet/
[5 October 2002]

Kennedy Center. *Kennedy Center ArtsEdge: Curriculum WebLinks: Visual Arts.*
http://artsedge.kennedy-center.org/teaching_materials/weblinks/weblinks.cfm?subject_id=VIA
[5 October 2002]

Kennedy Center. *Kennedy Center ArtsEdge: Professional Resources: Standards and Exemplars: National Standards for Arts Education.*
http://artsedge.kennedy-center.org/professional_resources/standards/nat_standards_main.html
[5 October 2002]

National PTA. *National PTA Arts in Education Resource Libraries.*
http://www.pta.org/programs/artslibr.htm
[5 October 2002]

Newquist, Colleen and Education World. *Education World: The Educator's Best Friend: Picture This: Art Every Day!: Enrich Learning with Discipline-Based Art Education.*
http://www.education-world.com/a_lesson/lesson002.shtml
[5 October 2002]

Suggested Web Sites for Teacher Resources and Lesson Plans

Art Teacher on the Net. *Art Teacher on the Net Home Page.*
http://www.artmuseums.com/
[5 October 2002]

Australian National University, Canberra, Australia. *ArtServe. Welcome to ArtServe: Art & Architecture Mainly from the Mediterranean Basin and Japan.*
http://www.anu.edu.au/
[5 October 2002]

ERIC Clearinghouse on Information & Technology. *AskERIC: Lesson Plans: Arts: Art History: How to Recognize a Painting by Frida Kahlo.*
http://www.askeric.org/Virtual/Lessons/Arts/Art_History/ARH0009.html
[5 October 2002]

ERIC Clearinghouse on Information & Technology. *AskERIC: Lesson Plans: Arts: Arts Lesson Plans: What Did They Say? Interpretation of Criticism.*
http://www.askeric.org/cgi-bin/printlessons.cgi/Virtual/Lessons/Arts/ART0002.html
[5 October 2002]

Lewestown Publishers. *Art and Education Gallery: Art & Education Links.*
http://www.lewestown.com/art_education/
[5 October 2002]

Morton, J. L. *Color Matters.*
http://www.colormatters.com/entercolormatters.html
[5 October 2002]

National Art Education Association. *NAEA: National Art Education Association: Charter Schools.*
http://www.nea.org/charter/
[5 October 2002]

National Art Education Association. *NAEA: National Art Education Association Home Page.*
http://www.naea-reston.org/
[5 October 2002]

Pacific Bell. *Eyes on Art.*
http://www.kn.pacbell.com/wired/art2/index.html
[5 October 2002]

Roland, Craig. University of Florida, Gainesville, FL. *@rt room Home Page.*
http://www.arts.ufl.edu/art/rt_room/resources.html
[5 October 2002]

Sanford. *Educational Web Adventures.*
http://www.sanford-artedventures.com/
[5 October 2002]

VSA arts. *VSA arts: Value of the Arts to People with Disabilities.*
http://www.vsarts.org/bestpractices/dag/valueofarts.html
[5 October 2002]

Young Audiences, Inc. *Young Audiences: A Bright Idea in Education Home Page.*
http://www.youngaudiences.org/
[5 October 2002]

References

Corwin, Sylvia K., ed. 2001. *Explore the Legends: Guideposts to the Future.* Reston, VA: National Art Education Association.

J. Paul Getty Trust. ArtsEdNet: The Getty Art Education Web Site Home Page. http://www.getty.edu/artsednet/ [17 November 2001].

Michael, J. A. 1982. *The Lowenfeld Lectures.* University Park: Pennsylvania State University Press.

CHAPTER 2

Developing Critical Thinking Skills in the Visual Arts

In 1968, the National Art Education Association (NAEA) published its philosophy of a subject-centered focus for art education in "The Essentials of a Quality School Art Program." Its primary goals were the following:

- Teaching art production

- Teaching art history

- Teaching art appreciation

These goals integrated production (studio art classes) with aesthetics, criticism, and art history. The NAEA-required art courses were to be taught by certified art teachers. Art classes were to be integrated into the general curriculum for elementary, middle, junior, and senior high schools. To graduate from high school, a student would have to complete a one-year visual arts course that included the study of aesthetics, art history, and criticism. General education requirements for a university or college are that students will take a one-year credit class in the visual arts (Parks 1994, 60). In 1985, the Getty Center for Education in the Arts released its report, "Beyond Creating: The Place for Art in America's Schools." This report recognized that an art curriculum should be a fundamental subject taught in schools. It served as an impetus to devise a curriculum that is rich in content and established standards for visual arts education in the United States. Students would learn about aesthetics and art history and develop critical thinking skills from such an art curriculum. By developing critical thinking skills in the visual arts, students will be able to consider problems more objectively, make better decisions, become sensitive and thoughtful, and broaden their creativeness for individual satisfaction.

Critical thinking requires a series of thought processes. One needs to understand how to ask relevant questions. By asking a series of questions, one gathers information about a topic in order to make a logical deduction. But not all inquiries result in cut-and-dried answers, especially when analyzing objects or concepts in the visual arts. Critical thinking is as abstract and conceptual as art itself can be. It is a deductive (analytic) and creative (synthetic) process that our minds undertake when we look at something. It is a skill that can be refined once one learns some design basics, history, aesthetics, and formal analysis methods for criticism. A whole new world of information opens up to the person who develops these skills, a world that one appreciates and cherishes once one learns how to look.

A crucial part in the critical thinking process is the ability to be open to other points of view. Objects and ideas are relative in nature, time, place, and situation. To exchange ideas people need to be able to discuss a topic reasonably. As you analyze an object, you have to stop, look, read, listen, and respect others' opinions. We often associate critical thinking with being negative, and most dictionaries define "critical" as "tending to find fault." Such cynicism and negativity makes students avoid learning how to think critically (Alexander 1999). The teacher is an important facilitator in students' active discussions. To promote critical thinking, sometimes the teacher has to step back and let the students engage in an exchange of ideas. The teacher has to be aware of cues that signal the need for an intervention and be prepared with possible answers or know how to pose additional probing questions. The idea is to promote a healthy and constructive discussion among the students when analyzing an art piece. By developing cognitive skills, the students learn to draw upon their own ideas as they experience the world around them. Teachers can help accomplish this by encouraging students to communicate, use their imagination, be sensitive to social issues, use good judgment, and develop perceptual awareness. Teachers should be aware that students may not initially interpret works of art in the same way that they themselves do. To promote critical thinking, teachers should not allow their own art historical knowledge about a piece to influence the students' discussion (Leshnoff 1995). Right or wrong, students will eventually learn how to find and understand ideas if they apply these skills themselves rather than being corrected during the process.

Diversity is another issue that teachers have to recognize and respect. Because of their different social, religious, political, ethical, and ethnic backgrounds, people have a variety of interpretations when discussing an idea or looking at something. We each have different ways of knowing, seeing, and learning about things. Art can help students function in cultures that are diverse and heavily dependent upon visual stimuli. Art teachers can nurture "critical thinking as a seedbed for diversity appreciation and multicultural understanding" (Stout 1997). This form of visual literacy affects "behavior and the psychological well-being of students, nurturing such traits as self-esteem, patience, and rigor" (J. Paul Getty Trust 2002).

Arts education can incorporate the following steps to develop critical thinking skills:

- State the problem.

- Formulate a hypothesis to solve the problem.

- Infer a conclusion from the hypothesis.

- Evaluate the strength of the conclusion.

Stating the problem gives students a clear understanding of expectations. Because students are expected to look, study, reflect, and interpret ideas and objects, they have to understand the purpose of analyzing a problem. Formulating a hypothesis states a theory about how to address the problem in order to attain or infer a conclusion or solution. Evaluating the strength of the conclusion draws upon the critical thinking process. Students learn how to look at things in a broader realm and then draw conclusions or make decisions. They need to ask whether the information is reliable and applicable within its context (White 2001). Doing these things also makes them aware of the possibility of multiple and equally valid interpretations.

It is not enough just to look at something; by developing cognitive skills, students learn to see and understand various aspects of an object. Art and artifacts offer insight about both past and present cultures. Our society is diverse, and in order to live harmoniously within such a community, certain relationships have to develop. The visual arts can cultivate this relationship within communities. It is important to develop respect for individuality, culture, and nature. Perception sensitizes students to multicultural differences and broadens their knowledge of the world in which we live. The ability to perceive is fundamental to art expression and appreciation. Aesthetics is the study of intellectual, philosophical, natural, and visual elements of beauty and taste. Because beauty and taste are relative concepts, learning about content, form, techniques, and purpose is crucial to the critical thinking process.

The age-old question "what is art?" can be one of aesthetics. People look at art in a variety of ways; some consider it a form of expression, a way to communicate emotion, the organization of formal properties, or the process of creation and its effect; sometimes people consider its status in society and the experience one has of an object or moment. There is also the question of objectivity and subjectivity and whether "beauty is in the eye of the beholder." This is an issue that scholars and philosophers have contemplated. Aesthetics can encompass ethics, which gives students an opportunity for moral debate. Students need to realize the power images can have but should not confuse one's control over it with censorship. Some of the ethical issues involving images that students should consider are "defamation, sensationalism, coercion, omission, offensiveness, and intrusion" (Green 2000). Students need to learn how to look at all images with a critical eye by developing their understanding, a means of analysis, and an evaluative process.

The aesthetic study of works of art may include general criteria for judging art, such as design, color, or composition. A comparative judgment does not restrict itself to a set of rules, and moral judgment analyzes defects in virtue. People base their opinions on certain aesthetic elements when evaluating a work of art. For example, a student who looks at an abstract painting of trees can possibly formulate other ideas about what they are looking at. Because of its abstract form and unnatural color, it may actually trigger conceptual ideas that go beyond the recognition that they are looking at trees. A discussion about what students think is beautiful when looking at an object will determine whether it has a bearing upon their lives. In other words, students will often comment about things they like to look at and are familiar with. This is why they find it easy to give reasons why they like it. But if you have them look at something unpleasant and unfamiliar, they often cannot give a reason or at least a good reason why they may not like something. Life experiences will often give relevance to why we may not like something. Students may not have had to deal with an unpleasant situation yet in order to form an opinion about something. Things we like are easy to form an opinion about; it is the unpleasant situations that make it harder to deal with. We all learn by experiences as we age; life itself teaches us many things. There can be questions about representation (realism versus conceptualism) or avant-garde deviations—those that break from tradition. Aesthetically, what is the significance of an original piece of art when a forgery is an exact duplicate? Are aesthetics compromised when artworks are repaired or archeological sites renovated? These are questions that stimulate thought and self-realization when analyzing works of art based on aesthetics.

A student learns how to look by understanding the elements and principles of design. These basic elements are color, line, space, shape, composition, texture, balance, proportion, perspective, medium, and technique. There is also the historical context, that is, how and why the artist created a piece within the context of a particular time period. The study of iconography and symbolism can give additional meaning to an artwork. Personal reaction depends on one's family background, religion, politics, past experiences, gender, social status, education, and so on. There is more to the visual arts than just the sense of seeing. The images in our mind are made in conjunction with our other senses. A thought, smell, emotion, sound, or feel of something will create images based on what we know. These are associations that our brain synthesizes to create an image in our mind. Our intellect often sharpens our senses to compensate for a sense that we lose. Helen Keller, Milton, and Homer were all blind, and they all saw the world quite differently because they used their imagination and other senses. Some people afflicted with autism may exhibit a unique talent or response when they are confronted with a certain stimulus that leaves others unaffected. We create a broader knowledge base of understanding when we focus on details. A minute detail can make a profound difference when we look at something. Teachers can teach students to be aware of and appreciate such details. For example, our looking at a leaf that has fallen from a tree in late October can trigger several images in our mind. The colors of the leaf will associate for us the autumn season and the coming of winter. Later on, memories of Halloween and Thanksgiving may be triggered. The smell of burning leaves and wet grass comes to mind. We may even seem to feel a brisk wind and a chill. All these images can be triggered simply by looking at the details of a leaf. This can be a very exciting experience for students to master and continue throughout life. Combining our outer physical world with our inner self often gives students a satisfying sense of being. This is yet another valuable result of teaching the visual arts and other forms of art to students.

Teaching elements and principles of design frames how one looks at a piece of art objectively. Just look around and consider that all things have shape, form, color, texture, and line and that these elements are organized into various arrangements. A house can be broken down into a combination of squares, rectangles, circles, or triangles. A cat has textures of both smooth softness and sharp cutting edges. A computer has mass, weight, and dimension. Line creates order, just as lines on a road psychologically keeps people driving in an orderly fashion and moving in the same direction. If someone deviates from the lines on the road, accidents occur. Jagged lines instill emotions of tension, nervousness, or anxiety. The thickness of a line indicates boldness or a sensation of weight. Lines placed in a certain direction can emulate motion and unconsciously point your eye in a particular direction. Receding lines render the illusion of perspective. Lines create dimensional space; forms create a shape and model through shading. Lines can shape the letters of an alphabet to create words that communicate thoughts. They can also create a textured effect that makes viewers want to touch something. Line can build areas of light and dark or create "negative" and "positive" space. Artists learn to manipulate line in a variety of ways to communicate ideas, emotions, and thoughts. An artist can also create the illusion of line that psychologically suggests that you see things that may or may not be there. Many of us are unaware of the suggestive power that a simple line can have and the influence artists have on their audience.

Shapes and forms create two- and three-dimensional areas. A shape has linear qualities (two-dimensional): Their contours and shading give shape to forms of mass or volume (three-dimensional). Overlapping two-dimensional shapes can give the illusions of a three-dimensional space. Making a form or shape smaller than another or showing more than one side of the form gives the illusion of perspective and space. Perspective is the science of optics that creates the illusion of deep space on a two-dimensional surface. Rendering perspective can be a complex process when combined with the manipulation of light, refraction, color, and shadow. Converging lines that meet at a single vanishing point create a linear one-point perspective perpendicular to the picture plane. This makes things look as though they are disappearing into the distance. A two-point perspective is created when parallel lines diverge toward two vanishing points at which the three-dimensional form is then viewed at a certain angle. For example, think of yourself standing in the middle of a four-road intersection. If you look down one road, the lines of the road converge to one point (one-point perspective). If you stand on one corner of the intersection and look at a building across the street, you will see most of the building from one side. Then, looking at the opposite side of the building, you obtain a different point of view (two-point perspective). Aerial perspective is an illusionary device that creates perspective by using value contrast (making things look fuzzy—as if you are looking into the distance). Perspective goes hand in hand with proportion because an object's size has a certain kind of relationship to the other components in the composition.

Shapes and forms can imply our experiences with reality. The pointed corners of a triangle can suggest the sharpness of an arrow or point toward a particular direction. A triangle can suggest the shape of a face or the roof of a house. A curved shape can be dynamic, in essence suggesting a life form that can move. Shapes can form patterns that can create compositions with symbolic meaning. The patterns and symbols found in Amish quilts, Scottish kilts, and Kente cloth represent concepts such as marriage and family. Geometric shapes are found in nature but possess cerebral qualities that are a product of our intellect (Feldman 1992). Nature in essence has its own sense of balance, proportion, symmetry, and asymmetry. Balance is a distribution of weight that can be either symmetrical (equal) or asymmetrical. Asymmetry has a unique quality of distributing dissimilar weights in such a way that they do not seem to be visually out of balance. Elements in nature are usually asymmetrical but still pleasing to look at; we call this quality informal balance.

Artists render natural or geometric shapes and forms and then organize them to create a composition. A scene or landscape is composed of organized shapes and forms that represent images of reality. Abstract art is an organization of shapes and forms as well, but it represents conceptual ideas. Shapes and forms create space, space is intangible, and mass takes up space. A form or shape can create negative space as well as negative emotions or the feeling of emptiness. The placement of a shape or form can fool the eye into thinking it is looking into a space that actually has presence and depth.

Medium is the physical material an artist uses to create something. Examples of media are paint, clay, stone, and wood. Each type of medium possesses unique characteristics that add beauty to a piece of art. For instance, stone will vary, depending on where it originates from and how much is available. Marble is a type of stone that varies in color, pattern, hardness, and origin. Expensive Carrara marble is one of fine quality known for its pure white color and translucency and comes from the quarries of Carrara, Italy. It was a favorite medium used by the Romans for the columns of the Pantheon and the statue of the Apollo Belvedere. Renaissance artists such as Michelangelo preferred Carrara marble because its properties of smoothness and warmth seemed to give life to the figurative pieces sculpted from it. Identifying the medium may indicate where and when something was created. This is an important element in determining the historical background and authenticity of an artwork or artifact. Some types of media no longer exist, are rare or endangered, or can be exotic in nature. Performance art and the use of the body are media that are conceptual and physical. Advances in technology have given rise to new types of media. Computer art and web-based art are recent examples of new media. Artists have either worked exclusively with one medium or combined different media in a single art piece.

Most media have qualities of texture or can create the semblance of texture. For example, an oil painting can be done in such a way as to represent the texture of fur, such as in *After the Hunt*, a still life done by painter William Michael Harnet (1885). Harnet depicts a rabbit's coat with such realism that you can almost feel the soft texture of the fur. Other artists, such as van Gogh, used paint to build up texture on the surface of the canvas. The heavy texture of the paint and brushstroke can indicate either mood or motion. The sculptor Méret Oppenheim, a Surrealist artist, used a medium that was out of context with the object it represented. Her piece titled *Object (Breakfast in Fur)* (1936) shows a teacup, saucer, and spoon covered in fur. The texture of the soft fur covering the cup and spoon made these items no longer functional and reduced them to mere objects.

Artists manipulate color by varying the range of hues, values, saturation, pigment, light, and blending. Colors have physical, spiritual, and psychological properties that artists can apply to almost any type of art-work. Physically, color is a "reflection of light of a certain wavelength off a surface that is received by the retina of the eye and perceived by the brain" (Zelanski 1991). The wavelengths create a spectrum (rainbow) of colors. The brain synthesizes the reception from the rods and cones of the retina and processes the information as a type of color. Hue is the name of a color, such as red, blue, yellow, or green; each hue has a particular position on the spectrum and on the color wheel. Saturation refers to the purity of a color, whereas brightness is a measure of the lightness of that color. The three primary colors (hues) that can be mixed are red, yellow, and blue. When mixed, primary colors create secondary colors such as orange (red and yellow), green (blue and yellow), and violet (blue and red). Complementary colors lie *opposite* each other on the color wheel. An artist can use a complementary color to enhance its opposite and create vivid effects. A complementary color of a primary is achieved by mixing the other two primary colors:

- Red is complemented by green (a mix of blue and yellow).

- Yellow is complemented by violet (a mix of red and blue).

- Blue is complemented by orange (a mix of red and yellow).

The vivid contrast between complementary colors is a device artists have often used to advantage in adver-tisements, logos, and package design. Controlling a color's saturation and physical placement next to another color can create other visual effects. Op art is an example of color saturation manipulation. The color seems to flicker as one views that area. The late-nineteenth-century artist George Seurat developed the theory of pointillism (also known as divisionism), which blends colors together based on where they are placed in relation to one another. Local color refers to colors that are seen realistically as they appear in nature under normal light conditions. Impressionists such as Claude Monet challenged the idea of local color and experimented with it under the conditions of changing light. Interpretive color is the use of a color that is not found under natural conditions in order to achieve a psychological response.

Color has psychological properties that can affect the way people react. How we perceive a color may vary as well; again, one's life experiences and the keenness of one's vision determine this. Color can direct one's mood or emotions and may even produce physiological changes. Charles Féré and Kurt Goldstein con-ducted experiments that found that the body responds to color stimuli (Arnheim 1954). Increased circulation and blood pressure, dilation of pupils, loss of balance, and dizziness are documented responses. Warm colors are those that are within the orange range of the color wheel, and cool colors are within the blue-green sector. A painting using warm or cool colors can determine the mood or tone of the artwork and enhance the viewer's experience. Greens are associated with nature and have a feeling of freshness; blues are regarded as cool or cold depending on their intensity. A calm-looking, tranquil seascape using blues and greens depicting the water and sky can be quite calming. In contrast, blues can suggest despair, depression, melancholy, and sadness, whereas a painting of a field of sunflowers at dusk, full of yellows and reds, is warming and vibrant. Red is recognized as fiery and stimulating and can be associated with ideas of revolution, blood, or danger. One's eyes tend to focus on red pigment that has been applied to a specific area on a sculpture piece or painting. Color that has been placed strategically on an artwork can guide the eye through its composition regardless of whether it is two- or three-dimensional in form.

Colors may also have a spiritual, religious, gender, or social context; for example, the colors of red and white were used on the crowns of Egyptian pharaohs. The color of the crown identified the pharaoh's rule over a specific geographic area of Egypt. The appearance of a green palm branch in Christian paintings signifies the promise of immortality. A red apple seen in many scenes depicting the Garden of Eden is the color of the fruit that tempted Adam and caused him to fall victim to the temptations of the devil, who enticed him to eat the red apple. A white lily is a symbol of purity and is often used in paintings depicting the Virgin Mary. But various interpretations of white can range from the Native American concept of wisdom and health to an Eastern culture's reference to death. Symbolic color used in art varies, depending upon customs, cultures, and religions.

Technically, colors do not have the physical properties of weight, movement, or temperature, yet visually it seems as if they do. The artist creates a feeling of weight, movement, and temperature by varying a color's level of brightness and the placement of other colors around it. We perceive the size of objects differently depending on their color. Lighter-shade colors make things look visually larger than darker-shade objects of the same size. Background colors of similar hue make other colors appear larger or to move forward. Showing gradations of color or directing the color on a surface creates movement and rhythm. Wassily Kandinsky was keenly aware of how colors conduct movement and establish rhythms similar to musical notes. Bright colors, such as yellow, give the effect of radiating outward and warmth. Blues and greens have the opposite effect, causing the eye to move inward and creating the sensation of coolness. Color can make things appear as if they have depth, imparting the sense that distance and dimensionality exist. The blurring of color makes things disappear within the distance. Color can appear to have texture, depending on the way light strikes and enters an object's surface. If an object reflects most of the light off its surface, then the color has a solid matte look. When an object allows most light to pass through it, a color becomes translucent. A more transparent, see-through appearance happens when an object allows light to pass through with little diffusion. When there is little diffusion of light off the surface, a smooth, glossy effect is achieved. Three-dimensional color is achieved through saturation, brightness, and hue. A system that shows a range of saturated colors that vary from one hue to another is known as the "Munsell Color Tree," which was developed by Albert Munsell, a color theorist. His system has become a commercial standard for naming and mixing pigments. Works of art have incorporated a number of different types of color theories. Each one deserves further investigation and study.

An artist creates a composition by arranging the elements of design. Compositional styles are subject to time, taste, and personal preferences as well. A common standard for compositions is the unifying structure of a conceptual triangle. Drawn figures, objects, or lines that are strategically placed can imply a compositional triangle. A triangle unifies other elements within the composition, adds balance and proportion, and can impart symbolic meaning. A composition may have multiple triangular components placed to create patterns or rhythms. A common theme, subject matter, gesture, or objects are other ways to unite the elements of a composition. An example is a painting of a group of men and women, all wearing riding clothes and seated on horses. A common object might be the horses and the way they all appear to be chasing a fox. Most of the men and women are engaged in chasing the fox, except for one woman who appears in the background. This figure is drawn into the composition because the fox is seen running toward her and the horse she is seated on. The motion of the horses riding together in a particular direction adds emphasis to the composition. These are the elements of composition of an artwork.

Mastering and understanding techniques to create an artwork is a component of the production. Each type of material is manipulated by a technique. The techniques the artist chooses vary according to one's training, the availability of materials, type of tools, and skill. A critique of an artwork is an analysis of its compositional elements and its aesthetic beauty. The appreciation of a work of art includes its symbolic and conceptual meaning, historical context, purpose, and relevance to culture and society. An artwork may be judged according to the level of skill that existed at the time it was created, such as the different ways the human figure has been drawn throughout history because of changing knowledge and techniques. Over time, humans began to understand the concepts of proportion, ratios, foreshortening, and perspective. Eventually, the study of anatomy enhanced techniques for drawing the human figure. Knowledge is the basis for technique, but do not confuse expression and creativity with skill and technique. Artists such as Pablo Picasso, who was skilled in the techniques of drawing, drew abstract forms resembling the human body. He took advantage of drawing techniques to create a new way of viewing things. We may admire an artist's technique if it can manipulate materials in ways that most people can't. For example, a one-inch miniature painting of a portrait may be so realistically done that you can count the hairs on the sitter's head. Another technique may involve manipulating the environment, as Christo did when he created *Valley Curtain* (1970–72), for which he hung an orange curtain between canyons in Colorado. A technique can be utilized to fool, violate, or challenge the viewer's interpretation. Claes Oldenburg turned everyday items into colossal sculptured pieces, such as the giant rubber stamp titled

Free Stamp (installed April 1990 at Willard Park), located on the lakefront in Cleveland, Ohio. Not only does he violate the look of its natural scale, but he also used materials that made the piece look like an actual rubber stamp. Artists, especially contemporary artists have a way of manipulating an image and placing it in a different context that makes you look and think differently about the object. Marcel Duchamp used common objects of his "ready mades" (circa 1917) in order to create a conceptual piece of artwork. Is this considered a technique? It is a process for which he created a type of artwork by placing a common object such as a shovel in an art museum. Not only did this outrage the audience, but it also made them think about the institution of a museum, the reverence with which society regards things, and the absurdities of the times.

Suggested Web Sites About Design and Techniques

> **Khouw, Natalia.** *The Meaning of Color for Gender* in Morton, J. L. *Color Matters: Research.*
> http://www.colormatters.com/khouw.html
> [5 October 2002]

> **Morton, J. L.** *Color Matters: The Brain: Car Color Stories.*
> http://www.colormatters.com/bbcar.html
> [5 October 2002]

> **Morton, J. L.** *Color Matters: The Bulletin Board: Colors and Education: Classroom Color and Autism.*
> http://www.colormatters.com/bubdarc12-educate.html
> [5 October 2002]

> **Morton, J. L.** *Color Matters: The Bulletin Board: Effects of Color on the Body and Brain.*
> http://www.colormatters.com/bubdarc9a-physio.html
> [5 October 2002]

> **Morton, J. L.** *Color Matters: Vision: How the Eye Sees Color.*
> http://www.colormatters.com/seecolor.html
> [5 October 2002]

> **Sanford.** *Educational Web Adventures: Create Art: Technique Demonstrations: Making 3D Forms; Drawing Techniques: Perspective Techniques: Color Techniques: Portrait and Figure Techniques.*
> http://www.sanford-artedventures.com/create/create.html
> [5 October 2002]

> **Willard, Christopher.** *A Dystopia of Color Education in a Utopia of Color Experience* (1998) in Morton, J. L. *Color Matters: Research.*
> http://www.colormatters.com/willard.html
> [5 October 2002]

Students will broaden their critical thinking skills when they have a knowledge base of various techniques and design basics. They will begin to question works of art more constructively before doing additional background research about an art piece. This is the process of art criticism, and we can break it down into several steps: Description, Formal Analysis, Interpretation, and Evaluation (Feldman 1992, 471). A description begins with identifying what one sees. One should not make inferences at this point and should not assume something exists within the composition. This is an objective observation, whose purpose is to identify the objects or figures, the medium, colors, size, and construction of the composition. Abstract art lacks a formal description, identifying recognizable objects other than shapes, line, color, space, and mass. Again, one should make no value judgments at this point. Identify the medium of the artwork, which if a painting might be identified as oil, watercolor, acrylic, tempera, or fresco. The medium of a drawing might be charcoal, pencil, pen, pastels, chalk, and so on. Sculpture can be made of marble, wood, jade, granite, steel, and so forth. Printmaking could include etchings, woodcuts, linocuts, and engravings. Is there a texture surface? If so, what kind is it? Identify the colors, size, and dimensionality (two or three dimensions) of an artwork.

Formal analysis is identifying the arrangement of the forms and their relationship to one another. Be more precise about the description; for example, mention that three of the five figures seen in a painting are male and situated in the background, and two female figures are in the foreground. This description can be more precise if you identify the clothes and stance of the figures. By paying attention to details, you will be surprised about how much information you can uncover from a detailed analysis. Describe how the objects or figures are arranged in the composition. What was the first thing that you noticed when you looked at the composition? Compositions will have a focal point, so be aware of how your eye found the focal point and then moved through the composition. This is especially important when describing abstract works of art.

After identifying the medium, try to determine the technique the artist applied to manipulate it. The technique is the process for which a piece of art was created. For example, questions that pertain to a Michelangelo figurative sculpture can include the following: Was the artist able to master the technique of the chosen medium? Was the technique an appropriate choice for that particular piece of art? Would a sculpture piece look better if it had been done in a different medium rather than the one the artist chose? Would Michelangelo's sculptures have been as successful if he had used wood for his figures rather than Carrara marble? What properties does Carrara marble possess that makes sculpture figures look dynamic? These are questions to ask during the descriptive process of criticism. Identify how an artist handled the medium, such as how the wood for a sculpture was cut. Was it cut smooth and polished or left rough and chipped? Or perhaps notice how paint was applied to a canvas; was it in small, smooth brushstrokes or thick and heavy (as if applied with a putty knife)? What kinds of tools might have been used based upon your observation of the art piece? Did the artist intend it to be viewed frontally, from the side, or in the round? Did the artist intend for people to touch it? Do the colors clash or complement one another? Are there variations of a shade of color, or does the artist use only one color? How does the artist create the illusion of space, perspective, or proportion? Most important, is the synthesis of all of these elements successful to the overall composition of the art piece?

Interpretation is the investigative process of finding meanings associated with the artwork. The piece may contain suggestive elements. The artist may have included something that the audience will notice based upon what they know and value. What I may see and interpret may be very different from what someone else may see. It may be a simple matter to identify some straightforward and objective elements. You may be able to interpret other meanings through symbolic images or iconography (the study of symbols). Iconography can be either secular or spiritual (religious), depending on history, cultures, and societies. An interpretive analysis will examine all of these elements in order to define a relationship between the ideas and the image. Other factors to consider are historical, social, religious, political, cultural, and personal context. Investigative research on an art piece can assist in its interpretation. Personal information about the artist is pertinent as well. How did the artist live, why did that person become an artist, who did the artist study with, where did this person live, who did he or she love, when did the artist create a particular piece, was the artist political or spiritual, and what events in the artist's life shaped that person's artistic style? This information alone can bring to light the meaning and relevance of an art piece. Forming a hypothesis begins the interpretive process of critical thinking. A hypothesis is a statement that identifies an idea that relates to the interpretation of an artwork. By looking at something, one formulates an idea about the piece. The hypothesis identifies an idea but also states a possible reason for the statement. You will formulate questions when looking, researching, and analyzing information, thus beginning the critical thinking process. Students will amaze themselves by discovering things they already know and uncovering more new information through research. The next step is for them to evaluate the information they gather.

Evaluation of an art piece combines the cognitive results of research and formal analysis along with one's emotional reaction based on one's own experiences. How and why we may or may not like something can be determined by an evaluative analysis. This is a union between the "logical and emotional, the objective and the subjective" (Olson 2000, 65). The evaluation process may include the authentication of a historical piece. The question of aesthetics comes into play insofar as what we consider "beautiful." In the evaluation process one needs to consider how the artist consciously ignored the rules of a technique in order to achieve personal creativity. Rather than answering many questions, the evaluation process may lead to still more questions. These questions show that the student is developing critical thinking skills and is seeking answers or an understanding. Some questions simply cannot be answered, but we cannot evaluate works of art on the basis of "not knowing." The more you know about something, the better is your chance of producing a more interesting and provocative evaluation. Critical thinking involves more than just memorization; students need to learn how to ask questions that will elicit the information they need to make informed decisions and opinions. Teachers can use art as a provocative tool in guiding students through this learning process. The results can be endless when students acquire the lifetime skill of thinking for themselves and appreciating the world around them.

Suggested Web Sites Regarding Critical Thinking Skills

Association for the Advancement of Arts Education. *Association for the Advancement of Arts Education: How the Arts Contribute to Education.*
http://www.aaae.org/archive/artsbro/arts_bro.htm
[5 October 2002]

Center for Critical Thinking. *Critical Thinking Consortium Home Page.*
http://www.criticalthinking.org/
[5 October 2002]

Horizon. *The Future of Secondary Education: The Arts, Critical Thinking, and Reform: Classrooms of the Future by Ivan Olson.*
http://horizon.unc.edu/projects/HSJ/Olson.asp
[5 October 2002]

Longview Community College, Lee's Summit, MO. *Critical Thinking Across the Curriculum Project: Are You Thinking Yet?*
http://www.kcmetro.cc.mo.us/longview/ctac/toc.htm
[5 October 2002]

North Carolina Public Schools. *Arts Education Curriculum: Arts Education Standard Course of Study and Grade Level Competencies: Visual Arts.*
http://www.ncpublicschools.org/curriculum/ArtsEd/visual.htm
[5 October 2002]

References

Alexander, Mary S. 1999. "The Art of Teaching Students to Think Critically." *The Chronicle of Higher Education* (6 August): B9.

Arnheim, Rudolf. 1954. *Art and Visual Perception: A Psychology of the Creative Eye.* Berkeley: University of California Press.

Feldman, Edmund Burke. 1992. *Varieties of Visual Experience.* New York: Harry N. Abrams.

J. Paul Getty Trust. ArtsEdNet: The Getty Art Education Web Site Home Page. http://www.getty.edu/artsednet/ [5 October 2002].

Green, Gaye Leigh. 2000. "Imagery as Ethical Inquiry." *Art Education* (November): 19–24.

Leshnoff, Susan K. 1995. "Art, Ambiguity and Critical Thinking." *Art Education* (September): 51–56.

Olson, Ivan. 2000. *The Arts and Critical Thinking in American Education.* Westport, CT: Greenwood.

Parks, Michael E. 1994. *The Art Teacher's Desktop Reference*. Englewood Cliffs, NJ: Prentice-Hall.

Stout, Candace Jesse. 1997. "Multicultural Reasoning and the Appreciation of Art." *Studies in Art Education* (Winter): 96–111.

White, David A. 2001. "Critical Thinking and Artistic Creation." *Journal of Aesthetic Education* (Summer): 77–85.

Zelanski, Paul, and Mary Pat Fisher. 1991. *The Art of Seeing*. Englewood Cliffs, NJ: Prentice-Hall.

CHAPTER 3

Using Primary Sources on the Internet in the Visual Arts

For the last forty years or so the field of arts education has regularly employed a multimedia approach to learning. Teachers have taken advantage of incorporating multimedia into their classroom teaching, including formats such as art reproductions, slides of images, curriculum kits, filmstrips, transparencies, puppets, videos, and films. The Internet is yet another multimedia teaching tool and is one that teachers, librarians, students, and parents need to understand and learn to use to their advantage. Technology and the Internet have introduced a new form of expression and creativity. "How children learn and how teachers teach, as well as how schools communicate with parents, will be improved with technological advances" (Getty Center for Education in the Arts 1993, 17).

Internet technology has opened a worldwide educational opportunity for developing creativity in the visual arts. But it is not enough to merely obtain money and equipment to install computers and provide Internet access in classrooms. Teachers need education, training, and guidance in order to make the Internet work for them. The teachers will be the ones who guide students in developing critical thinking skills to locate authoritative web sites of information on any subject. The questions in each of the primary source sites utilize different ways of searching the Internet, such as using a search engine, an image browser, museum sites, lesson plan sites, organizations, commercial sites, and private web pages. The purpose of this book is not just to identify the primary source web site according to the topic but also to teach, evaluate, and locate web sites. Retention relies on doing; the "hands on" approach reinforces what the student has learned. If you just show the students a web site, you are not teaching them how to find it for themselves, nor are you teaching the evaluation process of selection and assessment.

Web sites come and go quite quickly because of the pace of technology. Even though the web sites cited in this book were active prior to publication, by the time you read this a web site may be changed, disconnected, or no longer updated. Web sites cited in this publication include the copyright holder and the title of the web page, so it can easily be found using a search engine. Enclose a title of an artwork, title of a web site, the copyright holder, or keyword phrase within parentheses to return better results. This is especially helpful when a web address is very long and easy to mistype. There may also be a problem with connection time, software, hardware, "pay-to-play" conversion, filters, and copyright. The Internet is dynamic, yet it can be frustrating when users encounter obstacles that hinder their access to a web site. Critical thinking using the Internet will help overcome such obstacles, both for the teacher and the student. Some of the web sites may link only to an image, others may have only text, and others may have both text and images. The first step is to understand what a primary source is in the visual arts using the Internet.

A primary source is information that someone has recorded firsthand. It is the most direct way a person can formulate and record information. Primary sources include eyewitness accounts, letters, diaries, interviews, archives, vertical files, and so on. Primary sources in the visual arts include paintings, sculptures, prints, drawings, photographs, films and video, tapestries, ceramic pieces, and architecture. Technology has permitted access to such primary sources through digital images. Many primary sources of visual arts exist in the public domain and are available in digital format via the Internet. Museums, galleries, private collections, libraries, universities, arts organizations and associations, and archives that own the artwork are also the owners of its image. If someone creates a nonprofit personal web page and intends to use an image of an artwork, that person needs to request copyright permission and include an educational fair use statement on its web site. A hyperlink from a web site to the primary image source is also acceptable as long as you cite the primary source (Harnack 2000, 134). But keep in mind that even the image's copyright holder can alter the image. Computer technology using software such as PhotoShop can alter colors, crop an image, or even delete or add details. Written observation accounts assist in determining the quality of the image as a primary resource. Museums, galleries, archives (public and private), private art collections, and so on hold the copyright to the image of an artwork. The most obvious primary sources are the web sites that have posted Internet images from their own collections. Evaluating information about a web site entails investigation, research, and assessment. Teachers and students need to ask the following questions: Can I consider the web site's image and accompanying information as a primary source? Is it scholarly information? Is the information accurate? Does the web site sponsor a particular agenda? Is the information current or out of date?

Suggested Web Sites on Primary Sources, Collections, and Copyright

Colyer, Anita F. *A Copyright Guide for Librarians: A Subject Guide to Copyright Information on the Internet.*
http://slis.cua.edu/ihy/SP/GG.htm
[5 October 2002]

Library of Congress. *The Learning Page: Lesson Plans: Using Primary Sources in the Classroom.*
http://memory.loc.gov/ammem/ndlpedu/lessons/primary.html
[5 October 2002]

MuseumSpot. *MuseumSpot Home Page.*
http://www.museumspot.com/
[5 October 2002]

University of California Berkeley Library, Berkeley, CA. *UC Berkeley Library: Library Research Using Primary Sources.*
http://www.lib.berkeley.edu/TeachingLib/Guides/PrimarySources.html
[5 October 2002]

University of California Berkeley Library, Berkeley, CA. *UC Berkeley Library: Library Research Using Primary Sources: Primary Sources on the Web.*
http://www.lib.berkeley.edu/TeachingLib/Guides/PrimarySourcesOnTheWeb.html
[5 October 2002]

University of Connecticut History Online. *How to Use Primary Sources.*
http://www.cthistoryonline.org/classrm_primsource.html
[5 October 2002]

University of Idaho, Moscow, ID. *Repositories of Primary Sources.*
http://www.uidaho.edu/special-collections/Other.Repositories.html
[5 October 2002]

U.S. Copyright Office. *Copyright Act of 1976.*
http://www.law.cornell.edu/copyright/copyright.table.html
[5 October 2002]

Yale University Library, New Haven, CT. *Visual Materials As Primary Sources.*
http://www.library.yale.edu/instruction/vismats.html
[5 October 2002]

Web Site Evaluation Guidelines

Determine Your Objective

Identify what you are looking for and the type of information you need. Who is the intended audience? Question whether the web site is appropriate for a classroom setting. Always preview the site—not just once or twice, but also just prior to the class session to make sure the information you reviewed is still available. Review the entire web site. Decide whether you plan to include "for pay or register" sites or use only free web sites. Realize that search engines will actually sell space and rank listings to advertisers who are willing to pay. Determine what browser to use. Web sites are designed according to browsers, so the appearance of a web site may differ from one browser to another. Access to a web site may be limited because of a particular browser. A browser is a web program for navigating the Internet. Web sites that contain graphics and images will use graphic browsers. The web sites identified in this book used the Netscape Navigator 4.7 browser.

Evaluate the Source

Determine the accuracy, reliability, and value of the web site's information. This includes authorship, publishing body, and intent (reason for existing). Question whether the authorship is identified on the web site or at least linked to the site. Look for information about the author and the credentials that person has. Is the author an expert or at least very knowledgeable about the information posted on the web site? Does the author have a certain agenda, and is this agenda questionable? Does the author include an E-mail address or some other way to contact that person (telephone number, address)? The publishing body is the host of the web site, and authors can contribute to the site.

How a URL is posted helps to determine a publishing body and the author's affiliation as posted according to its domain. "URL" is an abbreviation for Uniform Resource Locator, which is an address for a web site posted on the World Wide Web. Examples of domains are the following: .gov sites are sponsored by government agencies; .edu sites are affiliated with educational institutions; .mil is used for the military; .net is used for networks; and .org sites are organizations Commercial.com sites run the gamut from good and credible to pornographic and unauthoritative resources to information. Some information that government and educational sites post may not be as accurate or credible as one may assume. There are also two-letter domain names for individual countries, such as .us (United States), .uk (United Kingdom), and so on. Determine whether there is a header, watermark, wallpaper, or logo that symbolizes the affiliation. If authorship is difficult to determine because the web site lacks some of these features, try truncating the web site's URL after the server name. It is also possible to obtain information through the server or domain. Some web sites identify the owner of a server and provide contact names and telephone numbers. Associations fall under the categories of education, organizations, government, commercial, and so on. Some web sites list scholarly and educational societies that include a list and a description of their publications (the full text of some publications may be available online).

Intent identifies the agenda or purpose of the web site, as well as its intended audience. The agenda may be educational, personal, religious, or political purposes, or it may be to spread deviant or unsavory propaganda. See whether the web site cites (acknowledges) its sources or plagiarizes from another web site. Commercial.com sites could contain valuable information, but their intent is concerned with marketing purposes. These web sites are often cluttered with advertisements or contain hidden links to products that are for sale. News sites contain valuable primary source information, but a disadvantage is that the information is temporarily posted and not digitally archived. Electronic journals continue to be a good source for scholarly research, but access may be limited to educational institutions or to those who pay a fee for access. A private/personal URL contains a tilde (~) symbol after the domain. Scrutinize these sites for their accuracy and agenda. There are some good personal web pages that cite and hyperlink to primary source sites.

Currency of Information

Web sites that have not been recently updated may contain inaccurate and outdated information. The web site may have ceased and no longer support current information. Most web sites will post the date of the most recent update, or you may find it posted under a feature of the browser (e.g., Netscape Navigator, Internet Explorer). The original date the web site was produced and an update listing is an indicator of the site's lasting power and future existence.

Practical to Use

Test the web site to see whether it is practical to use in your current classroom setting. Determine whether your computer software and hardware can support the special features of the web site. You may have to install plug-ins or PDF readers such as Adobe Acrobat Reader. Downloads may take some class time away if you do them on the spot. Consider whether you want the students to use a plug-in of some kind. A plug-in is a program helper that allows the browser to access a special feature of a web site (such as an image, audio, or printing). The most common plug-ins are Acrobat Reader for printing, Quick Time for videos, Real Player for audio, and ShockWave Flash for streaming video clips.

Frames in a web site may also take some time to load. Frames divide a screen into sections so that each section can be independently moved when viewed. Frames do take longer to load, and some browsers do not support the feature. Some web sites may allow you to "shut off" the frame. Using a right click on the mouse and selecting "open frame" can usually isolate a frame. Most images are scanned and saved as JPEG or GIF files. Joint Picture Experts Group (JPEG) is a graphic image format that compresses a graphic into a smaller file. JPEG images have a range of colors and load fairly quickly. Graphics Interchange Format (GIF) files are also compressed images used for fast loading, especially for images that have few colors, line drawings, or cartoons. A full image takes some time to load even though it may be a JPEG.

Look for web sites that have a preview "thumbnail image" feature. Thumbnails are smaller samples of an image that load quickly. One can then decide whether to view or download the full image from the thumbnail. To access the full view of a thumbnail, simply right click on the mouse. See whether the images (and text) can be printed. You can do this by selecting File and Print Preview. If none of the image (or text) is seen on the Print Preview screen, it is usually because of the design of the web site. In some instances, changing the Colors setting to "use my colors" of the Edit, Preferences file may allow for printing capabilities.

Access to the URL may be denied for various reasons. Some troubleshooting hints include checking for spelling errors in the URL; the web site may be under construction or in the process of update; too many simultaneous users on the same site; restricted access that is limited to registered or paying customers; the web site has been removed; the browser may not recognize the site; the URL has moved; or a fire wall or Internet filter may have been installed. Many web sites are free to access, but some research databases and electronic resources require registration or charge a fee. The *Grove Dictionary of Art Online* is an example of a wonderful art resource that charges thousands of dollars for licensed access. Only major institutions and libraries can afford such databases. Web sites cited in this text offered free access prior to publication, but of course some of them may eventually charge a fee.

Fire walls are network security systems designed to prevent unauthorized access to a local network. Unfortunately, this can also prevent a legitimate user (such as a teacher) from accessing the Internet via the local network. An Internet filter is software that blocks access to designated web sites, particularly those containing pornography and other offensive material. Most schools have installed some kind of Internet filter onto their classroom networks, and these may block some images and web sites of artwork. The Children's Internet Protection Act (CIPA) was approved in December 2000 and became law in April 2001. The law required that schools and libraries would have to install Internet content filters in order to receive any future federal e-rate funding. In addition, a policy that would enforce monitoring the online activities of minors had to be implemented. Schools and libraries were supposed to be in full compliance by July 1, 2002. The American Libraries Association (ALA) and the American Civil Liberties Union filed a lawsuit that argued that such restrictions to information was unconstitutional. In May 2002, a three-judge panel decided that the CIPA law was unconstitutional. The panel recommended that there should be less restrictive ways, other than Internet filters, to protect children. Some states are still pursuing similar state legislative laws that mirror the former CIPA law. Many schools have installed Internet filters, which will block access to many art images. Most commercial filters offer software updates as part of their service. You should always inquire and test a web site to check to see if your school has installed an Internet filter.

Suggested Web Sites About Filters and Filtering

American Library Association. *The Voice of America's Libraries: ALA: American Library Association: ALA Applauds Federal Court Ruling on the Children's Internet Protection Act.*
http://www.ala.org/cipa/cipatrial9.html
[5 October 2002]

American Library Association. *The Voice of America's Libraries: ALA: American Library Association: Filters and Filtering.*
http://www.ala.org/alaorg/oif/filtersandfiltering.html
[5 October 2002]

Kranz, Cindy. *Filtering Software Varies: Here's 4 of the Best by Cindy Kranz: The Cincinnati Enquirer.*
http://enquirer.com/editions/1999/11/04/loc_filtering_software.html
[5 October 2002]

SafetyEd International. *Internet Content Filters: Issues Facing Parents, Schools and Libraries.*
http://www.safetyed.org/help/filtering.html
[5 October 2002]

SafetyEd International. *Internet Safety Education, Child Advocacy & Child Protection.*
http://www.safetyed.org/
[5 October 2002]

Content and Layout Quality

The proper selection and use of information on a web site is fundamental. A number of good web sites may exist on a particular topic, but it may be necessary to select those that provide the best information. Use good judgment, critical thinking skills, and comparative authoritative resources such as print encyclopedias, dictionaries, directories, and so on. Determine whether the information is objective or biased. See whether the posted links are active and relevant. Decide whether the web site uses abusive language or slang or is grammatically incorrect; has too many spelling errors, offensive images, or advertisements; or is too difficult to navigate. The purpose of selecting a web site is to prevent students from missing the information because of clutter; if you must eliminate a site, choose another one on the same topic. See whether the graphic layout of the web page follows good design principles. Decide whether the graphics, fonts, and images complement the information on the web site. A good web site will identify either the title of an artwork, its medium, date of creation, size, and ownership (museum, gallery, or private collection) or cite (or hyperlink) to its primary source.

Suggested Web Sites That Discuss How to Evaluate a Web Site

Milton S. Eisenhower Library, Johns Hopkins University, Baltimore, MD. *Evaluating Information Found on the Internet.*
http://www.library.jhu.edu/elp/useit/evaluate/
[5 October 2002]

Trochim, William. Cornell University, Ithaca, NY. *Evaluating Web Sites.*
http://trochim.human.cornell.edu/webeval/webintro/webintro.htm
[5 October 2002]

University of California College Library, Los Angeles, CA. *UCLA College Library: Help Guides: Hoax? Scholarly Research? Personal Opinion? You Decide!*
http://www.library.ucla.edu/libraries/college/help/hoax/
[5 October 2002]

University of California College Library, Los Angeles, CA. *UCLA College Library: Help Guides: Thinking Critically about World Wide Web Resources by Esther Grassian.*
http://www.library.ucla.edu/libraries/college/help/critical/
[5 October 2002]

University of California College Library, Santa Barbara, CA. *How Do I Know What's Good on the Web? by Janet Martorana.*
http://www.library.ucsb.edu/libinst/lib101/webfaq08.html
[5 October 2002]

You need to select a browser before searching for web sites. A browser is software that navigates the Internet and then displays a web page. Graphic browsers such as Netscape Navigator, Microsoft Explorer, or HotJava view images and graphics and are updated in versions. Each browser and version will vary in its features. Most web sites include an information page describing how to best view the site according to a particular browser. Select a browser that will meet your classroom needs and is compatible with the local network.

A search engine is a program that has indexed web pages. It generates a list of sites based upon the keywords you type into the program. Keep in mind that a single search engine cannot identify all of the sites on the web. Thousands of new web sites are added daily, so no one search engine can keep up with all of the additions. Large search engines (such as Yahoo, AltaVista, Lycos, and Google) generally return a lengthy list of hits, but quantity does not always mean quality. Each search engine has its own basic structure and features for searching the Internet. Search engine strategies are often identified as Search Tips, Advanced Search, Help, or Frequently Asked Questions (FAQ). Tips for successful searching are constantly being updated and posted on the search engine.

Remember that a search engine does not replace your critical thinking skills. Search engines can neither comprehend nor understand what a word or concept may mean. The person who is doing the search has to rely on terminology to translate abstract ideas. This is something that cannot be built into a program other than the tags that are part of the site's metadata. Humans input data into the metatags, so not all of the concepts or ideas can be tagged by a person in a search engine. Plan your search by defining the concepts or phrases that you will use in a search engine. Some examples are the style or time period in art history, the artist's name (spelling may vary depending on nationality), titles of an artwork (titles sometimes appear in different languages), and location of the work of art (including architecture or public sculpture pieces). Use a variety of search engines (and image search engines) to obtain successful results. Learn how to use the various features of the search engine to maximize its benefits. Be careful with spelling and multiple-word searches. If you type the term "modern art painting" into the keyword search field, the search engine will search for any web site that contains one or all three words anywhere on the web page. The findings will be a list consisting of tens of thousands of web sites, which is too overwhelming to use logically. Try using quotation marks ("), Boolean operators (and, or, and not), or truncation to frame your query. Refer to the search engine's Advanced Search, FAQ, Help, or Tips screens for further assistance.

Metasearch engines are services that search several other search engines and then report the results from the query. This is an "all-in-one" approach to search the ever-expanding web. The service identifies which search engines are indexed, but each service is not fully comprehensive and thus has some drawbacks. Often a service misses good sites, or the search takes too long to execute. A metasearch engine is helpful when you use a unique single word or specific phrase and you expect a limited return of records. This is not a very useful tool for more general types of searches.

Suggested Web Sites of Metasearch Engines

CNET Networks, Inc. *Search.com.*
http://www.search.com/
[5 October 2002]

Fast Search & Transfer ASA. *AlltheWeb: All The Time.*
http://www.alltheweb.com/
[5 October 2002]

Highway61.com. *Highway61, Or: How I Learned To Stop Searching, And Love These Results!*
http://www.highway61.com/
[5 October 2002]

Indiana University Libraries, Bloomington, IN. *Guide to Meta-Search Engines by Jian Liu.*
http://www.indiana.edu/~librcsd/search/meta.html
[5 October 2002]

InfoSpace, Inc. *Dogpile.*
http://www.dogpile.com/
[5 October 2002]

InfoSpace, Inc. *MetaCrawler: Search the Search Engines.*
http://www.metacrawler.com/
[5 October 2002]

InfoSpace, Inc. *WebCrawler.*
http://www.webcrawler.com/info.wbcrwl/
[5 October 2002]

Intelliseek, Inc. *ProFusion: Powered by Intelliseek.*
http://www.profusion.com/
[5 October 2002]

Mamma.com. *Mamma Home Page.*
http://www.mamma.com/
[5 October 2002]

Software is available for purchase that locates images and arranges them into a gallery of thumbnails. The software labels the thumbnail with the original URL and provides full-image access. To access the full image, right click on the mouse. Some web sites offer shareware that identifies a limited number of images that may or may not have thumbnails. The more popular search engines include an Image Finder option. The search engine identifies the approximate number of images it has indexed. For example, Google's Image Search states that it has indexed more than 250 million images, and it cautions users about copyright and permission rights (Google Image Search, 19 November 2001). Usually a warning message states that some images may contain mature subjects and suggests using its filter. An image search engine filter can be turned on or off, but there is no guarantee that all mature subject images will be blocked. Consult the FAQ or HELP screens of each search engine to help locate specific images on the Internet. There are a number of search engines for images, multimedia, and video. A simple search using keywords such as "directory of . . ." or "list of image (or multimedia) search engines" will produce a number of sites.

Suggested Web Sites, Image Search Engines, and Directories

AccuNet. *AccuNet/AP Photo Archive Multimedia Archive.*
http://ap.accuweather.com/apphoto/
[5 October 2002]

AltaVista Company. *AltaVista Image Search.*
http://www.altavista.com/sites/search/mm_imageresults?pg=q&stype=simage&imgset=2&q=&avkw=qtrp
[5 October 2002]

AMICO. *AMICO: Art Museum Image Consortium: Thumbnail Catalog.*
http://search.amico.org/amico/apw/search/
[5 October 2002]

Cave Spring Middle School, Roanoke, VA. *MegaLinks: Art.*
http://www.rcs.k12.va.us/csjh/artlinks.htm
[5 October 2002]

Corbis. *Corbis: Discover the Perfect Image.*
http://www.corbis.com/
[5 October 2002]

Crosby-Muilenburg, Corryn. *Search Engines for Images, Multimedia, & Video.*
http://library.humboldt.edu/~ccm/searchmedia.html
[5 October 2002]

Excite Network. *Excite.*
http://www.excite.com/
[5 October 2002]

Fossick International. *Fossick.com: Fossick Online Multimedia.*
http://fossick.com/Multimedia.htm
[5 October 2002]

Google. *Google Image Search.*
http://www.google.com/imghp?hl=en&ie=ISO-8859-1&q=fossick+online+multimedia
[5 October 2002]

Jupitermedia Corporation. *How Search Engines Work by Danny Sullivan, Editor, SearchEngineWatch.com, Updated: October 14, 2002.*
http://searchenginewatch.com/webmasters/work.html
[5 October 2002]

Jupitermedia Corporation. *Search Engine Features for Webmasters by Danny Sullivan, Editor, SearchEngineWatch.com, Updated: October 14, 2002.*
http://searchenginewatch.com/webmasters/features.html
[5 October 2002]

Lycos, Inc. *HotBot (select "Advanced Search").*
http://hotbot.lycos.com/
[5 October 2002]

Lycos, Inc. *Lycos Multimedia Search.*
http://multimedia.lycos.com/
[5 October 2002]

Microsoft Corporation. *MSN Search: Advanced Search Options.*
http://search.msn.com/advanced.asp
[5 October 2002]

mister-pix.com. *Mister PiX.*
http://www.mister-pix.com/english/main.htm
[5 October 2002]

Nerdworld Media. *Nerdworld: Education: Arts.*
http://www.nerdworld.com/nw740o1o40.html
[5 October 2002]

Picsearch. *Picsearch Home Page.*
http://www.picsearch.com/
[5 October 2002]

Proteus Image Search. *Image Search Powered by Proteus.*
http://www.thrall.org/proimage.html
[5 October 2002]

TLS Technologies, LLC. *Ditto: See the Web Visual Search.*
http://www.ditto.com/
[5 October 2002]

Yahoo! Inc. *Yahoo! Picture Gallery.*
http://gallery.yahoo.com/
[5 October 2002]

Directories of a search engine help to categorize the sites by subject. This narrows a search to a more specific subdirectory subject area, such as the "Arts," "Visual Arts," or "Art and Architecture." Most visual arts primary sources are museums, galleries, private collections, archives, universities, libraries, arts organizations, and associations. There are some good personal web pages that link to primary source sites. These web pages identify the primary source (for copyright reasons). A subdirectory is adequate for browsing, but if you are looking for a specific image, an image finder will have more success. If you know the museum/gallery location of a specific artwork, go directly to the museum/gallery web site home page. Museum collections, galleries, private collectors, and so on who own a piece of art hold the copyright to the piece and its image. The site will often "exhibit" its online gallery or have some kind of "search box" feature. Many museums include helpful background information about the artwork and its creator. Some software packages are available for purchase, but most images can be found using a search engine or going directly to a web site that holds the copyright to the artwork. There are specialized art consortia that require registration or a paid licensure that specializes in image data banks. The Art Museum Image Consortium (AMICO) and the Bridgeman Art Library of Images featured in the *Grove Dictionary of Art Online* are examples of such image data banks. Some state digital media center consortia, such as the OhioLINK Digital Media Center, have excellent comprehensive image files but are restricted to registered members.

Suggested Web Sites of Primary Source Directories for Images and Art History Information

About.com. *Art History 101 with Andrea Mulder-Slater: Table of Contents.*
http://arthistory.about.com/library/bl101.htm?PM=ss14_arthistory
[5 October 2002]

About.com. *Photography with Peter Marshall.*
http://photography.about.com/library/weekly/
[5 October 2002]

Aliceville. *Welcome to Aliceville Home Page.*
http://www.aliceville.com/index.htm
[5 October 2002]

All About Artists. *All About Artists Home Page.*
http://www.allaboutartists.com/
[5 October 2002]

Alternate Realities in Art and Thought. *Art Gallery: Main Directory.*
http://www.EsotericArt.com/fringe/art/artndx.htm
[5 October 2002]

AMICO. *AMICO: Art Museum Image Consortium: Thumbnail Catalog.*
http://search.amico.org/amico/apw/search/
[5 October 2002]

Andrus, Kathryn. University of Colorado at Colorado Springs. *Digital Art Collections.*
http://harpy.uccs.edu/collect.html
[5 October 2002]

Andy Warhol Museum, Pittsburgh, PA. *The Warhol.*
http://www.warhol.org/
[5 October 2002]

Andy Warhol Museum, Pittsburgh, PA. *The Warhol: Education: Resources and Lessons.*
http://www.warhol.org/education/resources_lessons.html
[5 October 2002]

Annenberg. *The Western Tradition: The Renaissance.*
http://www.learner.org/exhibits/renaissance/index.html
[5 October 2002]

ARC Art Renewal Center. *ARC Art Renewal Center: Home Page.*
http://www.artrenewal.org/
[5 October 2002]

Art Institute of Chicago. *Art Institute of Chicago: Collections.*
http://www.artic.edu/aic/collections/index.html
[5 October 2002]

Art Institute of Chicago. *Art Institute of Chicago: Student and Teacher Programs: ArtAccess.*
http://www.artic.edu/artaccess/
[5 October 2002]

Art Institute of Chicago. *Art Institute of Chicago: Student and Teacher Programs: Cleopatra:*
    A Multimedia Guide to Art of the Ancient World.
http://www.artic.edu/cleo/
[5 October 2002]

Artcyclopedia. *Artcyclopedia: The Fine Art Search Engine.*
http://www.artcyclopedia.com/
[5 October 2002]

Artifice, Inc. *Great Buildings Online.*
http://www.greatbuildings.com/gbc.html
[5 October 2002]

ArtSceneCal. *ArtScene: The Guide to Art Galleries and Museums in Southern California.*
http://artscenecal.com/
[5 October 2002]

Ashmawy, Alaa K. *Seven Wonders of the Ancient World.*
http://ce.eng.usf.edu/pharos/wonders/
[5 October 2002]

Australian National University, Canberra, Australia. *ArtServe. Welcome to ArtServe: Art &*
    Architecture Mainly from the Mediterranean Basin and Japan.
http://www.anu.edu.au/
[5 October 2002]

Beniger, James R. University of Southern California, Los Angeles, CA. *Comm 544: Image*
    Library.
http://www.usc.edu/schools/annenberg/asc/projects/comm544/library/
[5 October 2002]

Brain-Juice.com, Inc. *Brain-Juice: The Best Biographies for 20th Century Art, Film, History,*
    Literature, and Music: Art.
http://www.brain-juice.com/cgi-bin/browse.cgi
[5 October 2002]

British Library, London, England. *British Library: Collections Site Map.*
http://www.bl.uk/sitemap.html#collections
[5 October 2002]

British Museum, London, England. *The British Museum: Compass: Explore the Collections On-line.*
http://www.thebritishmuseum.ac.uk/compass/
[5 October 2002]

Brkich, Lazar. Milwaukee Public Museum, Milwaukee, WI. *Milwaukee Public Museum: Welcome to the Collections and Research area of the Milwaukee Public Museum.*
http://www.mpm.edu/collect/
[5 October 2002]

Butler Institute of American Art, Youngstown, OH. *Butler Institute of American Art: America's Museum: The Butler Youngstown.*
http://www.butlerart.com/butler_youngstown.htm
[5 October 2002]

Cave Spring Junior High, Roanoke, VA. *CSMS Art Gallery.*
http://www.rcs.k12.va.us/csjh/artindex.htm
[5 October 2002]

Cedar Rapids Museum of Art, IA. *Cedar Rapids Museum of Art: Permanent Collection.*
http://www.crma.org/collection/collection.htm
[5 October 2002]

Centaro, Orazio. *Orazio Centaro's Art Images on the Web.*
http://www.ocaiw.com/indexing.htm
[5 October 2002]

Centre Georges Pompidou, Paris, France. *Centre Georges Pompidou: Museum.*
http://www2.centrepompidou.fr/english/museum/
[5 October 2002]

Christus Rex, Inc. *Christus Rex Project: Art Gallery.*
http://www.christusrex.org/www2/art/gallery.htm
[5 October 2002]

Cigola, Riccardo. *Art: Artists and Architects Home Page.*
http://www.italycyberguide.com/Art/artistsarchite/artists.htm
[5 October 2002]

Clardy, Brian. *NIRD Art History.*
http://www.jlc.net/~brian/art/art_history.html
[5 October 2002]

Cleveland Museum of Art. *Cleveland Museum of Art: Explore: Education and Research: For Schools and Teachers: Teachers Resource Center.*
http://www.clevelandart.org/educatn/trc-news/index.html
[5 October 2002]

Cleveland Museum of Art. *Cleveland Museum of Art: Explore Our Collections.*
http://www.clevelandart.org/Explore/

Crystalinks. *Ancient and Lost Civilizations.*
http://www.crystalinks.com/ancient.html
[5 October 2002]

Current Archeology. *Current Archeology: Welcome to the Wonderful World of Archaeology!*
http://www.archaeology.co.uk/
[5 October 2002]

Detroit Institute of Arts, Detroit, MI. *Detroit Institute of Arts: Collection.*
http://www.dia.org/collection/collection.html

Detroit Institute of Arts, Detroit, MI. *Detroit Institute of Arts: Education: Lesson Plans.*
http://www.dia.org/education/lesson.html
[5 October 2002]

Emory University, Atlanta, GA. *Michael C. Carlos Museum of Emory University Home Page.*
http://carlos.emory.edu/

Emory University, Atlanta, GA. *Michael C. Carlos Museum of Emory University: Programs for Schools and Teachers: Odyssey Online.*
http://carlos.emory.edu/ODYSSEY/MidElem_Home.html
[15 October 2002]

ERIC Clearinghouse on Information & Technology. *AskERIC: Lesson Plans: Arts.*
http://www.askeric.org/cgi-bin/lessons.cgi/Arts
[5 October 2002]

Exploring Ancient World Cultures. University of Evansville, Evansville, IN. *Exploring Ancient World Cultures: An Introduction to Ancient World Cultures on the World Wide Web.*
http://eawc.evansville.edu/
[5 October 2002]

Fleischer Museum of American and Russian Impressionism, Scottsdale, Arizona. *Welcome to the Fleischer Museum.*
http://www.fleischer.org/intro.html
[5 October 2002]

Frick Collection, New York, NY. *Frick Collection and Frick Art Reference Library.*
http://www.frick.org/
[5 October 2002]

Georgia O'Keeffe Museum, Santa Fe, NM. *Georgia O'Keeffe Museum: Education and Programs.*
http://www.okeeffemuseum.org/programs/index.html
[5 October 2002]

Georgia O'Keeffe Museum, Santa Fe, NM. *Georgia O'Keeffe Museum Home Page.*
http://www.okeeffemuseum.org/indexflash.html

Gerten-Jackson, Carol. *CGFA: A Virtual Art Museum: Alphabetical Index.*
http://sunsite.dk/cgfa/fineart.htm
[5 October 2002]

Giorgio Vasari's Lives of the Artists. *The Lives of the Most Eminent Painters, Sculptors and Architects.*
http://easyweb.easynet.co.uk/giorgio.vasari/list.htm
[5 October 2002]

Google. Google Directory: Arts: Visual Arts.
http://directory.google.com/Top/Arts/Visual_Arts/
[5 October 2002]

Harden Mark. *Artchive.*
http://www.artchive.com/ftp_site.htm
[5 October 2002]

Hellenic Ministry of Culture. *Hellenic Ministry of Culture. Museums, Monuments, Archaeological Sites in Greece.*
http://www.culture.gr/2/21/toc/index.html
[5 October 2002]

Hood Museum of Art. Dartmouth College, Hanover, NH. *Hood Museum of Art: Faculty and Student Resources.*
http://www.dartmouth.edu/~hood/cap/facultystudentre.html
[5 October 2002]

Hood Museum of Art. Dartmouth College, Hanover, NH. *Hood Museum of Art Home Page.*
http://www.dartmouth.edu/~hood/Menu.html

Howe, Jeffery. Boston College. *Digital Archive of Architecture.*
http://www.bc.edu/bc_org/avp/cas/fnart/arch/contents_europe.html
[5 October 2002]

IDSC: Information and Decision Support Center, Egyptian Cabinet. *Egyptian Museum Official Site, Cairo.*
http://www.egyptianmuseum.gov.eg/home.html
[5 October 2002]

Incursio, Inc. *WetCanvas: The Virtual Museum.*
http://www.wetcanvas.com/Museum/index.html
[5 October 2002]

Kelsey Museum of Archeology, University of Michigan, Ann Arbor, MI. *Kelsey Museum of Archeology: Educational Programs.*
http://www.lsa.umich.edu/kelsey/educational.html
[5 October 2002]

Kelsey Museum of Archeology, University of Michigan, Ann Arbor, MI. *Kelsey Museum of Archeology Home Page.*
http://www.lsa.umich.edu/kelsey/

Kimbell Art Museum, Fort Worth, TX. *Kimbell Art Museum.*
http://www.kimbellart.org/

Kimbell Art Museum, Fort Worth, TX. *Kimbell Art Museum: Education and Events: Programs for Educators and School Groups.*
http://www.kimbellart.org/education/educators.cfm?id=18
[5 October 2002]

Knechtel, Nancy. Niagara County Community College (SUNY). *Nancy Knechtel's Home Page: Courses: Art.*
http://www.sunyniagara.cc.ny.us/homepags/Knechtel/knechtel.html#courses
[5 October 2002]

Knight, Kevin. *Catholic Encyclopedia Online Edition (2002).*
http://www.newadvent.org/cathen/
[5 October 2002]

Kohl, Allan T. and Art Images for College Teaching (AICT) and the Minneapolis College of Art and Design. *AICT: AICT is a free-use image resource for the educational community.*
http://arthist.cla.umn.edu/aict/html/
[5 October 2002]

Krannert Art Museum, University of Illinois at Urbana-Champaign. *Krannert Art Museum and Kinkead Pavilion: Education and Resources.*
http://www.art.uiuc.edu/galleries/kam/index.html
[5 October 2002]

Krannert Art Museum, University of Illinois at Urbana-Champaign. *Krannert Art Museum and Kinkead Pavilion Home Page.*
http://www.art.uiuc.edu/galleries/kam/index.html

Kren, Emil and Daniel Marx. *Web Gallery of Art: Introduction.*
http://gallery.euroweb.hu/welcome.html (no frames)
http://gallery.euroweb.hu/index1.html (frames)
http://www.kfki.hu/~arthp/index1.html (mirror site—frames)
[5 October 2002]

Kyoto National Museum, Kyoto, Japan. *Kyoto National Museum (in English).*
http://www.kyohaku.go.jp/indexe.htm
[5 October 2002]

Leijenaar, Matthijs W. *the-artists.org: The Major Modern & Contemporary Visual Artists Home Page.*
http://www.the-artists.org/index.cfm
[5 October 2002]

Library of Congress. *Prints and Photographs (P&P) Online Catalog.*
http://lcweb.loc.gov/rr/print/catalog.html
[5 October 2002]

Liu, Alan, University of California, Santa Barbara, CA. *Voice of the Shuttle: Art and Art History.*
http://vos.ucsb.edu/browse-netscape.asp?id=2707
[5 October 2002]

Louvre Museum Official Website.
http://www.louvre.fr/louvrea.htm
[5 October 2002]

Lowe Art Museum, University of Miami, Miami, FL. *Lowe Art Museum Home Page.*
http://www.lowemuseum.org/lowe.shtml
[14 October 2002]

Macmillan Publishers Limited. *The Grove Dictionary of Art Online: Free Trials and Sample Searches.*
http://www.grovereference.com/TDA/online/freetrials.htm
[5 October 2002]

Metropolitan Museum of Art, New York. *Metropolitan Museum of Art: Educational Resources.*
http://www.metmuseum.org/education/index.asp
[5 October 2002]

Metropolitan Museum of Art, New York. *Metropolitan Museum of Art: Explore & Learn.*
http://www.metmuseum.org/explore/index.asp?HomePageLink=explore_l

Metropolitan Museum of Art, New York. *Metropolitan Museum of Art: Home Page.*
http://www.metmuseum.org/home.asp

Milwaukee Public Museum, Milwaukee, WI. *Milwaukee Public Museum: Collections.*
http://www.mpm.edu/collections.html
[5 October 2002]

Minneapolis Institute of Arts, MN. *Minneapolis Institute of Arts: Education: Interactive Programs for Teachers & Students.*
http://www.artsmia.org/interactive-media/teachers-students.cfm
[5 October 2002]

Minneapolis Institute of Arts, MN. *Minneapolis Institute of Arts: The Collection.*
http://www.artsmia.org/collection/

Minnesota State University, Mankato. *Emuseum Home Page.*
http://emuseum.mnsu.edu/index.shtml
[5 October 2002]

Musée d'Orsay, Paris. *Musée d'Orsay: Home Page (English).*
http://www.musee-orsay.fr:8081/ORSAY/orsaygb/HTML.NSF/By+Filename/mosimple+index?OpenDocument

Musée d'Orsay, Paris. *Musée d'Orsay: Students/Education: Online Resources.*
http://www.musee-orsay.fr:8081/ORSAY/orsaygb/PROGRAM.NSF/6757ef6dee474116802563cd004f90ca/1f3324d799074722c1256ba40046bb7f?OpenDocument
[5 October 2002]

El Museo del Barrio, New York, NY. *El Museo del Barrio: Educational Programs.*
http://www.elmuseo.org/edu.html
[15 October 2002]

El Museo del Barrio, New York, NY. *El Museo del Barrio Home Page.*
http://www.elmuseo.org/

Museum of Antiquities, University of Saskatchewan. *Museum of Antiquities: Educational Programming and Summer Children's Workshops.*
http://www.usask.ca/antiquities/Educational_Programming.html
[15 October 2002]

Museum of Antiquities, University of Saskatchewan. *Museum of Antiquities Home Page.*
http://www.usask.ca/antiquities/

Museum of Fine Arts, Boston. *Museum of Fine Arts, Boston Home Page.*
http://www.mfa.org/home.htm

Museum of Fine Arts, Boston. *Museum of Fine Arts, Boston: Museum Learning and Public Programs: Teachers.*
http://www.mfa.org/education/teachersandstudents.htm
[15 October 2002]

Museum of Modern Art, New York, NY. *Museum of Modern Art Home Page.*
http://www.moma.org/
[5 October 2002]

Museum of Spanish Colonial Art, Santa Fe, NM. *Museum of Spanish Colonial Art: Education Programs of the Museum of Spanish Colonial Art.*
http://www.spanishcolonial.org/schedule.shtml
[15 October 2002]

Museum of Spanish Colonial Art, Santa Fe, NM. *Museum of Spanish Colonial Art Home Page.*
http://www.spanishcolonial.org/

MuseumSpot. *MuseumSpot Home Page.*
http://www.museumspot.com/
[5 October 2002]

MyStudios. *MyStudios Home Page.*
http://www.mystudios.com/
[5 October 2002]

National Endowment for the Arts. *Welcome to the Arts: National Endowment for the Arts.*
http://www.nea.gov/
[5 October 2002]

National Gallery of Art, Washington, D.C. *National Gallery of Art: Education.*
http://www.nga.gov/education/education.htm
[5 October 2002]

National Gallery of Art, Washington, D.C. *National Gallery of Art Home Page.*
http://www.nga.gov/

National Museum of Women in the Arts, Washington, DC. *National Museum of Women in the Arts Home Page.*
http://www.nmwa.org/

National Museum of Women in the Arts: Resources for Educators.
http://www.nmwa.org/resources/edu_workshop.asp
[28 September 2002]

North Carolina Museum of Art Foundation, Raleigh, NC. *North Carolina Museum of Art: Education and Museum Services: Teacher Resources.*
http://ncartmuseum.org/education/teacher.shtml

North Carolina Museum of Art Foundation, Raleigh, NC. *North Carolina Museum of Art: Education and Museum Services: Teacher Resources: Teacher's Guide to Twelve Objects in the Museum Collection.*
http://ncartmuseum.org/education/teacher/guide.shtml
[5 October 2002]

North Carolina Museum of Art Foundation, Raleigh, NC. *North Carolina Museum of Art Home Page.*
http://ncartmuseum.org/

Oakland Museum of California. *Oakland Museum of California: Art.*
http://www.museumca.org/global/art/index.html
[5 October 2002]

Olga's Gallery. *Olga's Gallery Home Page.*
http://www.abcgallery.com/
[5 October 2002]

OnFineArt.com. *On Fine Art.com*
http://www.onfineart.com/index.htm
[5 October 2002]

Philadelphia Museum of Art, Philadelphia, PA. *Philadelphia Museum of Art: Education: Teaching Resources.*
http://www.philamuseum.org/education/resources.shtml
[5 October 2002]

Philadelphia Museum of Art, Philadelphia, PA. *Philadelphia Museum of Art Home Page.*
http://www.philamuseum.org/

Pioch, Nicolas. *WebMuseum, Paris: Famous Artworks Exhibition.*
http://www.ibiblio.org/wm/paint/
[5 October 2002]

Portland Museum of Art, Portland, ME. *Portland Museum of Art: Education Programs.*
http://www.portlandmuseum.org/educ.html
[5 October 2002]

Portland Museum of Art, Portland, ME. *Portland Museum of Art Home Page.*
http://www.portlandmuseum.org/

President and Fellows of Harvard College. *Harvard University Art Museums.*
http://www.artmuseums.harvard.edu/

President and Fellows of Harvard College. *Harvard University Art Museums: Arthur M.
Sackler Museum.*
http://www.artmuseums.harvard.edu/sackler/index.html

President and Fellows of Harvard College. *Harvard University Art Museums: Busch-Reisinger
Museum.*
http://www.artmuseums.harvard.edu/busch/index.html

President and Fellows of Harvard College. *Harvard University Art Museums: Fogg Art Museum.*
http://www.artmuseums.harvard.edu/fogg/index.html
[5 October 2002]

San Francisco Museum of Modern Art, CA. *San Francisco Museum of Modern Art.*
http://www.sfmoma.org/

San Francisco Museum of Modern Art, CA. *San Francisco Museum of Modern Art: Education:
Art as Experiment, Art as Experience.*
http://www.sfmoma.org/anderson/index.html
[5 October 2002]

San Francisco Museum of Modern Art, CA. *San Francisco Museum of Modern Art: Education: e.school: Content and Curriculum.*
http://www.sfmoma.org/eschool/curriculum.html

San Francisco Museum of Modern Art, CA. *San Francisco Museum of Modern Art: Education:
Making Sense of Modern Art.*
http://www.sfmoma.org/MsoMA/index.html

Sarphy Production. *ArtFile: Welcome.*
http://www.the-artfile.com/uk/
[5 October 2002]

Smithsonian Institution. *National Museum of African Art: Education Programs.*
http://www.nmafa.si.edu/educ/educprog.htm
[5 October 2002]

Smithsonian Institution. *National Museum of African Art Home Page.*
http://www.nmafa.si.edu/

Smithsonian Institution. *Smithsonian American Art Museum: Education.*
http://nmaa-ryder.si.edu/education/main.html
[5 October 2002]

Smithsonian Institution. *Smithsonian American Art Museum Home Page.*
http://nmaa-ryder.si.edu/

Solomon R. Guggenheim Museum, New York. *Guggenheim Museum Home Page.*
http://www.guggenheim.org/new_york_index.html
[5 October 2002]

State Hermitage Museum, St. Petersburg, Russia. *State Hermitage Museum Home Page (English).*
http://www.hermitagemuseum.org/html_En/index.html
[5 October 2002]

Sterling and Francine Clark Art Institute, Williamstown, MA. *Sterling and Francine Clark Art Institute.*
http://www.clarkart.edu/the_clark_story/index.cfm?ID=33
[5 October 2002]

Sullivan, Mary Ann. Bluffton College, Bluffton, OH. *Digital Imaging Project.*
http://www.bluffton.edu/~sullivanm/
[5 October 2002]

Tate Gallery, London. *Tate: E-Learning.*
http://www.tate.org.uk/elearning/default.htm
[5 October 2002]

Tate Gallery, London. *Tate Home Page.*
http://www.tate.org/uk/home/default.htm

Tigertail Associates. *Tigertail Virtual Art Museum.*
http://tvm.tigtail.org/TVM/M_View/E/Efp.html
[5 October 2002]

University Art Museum, University at Albany, New York. *University Art Museum: University at Albany Home Page.*
http://www.albany.edu/museum/home.html
[5 October 2002]

University of Michigan School of Art and Design, Ann Arbor, MI. *Mother of All Art and Art History Links.*
http://www.art-design.umich.edu/mother/
[5 October 2002]

University of Pennsylvania Museum of Archaeology and Anthropology, Philadelphia, PA. *University of Pennsylvania Museum of Archaeology and Anthropology: Educational Services.*
http://www.upenn.edu/museum/PublicServices/edservices.html
[5 October 2002]

University of Pennsylvania Museum of Archaeology and Anthropology, Philadelphia, PA. *University of Pennsylvania Museum of Archaeology and Anthropology Home Page.*
http://www.museum.upenn.edu/

Utah Museum of Fine Arts, Salt Lake City, UT. *Utah Museum of Fine Arts: Educational Services.*
http://www.utah.edu/umfa/edprograms.html
[5 October 2002]

Utah Museum of Fine Arts, Salt Lake City, UT. *Utah Museum of Fine Arts Home Page.*
http://www.utah.edu/umfa/index.html

Walker Art Center, Minneapolis, MN. *Walker Art Center: Visual Arts.*
http://www.walkerart.org/programs/va_prog_frindex.html
[5 October 2002]

Washington University in St. Louis, St. Louis, MO. *Washington University in St. Louis Gallery of Art.*
http://galleryofart.wustl.edu/
[5 October 2002]

Williams College Museum of Art. Williamstown, MA. *Artnet Speaks Out!*
http://www.williams.edu/WCMA/artnet/kids/
[5 October 2002]

Witcombe, Chris. *Art History Resources on the Web.*
http://witcombe.sbc.edu/ARTHLinks.html
[5 October 2002]

Worcester Art Museum, Worcester, MA. *Worcester Art Museum Web.*
http://www.worcesterart.org/
[5 October 2002]

Xrefer. *Xrefer, The Web's Reference Engine.*
http://www.xrefer.com/
[5 October 2002]

Teachers first have to learn to use their critical thinking skills and the tools of the Internet before teaching these skills to their students. The Internet can be a fun and useful teaching tool. Along with fun, teachers should stress courtesy, "netiquette," and ethics to the students as they use the Internet. Netiquette refers to appropriate behavior on the Internet. It includes observing copyright; avoiding copyright piracy (as in the case of violations by Napster); citing primary sources; avoiding plagiarism; observing license agreements; not using abusive or hateful language; computer hacking; e-commerce stealing; the stealing of personal identities; fraud; avoiding child pornography and other forms of pedophilia; posting accurate information; not inciting violence, panic, or hate; and using good grammar and spelling correctly. When Internet users engage in unsavory behavior, the cost can be personal, dangerous, hurtful, and financially damaging. One's ethics are based on one's personal, cultural, religious, political, and social values. Be true to yourself and what you consider truthful, fair, and honest when creating or viewing web sites. These are values that teachers should impart to all students regardless of whether they use the Internet frequently or just practice daily.

References

Getty Center for Education in the Arts. 1993. *Perspectives on Education Reform: Arts Education as Catalyst.* Santa Monica, CA: Getty Center for Education in the Arts.

Google Image Search. http://images.google.com/help.faq_images.html [19 November 2001].

Harnack, Andrew. 2000. *Online: A Reference Guide to Using Internet Sources.* New York: St. Martin's Press.

PART II

Applying Critical Thinking Skills in the Visual Arts

CHAPTER 4

Elements and Principles of Design

Images

Krater, terracotta, Greek, circa 750–700 B.C., approximately 42" high. New York: Metropolitan Museum of Art.

St. Jerome in His Study, by Albrecht Dürer, engraving, 1514, 24 cm. x 19 cm. Ball State University Museum of Art.

Sunflowers, by Vincent van Gogh, oil on canvas, circa 1888–1889, 92.1 cm. x 73 cm. London: National Gallery.

Waterlilies, by Claude Monet, oil on canvas, circa 1906. Chicago: Art Institute of Chicago.

Web Addresses

Elements and Principles of Design

Idaho 4-H, University of Idaho. *Kidspace Art.*
http://www.ets.uidaho.edu/4-H/kidspace/
[5 October 2002]

Pacific Bell. *Eyes on Art: ArtSpeak 101: Visual Glossary: Defining the Elements of Artistic Design.*
http://www.kn.pacbell.com/wired/art2/artspeak/visual_terms.html
[10 July 2002]

Sanford. *Educational Web Adventures: Study Art: Glossary Term: Elements of Art.*
http://www.sanford-artedventures.com/study/g_art_elements.html
[10 July 2002]

Sanford. *Educational Web Adventures: Study Art: Principles of Art.*
http://www.sanford-artedventures.com/study/g_art_principles.html
[10 July 2002]

Line

Jirousek, Charlotte. Cornell University, Ithaca, NY. *Art, Design, and Visual Thinking: Introduction to the Elements of Design: The Elements: Line.*
http://char.txa.cornell.edu/language/element/element.htm
[10 July 2002]

Metropolitan Museum of Art, New York. *Metropolitan Museum of Art: The Collection: Greek and Roman Art: Krater, ca. 750–700 B.C.; Geometric.*
http://www.metmuseum.org/collections/view1.asp?dep=13&full=0&item=14%2E130%2E14
[10 July 2002]

Sanford. *Educational Web Adventures: Study Art: Elements of Art: Glossary Term: Line.*
http://www.sanford-artedventures.com/study/g_line.html
[10 July 2002]

Skaalid, Bonnie. University of Saskatchewan, Canada. *Web Design for Instruction: Classic Graphic Design Theory. Elements of Design: Line.*
http://www.usask.ca/education/coursework/skaalid/theory/cgdt/line.htm
[10 July 2002]

Perspective

Garner, Jan. Drexel University, Philadelphia, PA. *Math Forum at Drexel University. Perspective Drawing.*
http://mathforum.org/sum95/math_and/perspective/perspect.html

Sanford. *Educational Web Adventures: Create Art: Technique Demonstrations: Perspective Techniques: One-Point Perspective.*
http://www.sanford-artedventures.com/create/tech_1pt_perspective.html
[11 July 2002]

Sanford. *Educational Web Adventures: Create Art: Technique Demonstrations: Perspective Techniques: Two-Point Perspective.*
http://www.sanford-artedventures.com/create/tech_2pt_perspective.html
[11 July 2002]

St. Jerome In His Study (St. Jerome dans sa Cellule), 1514, by Albrecht Durer.
http://www.ibiblio.org/wm/paint/auth/durer/engravings/st-jerome.jpg
[11 July 2002]

Color

Sanford. *Educational Web Adventures: Create Art: The Values of Color: Drawing Shades and Tints.*
http://www.sanford-artedventures.com/create/tech_value.html
[11 July 2002]

Sanford. *Educational Web Adventures: Study Art: Glossary Term: Color.*
http://www.sanford-artedventures.com/study/g_color.html
[11 July 2002]

Media

Olga's Gallery. *Mary Cassatt.*
http://www.abcgallery.com/C/cassatt/cassatt.html
[11 July 2002]

Sanford. *Educational Web Adventures: Study Art: Media: Acrylic Paint, Brush, Crayon, Fresco,*
Oil Paint, Paint, Paper, Pastel, Pen, Pencil, Photography, Pigments, Tempera.
http://www.sanford-artedventures.com/study/study.html
[11 July 2002]

Site Summary

Students need to understand basic design elements and principles before analyzing and criticizing works of art. By understanding how to look at things, they learn to accept and possibly appreciate things (and people) for what they are. All objects contain the elements of line, shape, mass, value, texture, and color. An artist creates works of art by arranging these elements into compositions. Compositions can be two- or three-dimensional. To develop critical thinking skills in the visual arts, students have to understand how design elements work together to create an artwork. Once they understand the basics, students can formulate investigative questions in order to reach a conclusion about or an understanding of the meaning of an artwork. An artist can arrange these elements so that they direct the viewers' eyes and thoughts. But it is the viewers who synthesize the compositional design elements along with their own perceptions when formulating an opinion of the art piece.

It all begins with a simple line. The way the artist draws a line can create a certain mood, imply motion, suggest weight and mass, and create illusions of depth. A two-dimensional shape can be transformed into a three-dimensional object that has mass and volume. The artist produces illusions of depth by overlapping shapes or by positioning shapes on a surface. Values of lightness and darkness can define shapes, create illusions, and suggest line and mass. Value can also set the mood or tone of the subject matter for works of art. Texture is the quality of a surface, whether it is on a flat picture plane or a three-dimensional object, such as sculpture. Texture can add an element of stimulation or surprise to our nonvisual senses. Color can create visual (e.g., optical illusions), psychological, spiritual, emotional, or even physiological effects. By arranging and varying these elements, an artist can suggest rhythm, balance, and empathy. The artist chooses to work in a particular medium and use a technique to manipulate it into an artwork. The following questions will help to heighten the awareness of design elements and principles and the way they work together to create works of art.

Discussion Questions and Activities

1. To obtain a better understanding of the elements of design, access the following web site: http://www .kn.pacbell.com/wired/art2/artspeak/visual_terms.html. The questions there address issues of color, line, value, shape and form, balance, texture, symmetry and asymmetry, contrast, rhythm, and theme and variation. Refer to http://www.ets.uidaho.edu/4-H/kidspace/E-P.htm. What are the differences between the *elements* of design and the *principles* of design?

2. The element of line is defined at http://www.ets.uidaho.edu/4-H/kidspace/E-P.htm and at http://www .usask.ca/education/coursework/skaalid/theory/cgdt/line.htm. What are the different ways one can draw a line? Read from http://char.txa.cornell.edu/language/element/element.htm. How can line suggest calm, movement, vitality, spirituality, and frenzy? Look at the image of the Greek terracotta *Krater* from the eighth century B.C. at http://www.metmuseum.org/collections/view1.asp?dep=13 &full=0&item=14%2E130%2E14 and click on the alternate views. Describe how line is used on the vase. How does the artist tell a story by using line? How many different types of line can you see on the vase?

3. Line can create perspective (see http://www.sanford-artedventures.com/create/tech_1pt_perspective.html and http://www.sanford-artedventures.com/create/tech_2pt_perspective.html). What is the difference between one-point and two-point perspective? Follow the directions from both sites to draw and understand how perspective works. View the image of *St. Jerome In His Study (St. Jerome dans sa Cellule)* at http://www.ibiblio.org/wm/paint/auth/durer/engravings/st-jerome.jpg and read about perspective at http://mathforum.org/sum95/math_and/perspective/perspect.html. Make a printout of the image. Use a ruler and line up the following from the empty chair near the table on the far right side of the image: chair to the ceiling rafters; chair to each row of the windows; chair to the table and window sill; chair to the edge of the window; chair to the top of the heads of the lion and dog; chair to the step near the dog's head; chair to the corner of the rug on the floor. Does this image follow the rules of perspective?

4. Artists can use color in a number of ways. Read http://www.sanford-artedventures.com/study /g_color.html and link to "cool" colors and "warm" colors. What are the colors of the spectrum? What are some of the warm colors? View the image of *Sunflowers* and describe how the color enhances the subject. Other than the flowers, how else does van Gogh use the color of yellow? What are considered cool colors? View the image of *Waterlilies* and tell how you think this painting can make you feel cooler. Techniques of blending, shading, and tinting can change how light or dark a color looks; refer to the following web site: http://www.sanford-artedventures.com/create/tech_value.html. Use colored pencils, follow the instructions, and learn some of these techniques.

5. Principles of design are discussed at http://www.ets.uidaho.edu/4-H/kidspace/E-P.htm and at http:// www.sanford-artedventures.com/study/g_art_principles.html and link to balance, pattern, and rhythm. How does an artist create balance in a composition? Use an image search engine and type the words "Kente cloth" and view some images. Choose a couple of patterns and describe how they are repeated. Read about Kandinsky and his art and music at http://www.artchive.com/artchive/K/kandinsky.html and then click on the link "View List of Kandinsky Images on the Web." How does Kandinsky tie in music with rhythm and painting? What is significant in the titles of the paintings? How does he create rhythm by using line and a sweep of the brush?

6. An artist chooses a medium and a certain technique to create an artwork. Refer to the web site at http://www.sanford-artedventures.com/study/study.html and under MEDIA choose pencil, pen, pastel, oil paint, tempera paint, fresco, pigments, and brush. How and by whom were ancient pencils made? What are pencils made of nowadays? What did people use as a pen before the ballpoint was invented? Why do artists like using pastels when drawing? View an image gallery of pastel drawings done by Mary Cassat at http://www.abcgallery.com/C/cassatt/cassatt.html. Do pastels look softer and seem to blend easily? Are the colors dull or bright? How do pastels create texture? Who invented oil paints? What is the advantage of working in them? What is tempera paint made of? What are some of the earliest examples of tempera painting? What type of painting is usually done in fresco? How does the artist prepare the surface before applying pigment? How does an artist make colors with different types of paints? What are the various ways a brush can be made?

Related Internet Sites

Cave Spring Junior High, Roanoke, VA. *The Elements of Design.*
- http://www.rcs.k12.va.us/csjh/elements_doc.htm
  [28 September 2002]

Lovett, John. *Design and Color.*
- http://www.johnlovett.com/test.htm
  [28 September 2002]

Morton, J. L. *Color Matters: Color Theory.*
- http://www.colormatters.com/colortheory.html
  [29 September 2002]

CHAPTER 5

Prehistoric and Ancient Middle Eastern Art

(Circa 35,000–331 B.C.)

Images

Code of Hammurabi, basalt, circa 1760 B.C., entire stele approximately 7'4" high. Paris: Louvre.

Lascaux Cave Paintings, wall painting, circa 15,000–13,000 B.C. Dordogne, France. Stonehenge, stone, circa 2000 B.C. Salisbury Plan, Wiltshire, England.

Luristan Bronzes, bronze, circa eighth century B.C. At various museums (Paris: Louvre; Cincinnati: Art Museum).

Palace of Persepolis, circa 500 B.C. Northeast of Shiraz, Iran.

Venus of Willendorf, stone, circa 15,000–10,000 B.C., approximately 4.5" high. Vienna: Museum of Natural History.

Web Addresses

Prehistoric Art (Circa 35,000–1500 B.C.)

Clardy, Brian. *NIRD Art History: Prehistoric Art.*
http://www.jlc.net/~brian/art/prehistoric.html
[11 July 2002]

Keyes, Bradley. *Stonehenge: Who Built Stonehenge? Why?*
http://www.activemind.com/Mysterious/Topics/Stonehenge/index.html
[1 July 2002]

Luengas, Anne S. de. ITESM Campus Tampico, Mexico. *Prehistory.*
http://www.tam.itesm.mx/art/preh/ipre1.htm

Luengas, Anne S. de. ITESM Campus Tampico, Mexico. *Prehistory: Neolithic Art.*
http://www.tam.itesm.mx/art/preh/ipre3.htm
[11 July 2002]

Luengas, Anne S. de. ITESM Campus Tampico, Mexico. *Prehistory: Paleolithic Art.*
http://www.tam.itesm.mx/art/preh/ipre2.htm

Ministry of Culture and Communication. *Cave of Lascaux.*
http://www.culture.fr/culture/arcnat/lascaux/en/
[11 July 2002]

Witcombe, Chris. *Art History Resources on the Web: Prehistoric Art.*
http://witcombe.sbc.edu/ARTHprehistoric.html
[11 July 2002]

Ancient Mesopotamia (Circa 10,000–331 B.C.)

Ashmawy, Alaa K. *Seven Wonders of the Ancient World: The Throne Hall of Persepolis (Takht-e-Jamshid).*
http://ce.eng.usf.edu/pharos/wonders/Forgotten/persepolis.html
[15 July 2002]

Kianush, K. *Art Arena: Luristan Bronzes.*
http://www.art-arena.com/luristan.html
[11 July 2002]

Kreis, Steven. *The History Guide: Lectures on Ancient and Medieval European History: The Code of Hammurabi.*
http://www.historyguide.org/ancient/hammurabi.html
[11 July 2002]

Louvre. *Louvre: Collections. Oriental Antiquities, Islamic Art: Selected Works: Mesopotamia and Anatolia: Law-Codex of Hammurabi Susa.*
http://www.louvre.fr/louvrea.htm (select *Collections*: select *Oriental Antiquities, Islamic Art*: select *Selected Works*; select *Mesopotamia and Anatolia*; select *Law-Codex of Hammurabi Susa*)
[11 July 2002]

Notebook. *The Art of Ancient Iran, Pre-Islamic Cultures: The Bronzes of Luristan.*
http://www.noteaccess.com/Texts/Porada/6.htm
[11 July 2002]

Oriental Institute. University of Chicago. *Persepolis and Ancient Iran Catalog of Expedition Photographs.*
http://www-oi.uchicago.edu/OI/MUS/PA/IRAN/PAAI/PAAI.html
[11 July 2002]

West Semitic Research Project. Southern California Archaeological Research Collection. *Ancient Texts Relating to the Bible: Cuneiform Tablet.*
http://www.usc.edu/dept/LAS/wsrp/educational_site/ancient_texts/Cuneiform.shtml
[11 July 2002]

Witcombe, Chris. *Art History Resources on the Web: Ancient Near East.*
http://witcombe.sbc.edu/ARTHancient.html#AncNearEast
[11 July 2002]

Site Summary

This chapter covers various time periods in world art: Paleolithic (circa 35,000–8000 B.C.), Mesolithic (circa 8000–3500 B.C.), Neolithic (3000–1500 B.C.), Sumerian (3000–2350 B.C.), Akkadian (2350–2150 B.C.), Babylon (1900–1600 B.C.), Assyrian (1150–625 B.C.), Neo-Babylonian (612–538 B.C.), and Persian (538–331 B.C.). Early Paleolithic art is distinguished by imaginative cave paintings that illustrate the magic of the hunt.

Human beings documented not only their daily lives but their spiritual and creative lives as well. Mural cave paintings found in Altamira (Spain) and Dordogne and Lascaux (France) are visual documents of how we once lived. But the unique aspect of these paintings is that whoever drew them used their imagination to manipulate the figures on the irregular surface of the wall to enhance the shape of the animals. This creates a three-dimensional effect that makes the creatures seem more alive and animated. These cave paintings show little evidence of a human presence, and if there is one, the figure is either crudely drawn or disguised in some manner.

By the Mesolithic period, the rock paintings found in the Gasulla gorge of Spain show human figures in different poses and settings and in groups. Humans are depicted in activities that show their dominance over the animals they hunt as well as a sense of movement and composition. Other paintings can be interpreted as pictographs (symbolic pictures) that tell a story of an event. Eventually other forms of writing evolve, such as hieroglyphs (symbols that represent letters of the alphabet) and the invention of a true alphabet.

The Neolithic age can be best recognized by the megalithic (great stones) structures of Stonehenge, England (circa 2000 B.C.) and the menhirs (single stones) of Carnac, Brittany. Not only is the size of these stone structures amazing, but their placement is also a symbolic reference to some type of ritual. Meanwhile, the ancient civilizations of the Middle East (Egypt, Israel, Syria, Iraq, Iran, and Turkey) began to develop near the fertile areas of the Nile, Tigris, and Euphrates Rivers. The city complex of Catal Hüyük (circa 7000–5000 B.C.) in Anatolia (Jordan, Iran, and Turkey) shows evidence of a flourishing Neolithic civilization. The Mesopotamian culture of Sumer built city-states, developed a religion centered on nature gods, and created a system of writing. The city plan located its ziggurat (temple tower) in the center of the compound. The former Sumerian cities then fell to the Akkadians, who grouped the cities under the rule of Sargon of Akkad (circa 2300 B.C.). Akkadians spoke a different language and introduced a new loyalty dedicated to the king rather than the city-state. Over several centuries of war, Mesopotamia returned to the concept of the city-state. Babylon became an independent city-state under the rule of its king, Hammurabi.

Hammurabi developed both a code of law to reestablish order among the other city-states and also a centralized government. The *Stele of Hammurabi* from Susa (circa 1760 B.C.) has the code inscribed on its black basalt surface. The top of the stele has a carved relief showing the sun god, Shamash, giving Hammurabi a ring and staff that represent divine power and inspiration for the code. This important sculptural reference attributes a human form to the gods. Again, over centuries of war, the Assyrians (circa 900 B.C.) eventually gained control of the Tigris and Nile Rivers and the Persian Gulf and Asia Minor areas. They were a military society that established royal citadel complexes to protect their king. The citadel of Sargon II at Khorsabad (circa 720 B.C.) was guarded by monumental sculptures of winged bulls with human heads. The ziggurat was built with a continuous ramp, and the palace façade was decorated with colorful glazed tiles.

Other Assyrian kings documented their victories through relief sculptures. All of these elements are symbols of the king's power and strength. Eventually the Assyrian empire fell to the Babylonians again, but this time under the rule of King Nebuchadnezzar (612–538 B.C.). Nebuchadnezzar rebuilt Babylon, known for its hanging gardens and its ziggurat temple to Bel (supreme god of the Babylonians), in grand style. Its Ishtar Gate (circa 575 B.C.) is known for its lapis blue–glazed tiles decorated with dragons and bulls in profile. But the mighty walls of Ishtar were not enough to defend Babylon from Cyrus of Persia (559–529 B.C.). The ruins of the palace at Persepolis (520–460 B.C.) are evidence of this great Persian ruler. The Persepolis complex sits on a high plateau that overlooks the area for miles. The compound consists of columned halls, terraces, and gateways decorated with sculptures and painted reliefs. Within its walls, craftsmanship flourished, and objects of silver and gold were created. The bronze industry peaked in the nearby mountain rage of Luristan. Luristan produced a number of portable bronze objects that are distinguished by their stylized animal drawings. The Persian Empire grew from the Indus to the Danube, until Alexander the Great defeated Darius at the Battle of Issus (circa 333–330 B.C.).

Discussion Questions and Activities

1. Paleolithic cave paintings are distinct visual representations of life as it was over 35,000 years ago. Refer to the following web site at http://www.tam.itesm.mx/art/preh/ipre1.htm to understand the art of the Paleolithic (paintings) and Neolithic (characteristics of the societies). What were the paintings made with, what did they represent, and where could they be found? What types of structures were built during the Neolithic period? What were these structures made of? Describe characteristics of Neolithic societies. Read about the Lascaux cave paintings at http://www.culture.fr/culture/arcnat/lascaux /en/ and view the various links about the discovery, map, tour, and closing. How and when were the caves first discovered? What is the name of the most impressive cave at Lascaux? How were the colors supposedly blended? How did the artist depict an aspect of the hunt even though no human figures were depicted?

2. Prehistoric sculptures and monuments were also created; refer to http://www.jlc.net/~brian/art /prehistoric.html and http://www.activemind.com/Mysterious/Topics/Stonehenge/index.html for more information and view the images. How large were most of the early prehistoric sculptures, and why were they made that size? What kinds of features were depicted on the human sculpture figures? What kind of sculpture is the *Venus of Willendorf* (circa 30,000–25,000 B.C.)? Where is Stonehenge located? How and with what type of material is this structure arranged? What are some of the theories about the purpose of Stonehenge?

3. Sumerian cuneiform writing is the oldest known written language. The web site at http://www.usc .edu/dept/LAS/wsrp/educational_site/ancient_texts/Cuneiform.shtml gives background information and an image of a clay tablet. What is a pictogram? How was cuneiform writing actually done? What were some of the other civilizations that adopted cuneiform? What were the uses of a writing system such as cuneiform?

4. One of the greatest kings of the Babylonian era was Hammurabi. Hammurabi erected a tall pillar (stele) inscribed with his code of laws. Refer to http://www.louvre.fr/louvrea.htm and select "Collections. Oriental Antiquities, Islamic Art: Selected Works: Mesopotamia and Anatolia: Law-Codex of Hammurabi" and read information at http://www.historyguide.org/ancient/hammurabi.html. What is the code written on and what is it made of? How many sections are there? What is the reason for the code? Describe the engraving of the top section. Who was Hammurabi?

5. The Achaemenids of the first Persian Empire built a splendid palace at Persepolis (circa 518 B.C.). View a map and images at http://ce.eng.usf.edu/pharos/wonders/Forgotten/persepolis.html and link to the Oriental Institute's web site about Persepolis and Ancient Iran at http://www-oi.uchicago.edu /OI/MUS/PA/IRAN/PAAI/PAAI.html and select the "Royal Tombs and Other Monuments" thumbnail image index. Who was the Persian King who began building at Persepolis? What is the name of the present-day location where the ancient site of Persepolis stands? When was the site discovered and excavated? What do some of the carved reliefs on doorways look like? Who destroyed the complex and when?

6. The Luristan bronzes are well known for their metalwork design and technique. The web sites at http://www.noteaccess.com/Texts/Porada/6.htm and http://www.artarena.force9.co.uk/luristan.html explain their origin. Where is Luristan, and what kind of people lived there? What are some of the objects that they created in bronze? Were these objects functional or used for some type of ritual? What did the ritual objects look like? What are the two different kinds of seals, and how were they decorated? What is the most distinct characteristic of any of these bronze objects (functional or ritual)?

Related Internet Sites

Ashmawy, Alaa K. *Seven Wonders of the Ancient World: The Hanging Gardens of Babylon.*
■ http://ce.eng.usf.edu/pharos/wonders/gardens.html
[15 July 2002]

Bashiri, Iraj. University of Minnesota, Minneapolis MN. *The Art of Achaemenian Iran.*
■ http://www.iles.umn.edu/faculty/bashiri/Achaemenid.html
[11 July 2002]

Crystalinks. *Ancient and Lost Civilizations: Language & Writing: Cuneiform.*
■ http://www.crystalinks.com/sumerlanguage.html
[11 July 2002]

Exploring Ancient World Cultures. University of Evansville, Evansville, IN. *Exploring Ancient World Cultures: Readings from the Ancient Near East: Hammurabi's Code of Laws Translated by L. W. King.*
■ http://eawc.evansville.edu/anthology/hammurabi.htm
[11 July 2002]

Providence College, Providence, RI. *Mesopotamian Art and Archaeology.*
■ http://www.providence.edu/dwc/mesopot1.htm
[11 July 2002]

Rymer, Eric. *History Link 101. Ancient Mesopotamia.*
■ http://www.historylink101.com/ancient_mesopotamia.htm
[11 July 2002]

Tigertail Associates. *Tigertail Virtual Art Museum: Prehistoric Art and Artifacts.*
■ http://tvm.tigtail.org/TVM/M_View/E/PreHistory/prehistory.html
[11 July 2002]

University of Pennsylvania Museum of Archaeology and Anthropology, Philadelphia, PA. *About Cuneiform Writing.*
■ http://www.upenn.edu/museum/Games/cuneiform.html
[11 July 2002]

CHAPTER 6

Ancient Egyptian Art

(Circa 6000–30 B.C.)

Images

Akhenaten and His Family, painted limestone relief, 1348–1336 B.C., 31 cm. x 39 cm. Berlin: Staatliche Museum.

Colossus of Ramses II, stone, circa 1290 B.C. Luxor, Egypt.

Hesira (Hesy) from Saqqara, wood relief, circa 2750 B.C., 45" high. Cairo: Egyptian Museum, Giza pyramids, circa 2500–480 B.C. Giza, Egypt.

Fowling Scene. From Nebamun's Tomb, painted plaster wall, 1400 B.C., 31 cm. London: British Museum.

Web Addresses

Canon of Proportions

Decosta, Michelle. **University of Toronto, Canada.** *The Idealized Body: The Portrait Panel of Hesira.*
http://citd.scar.utoronto.ca/VPAB04/VPAB04_98/student/Decosta/idealization.html
[15 July 2002]

IDSC: Information and Decision Support Center, Egyptian Cabinet. *Egyptian Museum, Cairo: The Collection: Sculpture.*
http://www.egyptianmuseum.gov.eg/collection_sculpture.html
[12 July 2002]

Legon, John. *The Egyptian Canon of Art: Canon of Proportions.*
http://www.legon.demon.co.uk/canon.htm
[12 July 2002]

Metropolitan Museum of Art, New York. *Metropolitan Museum of Art: Explore & Learn: Measured Proportions.*
http://www.metmuseum.org/explore/newegypt/htm/lk_rep.htm
[12 July 2002]

Pyramids and Tombs

Ashmawy, Alaa K. *Seven Wonders of the Ancient World: The Great Pyramid of Giza.*
http://ce.eng.usf.edu/pharos/wonders/pyramid.html
[15 July 2002]

Bolton, Ian. *Egypt: Land of Eternity: The Evolution of Tombs in Ancient Egypt.*
http://members.tripod.com/~ib205/tombs.html
[12 July 2002]

Sculpture

Detroit Institute of Arts. *Detroit Institute of Arts: Collection: Ancient Art: Egypt.*
http://www.dia.org/collections/ancient/egypt/egypt.html
[15 July 2002]

Rymer, Eric. *History Link 101: Egyptian Art Lesson #1 Sculpture.*
http://www.historylink101.com/lessons/art_history_lessons/egypt_art1.htm
[15 July 2002]

Hieroglyphs

Metropolitan Museum of Art, New York. *Metropolitan Museum of Art: Explore & Learn: Hieroglyphs and Art.*
http://www.metmuseum.org/explore/newegypt/htm/lk_hiero.htm
[15 July 2002]

Minnesota State University, Mankato. *Emuseum: Hieroglyphics: The Hieroglyphic Alphabet.*
http://emuseum.mnsu.edu/prehistory/egypt/images/heiroglyphicsimages/egypt150.gif
[15 July 2002]

Minnesota State University, Mankato. *Emuseum: The Story of the Rosetta Stone, "Finding a Lost Language": The following is a chapter from "Ancient Peoples: A Hypertext View," draft by Richard A. Strachan and Kathleen A. Roetzel (1997).*
http://emuseum.mnsu.edu/prehistory/egypt/hieroglyphics/rosettastone.html
[15 July 2002]

Museum of Fine Arts, Boston. *Museum of Fine Arts, Boston: Explore Ancient Egypt: Writing as Art: Hieroglyphs.*
http://www.mfa.org/egypt/explore_ancient_egypt/hiero_writing1.html
[15 July 2002]

Painting

Metropolitan Museum of Art, New York. *Metropolitan Museum of Art: Explore & Learn: Multiple Points of View.*
http://www.metmuseum.org/explore/newegypt/htm/lk_over.htm
[15 July 2002]

Metropolitan Museum of Art, New York. *Metropolitan Museum of Art: Explore & Learn: Pose and Gesture.*
http://www.metmuseum.org/explore/newegypt/htm/lk_pose.htm
[15 July 2002]

MyStudios. *Egyptian Art: Fowling Scene from Nebamun's Tomb.*
http://www.mystudios.com/art/ancient/egyptian/egypt-fowling-scene.html
[15 July 2002]

Wood, Sharon O. and Shadowmyst Web Designs. *Art Treasures of Egypt: Eye of Horus:*
     Painting.
http://www.arttreasuresofegypt.com/PaintingPage570.htm
[15 July 2002]

Amarna Style

Lorenz, Megaera. *Heptune: Art of the Amarna Period.*
http://www.heptune.com/art.html
[15 July 2002]

Metropolitan Museum of Art, New York. *Metropolitan Museum of Art: Explore & Learn:*
     The Amarna Style.
http://www.metmuseum.org/explore/newegypt/htm/lk_amarn.htm
[15 July 2002]

Site Summary

The Nile River served as a fertile resource for the development of the ancient Egyptian civilization. The earliest evidence tracing Egyptian art is a wall painting from the predynastic era found at Hierakonopolis (circa 3500 B.C.) in Upper Egypt. The mural illustrates human figures, animals, and barges that carry the dead, suggesting the funerary customs of Egypt. Most Egyptian art and architecture focuses on preparing for death and ensuring immortality in the afterlife. When someone died, the person's body was mummified and placed in a tomb filled with items it would need in the afterlife. The Early Dynastic Period (circa 3000–2665 B.C.) refers to the time when Upper and Lower Egypt were unified under Menes (possibly as King Narmer). The *Palette of Narmer* (circa 3000 B.C.) is a visual narrative that portrays Narmer as a deified figure with symbols representing the two regions. Thus, the king is divine and sets the tone of royal divinity throughout the dynasties of Egyptian rule. The Giza pyramids of the Old Kingdom (circa 2665–2155 B.C.) are a symbol of the timelessness and eternal nature of the pharaohs. The pyramids are located west of the Nile, the side where the sun sets and near the city of Heliopolis. Here is where the cult of Re, worshippers of the sun god, resided. Pharaohs considered themselves the sons of Re. The power of Re dwelled in the fetish stone of the *ben-ben*, shaped like a pyramid. The architectural structure of the pyramid represents the power and eternal home of the pharaohs.

The Middle Kingdom (circa 2050–1650 B.C.) suffered turbulent years of war and a power struggle between pharaohs and invading feudal lords. Tombs were built within the rock of Beni Hasan, fronted with porticos, and decorated with painted reliefs. Sculpture was massive and somber, reflecting the pessimism and weariness of war. The New Kingdom (circa 1550–1080 B.C.) finally nurtured new leaders who opened an era of prosperity for Egypt. Architectural tombs of the New Kingdom were designed as grandiose temples. The temple was home for the king in life and was also his mortuary after death. Wall paintings exhibited life with a new sense of naturalism.

The Amarna period (circa 1370–1350 B.C.) of the New Kingdom is distinct for recognizing only one god (Aten, the sun god), proclaimed by King Amenhotep IV. As a sign of a new beginning, Amenhotep IV changed his name to Akhenaton and moved the capital from Thebes to Tel el-Amarna. Sculptures and paintings of the human figure were represented with a livelier sense of movement, tenderness, and individuality. His queen, Nefertiti, is immortalized by elegant sculptures, wall paintings, and limestone reliefs of the palace walls. After the king's death, eventually the cult of Amun was restored, and the city was abandoned and monuments dedicated to Akhenaton were destroyed.

During the years of the Ramses era (circa 1350–1085 B.C.), Egypt remained powerful and enjoyed the standard of craftsmanship of its artisans. Architecture and sculpture were quite advanced and represented Egypt's power and wealth. However, during the Third Intermediate (1080–745 B.C.) and Late Periods (745–332 B.C.) military leaders weakened the Egyptian Empire. Artistic production became scarce and mediocre. By 525 B.C., the Persians took over Egypt and almost wiped out any trace of Egyptian cultural arts. Alexander the Great then conquered the Persians in 333 B.C. in the Battle of Issus. The Ptolemaic rule (332–30 B.C.) shows Greco-Roman influence in Egyptian art and architecture. Pharaohs of the Ptolemies were able to preserve some of their traditions and religious beliefs. Architecture incorporated new elements such as façades that were attached to annexes that led to vast sanctuaries enclosed by massive walls. Eventually the Egyptian flavor was influenced by other diverse cultures and became merely a way station under the rule of the Romans.

Discussion Questions and Activities

1. The Egyptians formulated a scale of proportion in order to depict human figures. Read the first page of the web site at http://www.legon.demon.co.uk/canon.htm#canon and from the Metropolitan Museum of Art at http://www.metmuseum.org/explore/newegypt/htm/lk_rep.htm. What is this system of proportion called? What did the artist do first before drawing a figure? How did the artist draw different parts of the body so that they were in proportion? How did an artist measure the height of a figure? How large should a face be drawn? View the image of *Hesira (Hesy) from Saqqara* and make a printout of the image at http://citd.scar.utoronto.ca/VPAB04/VPAB04_98/student/Decosta/idealization.html. Draw a grid across the figure according to the proportions that the other web sites described. Does the formula of human proportion follow as described? What is the Egyptian concept of the proper way to depict the ideal human form?

2. The Egyptian pyramid is one of the Seven Wonders of the World. Read the information about how early Egyptian tombs evolved into pyramid tombs at http://members.tripod.com/~ib205/tombs.html and at http://ce.eng.usf.edu/pharos/wonders/pyramid.html. Use an image search engine and type in the words "Giza pyramids" to view different angles of the site. What were early tombs before the pyramids called? Briefly describe each of these early tombs. How many pyramids are currently at Giza? Which is considered the greatest of them all? How long did it take to build this pyramid, and how many blocks of stone were used in its construction? Describe what it is like to go inside a pyramid.

3. Read about Egyptian sculpture at http://www.dia.org/collections/ancient/egypt/egypt.html and at http://www.historylink101.com/lessons/art_history_lessons/egypt_art1.htm and view the Colossus of Ramses II. Where was Egyptian sculpture usually displayed? What are some terms that describe this type of sculpture? What were the different kinds of media used? Why were the sculptures of pharaohs usually large? Describe the features of the Colossus of Ramses II. Look up the term "colossus" in the *Merriam-Webster Dictionary* online at http://www.m-w.com/netdict.htm and tell why the term applies to this statue. From what vantage point should one view this statue?

4. Read about Egyptian hieroglyphs at http://www.mfa.org/egypt/explore_ancient_egypt/hiero_writing1.html and at http://emuseum.mnsu.edu/prehistory/egypt/hieroglyphics/rosettastone.html. How are Egyptian letters represented? How many letters does the Egyptian alphabet contain? When and how were hieroglyphs finally translated? What is the name of the stone that archaeologists discovered that led to the translation of the text? Who was the French historian/linguist who made the translation? View the alphabet and use the hieroglyph symbols to spell out your name at http://emuseum.mnsu.edu/prehistory/egypt/images/heiroglyphicsimages/egypt150.gif. Look at the images of Egyptian art at http://www.metmuseum.org/explore/newegypt/htm/lk_hiero.htm. Identify some of the hieroglyphs in the images. Which image shows the name of the person the image represents on an item to be worn, and whose name is it? What is the purpose of a "scribe"?

5. Wall painting techniques are described at http://www.arttreasuresofegypt.com/PaintingPage570.htm (By Wood, Sharon O., and Shadowmyst Web Designs. [15 July 2002]). What is the name of the technique the site shows? How are the walls prepared, and what kind of paint is used? View some of the images from the links. What are some of the new features of the figures in New Kingdom painting? Do the paintings have any special significance, and if so, what are they? Certain gestures are often repeated in paintings in order to mean something; refer to http://www.metmuseum.org/explore/newegypt/htm/lk_pose.htm and try to identify the poses and gestures from the images.

6. The Amarna was a unique era and style in Egyptian history. Refer to the following web sites and images at http://www.metmuseum.org/explore/newegypt/htm/lk_amarn.htm and http://www.heptune.com /art.html. Which king created this style? On what god did this king focus his attention and why? What are some of this style's unique characteristics? What was the most common motif depicted? What are some of the endearing scenes of these images? Who was the wife of this king?

Related Internet Sites

Art Institute of Chicago. *Art Institute of Chicago: Cleopatra Lesson Plans: Building a Body: Scale, Proportion, and Ratio.*
■ http://www.artic.edu/cleo/Teachfolder/Paankhtml/FINAL/Paank.Science.2.html
[23 July 2002]

Bolton, Ian. *Egypt: Land of Eternity: Mummification: Herodotus—Mummification in Ancient Egypt.*
■ http://members.tripod.com/~ib205/herodotus_mummification.html
[23 July 2002]

Elliot, Roger. *Original Art School Online: Measurements and Perspective.*
■ http://www.angelfire.com/ar/rogerart/measure.html
[23 July 2002]

IDSC: Information and Decision Support Center, Egyptian Cabinet. *Egyptian Museum Official Site, Cairo.*
■ http://www.egyptianmuseum.gov.eg/
[22 July 2002]

Macmillan Publishers Limited. *Artnet Magazine: Research, Grove Dictionary of Art: Styles and Movements: Amarna Style.*
■ http://www.artnet.com/library/00/0022/T002248.ASP
[22 July 2002]

Metropolitan Museum of Art, New York. *Metropolitan Museum of Art: Explore & Learn: Lessons (L) and Activities (A) Related to Looking at Ancient Egyptian Art.*
■ http://www.metmuseum.org/explore/newegypt/htm/lk_less.htm
[23 July 2002]

Metropolitan Museum of Art, New York. *Metropolitan Museum of Art: Explore & Learn: Looking at Ancient Egyptian Art.*
■ http://www.metmuseum.org/explore/newegypt/htm/lk_.htm
[23 July 2002]

Minnesota State University, Mankato. *Emuseum: Prehistory Exhibits: The Ancient Egyptian Culture Exhibit.*
■ http://emuseum.mnsu.edu/prehistory/egypt/index.shtml
[23 July 2002]

Museum of Fine Arts, Boston. *Museum of Fine Arts, Boston: Explore Ancient Egypt: Pharaohs of the Sun: The Amarna Style.*
■ http://www.mfa.org/egypt/amarna/sift_amarna/sift_amarna.html
[23 July 2002]

Smithsonian Institution. *Encyclopedia Smithsonian: The Egyptian Pyramid.*
■ http://www.si.edu/resource/faq/nmnh/pyramid.htm
[23 July 2002]

Witcombe, Chris. *Art History Resources on the Web: Ancient Egypt & Near East.*
■ http://witcombe.sbc.edu/ARTHancient.html
[23 July 2002]

CHAPTER 7

Aegean and Greek Art

(Circa 2800–30 B.C.)

Images

Acropolis, circa fifth century B.C. Athens, Greece.

Altar of Zeus from Pergamon, marble (west front restored), circa 185–175 B.C. Berlin: Staatliche Museum.

Attica red and black figure pottery, circa 550–525 B.C. From various museums.

Cycladic Idols (male and female), mostly stone/marble, circa 3000–2000 B.C., sizes vary. From various museums.

Discobolus by Myron, Roman marble copy, circa 450 B.C., life-size. Rome: Museo Nazionale.

Gold Mask from Mycenae (also known as *Schliemann's Agamemnon*). Gold repoussé, circa 1500 B.C., approximately 12" high. From the royal tombs of Mycenae. Athens: National Museum.

Kouros and Kore Figures, circa 550 B.C., sizes vary from 34" to 6'4" high. From various museums.

Laocoön, marble, circa early first century B.C., 8' high. Rome: Vatican Museum.

Minoan Pottery, circa 1800–1500 B.C. Crete: Heraklion Museum.

Palace of Knossos, circa 1500 B.C. Knossos, Crete.

Vapheio (Vaphio) Cups, gold repoussé, circa 1500 B.C., approximately 3.5" high. Athens: National Museum.

Web Addresses

Cycladic (Circa 2500–1400 B.C.)

J. Paul Getty Trust. *ArtsEdNet: The Getty's Art Education Web Site: Explore Art: The Collections: Cycladic Female Figure: Attributed to the Schuster Master.*
http://www.getty.edu/art/collections/objects/o15192.html
[16 July 2002]

Hellenic Ministry of Culture. *Prehistoric Collection: Early Cycladic Figure and The Harp-Player from Keros.*
http://www.culture.gr/2/21/214/21405m/e21405m5.html
[16 July 2002]

Museum of Antiquities, University of Saskatchewan. *Museum of Antiquities Collection: Cycladic Art 3000–2000 B.C.*
http://www.usask.ca/antiquities/Collection/Cycladic_Art.html
[15 July 2002]

Minoan (Circa 2300–1100 B.C.)

Daedalus Informatics Ltd. *Knossos: The Palace of King Minos.*
http://www.daedalus.gr/DAEI/THEME/Knossos.htm
[16 July 2002]

Hellenic Ministry of Culture. *Palace of Knossos.*
http://www.culture.gr/2/21/211/21123n/e211wn01.html
[16 July 2002]

Hoover, M. San Antonio College, TX. *Minos and the Heroes of Homer: Art of the Aegean.*
http://www.accd.edu/sac/vat/arthistory/arts1303/Aegean1.htm
[16 July 2002]

Macrakis, Michele A. *Minoan Art: Palace of Knossos Kamaresware.*
http://home.earthlink.net/~macrakis/Minoan_Art_5.html
[16 July 2002]

Mycenaean (Circa 1580–1100 B.C.)

Hellenic Ministry of Culture. *Prehistoric Collection: Gold Mask from Mycenae (also known as Schliemann's Agamemnon) and Vapheio (Vaphio) Cups.*
http://www.culture.gr/2/21/214/21405m/e21405m5.html
[16 July 2002]

Macmillan Encyclopedia (2001). From *Xrefer, The Web's Reference Engine: Mycenae.*
http://www.xrefer.com/entry/510766
[16 July 2002]

Greek (Circa 1100–30 B.C.)

Andrus, Kathryn. University of Colorado at Colorado Springs. *Digital Art Collections: Greek Art and Architecture: Greek Sculpture.*
http://harpy.uccs.edu/greek/greeksculpt.htm
[16 July 2002]

Case, Eric and Judith de Luce. *Virtual Sculpture Gallery of Selected Greek and Roman Sculpture.*
http://mandarb.net/virtual_gallery/index.shtml
[16 July 2002]

Cigola, Riccardo. *Art: Artists and Architects: Myron.*
http://www.italycyberguide.com/Art/artistsarchite/myron.htm
[17 July 2002]

Krannert Art Museum, University of Illinois at Urbana-Champaign. *Krannert Art Museum and Kinkead Pavilion: Greek Vase Tour.*
http://www.art.uiuc.edu/galleries/kam/GreekKam/grkintro.html
[17 July 2002]

Marks, Tracy. *Ancient Greek Art & Architecture.*
http://www.geocities.com/Athens/Crete/9169/greek.html
[16 July 2002]

Marks, Tracy. *Classical and Hellenistic Greek Architecture: Altar of Zeus from Pergamon.*
http://www.geocities.com/Athens/Crete/9169/classical.html
[16 July 2002]

Marks, Tracy. *Greek Figure Sculpture of the Classical & Hellenistic Periods: Laocoön.*
http://www.geocities.com/Athens/Crete/9169/figure.html
[16 July 2002]

Marks, Tracy. *Greek Vases and Pottery.*
http://www.geocities.com/Athens/Crete/9169/vases.html
[16 July 2002]

Polliver. *Archeology on the Net Web Ring: Five Orders of Architecture.*
http://www.chch.school.nz/mbc/columns.htm
[17 July 2002]

Ricketson, Mary Ann. *Types of Greek Vases.*
http://www.arches.uga.edu/~mrickets/ricketson/Vases.htm
[17 July 2002]

ThinkQuest. *Art of Greece: The Archaic Period — The Age of Colonization.*
http://library.thinkquest.org/26264/art/periods/site004.htm?tqskip1=1&tqtime=0717
[17 July 2002]

ThinkQuest. *Art of Greece: The Classical Period.*
http://library.thinkquest.org/26264/art/periods/site100.htm?tqskip1=1&tqtime=0717
[23 July 2002]

ThinkQuest. *Art of Greece: The Geometrical Period — the Middle Ages of Greece (link to a Geometric Amphora).*
http://library.thinkquest.org/26264/art/periods/site003.htm?tqskip1=1&tqtime=0717
[17 July 2002]

ThinkQuest. *Art of Greece: The Hellenistic Period.*
http://library.thinkquest.org/26264/art/periods/site005.htm?tqskip1=1&tqtime=0717
[17 July 2002]

Universal Artists, Inc. *Ancient Greece Art and Architecture: Architecture in Ancient Greece (link to "Greek Temple Architecture").*
http://www.ancientgreece.com/art/art.htm
[17 July 2002]

University of Pennsylvania Museum of Archaeology and Anthropology, Philadelphia, PA. *University of Pennsylvania Museum of Archaeology and Anthropology: The Ancient Greek World: Economy: Attica Black Figure and Red Figure Manufacturing (links to "Pottery Images").*
http://www.museum.upenn.edu/Greek_World/Trade_craft/Pottery_attic.html
[17 July 2002]

Xrefer, The Web's Reference Engine.
http://www.xrefer.com/search.jsp
[17 July 2002]

Site Summary

Aegean cultures (Minoan, Cycladic, and Mycenaean) developed concurrently with the ancient Egyptian and Mesopotamian civilizations. Aegeans are considered to be the link to the Western world of Greece. The island of Crete is situated between Europe, Egypt, and Asia Minor. The Minoan civilization (circa 2800–1100 B.C.) established several major cities on Crete, where the palace of Knossos was located. Minoan pottery and wall paintings of the palace of Knossos (circa 1600–1400 B.C.) exhibit marine creatures, water flowers, bulls, and wavelike designs emulating water. Craftspersons on the smaller Cycladic islands (circa 2500–2000 B.C.) produced a number of marble statues (idols) that were stylized to represent mostly female figures.

The Mycenaean culture developed along the southeastern coast of mainland Greece. The palace of Tiryns (circa 1250 B.C.) was built as a fortress; two protective lions, carved in relief, flank its magnificent gate. Many aspects of Mycenaean art reflect an influence by the Minoans and Egyptians. Like the Egyptians, Mycenaeans used gold to create repoussé (inverted relief) death masks, plates, cups, and so on. Eventually tribespeople came from the northern regions of Greece and obliterated the Aegean and Mycenaean civilizations. Separate city-states were formed, and Athens became one of the most powerful among them. During this era art, philosophy, and democracy blossomed and became the foundation of the Greek civilization.

The people of Greece were also known as Hellenes, a culture that consists of peoples of the Aegean Islands and Indo-European backgrounds who spoke Greek. Athens built an acropolis over a former Mycenaean fortress, which consisted of stoas (covered colonnades), an agora (marketplace), theaters, and various temples dedicated to Greek deities. Daily life of the Greeks consisted of three things: man, nature, and reason. Everything revolved around these concepts, including philosophy, the arts, science, and history.

Early stages of Greek history are referred to as the Geometric and Archaic periods (circa 1100–480 B.C.). Geometric vase paintings reveal designs that consist of geometric shapes and stylized figures that were arranged in bands around the vase. Archaic vase painting adopted an oriental style, probably due to trade with ancient Eastern civilizations. Although this type of vase decoration was still arranged in bands, there were more human figures and animals incorporated to create a narrative. Archaic sculpture produced a number of statues representing young women (kore) and young men (kouros). Each is distinguished by a sweet frozen "Archaic" smile, stiff frontal position, and bulging eyes.

The fifth century B.C. was a transitional period where sculpture abandoned the stylized stiffness of Archaic figures. Although idealized, figures appear more natural looking and have a sense of movement. By the fourth century B.C., Classical sculptures appear even more natural (softer-looking hair and skin) and playful; the drapery is deeper cut, and the proportions are more slender. Later, Hellenistic (323–30 B.C.) sculpture exaggerates all of these elements and features a dramatic moment as well. In architecture, early Greek temples were considered as sculpture. Temples consisted of a simple chamber and a porch with two columns and were covered by a sloping roof. More ambitious temples added a back porch that was attached to the chamber; then the chamber was surrounded with columns (colonnade). The whole structure rested on a platform above the ground. When you look at a Greek temple plan, you perceive a sense of order and proportion. This is because the temples are based on the concept of "orders," a system of proportion that includes the architectural features of the entablature, columns, and pedestal of the temple façade.

As Greek culture was developing, the Romans were gaining strength in the western Mediterranean. By 146 B.C., the Romans invaded the Greek city of Corinth and took control of the smaller neighboring Greek city-states. By taking over this area, the Romans introduced Western ideas to Greece, as well as assimilating some of its Near Eastern influences into the Roman culture.

Discussion Questions and Activities

1. You can see the unique characteristics of Cycladic sculpture at http://www.culture.gr/2/21/214 /21405m/e21405m5.html and at http://www.getty.edu/art/collections/objects/o15192.html. Read some background information at http://www.usask.ca/antiquities/Collection/Cycladic_Art.html. What are these sculpture pieces typically called? What are they made of? What do they represent? How are the features rendered? Were these images ever painted?

2. Because of recurring earthquakes, the palace of Knossos was built in several stages. View some of the images of the palace and frescos at http://www.daedalus.gr/DAEI/THEME/Knossos.htm, and read background information from the "Emergence of the Minoan Civilization" link; also refer to the Hellenic Ministry of Culture web site at http://www.culture.gr/2/21/211/21123n/e211wn01.html. At what stage was the palace built? What were some of the architectural features of the complex? What was so special about the "Throne Room"? Refer to the following web site at http://home.earthlink.net /~macrakis/Minoan_Art_5.html. What technique was used to make these wall paintings, and how were the scenes arranged?

3. The Mycenaean civilizations built fortress palaces and produced skilled craftsmen of metalwork. Look up some definitions of the Mycenaeans at http://www.xrefer.com/entry/510766 and then link to the other cross-references about Heinrich Schliemann (1822–1890) and Agamemnon according to the *Oxford Paperback Encyclopedia.* View the *Gold Mask from Mycenae* at http://www.culture.gr /2/21/214/21405m/e21405m5.html. What did Schliemann have to do with this gold mask? Why was the mask referred to as "Agamemnon"? Go back to the Xrefer web site and do a new search with the term "repoussé." How does this term apply to the mask? View the Vapheio cups from the same web site as the mask. Were these cups made using the same technique? If so, how can you tell? Describe the scenes on the cups.

4. Ancient Greek sculpture evolves when rendering the human figure. View images of Archaic kouros and kore figures at http://mandarb.net/virtual_gallery/index.shtml and at http://harpy.uccs.edu/greek /archaicsculpt.html. Compare them to the Classical *Discobolus* figure by Myron at http://harpy .uccs.edu/greek/classicalsc.html and the Hellenistic figures of *Laocoön* at http://harpy.uccs.edu /greek/hellsculpt.html. How are the figures represented in each of these eras? How would you describe the kouros figures compared to that of *Laocoön*? At the GeoCities web site at http://www.geocities .com/Athens/Crete/9169/figure.html (Greek figure sculpture of the Classical and Hellenistic periods) is a description of the *Laocoön* piece. Who is Laocoön, and at what moment is he depicted in the sculpture? Why do you think that this particular moment is characteristic of the Hellenistic period? Refer to information about Myron at http://www.italycyberguide.com/Art/artistsarchite/myron.htm. Who is Myron, and why is he important to the era of Classical Greek sculpture? What are the significant characteristics of Myron's work?

5. Greek vase paintings are as beautiful as decorated palace murals. You can view various types of vases at http://www.arches.uga.edu/~mrickets/ricketson/Vases.htm and at the GeoCities web site at http://www.geocities.com/Athens/Crete/9169/vases.html. What is the difference between a kylix and a krater? What was a lekythos used for? View the images of red and black figures from Attica and read about the technique for making them at http://www.art.uiuc.edu/oldkam/GreekKam/grkintro.html and from the University of Pennsylvania Museum web site at http://www.museum.upenn.edu /Greek_World/Trade_craft/Pottery_attic.html. How many different styles of Greek vase painting are there? Name them. Describe the different techniques of each. View Minoan vases at http://www .accd.edu/sac/vat/arthistory/arts1303/Aegean1.htm and read about the Geometric style at http://library .thinkquest.org/26264/art/periods/site003.htm?tqskip1=1&tqtime=0717 (from ThinkQuest [Geometric

period]). Then click on the image link to the amphora. What kinds of motifs are depicted on the Minoan vases? How do they compare to the Geometric style? What is the design on the bands of the Geometric vase?

6. One of the tenets of Greek architecture is that of orders (types). Look up and read some definitions of "orders of architecture" from the Xrefer web site at http://www.xrefer.com/search.jsp. What are the three Greek orders? How many orders are there altogether, and what are the others called? What components of architecture are usually referred to when identifying orders? Refer to http://www .ancientgreece.com/art/art.htm to identify specific types of orders. Which order is identified by a scroll-like design? What temple at the Acropolis in Athens utilizes these scroll-like columns, and where are the columns located in that structure? What kinds of columns were used for the Parthenon? Greek temple designs were fairly standard with some exceptions; refer to a temple plan at http:// www.chch.school.nz/mbc/columns.htm. What are these exceptions? What are the basic elements of a temple plan? Where were the architectural decorations usually applied on a temple? View the *Altar of Zeus from Pergamon* (circa 185–175 B.C.) at http://www.geocities.com/Athens/Crete/9169/classical .html. Where is the frieze located on the structure, and what is its purpose? What is the theme of the frieze? What Greek period is this piece from? What types of columns are used?

Related Internet Sites

Andrus, Kathryn. University of Colorado at Colorado Springs. *Digital Art Collections: Greek Art and Architecture.*
■ http://harpy.uccs.edu/greek/greek.html
[23 July 2002]

Andrus, Kathryn. University of Colorado at Colorado Springs. *Digital Art Collections: Roman Art and Architecture.*
■ http://harpy.uccs.edu/greekromelinks.html
[23 July 2002]

Dobbins, John. University of Virginia, Charlottesville, VA. *History of Art I: Aegean Art: Mycenaean.*
■ http://cti.itc.virginia.edu/~arth101/html/mycenaean.html
[23 July 2002]

J. Paul Getty Trust. *ArtsEdNet: The Getty's Art Education Web Site: Explore Art: The Collections: Making Greek Vases.*
■ http://www.getty.edu/art/collections/presentation/p41_111649-1.html
[23 July 2002]

Howe, Jeffery. Boston College. *Digital Archive of Architecture: Greek Architecture: The Greek Orders: Doric, Ionic, Corinthian.*
■ http://www.bc.edu/bc_org/avp/cas/fnart/arch/greek_arch.html
[23 July 2002]

Swindale, Ian. *Knossos.*
■ www.uk.digiserve.com/mentor/minoan/knossos.htm
[23 July 2002]

ThinkQuest. *Ancient Civilizations: Art and Culture: The Use of Pottery.*
■ http://library.thinkquest.org/C004203/art/art03.htm
[24 July 2002]

Witcombe, Chris. *Art History Resources on the Web: Ancient Greece and Rome.*
■ http://witcombe.sbc.edu/ARTHgreecerome.html
[July 8, 2002]

Witcombe, Chris. *Women in the Aegean: Minoan Snake Goddess.*
■ http://witcombe.sbc.edu/snakegoddess/discovery.html
[23 July 2002]

CHAPTER 8

Etruscan and Roman Art

(Circa Eighth Century B.C.–A.D. 500)

Etruscan Images

Black-Figure Neck Amphora by the Micali Painter, late sixth century B.C., ceramic, 44.6 cm. high. Detroit: Detroit Institute of Arts.

Chimera of Arezzo, bronze, circa fourth century B.C., 31.5" high. Florence: Archeological Museum.

Reconstruction of the Portonaccio Temple, circa 515–490 B.C. Veii, Italy.

Sarcophagus from Cerveteri, painted terracotta, circa 520 B.C., 6'7" long. Rome: Museo Nazionale de Villa Giulia.

Tomb of the Leopards, wall painting, circa 520 B.C. Tarquinia, Italy.

Tomb of the Lionesses, wall painting, circa 520 B.C. Tarquinia, Italy.

Etruscan Web Addresses

Agmen. *Etruscan Virtual Museum: Etruscan Art: The Chimera of Arezzo.*
http://www.agmen.com/etruscans/pag_engl/museum/arte.htm
[18 July 2002]

Agmen. *Etruscan Virtual Museum: The Etruscan Temple: Religious Architecture: Scale model of an Etruscan temple.*
http://www.agmen.com/etruscans/pag_engl/museum/tempio.htm
[18 July 2002]

Agmen. *Etruscan Virtual Museum. The Noble Villas: The Banquet: The Tomb of the Leopards.*
http://www.agmen.com/etruscans/pag_engl/museum/ricchi3.htm
[18 July 2002]

Alacritude. *Encyclopedia.com: Etruscan Civilization.*
http://encyclopedia.com/html/E/Etruscan-c.asp
[18 July 2002]

Basic, Rozmeri. University of Oklahoma School of Art. *Etruscan Art: Architecture Page 1: Reconstruction of the Portonaccio Temple, Veii.*
http://www.ou.edu/class/ahi4163/files/arch1.html
[18 July 2002]

Basic, Rozmeri. University of Oklahoma School of Art. *Etruscan Art: Tomb Paintings Page 4: Tomb of the Lionesses.*
http://www.ou.edu/class/ahi4163/files/tomb04.html
[18 July 2002]

Detroit Institute of Arts. *Detroit Institute of Arts: Collection: Ancient Art: The Etruscans and Their Influence.*
http://www.dia.org/collections/ancient/theetruscans/theetruscans.html
[18 July 2002]

Petersen, Alan. Coconino Community College, Flagstaff, Arizona. *Art of Etruria: Etruscan Art.*
http://www.coco.cc.az.us/apetersen/_ART201/etruscan.htm
[18 July 2002]

Roman Images

Antonine Boy, marble bust, circa A.D. 170–180. Cedar Rapids: Cedar Rapids Museum of Art.

Arch of Constantine (part of the Roman Forum); circa A.D. 312–315. Rome.

Augustus of Primaporta, marble statue, circa 20 B.C., 70" high. Rome: Vatican Museum.

Colosseum (part of the Roman Forum); begun circa A.D. 70, completed circa A.D. 80. Rome.

Ixion Room Wall Paintings (from the House of the Vetti), Fourth Style wall paintings, circa A.D. 70–79. Pompeii.

Roman Forum, circa 54 B.C. Rome.

Tetrarchs, porphyry, circa A.D. 305, 4'3" high. Venice: corner of the façade of San Marco.

Villa of Mysteries Wall Paintings, Second Style wall painting, circa 60–50 B.C. Pompeii.

Roman Web Addresses

Andrus, Kathryn. University of Colorado at Colorado Springs. *Digital Art Collections: Roman Sculpture.*
http://harpy.uccs.edu/roman/html/augustus.html
[18 July 2002]

Cedar Rapids Museum of Art, IA. *Cedar Rapids Museum of Art: The Tom and Nan Riley Collection of Roman Portrait Sculptures.*
http://www.vroma.org/~riley/
[18 July 2002]

Detroit Institute of Arts. *Detroit Institute of Arts: Collection: Ancient Art: Rome.*
http://www.dia.org/collections/ancient/rome/rome.html
[18 July 2002]

Hoover, M. San Antonio College, TX. *The Fine Art of Roman Wall Painting.*
http://www.accd.edu/sac/vat/arthistory/arts1303/Rome4.htm
[18 July 2002]

Kelsey Museum of Archaeology Newsletter, University of Michigan, MI. *Kelsey Museum Newsletter: Fall Exhibition to Explore Pompeiian Mural Cycle.*
http://www.lsa.umich.edu/kelsey/research/Publications/spring2000/pompeii.html
[18 July 2002]

Kent School District, Kent, Washington State. *Ancient Rome: Colosseum.*
http://www.kent.wednet.edu/curriculum/soc_studies/rome/Colosseum.html
[18 July 2002]

Kent School District, Kent, Washington State. *Ancient Rome: Forum.*
http://www.kent.wednet.edu/curriculum/soc_studies/rome/Forum.html
[18 July 2002]

Marlborough Boy's College, Blenheim, New Zealand. *Arch of Constantine, Rome.*
http://www.chch.school.nz/mbc/constant.htm
[18 July 2002]

Petersen, Alan. Coconino Community College, Flagstaff, Arizona. *Pompeii and Herculaneum and Roman Domestic Architecture: Painting and Mosaic.*
http://www.coco.cc.az.us/apetersen/_ART201/wall_painting.htm
[18 July 2002]

Ross School, East Hampton, New York. *The Colosseum.*
http://ross.pvt.k12.ny.us/rome/colossem/colossem.html
[18 July 2002]

Sullivan, Mary Ann. Bluffton College, Bluffton, OH. *Digital Imaging Project: Tetrarchs, Corner of Façade*, San Marco.
http://www.bluffton.edu/~sullivanm/romantetrarchs/tetrarchs.html
[18 July 2002]

ThinkQuest. *The Forum: A Clickable Reconstruction.*
http://library.thinkquest.org/11402/homeforum.html?tqskip1=1&tqtime=0718
[18 July 2002]

Site Summary

The Etruscan civilization was a culture that settled in the mideastern and southern areas of Italy, perhaps because of Greek colonization. It is believed that they were originally from Asia Minor and immigrated to Italy in the eighth century B.C., bringing with them Greek influences. They adopted the Greek concept of the city-state and established several Etruscan cities along the Tyrrhenian coast by the sixth century B.C. But these cities were never united politically and lacked the strength of the Greek city-states. As a result of the Etruscans' autonomy, the Romans easily overcame the individual Etruscan cities in the second century B.C. The Etruscan home was the center of family life and was built as a simple rectangular structure with an opening in the roof for the central atrium.

Etruscan temples were similar to the Greek temple plan, but with the innovation of steps at one end and a highly decorated façade and interior murals. Unlike the Greeks, Etruscan temples were not viewed as sculpture but functioned as an interior space. Another important aspect of Etruscan life was their elaborate burial rituals, cemeteries, and tombs. The cemeteries were built away from the city and arranged in an orderly fashion, thus creating a necropolis. Tombs were built above ground or cut into tufa rock (hardened volcanic ash). Tufa became a standard type of construction material utilized later by the ancient Romans and modern Italian structures. The tomb walls were decorated with beautiful and lively murals perhaps illustrating rituals. The technique was a fresco painting style in which tinted slip was placed onto the creamy yellow walls. Funerary urns and sarcophagi were also placed within the tombs.

The Etruscans introduced to the Western world a vast array of Greek influences through their art, poetry, architecture, and literature. They also maintained the Eastern philosophy of believing that human beings exist within the context of nature. As the Romans began to gain strength and assimilate Etruscan cities into their own empire, they absorbed some of the Etruscan culture along with that of the Greeks. But the life of a Roman citizen was centered on government, order, and its expansion. Rome became its capital by A.D. 200, and the empire expanded by building cities, bridges, roads, and aqueducts throughout Europe and northern Africa. Roman generals and administrators decorated their homes with Greek sculptures that they had taken from invaded territories. Numerous bronze and marble copies were made of the Classical Greek statues that still exist today. The statue of *Augustus of Prima Porta* (circa 20 B.C.) is perhaps one of the most original examples of Roman sculpture that breaks away from Greek replications. This statue represents the power, individuality, and the character of Augustus himself.

During an era known as the Republican period (after the murder of Julius Caesar in 44 B.C.), Etruria was almost torn apart by war and civil strife. Roman art at this time reflected this life of authority, discipline, and practicality by clearly deviating from the Classical Greek style. Character and individuality were typical qualities portrayed in many portrait busts and statues of Roman citizens during this period. This strict Roman concept is even evidenced in their city planning designs and architecture. Roman buildings were functional, vast, and imposing and dominated the landscape. Thus, the Roman forum became an important symbol representing their civic life.

Roman citizens gathered in the forum to conduct business, practice rituals, and perform other civic functions. Roman leaders also recognized the power of architecture and built arches, forums, columns, and altars dedicated in their honor and glorifying the empire. Mosaics and paintings were popular decorations for the interiors of Roman homes. Walls were carefully prepared with plaster that was applied in several layers and then decoratively painted. Four major painting styles embellished domestic wall surfaces. The First Style painting (also known as incrustation) simply divided the wall space into individual registers painted with bright solid colors. Second Style painting depicted a scene as if one were watching an event taking place in its own architectural space. The infamous Villa of Mysteries wall paintings (circa 50 B.C.) show a number of figures engaged in a ritual-like dance that occurs on a somewhat painted stage. It is as if the artist wanted to create an illusion of activity already occurring as one walked into the room. Another aspect of Second Style painting is the incorporation of painted architectural elements such as columns that divided scenes of landscapes. Third Style (ornate style) painting exhibits painted decorative frames that surround a scene in a panel; the illusion of architectural elements disappears. The Fourth Style (intricate style) expands the aspect of the decorative frame and incorporates painted garlands and architecture, elements of incrustation, and trompe l'oeil ("fool the eye") still lifes and elaborate scenes of myths appear.

Floors and walls used mosaics as though they were a carpet or a mural. The earliest indication that Roman art was beginning to shift away from its symbols of glorification appeared around the fourth century A.D. Christians were considered threats to the empire and a subversive element contributing to its decline. Once the emperor Constantine recognized Christianity in A.D. 325, Roman art began to flourish. The component of naturalism began to stiffen, as seen in images on the Column of Trajan (circa A.D. 113) in Rome and the statues of the *Tetrarchs* (circa A.D. 305) on the Piazza of San Marco. Features are again more stylized but not classical looking, which is more typical of the Archaic period. Drapery is sharply cut into the stone and lacks the feel of comfort and ease. With the death of Theodosius I in A.D. 395, the empire was divided into the Western Roman Empire (with Rome as its capital) and the Eastern Roman Empire (Byzantine, with Constantinople as its capital). The common languages of Latin (west) and Greek (east) were a weak link between the two empires. The sack of Rome by the Visigoths in A.D. 410 helped to put an end to the Roman Empire and the last emperor, Romulus Augustulus, who was overthrown by A.D. 476.

Discussion Questions and Activities

1. Read information about Etruscan temples at http://www.agmen.com/etruscans/pag_engl/museum /tempio.htm and http://www.coco.cc.az.us/apetersen/_ART201/etruscan.htm. Also view the image of the Portonaccio Temple in Veii at http://www.ou.edu/class/ahi4163/files/arch1.html. What is the shape of an Etruscan temple floor plan? What are the components of the temple? What type of build- ing material was used? How was the roof shaped, and what did it consist of? Describe the façade (front) of the Etruscan temple. What is an acroterion? Where would the acroterion be located? What civilization influenced Etruscan art and architecture?

2. The Etruscans had great respect for the living and the dead. Tomb burial and rituals were part of their daily life. Read information at http://www.agmen.com/etruscans/pag_engl/museum/arte.htm and http://www.agmen.com/etruscans/pag_engl/museum/ricchi3.htm. What were the walls of the tomb decorated with? What is the significance of a banquet scene? Describe the scene from the *Tomb of the Leopards*. Read more about tomb painting at http://encyclopedia.com/html/E/Etruscan-c.asp. Compare the scenes to the paintings of the *Tomb of the Lionesses* at http://www.ou.edu/class/ahi4163/files /tomb04.html. How does the artist indicate movement in the dancer scenes?

3. Read about Etruscan cemeteries at http://www.coco.cc.az.us/apetersen/_ART201/etruscan.htm and the objects that were placed in the tombs at http://www.dia.org/collections/ancient/theetruscans /theetruscans.html. What is a necropolis? What kinds of materials were used to build the tombs? What kind of objects can be found there? What is the significance of placing the objects with the dead? Click on the link to the *Black-Figure Neck Amphora*. What is an amphora used for? How is it decorated? How does the artist use line to show movement? View the image of the *Sarcophagus from Cerveteri* at http://www.coco.cc.az.us/apetersen/_ART201/etruscan.htm. Describe the sarcophagus. Refer to http://www.xrefer.com and look up the word sarcophagus and explain what it is. What type of sculptures were the Etruscans famous for? Describe the creature of the *Chimera of Arezzo* at http://www.agmen.com/etruscans/pag_engl/museum/arte.htm. Is this a mythological figure? Describe the surface texture of this piece.

4. Read about Roman forums at http://www.kent.wednet.edu/curriculum/soc_studies/rome/Forum.html and at http://library.thinkquest.org/11402/homeforum.html?tqskip1=1&tqtime=0718. What does the word forum mean? What types of activities do you think occurred in this area? What other buildings surrounded a forum? Do you think this was a social and business area? Who designed the most famous forum? What were some of the public buildings that were important components of the forum? What were some of the common building materials used? What were the state archive and the state prison called as part of the forum? What was the name of the building that was considered the center of busi- ness or the royal palace of the forum? What was the purpose of the Roman temples of the forum?

5. Read about the Colosseum at http://www.kent.wednet.edu/curriculum/soc_studies/rome/Colosseum.html and at http://ross.pvt.k12.ny.us/rome/colosseum/collosseum.html. How is it shaped? How many arches does it have? How fast could a crowd get out of the Colosseum? What are the three components that compose the Colosseum? What was the floor made of? What kinds of shows were staged there? How many peopie could the Colosseum hold? View the structure and explain the architectural elements that give the building a sense of balance and proportion.

6. The forum also contained triumphal arches. Refer to background information at http://www.chch .school.nz/mbc/constant.htm and at http://library.thinkquest.org/11402/homeforum.html under the section "Triumphal Arches." What is the purpose of an arch? Who were they dedicated to? View images

of the Arch of Constantine and identify the elements that make these structures appear to be in proportion. Where is the Arch of Constantine located? What does the inscription on it say?

7. Roman portrait sculpture focused more on individuals and their characters compared to the idealized sculpture of the Greeks. Read background information and view images at http://harpy.uccs.edu/roman /html/augustus.html and http://www.dia.org/collections/ancient/rome/rome.html. Who was Augustus Caesar? What was the main function of Roman sculpture? Look up the word cuirass at http://www .xrefer.com and read the definition according to the *Oxford English Reference Dictionary* (1996). View the full image and details of the *Augustus of Primaporta* at http://harpy.uccs.edu/roman/html /augustus.html. What do the designs on the cuirass represent? Describe the figure's stance and gesture. How does the artist balance the composition of the statue to prevent it from falling over? View the *Head of Emperor Augustus* at http://www.dia.org/collections/ancient/rome/24.101.html. How old is the emperor as depicted? What does the artist do to the brow of the emperor's head? What emotion does it seem to depict? View the image of the *Antonine Boy* at http://www.vroma.org/~riley/boy/index.html. How do the hair and skin of this bust contrast with each other? What is unusual about the eyes? What elements indicate that this young boy was from a prominent family? Late Roman sculpture began to change under the influence of Christianity. View the figures at http://www.bluffton.edu/~sullivanm /romantetrarchs/tetrarchs.html. How does their appearance differ from that of the *Augustus of Primaporta*? What is porphyry, what color is it, and why is it used only for certain types of sculpture? Why are these figures stylized looking?

8. Roman wall painting featured four main styles. View the paintings from course web sites at http:// www.accd.edu/sac/vat/arthistory/arts1303/Rome4.htm and at http://www.coco.cc.az.us/apetersen /_ART201/wall_painting.htm. What are the differences between the First Style and the Third Style of Roman painting? View the image of the Ixion Room (from the House of the Vetti). Which style does this follow? What does it remind you of? Does this look cluttered to you? View the Villa of Mysteries paintings at http://www.umich.edu/~kelseydb/Publications/spring2000/pompeii.html. When were they discovered? What are the female figures doing? Look at the images and explain why this is considered the Second Roman Style of painting.

Related Internet Sites

Etruscan

Basic, Rozmeri. University of Oklahoma School of Art. *Etruscan Art.*
- http://www.ou.edu/class/ahi4163/files/main.html
  [28 September 2002]

Mysterious Etruscans. *The History of Etruria.*
- http://members.tripod.com/~Centime/Etruscans/history.html#orient
  [28 September 2002]

Petropoulos, George. University of Richmond, VA. *Etruscan Tombs.*
- http://oncampus.richmond.edu/academics/as/classics/students/TUSCANY/epics.htm
  [30 September 2002]

Witcombe, Chris. *Art History Resources on the Web: Ancient Greece & Rome: Etruscan.*
- http://witcombe.sbc.edu/ARTHgreecerome.html#Etruscan
  [28 September 2002]

Roman

Alacritude. *Encyclopedia.com: Roman Art: Painting.*
- http://www.encyclopedia.com/html/section/romanart_painting.asp
  [30 September 2002]

Andrus, Kathryn. University of Colorado at Colorado Springs. *Digital Art Collections: Roman Painting.*
- http://harpy.uccs.edu/roman/html/romptg.html
  [30 September 2002]

J. Paul Getty Trust. *ArtsEdNet: The Getty's Art Education Web Site: Lesson Plans & Curriculum Ideas: Trajan's Rome: The Man, The City, The Empire: An Interdisciplinary Middle School Curriculum Unit.*
- http://www.getty.edu/artsednet/resources/Trajan/index.html
  [30 September 2002]

Leo Masuda Architectonic Research Office. *History of Roman Architecture.*
- http://web.kyoto-inet.or.jp/org/orion/eng/hst/roma.html
  [30 September 2002]

Marlborough Boy's College, Blenheim, New Zealand. *The Colosseum, Rome.*
- http://www.chch.school.nz/mbc/colosseu.htm
  [30 September 2002]

Witcombe, Chris. *Art History Resources on the Web: Ancient Greece & Rome: Ancient Rome.*
- http://witcombe.sbc.edu/ARTHgreecerome.html#Roman
  [30 September 2002]

CHAPTER 9

Early Christian, Byzantine, and Islamic Art

(Circa 325 B.C.–A.D. 1390)

Early Christian Image

Good Shepherd, catacomb wall painting, circa second century A.D. Rome: Catacomb of Pricilla.

Old St. Peter's (reconstruction drawing), begun A.D. 333 (destroyed). Rome.

Early Christian Web Addresses

Alacritude. *Encyclopedia.com: Christian Iconography: Iconography.*
http://encyclopedia.com/html/section/iconogra_christianiconography.asp
[18 July 2002]

Alacritude. *Encyclopedia.com: Early Christian Art and Architecture.*
http://encyclopedia.com/html/section/EarlyChr_EarliestWorks.asp
[18 July 2002]

Alacritude. *Encyclopedia.com: Early Christian Art and Architecture: Architecture.*
http://www.encyclopedia.com/html/section/earlychr_architecture.asp
[20 July 2002]

Basic, Rozmeri. University of Oklahoma School of Art. *Early Christian Art: Page 3: Reconstruction of Constantine's Church of St. Peter.*
http://www.ou.edu/class/ahi4263/frameset.html
[20 July 2002]

Basic, Rozmeri. University of Oklahoma School of Art. *Early Christian Art: Page 4: Samson and the Lion, via Latina Catacomb, Rome.*
http://www.ou.edu/class/ahi4263/byzhtml/p01-04.html
[18 July 2002]

Istituto Salesiano S. Callisto, Rome. *The Christian Catacombs of Rome.*
http://www.catacombe.roma.it/welcome.html
[18 July 2002]

Petersen, Alan. Coconino Community College, Flagstaff, Arizona. *Early Christian Art.*
http://www.coco.cc.az.us/apetersen/_ART201/early_ch_art.htm
[18 July 2002]

Byzantine Image

Christ Pantocrator, A.D. 1363, egg tempera on gesso wood. St. Petersburg, Russia: State Hermitage Museum.

Hagia Sophia, circa A.D. 532–537 Constantinople.

Byzantine Web Addresses

Alacritude. *Encyclopedia.com: Byzantine Art: Mosaic.*
http://encyclopedia.com/html/section/ByzantinANA_ByzantineArt.asp
[30 September 2002]

Brkich, Lazar. Milwaukee Public Museum, Milwaukee, WI. *Milwaukee Public Museum: European History: Understanding Russian Icons.*
http://www.mpm.edu/collect/icon.html
[20 July 2002]

Knight, Kevin. *Catholic Encyclopedia: Byzantine Architecture.*
http://www.newadvent.org/cathen/03094a.htm
[20 July 2002]

Knight, Kevin. *Catholic Encyclopedia: Byzantine Art.*
http://www.newadvent.org/cathen/03095a.htm
[20 July 2002]

Metropolitan Museum of Art, New York. *Metropolitan Museum of Art: Explore & Learn: The Glory of Byzantium: A Brief Summary of Byzantine History.*
http://www.metmuseum.org/explore/Byzantium/byz_1.html
[20 July 2002]

Princeton University, Princeton, NJ. *Welcome to Istanbul: The Hagia Sophia.*
http://www.princeton.edu/~asce/const_95/ayasofya.html
[20 July 2002]

State Hermitage Museum, St. Petersburg, Russia. *State Hermitage Museum: Collection Highlights: Oriental Art: Byzantium: Christ Pantocrator.*
http://www.hermitagemuseum.org/html_En/03/hm3_5_3c.html
[20 July 2002]

Islamic Image

Mihrab from Iran, monochrome-glaze tiles on composite body set in plaster, circa 1354, approximately 343.1 cm. x 288.7 cm. New York: Metropolitan Museum of Art.

Islamic Web Addresses

Alacritude. *Encyclopedia.com: Architecture: Structure: Mosque.*
http://www.encyclopedia.com/html/section/mosque_structure.asp
[20 July 2002]

Detroit Institute of Arts. *Detroit Institute of Arts: Collection: Ancient Art: Islamic Art.*
http://www.dia.org/collections/ancient/islamicart/islamicart.html
[20 July 2002]

Macmillan Encyclopedia (2001). From *Xrefer, The Web's Reference Engine: Islamic Art and Architecture.*
http://www.xrefer.com/entry.jsp?xrefid=506794&secid=
[20 July 2002]

Macmillan Encyclopedia (2001). From *Xrefer, The Web's Reference Engine: Mohammed (or Muhammad).*
http://www.xrefer.com/entry.jsp?xrefid=510287&secid=
[20 July 2002]

Metropolitan Museum of Art, New York. *Metropolitan Museum of Art: The Collection: Islamic Art: Introduction to Islamic Art.*
http://www.metmuseum.org/collections/department.asp?dep=14
[20 July 2002]

Metropolitan Museum of Art, New York. *Metropolitan Museum of Art: The Collection: Islamic Art: Introduction to Islamic Art: Mihrab.*
http://www.metmuseum.org/collections/view1.asp?dep=14&item=39%2E20
[20 July 2002]

Oxford Paperback Encyclopedia (1998). From *Xrefer, The Web's Reference Engine: Islamic Art and Architecture.*
http://www.xrefer.com/entry.jsp?xrefid=217714&secid=
[20 July 2002]

Thames & Hudson Dictionary of Art and Artists (1994). From *Xrefer, The Web's Reference Engine: Islamic Art.*
http://www.xrefer.com/entry.jsp?xrefid=651389&secid=
[22 July 2002]

Thames & Hudson Dictionary of Art Terms (1984). From *Xrefer, The Web's Reference Engine: Mihrab (Arabic).*
http://www.xrefer.com/entry.jsp?xrefid=649214&secid=
[20 July 2002]

Xrefer, The Web's Reference Engine.
http://www.xrefer.com/
[22 July 2002]

Site Summary

Early Christian art was produced as early as the first century A.D. during an age of the persecution of Christians. Christian symbols had to be hidden, and rituals had to be performed in secret, or the participants would face death at the hands of the Romans. The Roman catacombs (mortuaries) were a significant aspect of early Christianity. The network of catacombs not only contained the dead but were also decorated with wall frescoes exhibiting stories from the Old Testament, the theme of the Good Shepherd, symbols such as the fish (Christ) and dove (the soul), and orans figures (Christian figures depicted in poses of prayer and raised hands). Although these wall paintings seem a bit Roman in style, the Christian references set this type of painting apart from Roman murals.

Christian sculpture during this era was mainly confined to sarcophagi. Emperor Constantine finally adopted Christianity as the official state religion circa A.D. 313–325. He encouraged architects to build a new type of structure for the practice of Christian devotion. The greatest early basilica was perhaps Old St. Peter's in Rome (circa A.D. 333), which was built over a cemetery and the tomb of St. Peter. It consisted of a timbered roof that covered a central nave and side aisles. The nave led to the apse, which was a large niche at the front of the basilica. Modifications over several hundreds of years have destroyed the original structure of Old St. Peter's.

Other Christian churches were built across Italy and Greece and in Constantinople and still stand today. Basilica interiors were filled with light and color using wall mosaics, gold, colored glass, and marble. The exterior was unadorned and simple; these elements symbolized the difference between earthly and spiritual needs. Constantine also developed libraries for manuscripts that were located in Constantinople. Manuscripts were collected and preserved and produced by copying. Eventually the long rotulus (scroll-type manuscript) was replaced by the codex (book format) made of vellum (veal/calf skin). Vellum proved to be a durable material as well as an excellent painting surface for illumination.

Early Christian art aesthetically preserved some Greco-Roman influences. The Roman Empire was divided into both an Eastern and a Western area and maintained the official languages (Latin in the West and Greek in the East) of these regions after the death of Theodosius in A.D. 395. Rome became the capital of the Western Empire, and Constantinople (Istanbul) became the capital of the Eastern Empire. The Visigoths weakened the Western Empire in A.D. 410 when they sacked Rome. The Eastern Empire flourished during this period and separated from the traditions of Rome.

By the sixth century, the Byzantine Empire under Justinian had experienced its golden age and renamed Constantinople as Byzantium. Justinian built one of the finest of Byzantine churches, known as Hagia Sophia (Holy Wisdom). The chief innovation of this structure was the incorporation of a dome situated in a square compartment of the nave. The dome flooded the interior with light and embellished the richly decorated mosaics and murals. Light became a symbol for divine inspiration and the spirit. The Eastern Empire favored a flat, stylized, and decorative format. By using symbols and deviating from three-dimensional rendering, artists exhibited a new concept of what was beautiful and what was celestial in the depiction of human figures. Their idea was to create a new reality—a new sense of regal spirituality—for those entering the Byzantine church.

During the eighth century, Emperor Leo III banned all depictions of religious images in the Byzantine Empire during an era of iconoclasm (image destroyers). The ban was finally lifted in A.D. 843, and a more formal and abstract Byzantine style emerged. Compositional space was symmetrically arranged, figures appeared motionless and elongated, and emotion is restrained and classical. This era is known as the Second Golden Age (circa A.D. 850–1200) in Byzantine art.

Icons (panel paintings of the Virgin, Christ, and saints) and carved ivories were abundantly produced during the Second Golden Age. Byzantine influences had reached as far as Russia and other Slavic lands such as Bulgaria. Meanwhile, in Arabia during the seventh century, the new religion of Islam appeared and swept across the Middle East and areas of Europe. Some characteristics of Islam are an acculturation from Judeo-Christian elements. These elements were probably assimilated when regions of the Byzantine Empire were captured. Islam sprang up when the prophet Mohammed fled from Mecca to Medinet-en-Nabi in 622. He began to preach his prophecy that one should surrender oneself to one God (Allah). The Koran (sacred scripture of Mohammed's revelations) includes basic concepts of the Bible and acknowledges the existence of Jesus.

Tenets of Islam specified the creation of a new social order that united religion and politics under one ruler, that is, a government of faith. Islamic followers are considered soldiers of Allah; their destiny (assignment) is to conquer the world for Allah. Mohammed's successors are known as caliphs, who claim to be family descendants of Mohammed.

Palestine, Syria, and Iraq (known as the Fertile Crescent) were the center of the early Moslem world. Islamic Arab soldiers expanded their empire by conquering Spain, Egypt, and Tunisia. Even though the Koran discourages a life of luxury, the caliphs' taste for opulence was not diminished.

Ornamentation is characteristic of Islamic art and is a symbol of Islamic values. Ornament became the Islamic signature utilized in calligraphy, manuscript painting, textile arts, and architecture. Typical Islamic ornamentation consisted of swirling plant formations and rosettes (known as an arabesque) as well as geometric figures representing human and animal forms. Arabic script created patterns that were sacred when scribes copied the Koran. Muslims believe that Allah's words are channeled through the Arabic language of the Koran. The act of copying the Koran in Arabic script is a sacred ritual practice.

Script is not limited to the book alone but also appears as wall decorations in mosques and on household objects and architectural components. Islamic architecture closely relates to prayer, so early mosques were built to contain a whole Moslem community. Mohammed's mosque was a courtyard in Medina, an adaptation of the rectangular Christian basilica. In the courtyard, the wall that faces closest toward Mecca is known as the qiblah (direction toward Mecca), where prayer is conducted in a niche known as a mihrab. The leader preaches from a minbar (pulpit) located near the qiblah. From a minaret (tower) a town crier summons the Moslem community to pray at particular times of the day.

During the twelfth century, the mosque assumed a more cruciform layout, with a niche on each side of the courtyard. The most recognizable mosque design today is one that has a rectangular hall capped with a dome, similar to Byzantine churches. Islamic art was symbolic and decorative, but individuality was not encouraged, for it was believed to be a deviation from the spirit of Islam. In any case, Islamic culture had far-reaching effects on science, astronomy, mathematics, poetry, and the visual arts of early medieval Europe.

Discussion Questions and Activities

1. Read http://www.encyclopedia.com/articlesnew/03904EarliestWorks.html about early Christian catacomb paintings. View images of these at http://www.ou.edu/class/ahi4263/byzhtml/p01-04.html and at http://www.catacombe.roma.it/welcome.html. What type of painting did early Christian catacomb wall paintings resemble? What early Christian themes were painted? What is the theme of the Catacomb of Pricilla wall paintings? Read the definition of Christian iconography at http://encyclopedia .com/html/section/iconogra_christianiconography.asp. What do you think some of the symbolic elements in these catacomb paintings are? View more catacomb paintings at http://www.coco.cc.az.us /apetersen/_ART201/early_ch_art.htm. What did the early Christians use the catacomb for? Why do you think that they had to use symbolic imagery?

2. Read about early Christian architecture at http://www.encyclopedia.com/html/section/earlychr _architecture.asp and at http://www.coco.cc.az.us/apetersen/_ART201/early_ch_art.htm. Also view the schematic drawings at http://www.ou.edu/class/ahi4263/frameset.html of the reconstruction of Constantine's Church of St. Peter, Rome. What happened to some of the Roman structures after the fall of the Roman Empire? What is the design of the basilica hall? Look at the reconstruction drawing and identify the nave and aisles. What was Old St. Peter's built over? What was the roof made of?

3. Read information about Byzantine history at http://www.metmuseum.org/explore/Byzantium/byz_1.html and at http://www.newadvent.org/cathen/03095a.htm. What was the capital of the Byzantine Empire? What countries were considered Byzantine? What other cultures influenced Byzantine art and architecture? Mosaics and icons flourished in Byzantine art. Refer to http://encyclopedia.com/html/section /ByzantinANA_ByzantineArt.asp and http://www.mpm.edu/collect/icon.html. Then view the image of the *Christ Pantocrator* icon from the Hermitage Museum at http://www.hermitagemuseum .org/html_En/03/hm3_5_3c.html. Where were mosaics usually found in Byzantine architecture? What are mosaics made of? Are they colorful, and if so, why? What were the themes of many of the mosaic designs? What is an icon? What kinds of figures were painted as icons, and what was the most popular figure? Describe the figure of *Christ Pantocrator* and its typical Byzantine characteristics.

4. Read about Byzantine architecture at http://www.newadvent.org/cathen/03094a.htm and http://www .princeton.edu/~asce/const_95/ayasofya.html about Hagia Sophia. Who built the structure? What kind of structure is it today? Where was Hagia Sophia built, and what is the city currently known as? What does "Hagia Sophia" mean? Why did the dome collapse? Was the second dome built like the original? What was unique about the dome, and what happened to it? How is the dome situated on the walls of the building? What is the dome a symbol of?

5. Mohammed founded the religion of Islam about A.D. 610. Look up encyclopedia articles in Xrefer at http://www.xrefer.com/ about Mohammed (or Muhammad [circa A.D. 570–632]). Then view images of Islamic art at http://www.dia.org/collections/ancient/islamicart/islamicart.html from the Detroit Institute of Arts and from the Metropolitan Museum of Art at http://www.metmuseum.org/collections /department.asp?dep=14 (click on the links to view the objects). How are Islamic architecture, objects, and manuscripts decorated? Why is the ornamentation stylized? What does the term arabesque mean? View the images and identify the arabesque ornamentation. What kind of design is on the open lacework of metal objects from the Detroit Institute of Arts? How is the design different from that on the glass bottle from the Metropolitan Museum of Art (New York)?

6. Read about the structure of a mosque at http://www.encyclopedia.com/html/section/mosque_structure.asp and http://www.xrefer.com/entry.jsp?xrefid=217714&secid=. Read the definition of a mihrab at http://www.xrefer.com/entry.jsp?xrefid=649214&secid=, and then view the image of one at http://www.metmuseum.org/collections/view1.asp?dep=14&item=39%2E20. What is the function of a mihrab? Where is it located within a mosque? What kind of decoration is on a mihrab? Describe the decoration and color of the mihrab from the Metropolitan Museum of Art. Why is the surface completely decorated? In what direction should a mihrab be placed? What is the significance of facing it in this direction?

Related Internet Sites

Early Christian

Museum of Antiquities, University of Saskatchewan. *Museum of Antiquities Collection: Medieval and Early Christian Art.*
■ http://www.usask.ca/antiquities/Collection/Medieval_Art.html
[April 29, 2002]

Witcombe, Chris. *Art History Resources on the Web: Art of the Middle Ages: Early Christian.*
■ http://witcombe.sbc.edu/ARTHmedieval.html#EarlyChristian
[July 14, 2002]

Byzantine

Luengas, Anne S. de. ITESM Campus Tampico, Mexico. *Byzantine Architecture.*
■ http://www.tam.itesm.mx/art/bizancio/ibizhtm2.htm
[21 July 2002]

Metropolitan Museum of Art, New York. *Metropolitan Museum of Art: Explore & Learn: Byzantium: Glossary of Terms.*
■ http://www.metmuseum.org/explore/Byzantium/glossary.html
[21 July 2002]

Metropolitan Museum of Art, New York. *Metropolitan Museum of Art: Explore & Learn: Byzantium: The Religious Sphere.*
■ http://www.metmuseum.org/explore/Byzantium/byzsub_1.html
[21 July 2002]

Metropolitan Museum of Art, New York. *Metropolitan Museum of Art: Explore & Learn: Byzantium: The Secular World: What Attributes Identify the Emperors?*
■ http://www.metmuseum.org/explore/Byzantium/byzsub_2.html
[21 July 2002]

St. Nicholas Russian Orthodox Church, Chisholm, MN. *Gallery of Icons.*
■ http://geminidom.com/stnicholaschurch/icongallery.html
[21 July 2002]

Islamic

Artifice, Inc. *Great Buildings Online: Islamic Architecture.*
■ http://www.greatbuildings.com/types/styles/islamic.html
[22 July 2002]

Islamic Arts and Architecture Organization. *Islamic Arts and Architecture (IAAO).*
■ http://www.islamicart.com/
[22 July 2002]

Macmillan Publishers Limited. *The Grove Dictionary of Art Online: Sample Articles: Islamic Architecture.*
- http://www.grovereference.com/TDA/samples/islam.htm
  [22 July 2002]

State Hermitage Museum, St. Petersburg, Russia. *State Hermitage Museum: Collection Highlights: Oriental Art: Islamic Art of Countries of the Near East.*
- http://www.hermitagemuseum.org/html_En/03/hm3_5_5.html
  [22 July 2002]

CHAPTER 10

Early Medieval and Medieval Art

(Circa A.D. 375–1500)

Images

Bayeux Tapestry, linen strip, executed between 1066 and 1077, wool embroidery and needle-work designs on linen, 48 cm. (19") wide and over 70 m. (231') long. Bayeux: Town Hall.

Book of Kells, illuminated manuscript, circa 760–820, approximately 13" x 9.5". Dublin: Trinity College.

Chartres Cathedral, circa 1194–1260. Chartres, France.

Ebbo Gospels, manuscript illumination, circa 816–835, Epernay, France: Bibliothèque Municipale.

Gospel Book of Otto II and Otto III, illuminated manuscripts, circa 983–1001. Munich: Bavarian State Library.

Lindisfarne Gospels, illuminated manuscript, circa late seventh century, approximately 13"x 10". London: British Library.

Palace Chapel of Aachen, designed by Odo of Metz, begun in A.D. 786. Aachen, Germany.

Sainte Madeleine Church, circa 1104–1132. Vézelay, France.

St. Denis, circa 1140–1144. Paris.

Sutton Hoo Burial Site and Treasures, circa 655, Anglo-Saxon wooden ship (rebuilt) and gold and enameled treasures. London: British Museum.

Web Addresses

Early Medieval (Circa 375–1015)

Andersen, Erik and Ole Crumlin-Pedersen. *Sutton Hoo Ship Recreated.*
http://www.natmus.dk/nmf/nb/8/english/art6.htm
[21 July 2002]

British Library, London, England. *British Library: Collections: Treasures: Lindisfarne Gospels.*
http://www.bl.uk/collections/treasures/lindis.html
[21 July 2002]

Clans of Ireland Ltd. *Irish History and Culture: The Book of Kells.*
http://www.irishclans.com/articles/bookofkells.html
[21 July 2002]

Current Archeology. *Current Archeology: Sutton Hoo: The Grandest Anglo-Saxon Burial of All (This is based on a fuller account in Current Archaeology 128).*
http://www.archaeology.co.uk/timeline/saxon/suttonhoo/suttonhoo.htm
[21 July 2002]

Keep, Christopher, Tim McLaughlin, and Robin Parmar. *Electronic Labyrinth: Institute for Advanced Technology in the Humanities, University of Virginia. Illuminated Manuscripts.*
http://www.iath.virginia.edu/elab/hfl0263.html
[21 July 2002]

Sutton Hoo Society. *Sutton Hoo Archeology.*
http://www.suttonhoo.org/archaeology.htm
[30 September 2002]

Carolingian (Circa 750–900)

About.com. *Art History 101 with Andrea Mulder-Slater: St. Matthew, Ebbo Gospels.*
http://arthistory.about.com/library/blslide_matthew_ebbo.htm
[21 July 2002]

Alacritude. *Encyclopedia.com: Aachen.*
http://www.newadvent.org/cathen/01001a.htm
[21 July 2002]

John F. Kennedy School, Berlin, Germany. *The Aachen Cathedral.*
http://www.jfks.de/slife/classtrips/france2000/aachencathedral.html
[21 July 2002]

Utah Museum of Fine Arts, Salt Lake City, UT. *Utah Museum of Fine Arts: Medieval Manuscripts: General Introduction, What is Illumination?*
http://www.utah.edu/umfa/mmgenintro.html
[21 July 2002]

Ottonian Period (Circa 955–1015)

Alacritude. *Encyclopedia.com: Ottonian Art.*
http://www.encyclopedia.com/html/O/Ottonian.asp
[21 July 2002]

University of California Regents. Berkeley Library, Berkeley, CA. *Digital Scriptorium: Ottonian Kingship Images: Otto II and Otto III.*
http://ishi.lib.berkeley.edu/history155/slides/kingship/Manuscripts/Ottonians/
[21 July 2002]

Romanesque (Circa 1000–1150)

Macmillan Encyclopedia (2001). From *Xrefer, The Web's Reference Engine: Bayeux Tapestry.*
http://xrefer.com/entry.jsp?xrefid=497669&secid=
[21 July 2002]

Macmillan Encyclopedia (2001). From *Xrefer, The Web's Reference Engine: Embroidery.*
http://xrefer.com/entry.jsp?xrefid=502871&secid=
[21 July 2002]

Thames & Hudson Dictionary of Art Terms (1984). From *Xrefer, The Web's Reference Engine: Tapestry.*
http://xrefer.com/entry.jsp?xrefid=649927&secid=
[21 July 2002]

Thames & Hudson Dictionary of Art and Artist (1994). From *Xrefer, The Web's Reference Engine: Romanesque.*
http://xrefer.com/entry.jsp?xrefid=652232&secid=
[21 July 2002]

University of Michigan, Ann Arbor, MI. *The Cultural Crusades: The War and Cultural Exchange Between the Christian and Islamic Worlds: Art of the Crusades Era.*
http://www.umich.edu/~marcons/Crusades/topics/art/art-article.html
[21 July 2002]

Gothic (Circa 1140–1500)

About.com. *Art History 101 with Andrea Mulder-Slater: Gothic Style: 1140–1500.*
http://arthistory.about.com/library/bl101_gothic.htm
[21 July 2002]

Artifice, Inc. *Great Buildings Online: Chartres Cathedral.*
http://www.greatbuildings.com/buildings/Chartres_Cathedral.html
[21 July 2002]

Howe, Jeffery. Boston College. *Digital Archive of Architecture: High Gothic Architecture: Chartres.*
http://www.bc.edu/bc_org/avp/cas/fnart/arch/chartres.html
[21 July 2002]

Medieval Glass

Alacritude. *Encyclopedia.com: From Bartleby: Stained Glass.*
http://www.bartleby.com/65/st/stainedg.html
[21 July 2002]

Art Glass Suppliers Association. *Community: History: General (links to chapters).*
http://www.agsa.org/community/history_general.asp
[21 July 2002]

Knight, Kevin. *Catholic Encyclopedia: Stained Glass.*
http://www.newadvent.org/cathen/14241a.htm
[21 July 2002]

Oxford Dictionary of Art (1997). From *Xrefer, The Web's Reference Engine: Stained Glass.*
http://xrefer.com/entry.jsp?xrefid=145562&secid=
[21 July 2002]

Site Summary

Artifacts, sculpture, painting, architecture, and so on all visually document the progress of a culture. These elements trace the evolution of a culture from one age to another. They also trace how people moved across a region and how they lived, worshipped, thought, and died. From the fourth to the ninth centuries A.D., Germanic tribespeople (Visigoths, Ostrogoths, Lombards, and Franks) overran weakened regions of the Roman Empire. Many of the objects they created were portable and often had a personal attachment. In addition to being functional, some of the objects were so ornamental that they were probably affiliated with a special ritual or perhaps were commemorative pieces.

These migratory people excelled in metalwork, goldsmithing, and enameling. They created beautiful buckles, purse covers, jewelry, and fibulae (pin clasps). The Anglo-Saxons, Hiberno-Saxons, and Celts settled in regions of Britain and Ireland beginning in the fifth century. They built monasteries attached to their churches. These monasteries not only spread the word of God but also became seats of learning. Monks were trained in various subjects as well as in the craft of creating illuminated manuscripts, such as the *Lindisfarne Gospels*. Celtic illumination focused on animal motifs that were more abstract and asymmetrical. With the demise of the Roman Empire during the fifth century, separate kingdoms emerged. The church became more powerful, and there was a renewed interest in Roman antiquities.

The Frankish Empire gained control over a major portion of Western Europe under the reign of Charlemagne (800–814). The pope recognized his success in creating a unified Christendom and was crowned Charlemagne, the First Holy Roman Emperor. His reign became known as the Carolingian era. Again, manuscripts prevailed; the monks developed a Roman type of lettering to illuminate Classical Latin text. Charlemagne's architectural masterpiece, the Palace Chapel in Aachen, Germany (792–805), reflects Roman influences but on a more massive level.

After Charlemagne's death in 814, the empire became divided and was thrown into turmoil until the tenth century. Otto I, a Saxon king, restored unity as well as retaining Charlemagne's fondness for Roman Classical culture. Otto I extended the empire to Italy and crowned himself emperor in 962. Again illumination and architecture flourished. Bishop Bernward of Hildesheim (960–1022) supported the idea of constructing the Church of St. Michael's, which would feature square piers alternating with pairs of columns. The church is similar to Charlemagne's design for the Palace Chapel in Aachen. Another distinctive feature is the cast-bronze doors exhibiting biblical scenes, which look similar to illuminated manuscripts.

During the eleventh and twelfth centuries—called the Ottonian age—elements of Classical Rome were restored, and the period became known as the Romanesque era. Christian religious devotion intensified and became the impetus for pilgrimages and armed crusades. The mission of the Crusades was to recapture the Holy Land from the Moslem world in the name of Christianity. A new class of merchants and craftsman emerged, and Europe became stronger militarily. Local feudal lords ruled the regions in which they lived. Thus, Romanesque art and architecture developed provincial designs that were stylized, classical looking, and linear and were dominated by Christian symbols and themes. There was a resurgence of monumental stone sculptures in preference to architectural structures.

By the twelfth century, developing towns would center around their cathedral. These cathedrals and their associated schools became the spiritual institutions of their citizens as well as institutions for learning. The Abbot Sugar was the driving force behind the development of the Gothic era, which originated in France. This began when he made innovative architectural changes to the original Romanesque structure of St. Denis (circa 1137–1144). Abbot Sugar expanded its interior by designing a more harmonious floor plan and opening up the massive walls to let light flow in. The most distinctive architectural feature was the development of the Gothic pointed arch.

Cathedrals that were built later incorporated other innovations such as soaring piers, stained glass, spires, high ceiling vaults, and flying buttresses. The emphasis of the cathedral was on its height and vertical line; combined with light, these elements give one the uplifting feeling of a spiritual life. Sculpture and stained glass became decorative features. At one time, stained glass became more popular than mural painting and manuscript illumination. But in the Gothic age, once again there was a sensation of harmony, order, and spirituality. The Gothic style began to soften in appearance around the turn of the century (circa 1400) and is referred to as the International Style. The International Style dominated Western Europe for about twenty years. Italy was not as strongly influenced by the style of the Germanic Gothic but had a closer affiliation to Classical Roman antiquity and early Christian art. This perhaps helped in the development of the early phase of Renaissance art in Italy.

Discussion Questions and Activities

1. Before the printing press was invented, the Bible was written by hand. The text was beautifully decorated with ornamentation and script. Read about illuminated manuscripts at http://www.iath.virginia.edu /elab/hfl0263.html. Where did the scribes work when they were copying text for manuscripts? What does the word illumination mean? What are the two most famous manuscripts done by the Irish School? Read information at http://www.irishclans.com/articles/bookofkells.html and link to the Trinity College Library to view the manuscripts. Who were the figures in the manuscripts? What made these figures look special? What kind of material was the illumination painted on? Describe the ornamentation that decorated the text. View another manuscript and read its information at http://www.bl.uk/collections/treasures/lindis.html. How is the first letter of the manuscript decorated? Who copied and decorated the text? What happened to the original binding, and what did it supposedly look like? What do both manuscripts share? In 1939, the site of Sutton Hoo was discovered; read more at http://www.natmus.dk/nmf/nb/8/english/art6.htm and http://www.archaeology.co.uk/timeline /saxon/suttonhoo/suttonhoo.htm and http://www.suttonhoo.org/archaeology.htm. What kind of site was Sutton Hoo? Why is it an important archeological find? What items were found there? Use a search engine and type the words "Sutton Hoo objects" to find images of the objects found. Describe the ornamentation on some of these treasures.

2. Charlemagne made the city of Aachen the new center of the Holy Roman Empire. At http://www .jfks.de/slife/classtrips/france2000/aachencathedral.html and at http://www.newadvent.org/cathen /01001a.htm, read about the home and chapel he built. Why is the Palace Chapel important? What type (style) of architecture is this? The chapel has a special feature; what is it? Why did people make pilgrimages to Aachen? Read information about Carolingian illumination at http://www.utah.edu /umfa/mmgenintro.html and view the image of St. Matthew at http://arthistory.about.com/library /blslide_matthew_ebbo.htm from the *Ebbo Gospels*. What was the importance of the Carolingian monastery? What types of letters developed then are still used today? What is St. Matthew doing in the *Ebbo Gospel* illumination? How does this manuscript look different from the *Book of Kells* manuscript?

3. Read http://www.utah.edu/umfa/mmgenintro.html about Ottonian illumination and at http://www .encyclopedia.com/html/O/Ottonian.asp and view images of manuscripts at http://ishi.lib.berkeley .edu/history155/slides/kingship/Manuscripts/Ottonians/ from the Berkeley Library. Besides illustrating the New Testament, other kinds of images were depicted on these manuscripts; what were they? Who were some of the most popular figures? What style influenced Ottonian manuscripts? Describe the glances and gestures of the figures from the manuscripts. How did the artists use line to depict drapery? What medium applied to manuscripts seems to make the images radiate?

4. Romanesque architecture incorporated sculpture into its structures. Read more information at http://xrefer.com/entry.jsp?xrefid=652232&secid= and http://www.umich.edu/~marcons/Crusades /topics/art/art-article.html. What styles influenced Romanesque churches? What is classical about the rounded arches? Why were the windows so small? View the tympanum images of La Madeleine at Vézelay church. What do the figures of the reliefs look like and whom do they represent? Do the figures look natural? What other kind of ornamentation is included? Describe the floor plan. Use an image search engine and view the *Bayeux Tapestry*. Go to http://www.xrefer.com and look up the following terms: Bayeux Tapestry, tapestry, and embroidery. What does the Bayeux Tapestry depict? Besides soldiers, what other creatures do you see? How many colors were used? Is the Bayeux Tapestry a real tapestry? If not, what is it?

5.   Read background information about the Gothic style at http://arthistory.about.com/library/bl101
     _gothic.htm and view images of Chartres Cathedral at http://www.bc.edu/bc_org/avp/cas/fnart
     /arch/chartres.html and at http://www.greatbuildings.com/buildings/Chartres_Cathedral.html. Name
     some of the architectural elements of Gothic architecture. View images of Chartres Cathedral and
     identify the location of these elements on the structure. What is the difference between Romanesque
     and Gothic churches? What was the purpose of a flying buttress, and where are they located on the
     Chartres Cathedral? What architectural feature opens up the interiors of Gothic cathedrals?

6.   Stained glass windows are one of the finest contributions of the medieval era. Refer to the web sites at
     http://www.bartleby.com/65/st/stainedg.html and http://www.newadvent.org/cathen/14241a.htm and
     view the images at http://www.agsa.org/community/history_general.asp (follow the links to chapters).
     What medieval period is known for its stained glass windows? What was the significance of having
     such a rich and colorful window? Was the glass really stained? If not, how was it colored? What ma-
     terial held the pieces of glass together? View some of the images and point out where this material is
     in the design. What kinds of designs do you see in these images? Using the terms "Chartres win-
     dows" and "St. Denis windows," use an image search engine to find more windows to view.

Related Internet Sites

About.com. *Art History 101 with Andrea Mulder-Slater: Ottonian Art.*
- http://arthistory.about.com/library/bl101_ottonian.htm
  [14 July 2002]

About.com. *Art History 101 with Andrea Mulder-Slater: Romanesque Art.*
- http://arthistory.about.com/library/bl101_romanesque.htm
  [14 July 2002]

Alacritude. *Encyclopedia.com: Romanesque Architecture and Art.*
- http://www.encyclopedia.com/html/section/romanesq_romanesquearchitecture.asp
  [2002]

Alternate Realities in Art and Thought. *The Book of Kells.*
- http://www.esotericart.com/fringe/art/symbolic/BookKell/kells.htm
  [14 July 2002]

British Broadcasting Company. *Tyne: Lindisfarne Gospels.*
- http://www.bbc.co.uk/tyne/features/gospels/gospels_tense_past.shtml
  [14 July 2002]

British Museum, London, England. *The British Museum: Compass: Explore the Collections On-line. (Do a Quick Search for Sutton Hoo)*
- http://www.thebritishmuseum.ac.uk/compass/
  [14 July 2002]

British Museum, London, England. *The British Museum: Compass: Explore the Collections On-line: Sutton Hoo Burial Site and Treasures.*
- http://www.thebritishmuseum.ac.uk/compass/ixbin/hixclient.exe?%7BUPPER%7D%3Av2_free_text_tindex=sutton+hoo&_IXDB_=compass&_IXSPFX_=graphical%2Fsummary%2F&_IXFPFX_=graphical%2Ffull%2F&_IXNOMATCHES_=graphical%2Fno_matches.html&%24+%28with+v2_searchable_index%29+sort=.&_IXsearchterm=sutton%2520hoo&submit-button=summary
  [14 July 2002]

Burgundy Tourism. *Vezelay the Eternal Hill.*
- http://www.burgundy-tourism.com/patrimoine/vezelay_.htm
  [14 July 2002]

Chartres, Sanctuary of the World Association. *Cathedral of Chartres.*
- http://www.chartres-csm.org/us_fixe/cathedrale/
  [14 July 2002]

Oxford University Press (1997). From *Xrefer, The Web's Reference Engine: Illuminated Manuscripts.*
- http://www.xrefer.com/entry.jsp?xrefid=144170&secid=
  [14 July 2002]

Pennington, Ken. Syracuse University, Syracuse, NY. *History of Charlemagne's Chapel in Aachen.*
- http://www.maxwell.syr.edu/maxpages/classes/his211/LectureTwo/PalaceChapelHistory.htm
  [14 July 2002]

Witcombe, Chris. *Art History Resources on the Web: Art of the Middle Ages.*
- http://witcombe.sbc.edu/ARTHmedieval.html
  [14 July 2002]

CHAPTER 11

Birth of the Renaissance: Early Renaissance Art

(Late Thirteenth Century–Early Fifteenth Century)

Giotto (Circa 1267–1337), Masaccio (1401–1428?), and Brunelleschi (1377–1446)

Early Renaissance Web Addresses

Annenberg. *The Western Tradition: The Renaissance.*
http://www.learner.org/exhibits/renaissance/
[24 July 2002]
A comprehensive, general information web site about the Renaissance. Provides links to information about how the Renaissance emerged from the Middle Ages and changed aspects of philosophy and science. Refer to the "Out of the Middle Ages" and "Printing and Thinking" sections of this site.

Annenberg. *The Western Tradition: The Renaissance: Florentine Art and Architecture.*
http://www.learner.org/exhibits/renaissance/florence_sub2.html
[24 July 2002]
Information about Florentine art and architecture. The web site includes information about Brunelleschi's architecture.

Annenberg. *The Western Tradition: The Renaissance: Printing and Thinking, Humanism Emerges.*
http://www.learner.org/exhibits/renaissance/printing.html
[24 July 2002]

Artifice, Inc. *Great Buildings Online: Filippo Brunelleschi.*
http://www.greatbuildings.com/architects/Filippo_Brunelleschi.html
[24 July 2002]

Christus Rex Inc. *Christus Rex Project: Art Gallery.*
http://www.christusrex.org/www2/art/gallery.htm
[24 July 2002]

Knechtel, Nancy. Niagra County Community College (SUNY). *Early Renaissance Art.*
http://www.sunyniagara.cc.ny.us/homepags/Knechtel/ren.html
[24 July 2002]
Provides general information and links about Early Renaissance art.

Kren, Emil and Daniel Marx. *Web Gallery of Art: Goujon, Jean.*
http://www.kfki.hu/~arthp/bio/g/goujon/biograph.html
[24 July 2002]

Market House Books Encyclopaedia of the Renaissance (1987). From *Xrefer, The*
Web's Reference Engine: Architecture (Renaissance).
http://www.xrefer.com/entry.jsp?xrefid=251576&secid=
[27 July 2002]
Definition of Renaissance architecture from the *Encyclopedia of the Renaissance* (1987).

Oxford Dictionary of Art (1997). From *Xrefer, The Web's Reference Engine: Renaissance.*
http://www.xrefer.com/entry.jsp?xrefid=145209&secid=
[27 July 2002]
Definition of "Renaissance" from *The Oxford Dictionary of Art* (1997).

Oxford Paperback Encyclopedia (1998). From *Xrefer, The Web's Reference Engine:*
Renaissance (French, rebirth).
http://www.xrefer.com/entry.jsp?xrefid=222863&secid=
[27 July 2002]
Encyclopedia article about the Renaissance ("rebirth"). Provides information about humanist philosophy,
Early Renaissance, High Renaissance, and Mannerism from the *Oxford Paperback Encyclopedia* (1998).

Pioch, Nicolas. *WebMuseum, Paris: La Renaissance.*
http://www.oir.ucf.edu/wm/paint/glo/renaissance/
[24 July 2002]
Information about Renaissance art in Europe.

Pioch, Nicolas. *WebMuseum, Paris: La Renaissance: Italy.*
http://www.oir.ucf.edu/wm/paint/glo/renaissance/it.html
[24 July 2002]
Background information about the Renaissance in Italy.

Pioch, Nicolas. *WebMuseum, Paris: The Northern Renaissance (1500–1615).*
http://www.ibiblio.org/wm/paint/tl/north-ren/
[23 July 2002]
General information on Northern Renaissance art.

Site Summary

The term Renaissance refers to the "rebirth" of the Classical age of the Greeks and Romans. The Renaissance philosophy of humanism formulated new ideas about science, religion, politics, and technology while referring to the Classical texts. These ideologies became evident in all aspects of the arts during the Renaissance period. Humanist texts spread quickly throughout Europe due to the invention of the printing press by Gutenberg circa 1445. The printed word helped disseminate knowledge about this rebirth and thus effected new ways to think, live, and observe one's natural surroundings.

The Renaissance emerged from the Middle Ages, beginning as early as the thirteenth century. Its influence affected different countries at different points in time, but its influence was contagious and inspired many artists, writers, musicians, philosophers, and scientists who were hungry for knowledge, experimentation, and discovery.

Because they had better access to printed books, more people became literate. Feudal life began to change when more people began to abandon the lands of the nobility and move to cities. People began to prosper on their own, and a new middle class emerged. This new middle class was able to afford and enjoy the arts; thus, the arts gained a wider audience and patronage. Two major Florentine artists of the Early Renaissance are

Giotto di Bondone (circa 1267–1337) and Masaccio (Tommaso de Giovanni, 1401–1428?) of Florence. Giotto introduced an innovative understanding of space, mass, and perspective into painting. Masaccio expanded these concepts later in fifteenth-century Italian painting. The architectural work of Brunelleschi (1377–1446) illustrates the mathematical ratio of building that the ancient Greeks and Romans used. Both architects and artists of the Renaissance incorporated the concept of proportion known as the "golden mean." The golden mean was a method of applying harmony and proportion to architectural structures, three-dimensional sculptures, and two-dimensional compositions. Other regions of Europe eventually began to adopt the concepts of humanism into their art. Germany, England, and France developed their own regional styles at different times. Some of the better-known artists who introduced ideas of the Italian Renaissance to northern Europe were Jan van Eyck, Martin Schongauer, and Albrecht Dürer.

Discussion Questions and Activities

1. Read the information from the Annenberg web site at http://www.learner.org/exhibits/renaissance /printing.html and the definitions from http://www.xrefer.com/entry.jsp?xrefid=222863&secid= and look up the word "humanism" in Xrefer at http://www.xrefer.com/ and answer the following questions. What historical events led to the Renaissance? What new philosophy helped to change medieval attitudes and develop conceptual changes by the fifteenth century? What kinds of texts did this philosophy refer to?

2. Refer to http://www.oir.ucf.edu/wm/paint/glo/renaissance/it.html and the web site that defines the Renaissance in Italy at http://xrefer.com/entry.jsp?xrefid=145209&secid=. What does the term "rebirth" mean? How did the status of artists change during the Renaissance? Who was Vasari, and why is he an important Renaissance figure?

3. Humanism is a concept associated with the Renaissance. Refer to the Annenberg web site that discusses humanist philosophy at http://www.learner.org/exhibits/renaissance/printing.html. Then log into an image gallery such as Christus Rex at http://www.christusrex.org/www2/art/gallery.htm and look at some paintings. What humanist concepts do you see in some of the works of Renaissance art? What are some natural elements in these paintings?

4. The golden mean is an important vehicle of Renaissance art and architecture. The golden mean uses mathematics and visual balance to create harmony. Read the article on architecture from Xrefer at http://xrefer.com/entry.jsp?xrefid=251576&secid= and view the architectural web sites of Brunelleschi at http://www.greatbuildings.com/architects/Filippo_Brunelleschi.html (from Great Buildings Online) or at http://web.kyoto-inet.or.jp/org/orion/eng/hst/renais.html. Make a printout of a building and trace the structure's outline. Which of the building's components create its balance and proportion? Why are these elements important for harmony in Renaissance art and architecture?

5. Renaissance art of Italy developed differently from its northern counterparts. View some of the web sites of Northern Renaissance art from Germany, England, and France. Use a search engine such as Google and the terms "Renaissance art and Germany," "Renaissance art and England," and "Renaissance art and France." Also view the biography web site about French Renaissance sculptor Jean Goujon at http://www.kfki.hu/~arthp/bio/g/goujon/biograph.html (from the Web Gallery of Art). Compare the dates of Renaissance development in different countries. Who were some of the artists who painted portraits in Germany? Who were popular English royalty that were depicted in portraits? What style is associated with Goujon's sculptures? What famous art museum did he create sculptures for?

6. After viewing artwork from different countries, choose the categories of landscape painting, portrait painting, and sculpture to compare. Do you find that Italian portraiture tends to be more idealized than German portraiture? How does landscape painting differ in Italian, German, and English painting? Does Northern Renaissance sculpture look more crude and dramatic than Italian Renaissance sculpture? If so, why? Do you find any nude sculpture pieces in Northern Renaissance art?

GIOTTO
(Circa 1267–1337)

Images

Arena Chapel frescoes, circa 1305–1306. Padua, Italy: Cappella dell'Arena (Arena Chapel).

Bardi Chapel frescoes, circa 1300. Florence: St. Croce.

Lamentation (Mourning of Christ), fresco, circa 1305–1306. Padua, Italy: Cappella dell'Arena (Arena Chapel).

The Ognissanti Madonna (Madonna in Glory), tempera on wood, 1310, Uffizi, Florence.

Web Addresses

Delahunt, Michael. *ArtLex Art Dictionary: Fresco.*
http://www.artlex.com/ArtLex/f/fresco.html
[24 July 2002]
Definition of fresco painting.

Gerten-Jackson, Carol. *CGFA: A Virtual Art Museum: Biography: Giotto.*
http://sunsite.dk/cgfa/giotto/ (images)
http://sunsite.dk/cgfa/giotto/giotto_bio.htm (biography)
[24 July 2002]

Gerten-Jackson, Carol. *CGFA: A Virtual Art Museum: Giotto: The Ognissanti Madonna (Madonna in Glory).*
http://sunsite.dk/cgfa/giotto/
[24 July 2002]

Harden, Mark. *Artchive: Giotto. Lamentation (Mourning of Christ).*
http://www.artchive.com/artchive/G/giotto/giotto_text.jpg.html
[24 July 2002]
Lamentation (Mourning of Christ) image and background information about the painting.

Kren, Emil and Daniel Marx. *Web Gallery of Art: The Art of Giotto.*
http://www.kfki.hu/~arthp/tours/giotto/
[24 July 2002]
Art of Giotto; includes information about the Arena Chapel, Padua.

Kren, Emil and Daniel Marx. *Web Gallery of Art: The Art of Giotto: The Arena Chapel in Padua.*
http://www.kfki.hu/~arthp/tours/giotto/arena.html
[24 July 2002]

Pioch, Nicolas. *WebMuseum, Paris: Giotto di Bondone.*
http://www.oir.ucf.edu/wm/paint/auth/giotto/
[24 July 2002]
Biography of Giotto.

Pioch, Nicolas. *WebMuseum, Paris: Giotto di Bondone: The Mourning of Christ.*
http://www.oir.ucf.edu/wm/paint/auth/giotto/mourning-christ/
[24 July 2002]
Image of the *Lamentation (Mourning of Christ).*

Site Summary

Giotto di Bondone (circa 1267–1337) was born near Florence, Italy, in the small village of Colle di Vespignano. He studied medieval, Byzantine, and Roman paintings from Rome, Padua, Assisi, and other nearby cities. His personal style evolved from the Classical Roman school of painting, which emphasized a more realistic interpretation of the human form. Giotto began to abandon the linear, flat shapes and decorative, jewel-like colors of Byzantine painting. His landscapes and human figures looked more realistic, natural, and sculptural compared to those of his contemporaries. His early fresco series of the Scrovegni (Arena Chapel) in Padua (circa 1304–1306) depicts the life cycle of the Virgin Mary and Christ. In the painting, *The Lamentation (Mourning of Christ)*, Giotto illustrates the moment when Christ is about to be laid to rest within the tomb. Mourners surround the dead figure of Christ while the Virgin Mary holds him in her arms. This fresco beautifully depicts Giotto's style of using human figures and landscape to create a spiritual landscape unlike those of the Byzantine or medieval icons of painting.

Discussion Questions and Activities

1. Refer to http://www.oir.ucf.edu/wm/paint/auth/giotto/ and http://sunsite.dk/cgfa/giotto/giotto_bio.htm. Why is Giotto called the "first genius" of early Renaissance art? What were his earliest works? What media did he work with? Refer to http://www.artlex.com/ArtLex/f/fresco.html and describe the technique used in working with the media. What former style of painting did Giotto abandon?

2. What was the usual theme of Giotto's paintings? View the image of the *Ognissanti Madonna (Madonna in Glory)* at http://sunsite.dk/cgfa/giotto/ (choose the image *Madonna in Glory*). Who was a major influence on Giotto? What was the difference between these two artists? Why did Giotto lack technical knowledge of anatomy and perspective? How does he render perspective in this painting? Of what did Giotto have a grasp that helped change the way artists depicted people?

3. What are the titles of the fresco series that Giotto is known for? What was the theme of the series he did in Assisi? What is a special feature of this saint, and how was Giotto able to depict the saint's characteristics? View the series at http://sunsite.dk/cgfa/giotto/ (the titles will include the place of Assisi). In how many scenes do you see this saint? Describe the saint's appearance. What kinds of events are shown in the scenes?

4. Refer to http://www.kfki.hu/~arthp/tours/giotto/arena.html for additional information. What is the theme of the other major series that Giotto painted? Who commissioned the frescoes? How many scenes are painted in this chapel? What kind of scene is depicted over the archway of the entrance wall? Do the compositions look cluttered? View images at http://sunsite.dk/cgfa/giotto/ (choose the images from this chapel). How does Giotto use space in these scenes? Do the scenes look flat? How does he imply perspective?

5. View the painting of the *Lamentation* at http://www.oir.ucf.edu/wm/paint/auth/giotto/mourning-christ/ or at http://www.artchive.com/artchive/G/giotto/giotto.jpg.html. What are some of the natural objects in the landscape? How can you tell which figures are the Virgin, apostles, and disciples of Christ in the *Lamentation*? Why does Giotto use the color gold for the halos? What does it signify? Which figures have halos? What makes the figures look realistic in this painting?

6. Refer to http://www.oir.ucf.edu/wm/paint/auth/giotto/mourning-christ/. The composition of the *Lamentation (Mourning of Christ)* has a foreground, a middle ground, and a background. What is in the foreground? How are the figures arranged there? Are they looking in a particular direction? What object dominates the middle ground? Why is your eye led toward the background? What objects do you see in the background?

MASACCIO (Tommaso di Giovanni) (1401–1428?)

Images

Brancacci Chapel frescoes, circa 1425. Florence: Santa Maria del Carmine.

The Holy Trinity with the Virgin and St. John, circa 1427. Santa Maria Novella, Florence.

Web Addresses

Gerten-Jackson, Carol. *CGFA: A Virtual Art Museum: Masaccio.*
http://btr0xw.rz.uni-bayreuth.de/cjackson/masaccio/
[24 July 2002]
Image gallery and biography link.

Gerten-Jackson, Carol. *CGFA: A Virtual Art Museum: Masaccio: The Holy Trinity.*
http://btr0xw.rz.uni-bayreuth.de/cjackson/masaccio/p-masaccio1.htm
[24 July 2002]
Image of *The Holy Trinity.*

Giorgio Vasari's Lives of the Artists. *The Lives of the Most Eminent Painters, Sculptors and Architects: Life of Masaccio.*
http://easyweb.easynet.co.uk/giorgio.vasari/masaccio/masaccio.htm
[24 July 2002]
Image gallery that includes brief information about *The Holy Trinity.*

Harden, Mark. *Artchive: Masaccio: The Holy Trinity (and details of St. John and the Virgin).*
http://www.artchive.com/artchive/M/masaccio/trinity.jpg.html
links to details of St. John and Mary at
http://www.artchive.com/artchive/M/masaccio.html
[24 July 2002]
Full-view image of *The Holy Trinity* and details of St. John and the Virgin.

Kren, Emil and Daniel Marx. *Web Gallery of Art: Masaccio.*
http://gallery.euroweb.hu/bio/m/masaccio/biograph.html
[24 July 2002]
Biography and images.

Kren, Emil and Daniel Marx. *Web Gallery of Art: Trinity, Fresco in the Santa Maria Novella in Florence by Masaccio (with thumbnails of perspective drawing and details).*
http://www.kfki.hu/~arthp/html/m/masaccio/trinity/index.html
[24 July 2002]
Full-view image of *The Holy Trinity,* details, and a perspective drawing schematic of *The Holy Trinity.*

MEGA. *Masaccio.*
http://www.mega.it/eng/egui/pers/masac.htm
[24 July 2002]
Biography, information, and image of *The Holy Trinity.*

Oxford Dictionary of Art (1997). From *Xrefer, The Web's Reference Engine: Polyptych.*
http://www.xrefer.com/entry.jsp?xrefid=145085&secid=
[27 July 2002]
Definition of "polyptych" from *The Oxford Dictionary of Art* (1997).

Science Museum, London. *Applications of the Method of Perspective in Renaissance Art.*
http://www.crs4.it/Ars/arshtml/arch2.html
[24 July 2002]
Applications of the method of perspective in Renaissance art.

Site Summary

Masaccio (Tommaso di Giovanni) was born in a small town near Florence called Valdarno in 1401. The earliest date associated with Masaccio's career in painting is circa 1422. This date indicates his affiliation with the Florentine Guild. As a fifteenth-century Italian painter, Masaccio clearly exhibited some of the traditions of Giotto. Such elements are the simplicity of forms, the use of chiaroscuro (use of light and shade), and the vitality of the figures in a composition. But what differentiates Masaccio from Giotto is his acute observation of perspective, the way a figure can move anatomically, and the realistic handling of components in nature. He also abandoned the medieval style of using gold ornamentation and the grand massiveness of human forms.

The first major fresco collaboration series that Masaccio created was for the Brancacci Chapel for Santa Maria del Carmine, Florence, circa 1425, for the Lenzi family. Masaccio's Brancacci frescoes illustrate events in the life of St. Peter and feature fresco paintings such as *The Tribute Money.* He also painted portraits and several polyptych panels such as the renowned *Pisa Polyptych* for the chapel in Santa Maria del Carmine, Pisa, in 1426. Another well-known fresco series was done for the church of Santa Maria Novella in Florence, circa 1427. The view of the fresco painting of *The Holy Trinity* is a study in linear perspective, which creates the illusion of space on a two-dimensional plane (like a painting or drawing). This is accomplished by converging lines that are perpendicular to the plane and meet at a vanishing point. The scene reveals the Virgin and St. John the Evangelist mourning while Christ hangs crucified on the cross. What makes the scene unusual is the perspective of the cross that is set within a barreled vault interior. It has been speculated that Masaccio created the linear perspective space according to architectural models that Brunelleschi made.

Although Masaccio died at the young age of twenty-seven, one cannot ignore his early influence on later Renaissance artists. Indeed, Masaccio influenced Michelangelo, who studied and drew from Masaccio's frescoes as did Fra Lippi, Fra Angelico, Castagno, Uccello, Mantegna, and Leonardo da Vinci.

Discussion Questions and Activities

1. Refer to biographical information of the web sites at http://www.mega.it/eng/egui/pers/masac.htm and http://gallery.euroweb.hu/bio/m/masaccio/biograph.html. Which artists influenced Masaccio? What are some of Masaccio's artistic characteristics and techniques? What is the most important of Masaccio's innovations that broke away from Gothic models?

2. What major artworks are attributed to Masaccio? What is the theme of his paintings? What is the subject of the panel painting? From http://gallery.euroweb.hu/bio/m/masaccio/biograph.html link to view the images of the paintings. See Xrefer at http://www.xrefer.com/entry.jsp?xrefid=145085&secid= and read the definition of "polyptych." Are any of these paintings by Masaccio considered to be polyptych panels? If so, which ones? Compare Masaccio's panel paintings to Giotto's panel of the *Ognissanti Madonna (Madonna in Glory)* at http://sunsite.dk/cgfa/giotto/p-giotto5.htm and discuss differences and similarities of the compositions.

3. Read more information at http://www.hol.gr/mirror/cgfa/masaccio/masaccio_bio.htm. What single painting is considered Masaccio's most important artwork? What did he depict for the first time in Western art? Masaccio also depicted light in a new way; how did he do this? View some of the images and describe the way he depicted light.

4. View the painting of *The Holy Trinity* at http://easyweb.easynet.co.uk/giorgio.vasari/masaccio/masaccio .htm and some of the painting details. What does this scene depict? Which figure looks directly at the viewer? Identify and discuss the figures of *The Holy Trinity*. How can you identify the Virgin? Discuss how the figures use hand gestures. Which figures have halos? Does Christ look as though he is in agony? Does the figure of Christ hang stiffly, or does it slump and shift on the cross in a more natural pose?

5. Visit the web sites http://easyweb.easynet.co.uk/giorgio.vasari/masaccio/masaccio.htm and http://www .kfki.hu/~arthp/html/m/masaccio/trinity/index.html to view a schematic drawing of the perspective view of *The Holy Trinity*. Read about perspective at http://www.crs4.it/Ars/arshtml/arch2.html. Discuss aspects of linear perspective and ways to draw an interior view using perspective. Make a photocopy of the painting and then draw lines of perspective from the vanishing point behind the figure of Christ. If you were looking at this painting, where would you think you were standing?

6. The fresco of *The Holy Trinity* was painted on a wall; discuss aspects of the illusionary architectural elements known as trompe l'oeil in the composition. What types of architectural elements do you see? In what kind of space or area is the cross located in the painting? If you took a ruler and lined up the figures, could you draw a triangle between them? Compositionally, there are triad elements in the fresco. How many triangles can you find in this composition? Discuss what the term "trinity" means and how it relates to the fresco of *The Holy Trinity*.

FILIPPO BRUNELLESCHI
(1377–1446)

Images

Cupola (dome) of the Cathedral of Santa Maria del Fiore (Florence Cathedral), completed in 1435, Florence.

Florence Baptistery Doors, bronze, 1401, approximately 21" x 17.5" inside molding. Florence: Bargello.

Web Addresses

Andrus, Kathryn. University of Colorado at Colorado Springs. *Digital Art Collections: Roman Art and Architecture.*
http://harpy.uccs.edu/roman/html/roman.html
[24 July 2002]
Images of Roman architecture.

Annenberg. *The Western Tradition: Renaissance, Florentine Art and Architecture.*
http://www.learner.org/exhibits/renaissance/florence_sub2.html
[24 July 2002]
Background information about Florentine art and architecture.

Annenberg. *The Western Tradition: Renaissance, Symmetry, Shape, Size.*
http://www.learner.org/exhibits/renaissance/symmetry.html
[24 July 2002]
Background information about proportions in architecture.

APT—Azienda di Promozione Turistica. *The Cupola of Brunelleschi.*
http://www.arca.net/db/brunell/cupola.htm
[24 July 2002]
Web site with text and links to images of the cupola of the Cathedral of Santa Maria del Fiore (Florence). Also biographical information.

Artcyclopedia. *Filippo Brunelleschi.*
http://www.artcyclopedia.com/artists/brunelleschi_filippo.html
[25 July 2002]
Directory of links to information and image galleries.

Artifice, Inc. *Great Buildings Online: Filippo Brunelleschi.*
http://www.greatbuildings.com/architects/Filippo_Brunelleschi.html
[24 July 2002]
Biographical information and links to images.

Artifice, Inc. *Great Buildings Online: Pantheon.*
http://www.greatbuildings.com/buildings/Pantheon.html
[24 July 2002]
Information and images of the Roman Pantheon.

Boston College, MA. *Competition Plaques: Ghiberti and Brunelleschi.*
http://www.bc.edu/bc_org/avp/cas/ashp/brunelleschi_ghiberti.html
[24 July 2002]

Forbes Technology Center, Ohio State University. *Columns, Arches, Vaults, and Domes.*
http://omega.cohums.ohio-state.edu/classes/cla506.W99.mlm/construction/arches_etc.html
[24 July 2002]
Information about elements of Classical architecture.

Kren, Emil and Daniel Marx. *Web Gallery of Art: Brunelleschi, Filippo.*
http://www.kfki.hu/~arthp/bio/b/brunelle/biograph.html
[24 July 2002]
Biography and links to images.

Market House Books Encyclopedia of the Renaissance (1987). From *Xrefer, The Web's
Reference Engine: Brunelleschi, Filippo (1377–1446).*
http://www.xrefer.com/entry.jsp?xrefid=251763&secid=
[27 July 2002]
Information about Brunelleschi and the influence of Roman architecture on his designs.

MEGA. *The Baptistery Doors: The Panels by Ghiberti and Brunelleschi at the Bargello.*
http://www.mega.it/eng/egui/monu/bo.htm
[24 July 2002]
The baptistery door panel designs by Ghiberti and Brunelleschi.

MEGA. *The Cathedral (Duomo of Florence).*
http://www.mega.it/eng/egui/monu/buq.htm
[24 July 2002]
Information about the Cathedral of Santa Maria del Fiore (Florence). Cathedral dome with images.

Science Museum, London. *Applications of the Method of Perspective in Renaissance Art.*
http://www.crs4.it/Ars/arshtml/arch2.html
[24 July 2002]
A description of Brunelleschi's theory of the applications of the method of perspective in Renaissance art.

Science Museum, London. From *Human Architecture to Architectural Structure: Part I:
Brunelleschi and the Origin of Linear Perspective.*
http://www.mcm.acu.edu/academic/galileo/ars/arshtml/arch1.html
[24 July 2002]

Sullivan, Mary Ann. Bluffton College, Bluffton, OH. *Digital Imaging Project: North
Doors, Florence Baptistry: Lorenzo Ghiberti.*
http://www.bluffton.edu/~sullivanm/ghibertinorth/ghibertinorth.html
[24 July 2002]
Baptistery doors by Ghiberti.

Westfall, C.W. University of Virginia, Charlottesville, VA. *Filippo Brunelleschi: Santa
Maria del Fiore and Ospedale degli Innocenti.*
http://www.lib.virginia.edu/dic/colls/arh102/two/two.html
[24 July 2002]
Images of Brunelleschi's cupola of the Cathedral of Santa Maria del Fiore (Florence) and the Ospedale
degli Innocenti (Florence).

Site Summary

Born in 1377 Brunelleschi was a Florentine sculptor and architect. One of his earlier-known sculptural pieces was for the competition to design the north bronze baptistery doors of the Cathedral of Santa Maria del Fiore, Florence, in 1403. The competition brought prominence to Brunelleschi, even though he lost the commission to his contemporary, Lorenzo Ghiberti. Brunelleschi was fascinated by Roman architectural structures and ornamental design. He easily incorporated elements of the Roman style and construction methods into his own buildings.

His greatest achievement was the design of the cupola (dome) of the Cathedral of Santa Maria del Fiore, Florence, in 1420, which was completed in 1436. Many believed that the intended size of this dome would preclude its construction; a large dome would collapse under its own weight. Brunelleschi took on the challenge, nevertheless, and created a structure of engineering ingenuity. In order to lighten the weight of a conventional dome, he designed a drum with large circular openings on each side of the octagonal crossings. This skeletal framework would be lighter and distribute the weight more evenly without reducing the dome's strength. An outer and inner shell would enclose the framework.

The size of the cupola (dome) of the Cathedral of Santa Maria del Fiore has become a symbol of Florence and the beginning of Renaissance architecture as well as an architectural feat. Brunelleschi continued to design other buildings incorporating Classical Roman influence, such as the reconstruction square plan of the Sacristy of San Lorenzo (circa 1418–1428) and the loggia of the Ospendale degli Innocenti (Foundling Hospital) (circa 1419–1424). Another Roman-inspired building was the Pazzi Chapel of Santa Croce (begun circa 1441), which is decorated with colorful sculpted roundel reliefs done by Lucca della Robbia. Brunelleschi's style of geometric line and perspective, as well as his use of decorative detail, is still used today in contemporary building.

Discussion Questions and Activities

1. Refer to the biographical web sites at http://www.greatbuildings.com/architects/Filippo_Brunelleschi.html and http://www.crs4.it/Ars/arshtml/arch1.html. For what was Brunelleschi originally trained? When and why did he begin his career as an architect? What is distinctive about his use of perspective? Refer to the web site of the Science Museum, London, at http://www.xrefer.com/entry.jsp?xrefid=251763 &secid= and to the activity at http://www.mcm.acu.edu/academic/galileo/ars/arshtml/arch2.html to learn how to use a central vanishing point and the horizon line to define the perspective of a building.

2. Identify some Classical Roman architectural elements in any of the buildings that Brunelleschi designed. Identify columns, porticos, facades, domes, and so forth and refer to a web site about Roman buildings at http://harpy.uccs.edu/roman/html/romarch.html and about columns, arches, vaults and domes at http://omega.cohums.ohio-state.edu/classes/cla506.W99.mlm/construction/arches_etc.html. Refer to image galleries of Brunelleschi's designs from *Great Buildings Online* at http://www.greatbuildings.com (search "Brunelleschi") and at http://www.mega.it/eng/egui/monu/buq.htm for views of the Cathedral of Santa Maria del Fiore (Florence). Identify Roman architectural components that Brunelleschi incorporated into his structures.

3. Read background information about Renaissance architecture from the Annenberg/CPB Project at http://www.learner.org/exhibits/renaissance/florence_sub2.html and about proportions at http://www.learner.org/exhibits/renaissance/symmetry.html. How is architecture a reflection of the culture in which we live? Why and how did Renaissance architecture reflect the ideologies of the time? View several images of the cupola of the Cathedral of Santa Maria del Fiore at http://www.mega.it/eng/egui/monu/buq.htm. Describe the shape of the dome. Observe how the cathedral looks among the other buildings in Florence. Does its dome dominate other structures in the area?

4. Refer to the web site about the Roman Pantheon at http://www.greatbuildings.com/buildings/Pantheon.html and identify reasons that the structure of a Roman dome influenced Brunelleschi's work. What was the Pantheon originally built as? How did natural light enter its interior? What architectural element do the Pantheon and the Florence cathedral have in common?

5. Read about the dome of the Florence Cathedral at http://www.arca.net/db/brunell/cupola.htm. What was the major problem in designing the dome for it? What happened to the dome of Hagia Sophia in Constantinople? Of what material was the Florence Cathedral cupola made? How many shells were built? What was the purpose of having multiple shells? What do people notice when they sightsee in Florence?

6. Compare the designs for the north bronze baptistery doors of the Cathedral of Santa Maria del Fiore at http://www.bluffton.edu/~sullivanm/ghibertinorth/ghibertinorth.html (Ghiberti) and at http://www.mega.it/eng/egui/monu/bo.htm (Brunelleschi and Ghiberti) of the *Sacrifice of Isaac* for the north doors. Describe how each artist enclosed a scene. Why do you think Ghiberti was awarded the commission? View more of the Ghiberti images. What do some of the scenes depict?

Related Internet Sites

Early Renaissance

Annenberg. *Western Tradition: Renaissance: Related Resources.*
- http://learner.org/exhibits/renaissance/resources.html
  [25 July 2002]
  Links to resources for information about the Renaissance.

Artcyclopedia. *Early Renaissance.*
- http://www.artcyclopedia.com/history/early-renaissance.html
  [25 July 2002]
  Directory of links to information and image galleries.

Cloud, Sarah E. University of Michigan, Ann Arbor, MI. *Northern Renaissance ArtWeb.*
- http://www.msu.edu/~cloudsar/nrweb.htm
  [25 July 2002]
  Directory of links on Northern Renaissance art.

Columbia Electronic Encyclopedia (1994, 2000). *Infoplease.com: Art of the Renaissance: The Italian Renaissance.*
- http://www.infoplease.com/ce6/ent/A0860692.html
  [25 July 2002]
  Information on the art of the Italian Renaissance.

Harden, Mark. *Artchive: Renaissance Art, Italian Renaissance, Northern Renaissance.*
- http://www.artchive.com/artchive/renaissance.html
  [25 July 2002]
  List of Renaissance and Northern Renaissance artists with links to images.

Leo Masuda Architectronic Research Office. *History of Renaissance Architecture.*
- http://web.kyoto-inet.or.jp/org/orion/eng/hst/renais.html
  [25 July 2002]
  Image gallery of Renaissance architecture by Brunelleschi, Bramante, Alberti, Michelangelo, and so on.

Maximillan, P. J. Institute of Art and Architectural History, Groningen, Netherlands. *Links in Medieval and Northern Renaissance Art History.*
- http://odur.let.rug.nl/~martens/links.htm
  [25 July 2002]
  Links to Medieval and Northern Renaissance art.

Pioch, Nicolas. *WebMuseum, Paris: La Renaissance.*
- http://www.ibiblio.org/wm/paint/glo/renaissance
  [25 July 2002]
  Background on Renaissance art and links to information about the Renaissance in Germany, France, and the Netherlands.

Witcombe, Chris. *Art History Resources on the Web: Renaissance Art and Architecture.*
- http://witcombe.sbc.edu/ARTHLinks2.html
  [25 July 2002]
  Resource directory that links to information on Renaissance art and image galleries.

Zwanger, Meryl. Columbia University, NYC. *Sister (feminist journal): Women and Art in the Renaissance.*
- http://www.cc.Columbia.edu/cu/sister/Renaissance.html
  [25 July 2002]
  An essay about women and art in the Renaissance.

GIOTTO

Artcyclopedia. *Giotto di Bondone.*
- http://www.artcyclopedia.com/artists/giotto_di_bondone.html
  [25 July 2002]
  Various links to Giotto sites for images in general.

Christus Rex Inc. *Christus Rex Project: Art Gallery: Giotto.*
- http://www.christusrex.org/www2/art/giotto.htm
  [25 July 2002]
  Image gallery.

MASACCIO

Christus Rex Inc. *Christus Rex Project: Art Gallery: Masaccio.*
- http://www.christusrex.org/www2/art/masaccio.htm
  [25 July 2002]
  Image gallery of several Masaccio works.

Kren, Emil and Daniel Marx. *Web Gallery of Art: Masaccio.*
- http://www.kfki.hu/~arthp/html/m/masaccio/index.html
  [25 July 2002]
  Gallery of images.

BRUNELLESCHI

Alinari. *Brunelleschi's Monographs.*
- http://arca.net/tourism/florence/brunelle.htm
  [25 July 2002]
  General information about and text on Brunelleschi with links to images.

Alinari. *The Construction of a New Classical Florence.*
- http://www.arca.net/db/brunell/classic.htm
  [25 July 2002]
  Web site of general information about fifteenth-century Florentine architecture. Includes text with links to images.

High Renaissance

Knechtel, Nancy. Niagara County Community College (SUNY). *High Renaissance Art.*
- http://www.sunyniagara.cc.ny.us/homepags/Knechtel/highren.html
  [25 July 2002]
  General information about the High Renaissance with links to images.

Mannerism

Thames and Hudson Dictionary of Art and Artists (1994). From *Xrefer, The Web's Reference Engine: Mannerism.*
- http://www.xrefer.com/entry.jsp?xrefid=651667&secid=
  [27 July 2002]
  Definition of mannerism from *The Thames and Hudson Dictionary of Art and Artists* (1994).

CHAPTER 12

High Renaissance Art

(Circa 1480–1527)

Leonardo da Vinci (1452–1519) and Michelangelo (1475–1564)

High Renaissance Web Addresses

Artcyclopedia. *The High Renaissance: Centered in Italy, Early 16th Century.*
http://www.artcyclopedia.com/history/high-renaissance.html
[25 July 2002]
Directory of links to information and image galleries.

Columbia Electronic Encyclopedia (1994, 2000). *Infoplease.com: Art of the Renaissance: The Italian Renaissance.*
http://www.infoplease.com/ce6/ent/A0860692.html
[25 July 2002]
Article on Italian Renaissance art.

Dictionary of Scientists (1999). From *Xrefer, The Web's Reference Engine: Vesalius, Andreas.*
http://www.xrefer.com/entry.jsp?xrefid=495301&secid=
[1 August 2002]
Definition of "Vesalius."

Gerten-Jackson, Carol. *CGFA: A Virtual Art Museum: Raphael.*
http://btr0xw.rz.uni-bayreuth.de/cjackson/raphael/
[25 July 2002]
Image gallery and biography link about Raphael.

Harden, Mark. *Artchive: Giorgione.*
http://www.artchive.com/artchive/ftptoc/giorgione_ext.html
[25 July 2002]
Background information and image links about Giorgione (circa 1478?–1510).

Harden, Mark. *Artchive: Renaissance Art: Italian Renaissance, Northern Renaissance.*
http://www.artchive.com/artchive/renaissance.html
[25 July 2002]
List of Renaissance and Northern Renaissance artists with links to images.

Knechtel, Nancy. Niagara County Community College (SUNY). *High Renaissance Art.*
http://www.sunyniagara.cc.ny.us/homepags/Knechtel/highren.html
[25 July 2002]
General information about the High Renaissance with links to images.

113

Oxford Paperback Encyclopedia (1998). From *Xrefer, The Web's Reference Engine: Renaissance (French, rebirth).*
http://www.xrefer.com/entry.jsp?xrefid=222863&secid=
[1 August 2002]
Encyclopedia article about the Renaissance. Cites information about the humanist philosophy and the High Renaissance from the *Oxford Paperback Encyclopedia* (1998).

Thames and Hudson Dictionary of Art Terms (1984). From *Xrefer, The Web's Reference Engine: Renaissance.*
http://www.xrefer.com/entry.jsp?xrefid=649636&secid=
[1 August 2002]
Definition of "Renaissance" from *The Thames and Hudson Dictionary of Art Terms* (1984).

Witcombe, Chris. *Art History Resources on the Web: 15th-Century Renaissance Art.*
http://witcombe.sbc.edu/ARTHLinks2.html
[25 July 2002]
Resource directory that links to information about the Renaissance and image galleries.

Site Summary

High Renaissance art is distinguished by the eloquent use of line, balance, and harmony. Once artists of the Early Renaissance era broke away from the strict and linear Gothic style, design elements were free to flow gracefully and evolve into the style that marks the High Renaissance. Although this is considered a brief period of the era (circa 1500–1520), it produced some of the most creative, inspirational, and technically skilled pieces of artwork of the time. Artists and architects such as Raphael, Donato Bramante, Leonardo da Vinci, and Michelangelo dominated the direction of artistic taste and style. Da Vinci epitomizes the term "Renaissance man." His artistic talents and intellect touched every aspect of art. He was not only an artist but also a scientist by nature. His knowledge of math and science helped him develop some of the most important innovations and discoveries of the millennium. Da Vinci recorded his studies in numerous notebook sketches.

Michelangelo was an artist who was passionate about his work. Although he was familiar with the art of the classics, he abandoned their idealism for the beauty of naturalism and realism. The Renaissance philosophy of humanism was coupled with an appreciation for harmony and balance.

Discussion Questions and Activities

1. Read background information about the High Renaissance from the Xrefer web sites at http://xrefer.com/entry.jsp?xrefid=649636&secid= and at http://www.xrefer.com/entry.jsp?xrefid=222863&secid=. Who were some of the leading High Renaissance architects? Refer to http://witcombe.sbc.edu/ARTHLinks2.html under the section "Sixteenth-Century Art Italy: The High Renaissance and Mannerism" and link to web sites about the architecture of Andrea Palladio (1508–1580). Harmony and balance were important in Renaissance architecture. When you look at the structures Palladio designed, identify the elements that depict balance. How does line create harmony (flow) in the building design?

2. Using information from the Xrefer web sites, answer the following questions. Masaccio was an important painter of the Early Renaissance because of one of his inventions. What did he invent that became important to Renaissance artists? How did Renaissance artists expand the technique used in Masaccio's invention? What three major Italian cities dominated the art world at this time? What other innovations in art occurred during this time? Besides religious themes, what other subjects were artists painting? What historical event effectively ended the era of the High Renaissance? Look up this event (type in the event) in the Xrefer web site at http://www.xrefer.com and explain what happened.

3. In the first paragraph about the Renaissance at http://www.xrefer.com/entry.jsp?xrefid=222863&secid= read about the importance of depicting nature. Choose a couple of artists from the Artcyclopedia site at http://www.artcyclopedia.com/history/high-renaissance.html and view their paintings of nature scenes. How did they paint clouds and mountains? Do these look realistic? Why do you think the artists incorporated so many details put into a background scene of nature? Do the mountains seem to disappear in the distance in some scenes? Are the trees painted more realistically than in paintings from the Early Renaissance (Giotto)?

4. Read about themes and portraiture (paragraphs 4 and 5) at http://www.infoplease.com/ce6/ent/A0860692.html. What new themes emerged in the Renaissance art of the fifteenth century? What were these themes derived from? What is a myth? Look up the word "mythology" at http://www.xrefer.com. Read the information and view the paintings by Giorgione (circa 1478–1510) at http://www.artchive.com/artchive/ftptoc/giorgione_ext.html. What are the titles of the paintings that depict myths? What mythological creatures do you see in these paintings?

5. Raphael painted religious scenes and portraits. View some of his portraits (there are several screens) at http://btr0xw.rz.uni-bayreuth.de/cjackson/raphael/. Why did portraits become popular during the High Renaissance? What segment of society did these portraits depict? Do the eyes of the sitter look at the viewer? How did Raphael depict the sitters (e.g., seated, three-quarter view, head and shoulders, full standing)?

6. At http://www.xrefer.com/entry.jsp?xrefid=222863&secid= read about the new discoveries that influenced High Renaissance art. What important Flemish treatise influenced the sciences? At http://xrefer.com/entry.jsp?xrefid=495301&secid=.-&hh=1 find out what other sciences expanded during this time (look for the name of a famous anatomist). Use an image search engine and type in the name of this anatomist to view some studies and then describe some of the details you see in the drawings.

LEONARDO DA VINCI
(1452–1519)

Images

Drawings of Machines, circa 1480–1482, pen and ink. Milan: Atlanticus Biblioteca Ambrosiana.

Muscles of the Neck and Shoulders, circa 1515, pen and ink, black chalk, wash, 29.2 cm. (11½") high. Anatomical Studies, fol. 137v. Windsor Castle, England: The Royal Library.

Study of Cat Movements and Positions, circa 1515, pen and ink. Windsor Castle, England: The Royal Library.

Vitruvian Man: A Study of Proportions from Vitruvius's De Architectura, circa 1515, pen and ink, 34.3 cm. x 24.5 cm. (13½" x 9⅝"). Venice: Accademia.

Web Addresses

Alvey, R. Kevin. *The Anatomical Drawings of Leonardo da Vinci.*
http://www.geocities.com/CollegePark/1070/leonardo.html
[25 July 2002]
Article about da Vinci's anatomical drawings.

Harden, Mark. *Artchive: Leonardo da Vinci.*
http://www.artchive.com/artchive/L/leonardo.html
[25 July 2002]
Background information and links to images.

Harden, Mark. *Artchive: Leonardo da Vinci: Muscles of the neck and shoulders.*
http://www.artchive.com/artchive/L/leonardo/leonardo_muscles.jpg.html
[25 July 2002]
Muscles of the Neck and Shoulders, circa 1515, pen and ink, black chalk, wash drawing.

Harden, Mark. *Artchive: Leonardo da Vinci: Study of Cat Movements and Positions.*
http://www.artchive.com/artchive/L/leonardo/leonardo_cats.jpg.html
[25 July 2002]
Study of Cat Movements and Positions, pen and ink drawing.

Harden, Mark. *Artchive: Leonardo da Vinci: Study of proportions from Vitruvius's De Architectura.*
http://www.artchive.com/artchive/L/leonardo/proports.jpg.html
[25 July 2002]
Vitruvian Man: A Study of Proportions from Vitruvius's De Architectura, pen and ink drawing.

Kren, Emil and Daniel Marx. *Web Gallery of Art: Drawings by Leonardo da Vinci.*
http://www.kfki.hu/~arthp/html/l/leonardo/drawings/index.html
[25 July 2002]
Web site links to images and biographical information featuring the drawings of Leonardo da Vinci.

Kren, Emil and Daniel Marx. *Web Gallery of Art: Drawings of machines by Leonardo da Vinci.*
http://www.kfki.hu/~arthp/html/l/leonardo/drawings/machines/index.html
[25 July 2002]
Drawings of Machines, pen and ink drawings.

Larmann, Ralph. University of Evansville, IN. *The Figure Drawing Lab: The Vitruvian Man.*
http://www2.evansville.edu/drawinglab/vitruvian.html
and *The Figure Drawing Lab: Standard Visual Human Body Proportions.*
http://www2.evansville.edu/drawinglab/body.html
[25 July 2002]
Standard visual human body proportions of ideal measurements based on da Vinci's *Vitruvian Man.*

McKie, Kelly. University of Calgary. *Exploring da Vinci: The Vitruvian Man.*
http://www.ucalgary.ca/~kamckie/davinci/vitruvian.html
[25 July 2002]

Museum of Science, Boston. *Exploring Leonardo: The Inventor's Workshop.*
http://www.mos.org/sln/Leonardo/InventorsWorkshop.html
[25 July 2002]
Information about da Vinci's inventions with images and links to classroom activities.

Olga's Gallery. *Leonardo da Vinci.*
http://www.abcgallery.com/L/leonardo/leonardo.html
[25 July 2002]
Image gallery and link to biography.

Pioch, Nicolas. *WebMuseum, Paris: Leonardo da Vinci.*
http://www.ibiblio.org/wm/paint/auth/vinci/
[25 July 2002]
Biography and links to images.

Site Summary

Leonardo da Vinci was an artist, scientist, architect, and inventor. All of his creations exhibit the concepts of Renaissance humanist philosophy. In the studio of Verrocchio he was trained at an early age to work in different artistic techniques and media. He received numerous painting commissions from wealthy patrons and the church. Paintings ranged from portraits and religious themes to visual documentation of historical events. His masterpieces include the *Madonna of the Rocks* (begun in 1483), the *Last Supper* fresco for Santa Maria delle Grazie in Milan (1495–1497), *Lady with the Ermine* (1483–1484), the *Mona Lisa* (1503–1507), and the commission for the fresco of the *Battle of Anghiari* (commissioned in 1503; today only the studies and engravings exist).

His interest in science and physiognomy is apparent in his drawing studies and their accompanying notations. In 1490, da Vinci began to write an important *Treatise on Painting* to explain his theories. Other projects included the architectural designs for the Milan Cathedral spire (1487) and the Cathedral at Pavia. In 1517, da Vinci was invited to become the engineer for the new king of France, Francis I, and he lived in Amboise until his death in 1519. Da Vinci left a legacy for other artists to emulate, especially through the documentation of his drawing studies for paintings, anatomical studies, and inventions.

Discussion Questions and Activities

1. View the anatomical drawings at http://www.kfki.hu/~arthp/html/l/leonardo/drawings/index.html and of *Muscles of the Neck and Shoulders* at http://www.artchive.com/artchive/L/leonardo/leonardo _muscles.jpg.html. Read the information at http://www.geocities.com/CollegePark/1070/leonardo.html. Why do you think it was important for da Vinci to study anatomy in order to depict human figures? Describe the detail of the drawings.

2. Refer to the web site explaining human proportion at http://www2.evansville.edu/drawinglab/body.html. Also visit the accompanying web site of http://www2.evansville.edu/drawinglab/vitruvian.html and read the theories at http://www.ucalgary.ca/~kamckie/davinci/vitruvian.html. How many heads high does the average human figure stand according to the Vitruvian theory? Who was Vitruvius, and why did da Vinci study his theories?

3. Refer to the following web site to see the drawing of the *Vitruvian Man: A Study of Proportions from Vitruvius's De Architectura* at http://www.artchive.com/artchive/L/leonardo/proports.jpg.html. How does this drawing represent the concepts of the Renaissance? Use a search engine and the phrase "Vitruvian man and advertising" to find advertisements that use the *Vitruvian Man* as a logo, such as Nokia's advertisement at http://www.pri.net/josh/nokia-asia_core_id.html.

4. View some of the paintings by da Vinci at http://www.abcgallery.com/L/leonardo/leonardo.html (from Olga's Gallery) and determine how anatomical studies helped him paint the figures realistically. View some of his paintings from the link at http://www.ibiblio.org/wm/paint/auth/vinci/. Do you see how drapery models around the figures? Describe how drapery falls on them.

5. Da Vinci based many of his studies and drawings on his observations of nature. View the image of the *Study of Cat Movements and Positions* at http://www.artchive.com/artchive/L/leonardo/leonardo_cats .jpg.html. Study the drawing and identify the different activities the cats are engaged in. As an activity, try to either draw or keep a journal describing your own pets' activities or those of other animals such as birds and squirrels, which you can watch in a park or from your own backyard.

6. Da Vinci was appointed as chief engineer and designed many mechanical devices. Read the information at http://www.mos.org/sln/Leonardo/InventorsWorkshop.html and refer to the image gallery web site at http://www.kfki.hu/~arthp/html/l/leonardo/drawings/machines/index.html to view his drawings of machines. Identify the various devices and their purposes. How do the drawings resemble blueprint drawings?

MICHELANGELO
(1475–1564)

Images

Bacchus, marble sculpture, over-life-size, circa 1496–1498. Florence: Bargello.

Florentine (Firenze) Pietà, marble sculpture, circa 1547–1555, approximately 7'8" high. Florence: Museo dell'Opera del Duomo.

Pietà (St. Peters), marble sculpture, circa 1498–1500, approximately 68½" high x 6'. Saint Peter's Basilica, Vatican.

Rondanini Pietà, marble sculpture, circa 1555–1664. Milan: Castello Sforzesco.

Sistine Chapel Frescoes, fresco, circa 1508–1512, approximately 63⅜" high. Rome: Vatican.

Web Addresses

Gerten-Jackson, Carol. *CGFA: A Virtual Art Museum: Michelangelo.*
http://sunsite.icm.edu.pl/cjackson/michelan/ (images)
http://sunsite.icm.edu.pl/cjackson/michelan/michelangelo_bio.htm (biography)
[25 July 2002]
Image gallery and a link to biographical information.

Gerten-Jackson, Carol. *CGFA: A Virtual Art Museum: Michelangelo: Pieta (Vatican).*
http://sunsite.icm.edu.pl/cjackson/michelan/p-michel11.htm
[25 July 2002]
Image of the *Pietà*, marble sculpture image.

Knight, Kevin. *Catholic Encyclopedia: Michelangelo Buonarroti: Sculpture, First Period.*
http://www.newadvent.org/cathen/03059b.htm
[25 July 2002]
Biography with information about the *Pietà*.

Kren, Emil and Daniel Marx. *Web Gallery of Art: Frescoes in the Sistine Chapel by Michelangelo.*
http://gallery.euroweb.hu/html/m/michelan/3sistina/index.html
[25 July 2002]

Kren, Emil and Daniel Marx. *Web Gallery of Art: Sculptures by Michelangelo (featuring The Pieta).*
http://gallery.euroweb.hu/html/m/michelan/1sculptu/index.html
[25 July 2002]
Biography link and image gallery (featuring the *Pietà*).

Olga's Gallery. *Michelangelo: Pieta (Vatican) with details of the Virgin and Christ.*
http://www.abcgallery.com/M/michelangelo/michelangelo.html
[25 July 2002]
Biography link and image gallery of the *Pietà* and details of the heads of the Virgin and the dead Christ.

Pioch, Nicolas. *WebMuseum, Paris: Michelangelo.*
http://www.ibiblio.org/wm/paint/auth/michelangelo/
[25 July 2002]
Background information about Michelangelo with information about the Sistine Chapel.

Thais. *1200 Years of Italian Sculpture: Michelangelo Buonarroti.*
http://translate.google.com/translate?hl=en&sl=it&u=http://www.thais.it/scultura/michelan.htm&prev
=/search%3Fq%3Dthais%2Bmichelangelo%26hl%3Den%26lr%3D%26ie%3DUTF-8
[25 July 2002]
Image gallery featuring the different versions of the *Pietà*.

Site Summary

Michelangelo Buonarroti was born in Caprese, Italy, in 1475. As a Renaissance artist, Michelangelo had a variety of talents that ranged from painting, architectural design, poetry, and sculpture. He began his training as a student in the studio of Domenico Ghirlandaio. He then became interested in the ideas of Neoplatonism (the body traps the soul) while studying the ancient sculptures in the Medici gardens near the monastery of San Marco. The Classical sculptures inspired Michelangelo to understand the beauty of form, mind, and soul. These ideals are elemental to Michelangelo's work, especially his sculptures. He studied anatomy and was particularly interested in the anatomical studies of Antonio Pollaiuolo.

His first major commission was to sculpt the *Pietà* (circa 1498–1500) for the tomb of Cardinal Jean de Villiers de La Grolais. The *Pietà* portrays the young mourning Virgin Mary holding the body of Christ after he was taken down from the cross. Michelangelo's masterpiece of serene tenderness depicts a mother holding her dead son. One observes tranquil and composed human grief that transcends spirituality. He enhanced these emotions with the simple gesture of the Virgin's left hand and her tilted head, the limp body of Christ within her lap, and the smooth warmth of the carved marble. Although this sculpture depicts the theme of death, Michelangelo breathed a sense of life into these figures. This particular piece was well received by his contemporaries and brought notoriety to his artistic career.

Other major commissions consisted of the marble statues of *David* (1503) and *Moses* (1516) and the figures for the Medici tombs (circa 1516–1534). As Michelangelo gained a reputation as a great artist, he attracted the interest of Pope Julius II, who commissioned the paintings for the Sistine Chapel in 1508. For the next several years, Michelangelo painted more than 300 figures for the chapel. The figures consisted of biblical prophets and pagan sibyls (prophetesses) and scenes from the *Creation* and the *Last Judgment*. Architectural projects included the design for the Laurentian Library in Florence (begun in 1524) and the plan of the Piazza del Campidoglio in Rome (1544–1552). His last major projects were more versions of the *Pietà* and are known as the *Rondanini Pietà* (circa 1555–1564) and the *Florentine (Firenze) Pietà* (circa 1547–1555).

Discussion Questions and Activities

1. Read the biographical information at http://gallery.euroweb.hu/bio/m/michelan/biograph.html and at http://sunsite.icm.edu.pl/cjackson/michelan/michelangelo_bio.htm. What artist did Michelangelo first study with? Where did Michelangelo study sculpture? What type of sculpture did he copy? What is the name of the influential family whom Michelangelo met and who later became his patron? Who were some of the other influential people that he knew, and why were they important to his artistic career?

2. Read the information from the *Catholic Encyclopedia* at http://www.newadvent.org/cathen/03059b.htm. What was the first large-scale sculpture that Michelangelo produced? View the piece from the image gallery at http://sunsite.icm.edu.pl/cjackson/michelan/. What is the subject of this piece? Why was this theme important to Michelangelo? Is this sculpture based on a pagan or religious theme? How did Michelangelo learn about anatomy?

3. While in Rome, Michelangelo produced the marble statue of the *Pietà.* View the image and details at http://www.abcgallery.com/M/michelangelo/michelangelo.html. Having read the articles from *Encarta* and the *Catholic Encyclopedia* answer the following questions: Where is the sculpture located? How old was Michelangelo when he produced the piece? What is the theme of the *Pietà*? What is unusual about the age of Mary as shown in this sculpture? What emotion does she depict? View the details of the artwork. Can you see Christ's wounds? Describe Mary's hands. What are some of the distinct anatomical features of this piece? What is the shape of the composition as a whole? Is this piece signed by Michelangelo? If so, why?

4. Later in life, Michelangelo created different versions of the *Pietà* theme. View the *Florentine (Firenze) Pietà* and the *Rondanini Pietà* at http://translate.google.com/translate?hl=en&sl=it&u=http://www .thais.it/scultura/michelan.htm&prev=/search%3Fq%3Dthais%2Bmichelangelo%26hl%3Den%26lr %3D%26ie%3DUTF-8. What is the difference between the *Florentine (Firenze) Pietà* and the earlier version? How is the figure of Christ depicted in these two later versions? Describe the marble surface of the earlier and later versions. Do these late versions portray any emotions? Compare the compositions of the late versions.

5. The statue of the *Pietà* in Saint Peter's Basilica, the Vatican, was attacked by vandals in the twentieth century. Use a search engine, such as http://www.google.com, and type in the phrase "vandalism *Pietà.*" Look for articles about the vandalism and answer the following questions: Why did the vandalism occur? What happened to the statue after the attack? What information did you find about the restoration?

6. Read the information about the Sistine Chapel at http://www.ibiblio.org/wm/paint/auth/michelangelo/ and view images at http://gallery.euroweb.hu/html/m/michelan/3sistina/index.html. Who commissioned the frescoes of the Sistine Chapel? Where exactly were these paintings located in the chapel? What is the first fresco of the series? What types of images surround the main scenes? Look at some of the details and describe these figures. What is the most dramatic element in the *Creation of Adam*? How did Michelangelo paint these frescoes?

Related Internet Sites

High Renaissance

Annenberg. *The Western Tradition: Renaissance: Introduction.*
- http://www.learner.org/exhibits/renaissance/
  [26 July 2002]
  A general and comprehensive information web site about the Renaissance.

Annenberg. *The Western Tradition: Renaissance: Printing and Thinking, Humanism Emerges.*
- http://www.learner.org/exhibits/renaissance/printing.html
  [26 July 2002]
  Brief summary of the humanist philosophy.

Google Web Directory. *Renaissance: Arts: Art History, Movements, Renaissance.*
- http://directory.google.com/Top/Arts/Art_History/Movements/Renaissance/
  [26 July 2002]

Moorhouse, Dan. *Schools History: Andreas Vesalius, A series of activities on the life and work of Andreas Vesalius.*
- http://www.schoolshistory.org.uk/vesaliusactivities.htm
  [26 July 2002]
  Learn more about the life and work of Andreas Vesalius.

The Oxford Dictionary of Art. (1997). From *Xrefer, The Web's Reference Engine: Renaissance.*
- http://www.xrefer.com/entry.jsp?xrefid=145209&secid
  [26 July 2002]
  Definition of "Renaissance" from the *Oxford Dictionary of Art* (1997).

Pioch, Nicolas. *WebMuseum, Paris: La Renaissance.*
- http://www.oir.ucf.edu/wm/paint/glo/renaissance/
  [25 July 2002]
  Information about Renaissance art in Europe.

Pioch, Nicolas. *WebMuseum, Paris: La Renaissance: Italy.*
- http://www.oir.ucf.edu/wm/paint//glo/renaissance/it.html
  [25 July 2002]
  Background information about the Renaissance in Italy.

Leonardo da Vinci

Alejandre, Suzanne. Drexel University, Philadelphia, PA. *Math Forum at Drexel: Leonardo da Vinci Activity.*
- http://www.mathforum.com/alejandre/frisbie/math/leonardo.html
  [26 July 2002]
  Information that explains the basis of da Vinci's theories of how to draw human proportions.

Kausal, Martin. *Leonardo da Vinci.*
- http://www.kausal.com/leonardo/index.html
  [26 July 2002]
  Background information about Leonardo da Vinci.

Knechtel, Nancy. Niagara County Community College (SUNY). *High Renaissance Art: Links to Web Sites: Leonardo da Vinci.*
- http://www.sunyniagara.cc.ny.us/homepags/Knechtel/highren.html
  [26 July 2002]
  Provides background information about the High Renaissance and features Leonardo da Vinci.

Museum of Science, Boston. *Exploring Leonardo.*
- http://www.mos.org/sln/Leonardo/
  [26 July 2002]
  Home page of the da Vinci web site. Has links and images.

Museum of Science, Boston. *Exploring Leonardo: The Inventor's Workshop.*
- http://www.mos.org/sln/Leonardo/InventorsWorkshop.html
  [26 July 2002]
  Learn about the inventions and devices da Vinci designed.

Michelangelo

Alacritude. *Encyclopedia.com: Sistine Chapel Restoration.*
- http://www.encyclopedia.com/html/s/sistinec1.asp
  [26 July 2002]
  Article about the Sistine Chapel restoration project.

Artcyclopedia. *Michelangelo Buonarroti.*
- http://www.artcyclopedia.com/artists/michelangelo_buonarroti.html
  [26 July 2002]
  Comprehensive list of links to works of art at various museums.

Christus Rex Inc. *Christus Rex Project: Art Gallery: Cappella Sistina (The Sistine Chapel).*
- http://www.christusrex.org/www1/sistine/0-Tour.html
  [26 July 2002]
  Image gallery of the Sistine Chapel paintings.

Harden, Mark. *Artchive: Michelangelo: Pieta.*
- http://www.artchive.com/artchive/M/michelangelo.html
  [26 July 2002]
  Biography and general information about the *Pietà*.

Hoover, M. San Antonio College, TX. *Roman Sculpture: Glorious Verism, Royal Imperialism.*
- http://www.accd.edu/sac/vat/arthistory/arts1303/Rome3.htm
  [26 July 2002]
  Image gallery of Classical Roman sculpture.

Kren, Emil and Daniel Marx. *Web Gallery of Art: Michelangelo.*
- http://gallery.euroweb.hu/html/m/michelan/index.html
  [26 July 2002]
  Image gallery.

Michelangelo.com. *Michelangelo Buonarroti: Early Life, Mid Years, Final Days.*
- http://www.michelangelo.com/buon/bio-index2.html
  [26 July 2002]
  Comprehensive biography.

CHAPTER 13

Mannerism

(Circa 1515–1610)

*Titian (Tiziano Vecellio) (Circa 1485–1576) and
Parmigianino (Girolamo Francesco Maria Mazzola)
(1503–1540)*

Mannerism Web Addresses

**Market House Books Encyclopaedia of the Renaissance (1987). From *Xrefer, The
Web's Reference Engine: Chiaroscuro*.**
http://www.xrefer.com/entry.jsp?xrefid=251886&secid=.-
[27 July 2002]
Definition of "chiaroscuro."

National Gallery of Art, Washington, D.C. *National Gallery of Art: Tour: Mannerism
Overview.*
http://www.nga.gov/collection/gallery/gg21/gg21-over1.html#jump
[27 July 2002]
Information about Mannerism.

Pioch, Nicolas. *WebMuseum, Paris. La Renaissance: Italy.*
http://www.oir.ucf.edu/wm/paint/glo/renaissance/it.html
[27 July 2002]
Background information about the Renaissance and Mannerism.

**Thames and Hudson Dictionary of Art and Artists (1994). From *Xrefer, The Web's
Reference Engine: Mannerism*.**
http://www.xrefer.com/entry.jsp?xrefid=651667&secid=
[27 July 2002]
Definition of "Mannerism" from *The Thames and Hudson Dictionary of Art and Artists* (1994).

TITIAN (Tiziano Vecellio)
(Circa 1485–1576)

Images

Christ Crowned with Thorns, oil on canvas, 1540. Paris: Louvre.

Crowning with Thorns, oil on canvas, circa 1573–1575, Munich: Alte Pinakothek.

Web Addresses

Gerten-Jackson, Carol. *CGFA: A Virtual Art Museum: Titian.*
http://sunsite.icm.edu.pl/cjackson/titian/index.html
[27 July 2002]
Image gallery and biography link.

Gerten-Jackson, Carol. *CGFA: A Virtual Art Museum: Titian-3: Crowning with Thorns (1573–1575, Alte Pinakothek).*
http://sunsite.icm.edu.pl/cjackson/titian/p-titian9.htm
[27 July 2002]
Crowning with Thorns (1573–1575, Alte Pinakothek) image.

Kren, Emil and Daniel Marx. *Web Gallery of Art: Tiziano (Titian) Crowning with Thorns (1573–1575, Alte Pinakothek).*
http://www.kfki.hu/~arthp/html/t/tiziano/5religio/crowning.html
[27 July 2002]
Biography and image gallery that features the image of *Crowning with Thorns* (1573–1575).

Olga's Gallery. *Titian.*
http://www.abcgallery.com/T/titian/titian.html
[27 July 2002]
Biography and image gallery.

Olga's Gallery. *Titian: Christ Crowned with Thorns (1540, Louvre).*
http://www.abcgallery.com/T/titian/titian42.html
[27 July 2002]
Christ Crowned with Thorns (1540, Louvre) image.

Pioch, Nicolas. *WebMuseum, Paris. Titian.*
http://www.ibiblio.org/wm/paint/auth/titian/
[27 July 2002]
Biography.

PARMIGIANINO
(Girolamo Francesco Maria Mazzola)
(1503–1540)

Images

Madonna of the Long Neck (Madonna dal Collo Longo), oil on wood, 1534–1540, 219 cm. x 135 cm. Galleria degli Uffizi, Florence.

Web Addresses

Harden, Mark. *Artchive: Parmigianino.*
http://www.artchive.com/artchive/P/parmigianino.html
[27 July 2002]
Biography, image gallery, and link to the image of the *Madonna of the Long Neck.*

Harden, Mark. *Artchive: Parmigianino: Madonna of the Long Neck.*
http://www.artchive.com/artchive/P/parmigianino/long_neck.jpg.html
[27 July 2002]
Madonna of the Long Neck image.

Kren, Emil and Daniel Marx. *Web Gallery of Art: Parmigianino: Biography.*
http://www.kfki.hu/~arthp/bio/p/parmigia/biograph.html
[27 July 2002]
Brief biography and image of the *Madonna of the Long Neck.*

Kren, Emil and Daniel Marx. *Web Gallery of Art: Parmigianino: Madonna of the Long Neck.*
http://www.kfki.hu/~arthp/html/p/parmigia/longneck.html
[27 July 2002]
Madonna of the Long Neck image.

Site Summary

The artists Titian and Parmigianino represent two different aspects of Italian Mannerism of the sixteenth century. Mannerism is the name given to the stylistic transition between the Renaissance and the Baroque periods. Mannerist painting can be distinguished by its use of strong acidlike colors, dramatic use of light and shadow (chiaroscuro), illogical use of space with possible trompe l'oeil effects (images painted to fool the eye), an emphasis on unusual compositional views, and elongated and contorted figures characterized as serpentine. This style is considered to possibly be a reaction to Renaissance art.

Titian apprenticed under Gentile Bellini and Giorgione while in Venice. His first masterpiece was an allegory known as *Sacred and Profane Love,* circa 1515. He was commissioned to paint numerous frescos and altarpieces and was eventually appointed as court painter to the Holy Roman Emperor in 1533. Titian developed a stronger use of color and light and featured dramatic moments that were distinct from Giorgione's. Both versions of his paintings of *Christ Crowned with Thorns* (1540, Louvre) and *Crowning with Thorns* (1573–1575, Alte Pinakothek) illustrate the Mannerist style. The contrasting use of light and shadow and the crossing of spears over the head of Christ emphasize the drama of the moment and indicate the key figure in this composition.

Parmigianino uses another Mannerist technique: that of the serpentine and elongated figure along with strange perspective views and out-of-proportion architectural elements. This is illustrated in his painting, *Madonna of the Long Neck (Madonna dal Collo Longo)*. The Madonna is extremely elongated, figures are crammed to one side of the composition, and the architectural components (such as the column in the background) are oddly proportioned. Both paintings use strong, acidlike colors that impart an almost surreal effect to the space and to the particular moment; these are distinct examples of the Mannerist style.

Discussion Questions and Activities

1.   Read the background information about Mannerism (under "The Late Renaissance" paragraph) at http://www.oir.ucf.edu/wm/paint/glo/renaissance/it.html and from the Xrefer web site at http://www.xrefer.com/entry.jsp?xrefid=651667&secid=. What happened in 1527 that caused most of the artists to flee to other cities? How did the style of Mannerism get its name? What time period did Mannerism follow? What are the distinct elements of Mannerist painting?

2.   Read background information on the Mannerist style at http://www.nga.gov/collection/gallery/gg21/gg21-over1.html#jump. View the images of *Christ Crowned with Thorns* (1540, Louvre) at http://www.abcgallery.com/T/titian/titian42.html by Titian. Then view Parmigianino's *Madonna of the Long Neck* at http://www.artchive.com/artchive/P/parmigianino/long_neck.jpg.html and identify the strange colors used in these paintings. How are the colors different from those used by other Renaissance artists such as Leonardo da Vinci?

3.   Identify illogical uses of space in these compositions. What makes the scenes look illogical? Are the foreground and background in perspective and/or in proportion to the composition of the rest of the paintings?

4.   Compare the two versions of Titian's paintings of *Christ Crowned with Thorns* (1540, Louvre) at http://www.abcgallery.com/T/titian/titian42.html and the *Crowning with Thorns* (1573–1575, Alte Pinakothek) at http://www.kfki.hu/~arthp/html/t/tiziano/5religio/crowning.html and http://sunsite.icm.edu.pl/cjackson/titian/p-titian9.htm. Minimize both images on the tool bar so you can look at them. What are the differences in the use of color between the two versions? Which version is more intense in color? Which version is dated earlier? What is common to both versions? Which painting has a more close-up view than the other? How can you tell which figure is Christ since none of the figures has a halo?

5.   Identify the use of light and shadow and tell how it adds to the drama in both versions of Titian's *Christ Crowned with Thorns* and *Crowning with Thorns*. Read the article about chiaroscuro at http://www.xrefer.com/entry.jsp?xrefid=251886&secid= from the *Encyclopaedia of the Renaissance* (1987). Why is this technique so successful in Mannerist paintings?

6.   View Parmigianino's *Madonna of the Long Neck* at http://www.kfki.hu/~arthp/html/p/parmigiam/longneck.html and identify what makes the figure of the Madonna serpentine-like. Does the drapery of her clothes emphasize the serpentine aspect of her figure? Does the figure of the baby depicting Christ look serpentine and in proportion?

7.   Compare the foreground and background of the *Madonna of the Long Neck*. Is there a middle ground to this painting? Does the background sit on the same plane of the foreground, and if not, does this make logical sense of the use of perspective and space? Is the small figure by the column meant to be seen in the distance even though it stands on the same plane of the foreground? Why are these elements considered Mannerist rather than Renaissance in style?

Related Internet Sites

Mannerism

Artcyclopedia. *Artists by Movement: Mannerism: Europe, Mid to Late 16th Century.*
■ http://www.artcyclopedia.com/history/mannerism.html
  [27 July 2002]
  Directory of links to information and image galleries about Mannerism.

Oxford Dictionary of Art (1997). From *Xrefer, The Web's Reference Engine: trompe l'oeil.*
■ http://www.xrefer.com/entry.jsp?xrefid=145724&secid
  [1 August 2002]
  Web site that provides a definition of trompe l'oeil from the *Oxford Dictionary of Art* (1997).

Televisual. *Uffizi Gallery: Mannerism.*
■ http://www.televisual.it/uffizi/manneris.html
  [1 August 2002]

Tigertail Associates. *Tigertail Virtual Art Museum: Mannerism.*
■ http://www.tigtail.org/TVM/M_View/X1/c.Mannerism/mannerism.html
  [1 August 2002]

Titian

Artcyclopedia. *Titian.*
■ http://www.artcyclopedia.com/artists/titian.html
  [1 August 2002]
  Directory of links to information and image galleries.

Harden, Mark. *Artchive. Titian.*
■ http://www.artchive.com/artchive/T/titian.html
  [1 August 2002]
  Background information featuring portraiture and an image gallery.

Tigertail Associates. *Tigertail Virtual Art Museum: High Italian Renaissance 1490 to 1520: Titian.*
■ http://tvm.tigtail.org/TVM/M_View/X1/b.High%20Italian/titian/titian.html
  [1 August 2002]
  Image gallery.

Parmigianino

J. Paul Getty Trust. *ArtsEdNet. Explore Art: The Collections: Parmigianino.*
■ http://www.getty.edu/art/collections/bio/a726-1.html
  [1 August 2002]
  Biography.

CHAPTER 14

Northern Renaissance Art

(Fifteenth Century-Sixteenth Century)

Jan van Eyck (Circa 1390-1441), Martin Schongauer (Circa 1450-1491), Pieter (the Elder, I) Bruegel (1525?-1569), and Albrecht Dürer (1471-1528)

Northern Renaissance Web Addresses

Annenberg. *The Western Tradition: The Renaissance: Printing and Thinking.*
http://www.learner.org/exhibits/renaissance/printing.html
[15 August 2002]
Information on printing and thinking as spiritual matters.

Artcyclopedia. *Artists by Movement: The Northern Renaissance: Centered in Germany and the Netherlands, 15th–16th Centuries.*
http://www.artcyclopedia.com/history/northern-renaissance.html
[15 August 2002]

Hemus Fine Arts. *Early Northern Renaissance.*
http://www.hermus.com/northern.htm
[15 August 2002]
Information about the early Northern Renaissance.

National Gallery of Art, Washington, DC. *National Gallery of Art: Collection: Northern European Painting of the 15th–16th Centuries.*
http://www.nga.gov/collection/gallery/euro15.htm
[15 August 2002]
Northern European paintings of the fifteenth and sixteenth centuries.

Oxford Dictionary of Art (1997). From *Xrefer, The Web's Reference Engine: Renaissance.*
http://www.xrefer.com/entry.jsp?xrefid=145209&secid=.-
[15 August 2002]
Definition of the Renaissance.

Witcombe, Chris. *Art History Resources on the Web: 15th Century Art in Northern Europe and Spain.*
http://witcombe.sbc.edu/ARTHLinks2.html#Northern15
[15 August 2002]
Resource directory that links to information about the Northern Renaissance and image galleries.

JAN VAN EYCK
(Circa 1390–1441)

Images

Giovanni Arnolfini and His Wife, oil on panel, 1434, approximately 33" x 22½". London: National Gallery.

Man in a Red Turban (Self-Portrait), oil on panel, 1433, approximately 10" x 7". London: National Gallery.

Web Addresses

Kren, Emil and Daniel Marx. *Web Gallery of Art: Jan van Eyck Biography.*
http://gallery.euroweb.hu/bio/e/eyck_van/jan/biograph.html
[15 August 2002]
Biography and image link.

Kren, Emil and Daniel Marx. *Web Gallery of Art: Jan van Eyck Biography. Portrait of Giovanni Arnolfini and his Wife.*
http://gallery.euroweb.hu/html/e/eyck_van/jan/15arnolf/15arnol.html
[15 August 2002]

Kren, Emil and Daniel Marx. *Web Gallery of Art: Portrait of Giovanni Arnolfini and his Wife (1434) by Hubert and Jan van Eyck.*
http://gallery.euroweb.hu/html/e/eyck_van/jan/15arnolf/index.html
[15 August 2002]
Image and details of *Giovanni Arnolfini and His Wife.*

Pioch, Nicolas. *WebMuseum, Paris: Eyck, Jan van: The Arnolfini Marriage.*
http://www.ibiblio.org/wm/paint/auth/eyck/arnolfini/
[15 August 2002]
Information about and image link to *Giovanni Arnolfini and His Wife.*

MARTIN SCHONGAUER
(Circa 1450–1491)

Images

Christ Carrying the Cross, engraving, circa 1445–1491, approximately 12" x 17". New York: Metropolitan Museum of Art.

The Temptation of St. Anthony, engraving, circa 1480–1490. New York: Metropolitan Museum of Art.

Web Addresses

Kren, Emil and Daniel Marx. *Web Gallery of Art: Schongauer, Martin: Biography.*
http://www.kfki.hu/~arthp/bio/s/schongau/biograph.html
[15 August 2002]
Biography and link to "Pictures."

Kren, Emil and Daniel Marx. *Web Gallery of Art: Graphics by Martin Schongauer.*
http://www.kfki.hu/~arthp/html/s/schongau/graphics/index.html
[15 August 2002]
Image gallery of "Graphics" print images.

Metropolitan Museum of Art, New York. *Metropolitan Museum of Art: The Collection: Christ Carrying the Cross, ca.1475–80 made by Martin Schongauer.*
http://www.metmuseum.org/collections/view1.asp?dep=9&full=1&item=35%2E27
[15 August 2002]
Image and information about *Christ Carrying the Cross.*

PIETER (the Elder, I) BRUEGEL
(1525?–1569)

Images

The Beggars, oil on wood, circa 1568, approximately 165 cm. x 215 cm. Paris: Louvre.

The Harvesters, oil on wood, 1565, approximately 119 cm. x 162 cm. New York: Metropolitan Museum of Art.

Web Addresses

Artcyclopedia. *Pieter Bruegel the Elder.*
http://www.artcyclopedia.com/artists/bruegel_the_elder_pieter.html
[18 August 2002]

Kren, Emil and Daniel Marx. *Web Gallery of Art: Paintings by Pieter Bruegel, the Elder.*
http://www.kfki.hu/~arthp/html/b/bruegel/pieter_e/painting/index.html
[18 August 2002]
Image gallery and biography link.

Louvre. *Louvre: Collections: Paintings: Selected Works; Netherlands 15th–16th Centuries: Pieter Bruegel the Elder. The Beggars (1568).*
http://www.louvre.fr/anglais/collec/peint/rf0730/peint_f.htm
[18 August 2002]
Image and information about *The Beggars.*

Metropolitan Museum of Art, New York. *Metropolitan Museum of Art: Explore & Learn: From Van Eyck to Bruegel: Pieter Bruegel the Elder: The Harvesters (1565).*
http://www.metmuseum.org/explore/Vaneyck/van_eyck19.htm
[18 August 2002]
Image and information about *The Harvesters.*

Site Summary

Northern Renaissance art developed independently from that of the Italian Renaissance. One of the best-known artists of the North was Albrecht Dürer (1471–1528) of Germany. Dürer helped to expand the idea of artistic rebirth to his northern homeland. Although Dürer embraced the ideas of the Italian Renaissance, his own art reflects his Germanic background. Earlier influential northern artists contributed to the evolution of Gothic imagery and introduced innovations in the natural sciences that enhanced imagery. Anatomy, perspective, alchemy, physics, and technology became evident in artworks. Artists began to incorporate more natural and realistic settings with an overtone of symbolic imagery.

Wanting a wider range of colors, painters developed the technique of underpainting in gray tempera. A thin transparent layer of oil-base color was then applied on top of the gray tempera so that colors of paint would blend. Jan van Eyck experimented with this technique of oil painting and achieved a wide range of rich colors, which glistened from his canvases where the effects of light appeared not only realistic but also spiritual.

Printmaking especially flourished throughout northern Europe. One of the finest fifteenth-century printmakers was Martin Schongauer, who featured emotional and dramatic lines in his engravings. A variety of subjects began to be depicted, especially since the posting of Martin Luther's list (1517) of his concerns about the church. Secular subjects (not religious) became more popular. Pieter Bruegel the Elder (1525?–1569) painted scenes that resembled visual fables, which were humorous yet provoking.

Discussion Questions and Activities

1. Read the biography of Jan van Eyck at http://gallery.euroweb.hu/bio/e/eyck_van/jan/biograph.html and view the images from the "Pictures" link. What nationality is van Eyck? What technique is he credited with inventing? How did he use this technique in his paintings? View some of the paintings from the link and describe the minute details. Did he paint them realistically? How does light affect the look of the paintings? View the link to "Paintings until 1434" and look at the portrait of *Man in a Red Turban (Self-Portrait)*. Does it seem that you can see almost every crease in the turban? How does the light affect the look of his face?

2. Details were very important in van Eyck's paintings. Read from http://www.hermus.com/northern.htm and http://www.ibiblio.org/wm/paint/auth/eyck/arnolfini/. Then view the full image and various details at http://gallery.euroweb.hu/html/e/eyck_van/jan/15arnolf/index.html of the *Giovanni Arnolfini and His Wife* painting. Why might van Eyck have paid so much attention to details in his paintings? What kind of document is this painting supposed to represent? What moment is the artist capturing? What does the lit candle represent? What is reflected in the mirror on the wall? What are the symbols of faithfulness?

3. Refer to http://www.kfki.hu/~arthp/bio/s/schongau/biograph.html for biographical information about Martin Schongauer. What is he best known for? What kind of prints did he produce? Whom did he influence? View images of his graphic work at http://www.kfki.hu/~arthp/html/s/schongau/graphics/index.html. How did he use line to contrast light and dark areas of the prints? Is the line soft or hard looking? What details do you see in these compositions?

4. View the image at http://www.metmuseum.org/collections/view1.asp?dep=9&full=0&item=35%2E27 of *Christ Carrying the Cross*. What type of print is this? What is unique about this print when compared with his others? What kind of line does he use to depict density? What inspired him to make this print? What is unusual about the figure of Christ? What did Schongauer do to fill in the composition to make the cross stand out?

5. Pieter Bruegel, the Elder, liked to use secular (nonreligious) themes in his paintings. Use the link at http://www.kfki.hu/~arthp/html/b/bruegel/pieter_e/painting/index.html. to refer to his biography. What were the various themes of his paintings? What type of people did he usually depict? View the image gallery and name some titles that compose this group. Where did he travel to in the 1550s that helped to develop his artistic style? View http://www.metmuseum.org/explore/Vaneyck/van_eyck19.htm of *The Harvesters*. What series is this painting from? What season is depicted? Explain the elements that identify the season. How do the figures look within the landscape?

5. Bruegel often uses a narrative (storytelling) painting style. View the image of *The Beggars* from the Louvre at http://www.louvre.fr/anglais/collec/peint/rf0730/peint_f.htm. What type of scene does it depict? What is the cluster of figures doing? What physical condition are these figures in? What is the figure in the background doing? What kind of space does Bruegel paint? How does he enclose the figures in the composition so that you are not distracted from the action? What do you think Bruegel is trying to say about painting such a scene?

ALBRECHT DÜRER
(1471–1528)

Images

The Four Horsemen of the Apocalypse, woodcut, 1498, 39 cm. x 28 cm. London: British Museum.

Self-Portrait at 28, oil on panel, 1500, 67 cm. x 49 cm. Munich: Alte Pinakothek.

Web Addresses

Artcyclopedia. *Albrecht Dürer.*
http://www.artcyclopedia.com/artists/durer_albrecht.html
[18 August 2002]
Directory of links to information and image galleries.

Gerten-Jackson, Carol. *CGFA: A Virtual Art Museum: Dürer.*
http://sunsite.dk/cgfa/durer/index.html
[18 August 2002]
Biography and images.

Harden Mark. *Artchive: Albrecht Dürer, from Martin Bailey, "Dürer".*
http://www.artchive.com/artchive/D/durer.html
[18 August 2002]

Harden Mark. *Artchive: Albrecht Dürer: The Four Horsemen of the Apocalypse (1498).*
http://www.artchive.com/artchive/D/durer/4horse.jpg.html
[18 August 2002]
Background information and links to images including *The Four Horsemen of the Apocalypse.*

Hart, George W. *Dürer's Polyhedra.*
http://www.georgehart.com/virtual-polyhedra/durer.html
[18 August 2002]
Information about Dürer's theories on perspective.

Kren, Emil and Daniel Marx. *Web Gallery of Art: Portraits by Albrecht Dürer.*
http://gallery.euroweb.hu/html/d/durer/painting/portrait/index.html
[18 August 2002]

Macmillan Encyclopedia (2001). From *Xrefer, The Web's Reference Engine: Engraving.*
http://www.xrefer.com/entry.jsp?xrefid=502938&secid=
[13 September 2002]

National Gallery of Art, Washington, DC. *National Gallery of Art: Tour: 15th and Early-16th-Century Germany.*
http://www.nga.gov/collection/gallery/gg35a/gg35a-over1.html#jump
[18 August 2002]
General information about Northern Renaissance art and a link to biographical information about Dürer.

Olga's Gallery. *Albrecht Dürer. The Four Horsemen of the Apocalypse.*
http://www.abcgallery.com/D/durer/durer5.html
[18 August 2002]

Olga's Gallery. *Old Testament Notes: Apocalypse.*
http://www.abcgallery.com/religion/apocalypse.html
[18 August 2002]
Information about *The Four Horsemen of the Apocalypse.*

Pioch, Nicolas. *WebMuseum, Paris: Dürer, Albrecht: Engravings: The Four Horsemen of the Apocalypse (1498) woodcut.*
http://www.ibiblio.org/wm/paint/auth/durer/engravings/
[18 August 2002]
The Four Horsemen of the Apocalypse image.

Pioch, Nicolas. *WebMuseum, Paris: Dürer, Albrecht: Self-Portraits.*
http://www.ibiblio.org/wm/paint/auth/durer/self/
[18 August 2002]

Thames & Hudson Dictionary of Art and Artists (1994). From *Xrefer, The Web's Reference Engine: Woodcut.*
http://www.xrefer.com/entry.jsp?xrefid=652751&secid=
[13 September 2002]

Site Summary

Albrecht Dürer was born in Nuremberg, Germany, in 1471. He was the first major northern European artist to gravitate away from the medieval Gothic tradition of painting and artistic rendering. His work flourished throughout Europe, especially his graphic prints. At an early age, Dürer apprenticed in the workshop of Michael Wolgemut, a renowned painter and printer. There he learned the art of woodcuts and engravings, mastering the technique of enhancing every detail with line throughout his compositions. He has been credited with the creation of some of the woodcut illustrations for the monumental work of the *Nuremberg Chronicle,* which was produced from Wolgemut's workshop in 1493. Although Dürer was an accomplished painter, his graphic career is considered his masterpiece.

Dürer admired the work of Martin Schongauer and spent some time traveling, including visits to Italy. He studied firsthand the graphic works of Antonio Pollaiuolo and Andrea Mantegna as well as admiring the anatomical works of Leonardo da Vinci. The Italian handling of the graphic line and interest in nature and anatomy influenced Dürer's art.

Dürer's first major woodcut masterpiece, *The Four Horsemen of the Apocalypse* (1498), exhibits a deviation from the stiff Gothic depiction of figures and religious themes. The theme of the *Apocalypse* comes from the *Book of Revelation* by St. John. It describes the end of the world and the Final Day of Judgment. The scene of the *Four Horsemen of the Apocalypse* is one of fifteen large woodcuts, a technical feat accomplished for the first time in graphic format. Dürer's depiction of the *Apocalypse* illustrates his frustration and disillusionment with the church. The four horsemen are said to represent conquest, war, famine, and death by pestilence. The scene is filled with energetic lines that create emotions of panic, fear, confusion, discouragement, and intimidation. The creation of this series and its mass distribution launched his international reputation and influenced a shift from the northern Gothic style of art.

Dürer's travels to Italy also affected the way he painted figures, especially self-portraits. As a northern artist, Dürer was able to introduce a new concept of self-portraiture to Renaissance painting. His own *Self-Portrait at 28,* an oil on panel done in 1500 (Alte Pinakothek, Munich), depicts Dürer subliminally suggesting that he possesses Christlike qualities. His later masterpieces include these engravings: *The Knight, Death, and the Devil* (1513), *Melencolia I* (1514), and *St. Jerome in His Study* (1514). His last major painting was of two large panels depicting the *Four Apostles* (1526). One of his greatest written contributions is a treatise on his theories of human proportion and perspective, written in the 1520s. A significant identifiable component of Dürer's art is his famous monogram "AD" seen on hundreds of his woodcuts, engravings, and paintings.

Discussion Questions and Activities

1. Read biographical information at http://sunsite.dk/cgfa/durer/index.html, and read about his other major contributions at http://www.georgehart.com/virtual-polyhedra/durer.html. What European countries did Dürer have an influence on? What elements of Italian art was Dürer interested in? What is the title of the treatise he wrote? Why was this concept of the treatise important to Renaissance ideals? What was the title of his 1525 book? What did it teach other artists?

2. Read the definition of a woodcut at http://www.xrefer.com/entry.jsp?xrefid=652751&secid= and the definition of an engraving at http://www.xrefer.com/entry.jsp?xrefid=502938&secid= then view some of Dürer's prints at http://www.ibiblio.org/wm/paint/auth/durer/engravings/ from the WebMuseum, Paris. Which type of print has a softer look—an engraving or a woodcut? How do you think the print technique affects the way line looks? Could you distinguish the woodcut prints from the prints made by engravings?

3. Refer to http://www.abcgallery.com/religion/apocalypse.html and view the woodcut of *The Four Horsemen of the Apocalypse.* Also read http://www.nga.gov/collection/gallery/gg35a/gg35a-over1 .html#jump for background information of the Reformation. How did the Reformation affect the graphic arts of northern Europe? What became the focus (theme) of art in the north? Dürer's *Apocalypse* is a statement about his opinions of the church. Which details in this woodcut indicate these opinions? Which figure represents war? Which horseman represents death by pestilence (disease)? Which symbols identify the elements of war and disease? How does line emphasize the drama of this scene?

4. Refer to http://artcyclopedia.com/artists/durer_albrecht.html and an excerpt from an article at http://www.artchive.com/artchive/D/durer.html. How did Dürer's travels to Italy affect Northern Renaissance art? Who was the Italian artist that Dürer admired? What is a monogram? Identify Dürer's monogram signature on the woodcut of *The Four Horsemen.* Look at other prints and paintings by Dürer and try to find the monogram signature.

5. View Dürer's *Self-Portraits* at http://www.ibiblio.org/wm/paint/auth/durer/self/ and at http://gallery .euroweb.hu/html/d/durer/painting/portrait/index.html. Read more about his self-portraits at http://www .artchive.com/artchive/D/durer.html. Which ones are three-quarter views? Which painting is a full frontal view? Can you tell that these self-portraits represent Dürer at different ages? If so, how?

6. What did you find striking about Dürer's *Self-Portrait at 28*? How does Dürer depict himself in this painting? What is different about this painting compared to his earlier self-portraits? Why do you think he painted his eyes to appear so intense? Does the figure dominate the composition? Do you think that this painting has a psychological effect upon the viewer? How would you feel if someone looked at you this intensely?

Related Internet Sites

Albrecht Dürer

Knight, Kevin. *Catholic Encyclopedia: Albrecht Dürer.*
- http://www.newadvent.org/cathen/05209c.htm
  [24 August 2002]
  Encyclopedia article.

Kren, Emil and Daniel Marx. *Web Galley of Art: Dürer, Albrecht.*
- http://www.kfki.hu/~arthp/bio/d/durer/biograph.html
  [24 August 2002]
  Biography and image link.

Kren, Emil and Daniel Marx. *Web Galley of Art: Portraits by Albrecht Dürer: Selbstbildnis im Pelzrock (Self-Portrait in Furcoat, Self-Portrait at 28).*
- http://www.kfki.hu/~arthp/html/d/durer/painting/portrait/
  [24 August 2002]
  Self-Portrait at 28 image.

Olga's Gallery. *Albrecht Dürer.*
- http://www.abcgallery.com/D/durer/durer.html
  [24 August 2002]
  Biography and image gallery.

Pioch, Nicolas. *WebMuseum, Paris: Dürer, Albrecht: Engravings: The Four Horsemen of the Apocalypse.*
- http://ibiblio.org/wm/paint/auth/durer/engravings/
  [24 August 2002]
  Image gallery of prints, including *The Four Horsemen of the Apocalypse.*

School of Mathematics and Statistics, University of St Andrews, Scotland. *Albrecht Dürer.*
- http://www-gap.dcs.st-and.ac.uk/~history/Mathematicians/Durer.html
  [24 August 2002]
  Biography and links to images.

Tigertail Associates. *Tigertail Virtual Art Museum: Northern Renaissance.*
- http://tigtail.org/M_View/TVM/X1/e.Northern/northern.html
  [24 August 2002]
  Information and links to images about Northern Renaissance art.

Tigertail Associates. *Tigertail Virtual Art Museum: Northern Renaissance, 1500 to 1550: Albrecht Dürer: Four Horsemen of the Apocalypse.*
- http://tigtail.org/M_View/TVM/X1/e.Northern/durer/durer.html
  [24 August 2002]
  Image gallery with a link to *The Four Horsemen of the Apocalypse.*

Jan van Eyck

Artcyclopedia. *Jan van Eyck.*
- http://www.artcyclopedia.com/artists/eyck_jan_van.html
  [24 August 2002]
  Directory of links to information and image galleries.

Gerten-Jackson, Carol. *CGFA: A Virtual Art Museum: Jan van Eyck.*
- http://sunsite.icm.edu.pl/cjackson/eyck
  [24 August 2002]
  Image gallery and biography link.

Harden, Mark. *Artchive: Jan van Eyck.*
- http://www.artchive.com/artchive/V/van_eyck.html
  [24 August 2002]
  Background information and image link.

Louvre. *Louvre: Collections: Paintings: Selected Works; Netherlands 15th–16th Centuries.*
- http://www.louvre.fr/anglais/collec/peint/pb15_16.htm
  [24 August 2002]
  An image gallery of art from the Netherlands in the fifteenth and sixteenth centuries.

Olga's Gallery. *Jan van Eyck.*
- http://www.abcgallery.com/E/eyck/eyck.html
  [24 August 2002]
  Image gallery and biography link.

Pioch, Nicolas. *WebMuseum, Paris: Eyck, Jan van.*
- http://www.ibiblio.org/wm/paint/auth/eyck
  [24 August 2002]
  Biography and link to images.

Martin Schongauer

Artcyclopedia. *Martin Schongauer.*
- http://www.artcyclopedia.com/artists/schongauer_martin.html
  [24 August 2002]
  Directory of links to information and image galleries.

Olga's Gallery. *Martin Schongauer.*
- http://www.abcgallery.com/S/schongauer/schongauer.html
  [24 August 2002]
  Image gallery and biography link.

Pieter (the Elder) Bruegel

Artcyclopedia. *Pieter Bruegel the Elder.*
- http://www.artcyclopedia.com/artists/bruegel_the_elder_pieter.html
  [24 August 2002]
  Directory of links to information and image galleries.

CHAPTER 15

The Baroque of Italy, Spain, and France

(Seventeenth Century)

*Caravaggio (Michelangelo Merisi da) (1573–1610),
Gianlorenzo Bernini (1598–1680), Artemisia Gentileschi
(1598–1652/1653), Diego Velázquez (1599–1660), and
Château of Versailles (Begun in 1623)*

Baroque Web Addresses

National Gallery of Art, Washington, DC. *National Gallery of Art: Tour: The Emergence of
New Genres.*
http://www.nga.gov/collection/gallery/gg33/gg33-main1.html
[24 August 2002]
Background information about the emergence of new genres in seventeenth-century Baroque painting.

Pioch, Nicolas. *WebMuseum, Paris: Baroque.*
http://www.ibiblio.org/wm/paint/glo/baroque/
[24 August 2002]
Background information about the Baroque.

Witcombe, Chris. *Art History Resources on the Web: 17th-Century Baroque Art.*
http://witcombe.sbc.edu/ARTHbaroque.html
[24 August 2002]
Resource directory that lists links to information about Baroque art and artists.

CARAVAGGIO
(Michelangelo Merisi da)
(1573–1610)

Image

The Calling of St. Matthew, oil on canvas, 1599–1600, 10'7½" x 11'2". Rome: Contarelli Chapel, Church of San Luigi dei Francesi.

Web Addresses

Gerten-Jackson, Carol. *CGFA: A Virtual Art Museum: Caravaggio.*
http://sunsite.dk/cgfa/caravagg/ (images)
http://sunsite.dk/cgfa/caravagg/caravaggio_bio.htm (biography)
[24 August 2002]
Biography and image gallery.

Market House Books Encyclopaedia of the Renaissance (1987). From *Xrefer, The Web's Reference Engine: Chiaroscuro.*
http://www.xrefer.com/entry.jsp?xrefid=251886&secid=
[13 September 2002]

Pioch, Nicolas. *WebMuseum, Paris: Caravaggio: The Calling of Saint Matthew.*
http://www.ibiblio.org/wm/paint/auth/caravaggio/calling/
[24 August 2002]
Information and image of *The Calling of St. Matthew.*

GIANLORENZO BERNINI
(1598–1680)

Image

Chair (Throne) of St. Peter (Cathedra Petri), gilt bronze, marble, and stucco, circa 1657–1666. Rome: St. Peter's Cathedral, the Vatican.

Web Addresses

Kren, Emil and Daniel Marx. *Web Gallery of Art: Bernini, Gian Lorenzo.*
http://www.kfki.hu/~arthp/bio/b/bernini/gianlore/biograph.html (biography)
http://www.kfki.hu/~arthp/html/b/bernini/gianlore/index.html (pictures) ("pictures" is used on the site)
[24 August 2002]
Biography and image gallery.

Kren, Emil and Daniel Marx. *Web Gallery of Art: Bernini, Gian Lorenzo: The Throne of Saint Peter.*
http://www.kfki.hu/~arthp/html/b/bernini/gianlore/sculptur/1650/throne.html
[24 August 2002]
Background information about the *Chair (Throne) of St. Peter.*

ARTEMISIA GENTILESCHI (1598–Circa 1652)

Image

Self-Portrait as the Allegory of Painting, oil on canvas, 1630s. Windsor: The Royal Collection.

Web Addresses

Brash, Larry. *The Life and Art of Artemisia Gentileschi.*
http://members.ozemail.com.au/~drbrash/artemisia/index.html
[24 August 2002]
Biography and links.

Marks, Tracy. *Artemisia.*
http://www.geocities.com/tmartiac/artemisia/artemisia.htm
[24 August 2002]
Biography and links to images.

DIEGO VELÁZQUEZ
(1599–1660)

Image

Las Meniñas (Maids of Honor), oil on canvas, 1656. Prado, Spain: Museo del Prado.

Web Addresses

Gerten-Jackson, Carol. *CGFA: A Virtual Art Museum: Velázquez.*
http://sunsite.dk/cgfa/velazque/index.html (images)
http://sunsite.dk/cgfa/velazque/velazquez_bio.htm (biography)
[24 August 2002]
Biography and image gallery.

Gerten-Jackson, Carol. *CGFA: A Virtual Art Museum: Velázquez: Las Meninas (Maids of Honor).*
http://btr0xw.rz.uni-bayreuth.de/cjackson/velazque/p-velazq18.htm
[24 August 2002]
Las Meniñas (Maids of Honor).

Olga's Gallery. *Diego Velázquez.*
http://www.abcgallery.com/V/velazquez/velazquez.html (biography)
http://www.abcgallery.com/V/velazquez/velazquez.html (images)
[24 August 2002]
Biography and image gallery.

CHÂTEAU OF VERSAILLES, FRANCE
(Begun in 1623)

Images

Chateau of Versailles, France (Began in 1623)

Web Addresses

Castles of the World. *Versailles.*
http://www.castles.org/castles/Europe/Western_Europe/France/france6.htm
[24 August 2002]
Background information and images.

Knechtel, Nancy. Niagara County Community College (SUNY). *Palace of Versailles.*
http://hometown.aol.com/nknechtel/index.html
[24 August 2002]

Official Website of the Chateau de Versailles. *Panoramas: Hall of Mirrors and King's Bedchamber.*
http://www.chateauversailles.fr/en/
[24 August 2002]
Official web site of Versailles with links to panoramic views of the Court of the Château, the Hall of Mirrors, and the King's Chamber.

Site Summary

The Baroque era stylistically emerged from Mannerism and Renaissance aesthetics. The term baroque originally meant irregular, bizarre, grotesque, and absurd. Fusing the Mannerists' elements of movement and emotion with Renaissance elegance and grandeur gave birth to what is known as the Baroque period. The Counter Reformation played into its development by creating a reaction to the former styles. The Reformation of the early sixteenth century challenged the Catholic Church and its teachings. As a result, the church needed to regain its followers and used the arts to publicize its grandiose image as emotional, highly spirited, and mystical. Painting, sculpture, and architecture adopted these elements in the seventeenth century.

Baroque elements varied from country to country due to regional taste, monarchy, and religion. Protestant Holland (Dutch) focused on still lifes, genre scenes, and landscapes in contrast to fervently religious Spain and traditional Italy. Biblical scenes varied in theme, composition, depiction, and emotion due to possible threats of iconoclasm (where Protestants destroyed religious images in protest against Catholicism). Scenes were more focused on a dramatic moment, emphasized by severe gestures and extreme contrast between light and dark. Still lifes and landscapes had their own sense of drama by using composition, line, and color for emphasis. Portrait painting became more natural, personal, and psychological. Scenes of everyday life (genre) were more common because a new buying market that consisted of a prosperous middle class had emerged. England never really grasped the lavishness, decorative, and grandiose concepts of the Baroque period.

The work of Caravaggio and Gianlorenzo Bernini of Rome are key to the beginnings of the Baroque style in painting, sculpture, and architecture. From Italy, the taste for decorative elegance, exquisite detail, high emotion, and drama were adopted across Europe and the new world of Latin America.

Discussion Questions and Activities

1. Read the background information about the Baroque era from the National Gallery of Art (Washington, D.C.) at http://www.nga.gov/collection/gallery/gg33/gg33-main1.html and from the WebMuseum, Paris, at http://www.ibiblio.org/wm/paint/glo/baroque/. What three types of painting themes became popular during the late sixteenth and seventeenth centuries? What did the artists include in portrait paintings that was significant? What was the historic event that helped to change the artists' style from Mannerism?

2. Read the biography of Caravaggio at http://sunsite.dk/cgfa/caravagg/caravaggio_bio.htm from CGFA. What elements in his painting made him popular? View the painting of *The Calling of St. Matthew* from the WebMuseum, Paris, at http://www.ibiblio.org/wm/paint/auth/caravaggio/calling/. Describe and identify the era indicated by the clothing that Christ and St. Peter are wearing? What era is indicated by the clothing the other figures in the painting are wearing? Why do you think that figures wear clothing from different eras? Read the definition of chiaroscuro at http://www.xrefer.com/entry.jsp?xrefid =251886&secid=. How does Caravaggio use this technique in this painting? How does he use hand gestures to emphasize the drama of the moment? Which figure do you think is St. Matthew and why?

3. Read Bernini's biography at http://www.kfki.hu/~arthp/bio/b/bernini/gianlore/biograph.html and background information about the *Chair (Throne) of St. Peter (Cathedra Petri)* from the Web Gallery of Art at http://www.kfki.hu/~arthp/html/b/bernini/gianlore/sculptur/1650/throne.html. Besides sculpture, what other aesthetic aspects did Bernini excel in? What type of classical sculpture inspired him and why? What does the chair (throne) symbolize? What is the significance of having such a monumental sculpture dedicated to St. Peter and having it placed above his tomb? Identify the intricate architectural components in this piece.

4. Artemesia Gentileschi is one of the first female artists whose life and work have been extensively documented. She established herself as a professional painter and did not limit her subjects to portraits and still lifes. Read the biographies at http://www.geocities.com/tmartiac/artemisia/artemisia.htm and http://members.ozemail.com.au/~drbrash/artemisia/index.html. View some of the image galleries. What major event in her early career brought on her turbulent reputation? What was the title of the painting that she created as a cathartic act? What are some of the titles of her other paintings? Why do you think she continuously painted images of powerful women? In what aspect of her work do you see an influence from Caravaggio?

5. Read the Diego Velázquez biographies and view the painting of *Las Meniñas (Maids of Honor)* at http://btr0xw.rz.uni-bayreuth.de/cjackson/velazque/p-velazq18.htm and http://www.abcgallery.com/V /velazquez/velazquezbio.html. What type of painter was he considered to be when he was in service to King Philip IV of Spain? What type of paintings did he do at this time? Which famous artist inspired Velázquez to visit the art collections in Italy? Who is the focus of the painting *Las Meniñas*? What are the other figures doing around the child? What is Velázquez himself doing in this painting? What kind of brushwork and color of paint did he use? Is the style of this painting reminiscent of Italian Baroque painters?

6. Outside of Italy, one of the most extensive architectural projects in France that dominated the seventeenth century was the gardens and additions to the Château of Versailles. Read background information and view the images at http://www.castles.org/castles/Europe/Western_Europe/France/france6.htm and from Dynasty Online at http://hometown.aol.com/nknechtel/index.html and http://www.chateauversailles.fr/en/. What designer began the initial project, and who was his successor? Who designed the gardens of Versailles? What patterns do they create? What painter decorated the interiors of the palace? What aesthetic elements of this structure do you consider to be Baroque?

Related Internet Sites

Baroque

Harden, Mark. *Artchive: Sculpture Garden: Baroque.*
- http://www.artchive.com/sculpture/baroque_sculpture.html
  [2 September 2002]
  Images of Baroque sculpture.

Kohl, Allan T. and Art Images for College Teaching (AICT), Minneapolis College of Art & Design. *Baroque Architecture.*
- http://www.mcad.edu/AICT/html/renbrq/brqarch.html
  [2 September 2002]
  Image gallery of Baroque architecture.

Leo Masuda Architectonic Research Office. *History of Baroque Architecture.*
- http://web.kyoto-inet.or.jp/org/orion/eng/hst/baroque.html
  [2 September 2002]
  History and image gallery of Baroque architecture.

National Gallery of Art, Washington, D.C. *National Gallery of Art: Collection: French and Italian Painting of the 17th Century.*
- http://www.nga.gov/collection/gallery/french17-2.html
  [2 September 2002]
  French and Italian Baroque painting images.

Thais. *1200 Anni di Scultura Italiana: Periodo Barocco.*
- http://www.thais.it/scultura/barocca.htm
  [2 September 2002]
  Image gallery of Baroque sculpture.

Tigertail Associates. *Tigertail Virtual Art Museum: Baroque Room.*
- http://tigtail.org/TVM/X1/f.Baroque/baroque.html
  [2 September 2002]
  Image gallery of Italian and Spanish Baroque images.

Xrefer: The Web's Reference Engine: Iconoclasm Definition of iconoclasm from The Bloomsbury Guide to Art. Xrefer.com.
- http://www.xrefer.com/entry.jsp?xrefid=438682&secid=

Caravaggio

ARC Art Renewal Center. *ARC Art Renewal Center: Michelangelo Merisi da Caravaggio.*
- http://www.artrenewal.org/museum/c/Caravaggio_Michelangelo_Merisi_da/page1.html
  [2 September 2002]
  Image gallery.

Christus Rex Inc. *Christus Rex Project: Art Gallery: Caravaggio.*
- http://www.christusrex.org/www2/art/caravaggio.htm
  [2 September 2002]
  Caravaggio image gallery.

Kren, Emil and Daniel Marx. *Web Gallery of Art: Paintings between 1593 and 1596 by Caravaggio.*
- http://www.kfki.hu/~arthp/html/c/caravagg/01/index.html
  [2 September 2002]
  Biography and image gallery.

Olga's Gallery. *Caravaggio.*
- http://www.abcgallery.com/C/caravaggio/caravaggio.html
  [2 September 2002]
  Image gallery and biography link.

Olga's Gallery. *Caravaggio. The Calling of St. Matthew.*
- http://www.abcgallery.com/C/caravaggio/caravaggio24.html
  [2 September 2002]
  The Calling of St. Matthew image.

Pioch, Nicolas. *WebMuseum, Paris: Caravaggio, Michelangelo Merisi da.*
- http://www.ibiblio.org/wm/paint/auth/caravaggio/
  [2 September 2002]
  Biography and image gallery.

World Art Treasures. *The Miraculous Caravaggio.*
- http://www.bergerfoundation.ch/Home/high_caravage.html
  [2 September 2002]
  Caravaggio biography and image gallery.

Gianlorenzo Bernini

ARC Art Renewal Center. *ARC Art Renewal Center: Gian Lorenzo Bernini.*
- http://www.artrenewal.org/museum/b/Bernini_Gian_Lorenzo/page1.html
  [2 September 2002]
  Image gallery.

Artifice, Inc. *Great Buildings Online: Bernini.*
- http://www.greatbuildings.com/architects/Bernini.html
  [2 September 2002]
  Biography and architectural image gallery.

Christus Rex Inc. *Christus Rex Project: Art Gallery: Basilica di San Pietro: Cathedra Petri (Basilica of St. Peter and Chair).*
- http://www.christusrex.com/www1/citta/B3-Cathedra.html
  [2 September 2002]
  Chair (Throne) of St. Peter (Cathedra Petri) image.

Harden, Mark. *Artchive: Bernini.*
- http://www.artchive.com/artchive/B/bernini.html
  [2 September 2002]
  Biography and image gallery.

Artemisia Gentileschi

Artcyclopedia. *Artemisia Gentileschi.*
- http://www.artcyclopedia.com/artists/gentileschi_artemisia.html
  [2 September 2002]
  Directory of links to information and image galleries.

Corbell, Rebecca and Samantha Guy. Australian National University. *Artemisia Gentileschi and The Age of Baroque.*
- http://rubens.anu.edu.au/student.projects/artemisia/Artemisia.html
  [2 September 2002]
  Biography and links to additional information.

Russ, Wendy and Carrie Carolin. *Women Artists in History: Seventeenth Century (including Artemisia Gentileschi).*
- http://www.wendy.com/women/artists.html#15
  [2 September 2002]
  A list of other seventeenth-century women artists.

Diego Velázquez

Artcyclopedia. *Diego Velázquez.*
- http://www.artcyclopedia.com/artists/velazquez_diego.html
  [2 September 2002]
  Directory of links to information and image galleries.

Kren, Emil and Daniel Marx. *Web Gallery of Art: Paintings between 1651 and 1660 by Velázquez.*
- http://www.kfki.hu/~arthp/html/v/velazque/1651-60/index.html
  [2 September 2002]
  Biography link and image gallery of paintings done between 1651 and 1660; includes the image of *Las Meninas.*

Kren, Emil and Daniel Marx. *Web Gallery of Art: Velázquez, Diego Rodriguez de Silva y.*
- http://www.kfki.hu/~arthp/html/v/velazque/index.html
  [2 September 2002]
  Velázquez image gallery.

Pioch, Nicolas. *WebMuseum, Paris: Velázquez (or Velásquez), Diego.*
- http://www.ibiblio.org/wm/paint/auth/velazquez/
  [2 September 2002]
  Biography and image gallery.

Versailles

Evans, C. T. Northern Virginia Community College. *Louis XIV and the Palace.*
- http://www.nv.cc.va.us/home/cevans/Versailles/site/mainbuild.html
  [2 September 2002]
  Background information and images of the Château of Versailles.

Howe, Jeffery. Boston College. *Digital Archive of Architecture: Baroque Architecture: Versailles.*
- http://www.bc.edu/bc_org/avp/cas/fnart/arch/versailles.html
  [2 September 2002]
  Image gallery of the Château of Versailles.

Vitruvio. *Architecture on the Web: Versailles.*
- http://www.vitruvio.ch/arc/baroque/french/versailles.htm
  [2 September 2002]
  Versailles resource directory to links.

CHAPTER 16

Flemish and Dutch Art

(Seventeenth Century)

Peter Paul Rubens (1577–1640), Jan Vermeer (1632–1675), and Rembrandt Harmenszoon van Rijn (1606–1669)

Flemish and Dutch Web Addresses

MyStudios. *Religious Works of the Dutch Masters.*
http://www.mystudios.com/gallery/dutch/enter.html
[6 September 2002]
Image gallery of religious works of the Dutch masters.

National Gallery of Art, Washington, D.C. *National Gallery of Art: Collection: Dutch and Flemish Painting of the 16th–17th Centuries.*
http://www.nga.gov/collection/gallery/dutch.htm
[6 September 2002]
Background information and image gallery of Dutch and Flemish painting of the sixteenth and seventeenth centuries with additional links featuring Dutch landscapes, seascapes, and still lifes of the 1600s.

Tigertail Associates. *Tigertail Virtual Art Museum: Flemish and Netherlands Baroque Art.*
http://tvm.tigtail.org/TVM/M_View/X1/f.Baroque/a.low/baroque-lowlands.html
[6 September 2002]
Image gallery of Flemish and Netherlands Baroque art.

PETER PAUL RUBENS
(1577–1640)

Image

The Landing (Debarkation) of Marie de Médici at Marseilles, oil on canvas, circa 1623–1625, approximately 25" x 20". Paris: Louvre.

Web Addresses

Gerten-Jackson, Carol. *CGFA: A Virtual Art Museum: Rubens.*
http://sunsite.dk/cgfa/rubens/ (images)
http://sunsite.dk/cgfa/rubens/rubens_bio.htm (biography)
[6 September 2002]
Image gallery and biography link.

Kren, Emil and Daniel Marx. *Web Gallery of Art: Other Paintings by Pieter Pauwel Rubens: The Landing of Marie de' Médici at Marseilles.*
http://www.kfki.hu/~arthp/html/r/rubens/61other/index.html
[7 September 2002]
Image gallery that includes the painting of *The Landing of Marie de Médici at Marseilles.*

Kren, Emil and Daniel Marx. *Web Gallery of Art: Rubens, Pieter Pauwel.*
http://www.kfki.hu/~arthp/bio/r/rubens/biograph.html
[6 September 2002]
Biography and link to images of pictures.

Olga's Gallery. *Peter Paul Rubens.*
http://www.abcgallery.com/R/rubens/rubens.html
[6 September 2002]
Image gallery and biography.

JAN VERMEER
(1632–1675)

Web Addresses

Gerten-Jackson, Carol. *CGFA: A Virtual Art Museum: Vermeer.*
http://sunsite.dk/cgfa/vermeer/ (images)
http://sunsite.dk/cgfa/vermeer/vermeer_bio.htm (biography)
[6 September 2002]
Image gallery and biography link.

Kren, Emil and Daniel Marx. *Web Gallery of Art: Paintings between 1661–1670 (page 4)*
        by Vermeer, van Delft.
http://www.kfki.hu/~arthp/html/v/vermeer/03d/index.html
[6 September 2002]
Image gallery of paintings done between 1661–1670; also a biography link.

Kren, Emil and Daniel Marx. *Web Gallery of Art: Vermeer van Delft, Jan.*
http://www.kfki.hu/~arthp/bio/v/vermeer/biograph.html
[6 September 2002]
Biography and image gallery link to pictures.

National Gallery of Art, Washington, D.C. *National Gallery of Art: Collection: Johannes*
        Vermeer.
http://www.nga.gov/cgi-bin/pbio?31800 (biography)
http://www.nga.gov/cgi-bin/psearch?Request=A&Person=31800 (painting)
[6 September 2002]
Background information and image gallery.

REMBRANDT HARMENSZOON VAN RIJN (1606–1669)

Image

Self-Portrait, medium varies from oil on canvas to oil on wood, circa 1626–1669, at various museums.

Web Addresses

Kren, Emil and Daniel Marx. *Web Gallery of Art: Rembrandt Harmenszoon van Rijn.*
http://www.kfki.hu/~arthp/bio/r/rembran/biograph.html *Biography.*
http://www.kfki.hu/~arthp/html/r/rembran/graphics/index.html *Graphics by Rembrandt.*
http://www.kfki.hu/~arthp/html/r/rembran/painting/index.html *Paintings by Rembrandt.*
Biography and image gallery link to pictures.

Olga's Gallery. *Rembrandt Harmenszoon van Rijn.*
http://www.abcgallery.com/R/rembrandt/rembrandt.html
[6 September 2002]
Image gallery and biography link.

Gerten-Jackson, Carol. *CGFA: A Virtual Art Museum: Rembrandt.*
http://sunsite.dk/cgfa/rembrand/
[6 September 2002]
Image gallery and biography link.

Kren, Emil and Daniel Marx. *Web Gallery of Art: Self-Portraits in Chronological Order by Rembrandt.*
http://www.kfki.hu/~arthp/html/r/rembran/painting/selfport/index.html
[6 September 2002]
Image gallery of S*elf-Portraits.*

Site Summary

Seventeenth-century Flemish (country of Flanders) art flourished in an area in the southern region of the Netherlands, in the approximate areas of modern-day Belgium and Luxembourg. Because of their proximity, Holland (Dutch), of the northern Netherlands, and Flanders had close ties, but there were artistic differences. Religion had split these regions between Catholics and Protestants. Flanders remained loyal to the church and glorified the monarchy visually. The Dutch, on the other hand, preferred to depict images that relayed symbolic moral ideas through images of natural landscapes, simple scenes of daily life, and still lifes. Dutch portraits depict the naturalness of the sitter, which often reveals the sitter's character. Flemish painting, however, was filled with energy, movement, and detail that was enhanced with rich jewel-like colors.

Peter Paul Rubens helped to introduce to Flanders a taste for the Baroque. He had studied painting in Italy and was especially interested in the work of Carracci and Caravaggio. He became the court painter to the Spanish regent, as well as accepting numerous commissions from royalty and diplomats of English and French society. His highly acclaimed painting, *The Landing of Marie de Médici at Marseilles* (the Queen Mother of France, born in Florence), glorifies the queen's persona quite dramatically. He used a transparent painting technique that enhances the movement of his images with emotion.

Dutch painters such as Franz Hals, Jan Vermeer, and Rembrandt were also influenced by the Italian Baroque and Caravaggio's use of light and naturalism. Yet they adhered somewhat to a stricter sense of the Protestant attitude. They preferred to paint images of a simpler lifestyle and an informal, yet dignified depiction of a sitter in portraiture. Rembrandt especially exploited this idea of portraiture in paintings of his own likeness. His numerous self-portraits reveal not only his age but also his state of mind as he aged. A Dutch scene by Vermeer utilizes light and detail, which makes images very clear and crisp. They can be so clear that people and objects seem almost unreal and timeless. In the middle of the seventeenth century, the focus of the art world moved from Italy to Paris. The French monarchy cultivated the classical arts in their music, architecture, painting, and sculpture. Numerous private art academies prospered, and Classicism became the official royal style at the end of the century.

Discussion Questions and Activities

1. Read about Dutch and Flemish painting at http://www.nga.gov/collection/gallery/dutch.htm from the National Gallery of Art (Washington, D.C.). What are some of the artistic, religious, and political differences between Flanders and the Netherlands? What kinds of scenes did the Dutch like to paint? View the Rubens image gallery at http://www.nga.gov/collection/gallery/gg45/gg45-main1.html and Dutch landscapes and seascapes at http://www.nga.gov/collection/gallery/gg50/gg50-main1.html. Do you find that the background scenes by Rubens seem to be more animated than those of other artists? What makes the compositions move with energy and emotion? Why do you find the Dutch scenes more calming than others?

2. Read the biographies of Peter Paul Rubens at http://www.abcgallery.com/R/rubens/rubens.html and at http://www.kfki.hu/~arthp/bio/r/rubens/biograph.html. Describe his upbringing. What influences did he experience when he was young? What happened after 1600 that influenced the artistic development of his career? Which Italian artists did Rubens admire? Which of their stylistic attributes did Rubens assimilate into his own work?

3. In 1622, Rubens received a major commission to paint the life of which queen? How many paintings were in the series? How was Rubens able to make her life seem interesting? View the painting from the Web Gallery of Art at http://www.kfki.hu/~arthp/html/r/rubens/61other/index.html. Identify some of the mythological references of this painting. What are some of the swirling elements of the composition that enhance movement? What kind of event is Rubens dramatizing? Do you think this kind of event deserves such attention and pomp?

4. Read the biographies of Rembrandt at http://www.kfki.hu/~arthp/bio/r/rembran/biograph.html, at http://www.abcgallery.com/R/rembrandt/rembrandt.html, and at http://sunsite.dk/cgfa/rembrand/. What type of paintings did Rembrandt create early in his career when he was living in Leiden and Amsterdam? What other themes did he paint? Why were the biblical scenes unusual for Rembrandt to paint? Were the landscapes painted from actual areas that he visited? Describe Rembrandt's late paintings. What technique did he use in them? What other medium did Rembrandt excel in?

5. Rembrandt's many self-portraits are considered to be the most ever produced by an artist. View the image gallery at http://www.kfki.hu/~arthp/html/r/rembran/painting/selfport/index.html. What quality of his self-portraits is unique? What painting technique did he like to demonstrate with his self-portraits? Does he try to idealize his own image? What kind of eye contact does Rembrandt have with his audience? Does this have a psychological effect? If so, why?

6. Genre paintings that depict scenes of daily life were popular in Dutch art. Read the biographies of Jan Vermeer at http://www.kfki.hu/~arthp/bio/v/vermeer/biograph.html and http://www.nga.gov/cgi-bin/pbio?31800. What phases of painting mark his career? What was his favorite and most famous theme? How did Vermeer apply paint to the canvas in order to create effects with light? What perspective did he use to create compositional space? Look up this term in the Xrefer web site at http://xrefer.com and view the image gallery at http://www.kfki.hu/~arthp/html/v/vermeer/03d/index.html. Can you identify the paintings that utilize this type of perspective?

Related Internet Sites

Flemish and Dutch

Artcyclopedia. *Artists by Nationality: Dutch Artists.*
■ http://www.artcyclopedia.com/nationalities/Dutch.html
  [7 September 2002]

Artcyclopedia. *Artists by Nationality: Flemish Artists.*
■ http://www.artcyclopedia.com/nationalities/Flemish.html
  [7 September 2002]

Russ, Wendy and Carrie Carolin. *Women Artists in History: Seventeenth Century.*
■ http://www.wendy.com/women/artists.html#17
  [7 September 2002]
  A list of seventeenth-century women artists.

Peter Paul Rubens

Artcyclopedia. *Peter Paul Rubens.*
■ http://www.artcyclopedia.com/artists/rubens_peter_paul.html
  [7 September 2002]

National Gallery of Art, Washington, D.C. *National Gallery of Art: Tour: Sir Peter Paul Rubens.*
■ http://www.nga.gov/collection/gallery/gg45/gg45-main1.html
  [8 September 2002]
  Background information and image gallery.

Jan Vermeer

Artcyclopedia. *Jan Vermeer.*
■ http://www.artcyclopedia.com/artists/vermeer_jan.html
  [7 September 2002]

Harden, Mark. *Artchive: Vermeer & the Art of Painting: Presented on the occasion of the Vermeer exhibit at the National Gallery of Art in Washington, D.C., November 12, 1995 to February 11, 1996 from "Vermeer & the Art of Painting", by Arthur K. Wheelock, Jr.*
■ http://www.artchive.com/vermeer/vermeer1.html
  [8 September 2002]
  Excerpt from the book, *Vermeer and the Art of Painting* by Arthur K. Wheelock Jr.

MyStudios. *Vermeer: The Complete Works.*
■ http://www.mystudios.com/vermeer/index.html
  [8 September 2002]
  Vermeer image gallery.

Rembrandt

Artcyclopedia. *Rembrandt van Rijn.*
- http://www.artcyclopedia.com/artists/rembrandt_van_rijn.html
  [7 September 2002]

Harden, Mark. *Artchive: Rembrandt.*
- http://www.artchive.com/rembrandt/rembrandt.html
  [8 September 2002]
  Rembrandt image gallery.

Internet 1996 World Exposition. *The Rembrandt Research Project.*
- http://parallel.park.org/Netherlands/pavilions/culture/rembrandt/
  [8 September 2002]
  Rembrandt resources and activities.

MyStudios. *Rijn van Rembrandt.*
- http://www.mystudios.com/art/bar/rembrandt/rembrandt.html
  [8 September 2002]
  Rembrandt background information and image gallery.

CHAPTER 17

European Art

(Eighteenth Century)

François Boucher (1703–1770), Jean Honoré Fragonard (1732–1806), Antoine Watteau (1684–1721), Giovanni Paolo Panini (Circa 1692–1765), Giovanni Battista (Giambattista) Tiepolo (1696–1770), William Hogarth (1697–1764), Thomas Gainsborough (1727–1788), Jean-Baptiste-Siméon Chardin (1699–1779), Jacques-Louis David (1748–1825), and Francisco José de Goya (1746–1828)

Rococo (Circa 1700–1750) Web Addresses

National Gallery, Washington, D.C. *National Gallery of Art: Tour: 18th-Century France—Boucher and Fragonard Overview.*
http://www.nga.gov/collection/gallery/gg55/gg55-over1.html#jump
[9 September 2002]

National Gallery, Washington, D.C. *National Gallery of Art: Tour: 18th-Century France—The Rococo and Watteau.*
http://www.nga.gov/collection/gallery/gg54/gg54-main1.html
[9 September 2002]
An overview of Watteau and the rococo style.

FRANÇOIS BOUCHER
(1703–1770),
JEAN HONORÉ FRAGONARD
(1732–1806),
and
ANTOINE WATTEAU
(1684–1721)

Web Addresses

Kren, Emil and Daniel Marx. *Web Gallery of Art: Fragonard, Jean-Honoré.*
http://www.ibiblio.org/wm/paint/auth/fragonard/
[9 September 2002]
Boucher biography and link to "Pictures."

Pioch, Nicolas. *WebMuseum, Paris: Fragonard, Jean-Honoré.*
http://www.ibiblio.org/wm/paint/auth/fragonard/
[9 September 2002]
Fragonard biography and image gallery.

GIOVANNI PAOLO PANINI
(Circa 1692–1765)
and
GIOVANNI BATTISTA (Giambattista)
TIEPOLO
(1696–1770)

Web Addresses

J. Paul Getty Trust. *ArtsEdNet: The Getty's Art Education Web Site: Explore Art: The Collections: Giovanni Paolo Panini.*
http://www.getty.edu/art/collections/bio/a650-1.html
[9 September 2002]
Panini biography.

Kren, Emil and Daniel Marx. *Web Gallery of Art: Panini, Paolo.*
http://www.kfki.hu/~arthp/html/p/pannini/index.html
[9 September 2002]

Kren, Emil and Daniel Marx. *Web Gallery of Art: Tiepolo, Giovanni Battista.*
http://gallery.euroweb.hu/bio/t/tiepolo/gianbatt/biograph.html (biography)
http://gallery.euroweb.hu/html/t/tiepolo/gianbatt/index.html Tiepolo (images)
[9 September 2002]
Tiepolo image gallery and biography link.

WILLIAM HOGARTH
(1697–1764)
and
THOMAS GAINSBOROUGH
(1727–1788)

Web Addresses

Olga's Gallery. *William Hogarth.*
http://www.abcgallery.com/H/hogarth/hogarth.html
[9 September 2002]
Hogarth image gallery and biography link.

Pioch, Nicoloas. *WebMuseum, Paris: Gainsborough, Thomas.*
http://www.ibiblio.org/wm/paint/auth/gainsborough/
[9 September 2002]
Gainsborough biography and image gallery.

JEAN-BAPTISTE-SIMÉON CHARDIN (1699–1779)

Web Addresses

Gerten-Jackson, Carol. *CGFA: A Virtual Art Museum: Chardin.*
http://sunsite.dk/cgfa/chardin/index.html (images)
http://sunsite.dk/cgfa/chardin/chardin_bio.htm *Jean-Baptiste Chardin* (biography)
[9 September 2002]
Image gallery and biography link.

Kren, Emil and Daniel Marx. *Web Gallery of Art: Chardin, Jean-Baptiste-Siméon.*
http://gallery.euroweb.hu/bio/c/chardin/biograph.html (biography)
http://gallery.euroweb.hu/html/c/chardin/index.html (paintings)
[9 September 2002]
Image gallery and biography link.

Pioch, Nicolas. *WebMuseum, Paris: Chardin, Jean-Baptiste-Siméon.*
http://www.ibiblio.org/wm/paint/auth/chardin/
[9 September 2002]
Biography and image gallery.

Neoclassicism (Circa 1750–1810) Web Addresses

Oxford Dictionary of Art (1997). From *Xrefer, The Web's Reference Engine: Neoclassicism.*
http://xrefer.com/entry.jsp?xrefid=144818&secid=
[9 September 2002]
Definition of *neoclassicism* from the *Oxford Dictionary of Art* (1997).

Thames and Hudson Dictionary of Art and Artists (1994). From *Xrefer, The Web's Reference Engine: Neoclassicism.*
http://xrefer.com/entry.jsp?xrefid=651892&secid=
[9 September 2002]
Definition of *neoclassicism* from *The Thames and Hudson Dictionary of Art and Artists* (1994).

JACQUES-LOUIS DAVID
(1748–1825)

Web Addresses

Gerten-Jackson, Carol. *CGFA: A Virtual Art Museum: Jacques-Louis David.*
http://sunsite.dk/cgfa/jdavid/index.html (images)
http://sunsite.dk/cgfa/jdavid/jdavid_bio.htm J. L. David (biography)
[9 September 2002]
Image gallery and biography link.

Harden, Mark. *Artchive: Jacques-Louis David.*
http://www.artchive.com/artchive/D/david.html
[9 September 2002]
Background information and links to "View Image List."

FRANCISCO JOSÉ DE GOYA
(1746–1828)

Image

Family of Charles IV, oil on canvas, 1800, approximately 9'2" x 11'. Madrid: Prado.

Web Addresses

Gerten-Jackson, Carol. *CGFA: A Virtual Art Museum: Francisco de Goya.*
http://btr0xw.rz.uni-bayreuth.de/cjackson/goya/ (images)
http://btr0xw.rz.uni-bayreuth.de/cjackson/goya/goya_bio.htm *Francisco de Goya* (biography)
[10 September 2002]
Image gallery and biography link.

Pioch, Nicolas. *WebMuseum, Paris: Goya (y Lucientes), Francisco (José) de.*
http://www.ibiblio.org/wm/paint/auth/goya/
[10 September 2002]
Biography and image gallery.

Site Summary

Paris remained the center for the arts in Europe in the beginning of the eighteenth century. From the Baroque of the previous century emerged a more delicate and ornate style known as Rococo. This style is associated with the reigns of Louis XIV and Louis XV—an era of splendid luxury. French Rococo painting uses elegant figures, decorative motifs of shells, delicate brushstrokes, pastel colors, and themes of frivolous and playful activities. The best-known French Rococo artists were François Boucher, Jean Honoré Fragonard, and Antoine Watteau. In Italy, Rococo painters exhibited tranquil fairy tale–like landscapes as seen in the work of Giovanni Battista Tiepolo and Giovanni Paolo Panini. English art never really acquired the Rococo flavor of art and ornamentation.

English painters, such as Thomas Gainsborough (he painted portraits with landscape backgrounds) and William Hogarth (he used curved lines), came closest to adopting a Rococo influence. The genre and still-life paintings of Jean-Baptiste-Siméon Chardin are more or less an entity of their own beyond the Rococo and Neoclassicism of the eighteenth century. Chardin favored the depiction of a simpler lifestyle characterized by realism and humanity; his mastery of brushwork and color enhanced his works of art.

As a result of the spoils and decadence of the French aristocracy, Rococo eventually gave way to the age of enlightenment, reason, and reaction. This era returned to the age of antiquity and democracy known as Neoclassicism. A new generation of painters, sculptors, and architects returned their attention to antiquity and were infused with a new spirit of patriotism. Artists such as Jacques-Louis David (1748–1825), Antonio Canova (1757–1822), and Jean-Antoine Houdon (1741–1828) depicted Classical figures as well as contemporary leaders who possessed qualities of Classical heroism and grandeur.

Early-eighteenth-century English architecture adopted the term Palladianism to characterize the designs of Renaissance architect Andrea Palladio. Palladian buildings are characterized by their Classical portico of the façade. These Classical architectural components opened the door to the Neoclassic development of the midcentury. In Spain, Francisco José de Goya y Lucientes (1746–1828) marks his work with a stark representation of the Spanish monarchy. He also uses tenderness and character analysis to portray other factions of society. Goya used his talents as well as his active imagination to express his disapproval of war and its atrocities. Goya's work bridges the period between the end of the eighteenth century and the beginning of the nineteenth century, as does the Neoclassic style that stands at its threshold. After 1810, a countermovement arose primarily in Germany, England, and, to a lesser extent, France and adopted a Romantic sentiment.

Discussion Questions and Activities

1. Read background information about Rococo art at http://www.nga.gov/collection/gallery/gg54/gg54 -main1.html from the National Gallery, Washington, D.C. Where does the term "Rococo" derive from, and what is its meaning in relation to this style of art? Who is the painter that once painted theatrical scenes? What artists influenced him? What are "fête galante" scenes? Refer to http://www.nga.gov /collection/gallery/gg55/gg55-over1.html#jump and read the section on "Boucher and Fragonard." Who and what influenced Boucher's style? Who was the woman that became his patron and why is she important? Who did Fragonard first study painting with? What did his brushwork look like? Where did Fragonard go to study and sketch Renaissance gardens? Read background information about Jean Honoré Fragonard at http://www.ibiblio.org/wm/paint/auth/fragonard/ from WebMuseum, Paris. What type of subjects did Fragonard like to paint? How did he handle coloring and brushwork?

2. View http://www.kfki.hu/~arthp/html/p/pannini/index.html of Panini's work and http://gallery.euroweb .hu/html/t/tiepolo/gianbatt/index.html of Tiepolo's paintings. What kind of scenes did Panini like to paint? What city inspired him to paint the structures in many of his masterpieces? What city influenced Tiepolo's work? What natural elements are characteristic of his paintings? Why do you think Panini's and Tiepolo's paintings are considered Rococo?

3. Read the background information about the English painters William Hogarth at http://www.abcgallery .com/H/hogarth/hogarth.html and Thomas Gainsborough at http://www.ibiblio.org/wm/paint/auth /gainsborough/. Give the titles of Hogarth's three most famous series of "pictorial drama" paintings. What was the theme of these paintings? What other medium did Hogarth excel in? What type of paintings did Gainsborough create? How did he become acquainted with the Rococo pastoral style of landscape painting? What artist influenced Gainsborough and how did this happen?

4. Refer to Chardin's image gallery at http://sunsite.dk/cgfa/chardin/index.html and biography at http:/ /sunsite.dk/cgfa/chardin/chardin_bio.htm and at http://gallery.euroweb.hu/html/c/chardin/index.html from the Web Gallery of Art. What kind of still lifes did Chardin depict? What other painting style can you identify with Chardin? What technique did Chardin use to paint realistic images?

5. Read background information about the Neoclassic era of art from the *Oxford Dictionary of Art* at http://www.xrefer.com/entry.jsp?xrefid=144818&secid= and *The Thames and Hudson Dictionary of Art and Artists* at http://www.xrefer.com/entry.jsp?xrefid=651892&secid= from the Xrefer web site. What major discovery prompted interest in the antiquities? Which scholar/archeologist studied and wrote about the art of the ancients? Which two major artists emulated the Neoclassic ideal in painting and sculpture? What is characteristic of Neoclassic architecture?

6. One of the most famous of all the Neoclassical painters was Jacques-Louis David. Read his biographies at http://www.artchive.com/artchive/D/david.html and http://sunsite.dk/cgfa/jdavid/jdavid_bio.htm then refer to images at http://sunsite.dk/cgfa/jdavid/index.html. How did David become acquainted with Classical art and antiquities? What are some of David's paintings that reflect tragedy and heroism? Who were the figures of the French Revolution that David admired? What are some of the Classical elements of his portraitures?

7. The second half of the eighteenth century experienced the expressive and imaginative art of Francisco José de Goya y Lucientes. Read his biography at http://www.ibiblio.org/wm/paint/auth/goya/ and http://btr0xw.rz.uni-bayreuth.de/cjackson/goya/goya_bio.htm then view images at http://btr0xw.rz .uni-bayreuth.de/cjackson/goya/. For which Spanish king did Goya paint? What is unique about the royal *Family of Charles IV* (1800) group portrait? What major political event began to change Goya's work? What is the title of the painting that commemorates this event? What is the title of the etching series Goya created to illustrate his condemnation of war?

Related Internet Sites

Rococo (Circa 1700–1750)

About.com. *Art History 101 by Art History 101 by Andrea Mulder-Slater: Rococo Art 1700–1750.*
- http://arthistory.about.com/library/bl101_rococo.htm
  [10 September 2002]
  Rococo background information.

Artcyclopedia. *Artists by Movement: Rococo Art Europe, 1715 to 1774.*
- http://www.artcyclopedia.com/history/rococo.html
  [10 September 2002]
  Directory of links to information and image galleries of Rococo artists.

Knight, Kevin. *Catholic Encyclopedia Online Edition (1999): Rococo Style.*
- http://arthistory.about.com/gi/dynamic/offsite.htm?site=http%3A%2F%2Fwww.knight.org%2Fadvent%2Fcathen%2F13106a.htm
  [10 September 2002]

Pacific Bell. *Eyes on Art: No Fear o' Eras: Rococo.*
- http://www.kn.pacbell.com/wired/art2/eras/rococo.html
  [10 September 2002]
  Rococo activities and sources.

Russ, Wendy and Carrie Carolin. *Women Artists in History: Eighteenth Century.*
- http://www.wendy.com/women/artists.html#18
  [10 September 2002]
  A list of eighteenth-century women artists.

Tigertail Associates. *Tigertail Virtual Art Museum: French Baroque 1600 to 1700.*
- http://tigtail.org/M_View/TVM/X1/g.Rococo/rococo-2.html
  [10 September 2002]

Tigertail Associates. *Tigertail Virtual Art Museum: Rococo Part 1: The French Rococo: 1700 to 1750.*
- http://tigtail.org/M_View/TVM/X1/g.Rococo/rococo.html
  [10 September 2002]
  French Rococo image gallery.

François Boucher, Jean Honoré Fragonard, and Antoine Watteau

Artcyclopedia. *Jean-Antoine Watteau.*
- http://www.artcyclopedia.com/artists/watteau_jean-antoine.html
  [10 September 2002]
  Watteau directory of links to information and image galleries.

Gerten-Jackson, Carol. *CGFA: A Virtual Art Museum: Boucher.*
- http://sunsite.icm.edu.pl/cjackson/boucher/
  http://sunsite.icm.edu.pl/cjackson/boucher/boucher_bio.htm *Bio: François Boucher*
  [10 September 2002]
  Boucher image gallery and biography link.

Gerten-Jackson, Carol. *CGFA: A Virtual Art Museum: Fragonard.*
■ http://sunsite.icm.edu.pl/cjackson/fragonar/
http://sunsite.icm.edu.pl/cjackson/fragonar/fragonard_bio.htm *Bio: Jean Honoré Fragonard*
[10 September 2002]
Fragonard image gallery and biography link.

Gerten-Jackson, Carol. *CGFA: A Virtual Art Museum: Watteau.*
■ http://sunsite.tus.ac.jp/cgfa/watteau/index.html
[10 September 2002]
Watteau image gallery and biography link.

Kren, Emil and Daniel Marx. *Web Gallery of Art: Watteau, Jean-Antoine: The Embarkation for Cythera.*
■ http://gallery.euroweb.hu/html/w/watteau/antoine/1/07cythe1.html
[10 September 2002]
Background information on Watteau's painting *Embarkation for Cythera.*

Pioch, Nicolas. *WebMuseum, Paris: Boucher, Francois.*
■ http://www.ibiblio.org/wm/paint/auth/boucher/
[10 September 2002]
Boucher biography and image gallery.

Pioch, Nicolas. *WebMuseum, Paris: Watteau, Jean-Antoine.*
■ http://www.ibiblio.org/wm/paint/auth/watteau/
[10 September 2002]
Watteau biography and images.

Giovanni Paolo Panini and Giovanni Battista (Giambattista) Tiepolo

Artcyclopedia. *Giovanni Battista Tiepolo.*
■ http://www.artcyclopedia.com/artists/tiepolo_giovanni_battista.html
[10 September 2002]
Tiepolo directory of links to information and image galleries.

Gerten-Jackson, Carol. *CGFA: A Virtual Art Museum: Tiepolo.*
■ http://sunsite.icm.edu.pl/cjackson/tiepolo/
http://sunsite.icm.edu.pl/cjackson/tiepolo/tiepolo_bio.htm *Bio: Giovanni Battista Tiepolo*
[10 September 2002]
Tiepolo image gallery and biography link.

Kren, Emil and Daniel Marx. *Web Gallery of Art: Tiepolo, Giovanni Battista Biography.*
■ http://www.kfki.hu/~arthp/bio/t/tiepolo/gianbatt/biograph.html
[10 September 2002]
Tiepolo image gallery and biography link.

William Hogarth and Thomas Gainsborough

Artcyclopedia. *Thomas Gainsborough.*
■ http://www.artcyclopedia.com/artists/gainsborough_thomas.html
[10 September 2002]
Gainsborough directory of links to information and image galleries.

Artcyclopedia. *William Hogarth.*
- http://www.artcyclopedia.com/artists/hogarth_william.html
  [10 September 2002]
  Hogarth directory of links to information and image galleries.

Gerten-Jackson, Carol. *CGFA: A Virtual Art Museum: Gainsborough.*
- http://sunsite.icm.edu.pl/cjackson/gainsbor/
  http://sunsite.icm.edu.pl/cjackson/gainsbor/gainsborough_bio.htm *Thomas Gainsborough (Biography)*
  [10 September 2002]
  Gainsborough image gallery and biography link.

Gerten-Jackson, Carol. *CGFA: A Virtual Art Museum: Hogarth.*
- http://sunsite.dk/cgfa/hogarth/
  http://sunsite.dk/cgfa/hogarth/hogarth_bio.htm *William Hogarth (Biography)*
  [10 September 2002]
  Hogarth image gallery and biography link.

Olga's Gallery. *Thomas Gainsborough.*
- http://www.abcgallery.com/G/gainsborough/gainsborough.html
  [10 September 2002]
  Gainsborough image gallery and biography link.

Jean-Baptiste-Siméon Chardin

Artcyclopedia. *Jean-Baptiste-Siméon Chardin.*
- http://www.artcyclopedia.com/artists/chardin_jean-baptiste-simeon.html
  [10 September 2002]
  Directory of links to information about Chardin and image galleries.

Neoclassicism (Circa 1750–1810)

National Gallery of Art, Washington, D.C. *National Gallery of Art: Tour: 18th- and 19th-Century France: Neoclassicism Overview.*
- http://www.nga.gov/collection/gallery/gg56/gg56-over1.html
  [10 September 2002]
  Background information of eighteenth- and nineteenth-century Neoclassicism.

Witcombe, Chris. *Art History Resources on the Web: 18th-Century Art.*
- http://witcombe.sbc.edu/ARTH18thcentury.html
  [10 September 2002]
  Directory of links about eighteenth-century art.

Jacques-Louis David

Artcyclopedia. *Jacques-Louis David.*
- http://www.artcyclopedia.com/artists/david_jacques-louis.html
  [10 September 2002]
  Directory of links to information about David and image galleries.

Pioch, Nicolas. *WebMuseum, Paris: David, Jacques-Louis.*
- http://www.ibiblio.org/wm/paint/auth/david/
  [10 September 2002]
  Biography and image gallery.

Wilson, Elizabeth. *Smithsonian Magazine (August 1999): Jacques-Louis David: Stage Manager of the Revolution.*
- http://www.smithsonianmag.com/smithsonian/issues98/aug98/david.html
  [10 September 2002]
  Article titled "Jacques-Louis David: Stage Manager of the Revolution."

Francisco José de Goya

Artcyclopedia. *Francisco de Goya.*
- http://www.artcyclopedia.com/artists/goya_francisco_de.html
  [10 September 2002]
  Directory of links to Goya information and image galleries.

Harden, Mark. *Artchive: Francisco de Goya: Excerpted from "About Modern Art" by David Sylvester.*
- http://www.artchive.com/artchive/G/goya.html
  [10 September 2002]
  Excerpt from Goya's paintings from *About Modern Art* by David Sylvester.

Romanticism and Realism

(Nineteenth Century)

William Blake (1757–1827), Barbizon School (Circa 1830–1870), Hudson River School (Circa 1835–1870), Eugène Delacroix (1798–1863), Caspar David Friedrich (1774–1840), Jean François Millet (1814–1875), Gustave Courbet (1819–1877), Édouard Manet (1832–1883), and Thomas Eakins (1844–1916)

Romanticism (Late-Eighteenth Century– Early-Nineteenth Century) Web Addresses

Artcyclopedia. *Artists by Movement: Romanticism: Late 18th Century to Mid 19th Century.*
http://www.artcyclopedia.com/history/romanticism.html
[14 September 2002]
Directory of links to information and image galleries.

Pioch, Nicolas. *WebMuseum, Paris: Romanticism.*
http://www.ibiblio.org/wm/paint/glo/romanticism/
[14 September 2002]
Background information.

WILLIAM BLAKE (1757–1827)

Web Addresses

Artcyclopedia. *William Blake.*
http://www.artcyclopedia.com/artists/blake_william.html
[14 September 2002]
Directory of links to information and image galleries.

Gerten-Jackson, Carol. *CGFA: A Virtual Art Museum: Blake.*
http://sunsite.dk/cgfa/blake/index.html (images)
http://sunsite.dk/cgfa/blake/blake_bio.htm *William Blake* (biography)
[14 September 2002]
Image gallery and biography link.

BARBIZON SCHOOL
(Circa 1830–1870)

Web Addresses

Artcyclopedia. *Artists by Movement: The Barbizon School: France, Mid-19th Century.*
http://www.artcyclopedia.com/history/barbizon-school.html
[14 September 2002]
Directory of links to information and image galleries of Barbizon artists.

Thames and Hudson Dictionary of Art and Artists (1994). From *Xrefer, The Web's Reference Engine: Barbizon School.*
http://xrefer.com/entry.jsp?xrefid=650323&secid=
[26 September 2002]

HUDSON RIVER SCHOOL
(Circa 1835–1870)

Web Addresses

Artcyclopedia. *Artists by Movement: The Hudson River School: America, 1835 to 1870.*
http://www.artcyclopedia.com/history/hudson-river-school.html
[14 September 2002]
Directory of links to information and image galleries of Hudson River artists.

Oxford Dictionary of Art (1997). From *Xrefer, The Web's Reference Engine: Hudson River School.*
http://xrefer.com/entry.jsp?xrefid=144146&secid=
[26 September 2002]
Definition of the Hudson River School from the *Oxford Dictionary of Art* (1997).

EUGÈNE DELACROIX
(1798–1863)

Images

Liberty Leading the People (July 28, 1830), oil on canvas, approximately 10'8" x 8'6". Paris: Louvre.

Web Addresses

Artcyclopedia. *Eugène Delacroix.*
http://www.artcyclopedia.com/artists/delacroix_eugene.html
[14 September 2002]
Directory of links to information and image galleries.

Gerten-Jackson, Carol. *CGFA: A Virtual Art Museum: Delacroix.*
http://sunsite.dk/cgfa/delacroi/index.html (images)
http://sunsite.dk/cgfa/delacroi/delacroix_bio.htm *Eugène Delacroix* (biography)
[14 September 2002]
Eugène Delacroix image gallery and biography link.

Olga's Gallery. *Eugène Delacroix.*
http://www.abcgallery.com/D/delacroix/delacroix.html (images)
http://www.abcgallery.com/D/delacroix/delacroixbio.html (biography)
[14 September 2002]
Image gallery and biography link.

CASPAR DAVID FRIEDRICH
(1774–1840)

Images

The Cross in the Mountains, oil on canvas, 1811. Dusseldorf: Museum Kunst Paast.

Web Addresses

Artcyclopedia. *Caspar David Friedrich.*
http://www.artcyclopedia.com/artists/friedrich_caspar_david.html
[14 September 2002]
Directory to links of information and image galleries.

ArtMagick. *ArtMagick: Caspar David Friedrich.*
http://artmagick.com/artists/friedrich.aspx
[14 September 2002]
Biography and image gallery.

Gerten-Jackson, Carol. *CGFA: A Virtual Art Museum: Friedrich.*
http://sunsite.dk/cgfa/friedric/index.html (images)
http://sunsite.dk/cgfa/friedric/friedrich_bio.htm *Caspar David Friedrich* (biography)
[14 September 2002]
Image gallery and biography link.

Museum Kunst Palast, Düsseldorf. *Museum Kunst Palast: Collections: Das Kreuz im Gebirge (The Cross in the Mountains), Caspar David Friedrich, 1811.*
http://www.museum-kunst-palast.de/eng/sites/s2s3s1c.asp
[14 September 2002]

Pioch, Nicolas. *WebMuseum, Paris: Friedrich, Caspar David: The Cross in the Mountains.*
http://www.ibiblio.org/wm/paint/auth/friedrich/
[14 September 2002]
Background information about and image of *The Cross in the Mountains.*

REALISM
(Mid–Nineteenth Century)

Web Addresses

Artcyclopedia. *Artists by Movement: Realism: Mid-19th Century.*
http://www.artcyclopedia.com/history/realism.html
[14 September 2002]
Directory of links to information and image galleries.

Thames & Hudson Dictionary of Art and Artists (1994). From *Xrefer, The Web's Reference Engine: Realism.*
http://xrefer.com/entry.jsp?xrefid=652172&secid=
[14 September 2002]
Definition of *realism* from *The Thames and Hudson Dictionary of Art and Artists* (1994).

JEAN FRANÇOIS MILLET
(1814–1875)

Web Addresses

Artcyclopedia. *Jean-Francois Millet.*
http://www.artcyclopedia.com/artists/millet_jean-francois.html
[14 September 2002]
Directory of links to information and image galleries.

Incursio, Inc. *WetCanvas: Jean Francois Millet.*
http://www.wetcanvas.com/Museum/Artists/m/Jean_Francois_Millet/index.html
[14 September 2002]
Jean-François Millet biography and links to images.

Pioch, Nicolas. *WebMuseum, Paris: Millet, Jean-Francois.*
http://www.oir.ucf.edu/wm/paint/auth/millet/
[14 September 2002]
Background information and images.

GUSTAVE COURBET (1819–1877)

Images

The Artist's Studio: A Real Allegory, oil on canvas, 1855, approximately 11'10" x 19'8". Paris: Musée d'Orsay.

Web Addresses

Artcyclopedia. *Gustave Courbet.*
http://www.artcyclopedia.com/artists/courbet_gustave.html
[14 September 2002]
Directory to links of information and image galleries.

Gerten-Jackson, Carol. *CGFA: A Virtual Art Museum: Courbet.*
http://sunsite.dk/cgfa/courbet/index.html (images)
http://sunsite.dk/cgfa/courbet/courbet_bio.htm (biography)
[14 September 2002]

Incursio, Inc. *WetCanvas: Gustave Courbet.*
http://www.wetcanvas.com/Museum/Artists/c/Gustave_Courbet/index.html
[14 September 2002]
Biography and links to images.

Musée d'Orsay, Paris. *Musée d'Orsay: Gustave Courbet: The Artist's Studio.*
http://www.musee-orsay.fr:8081/ORSAY/orsaygb/HTML.NSF/By+Filename/mosimple
+collect+courbet+index?OpenDocument
[14 September 2002]
Image of the painting titled *The Artist's Studio: A Real Allegory* (1855).

ÉDOUARD MANET
(1832–1883)

Images

Luncheon on the Grass (Le Déjeuner sur l'Herbe), oil on canvas, 1863, approximately 7' x 8'10".
Paris: Musée d'Orsay.

Web Addresses

Artcyclopedia. *Édouard Manet.*
http://www.artcyclopedia.com/artists/manet_edouard.html
[14 September 2002]
Directory to links of information and image galleries.

Gerten-Jackson, Carol. *CGFA: A Virtual Art Museum: Manet.*
http://sunsite.dk/cgfa/manet/index.html (images)
http://sunsite.dk/cgfa/manet/manet_bio.htm *Édouard Manet* (biography)
[14 September 2002]
Image gallery and biography link.

Incursio, Inc. *WetCanvas: Édouard Manet.*
http://www.wetcanvas.com/Museum/Artists/m/Edouard_Manet/index.html
[14 September 2002]
Biography and links to images.

Musée d'Orsay, Paris. *Musée d'Orsay: Édouard Manet: Le Déjeuner sur l'herbe (Luncheon on the Grass).*
http://www.musee-orsay.fr:8081/ORSAY/orsaygb/COLLEC.NSF/3773d3f987a94472c12567240053e8be
/7410c7025bfe7580c125675400532018?OpenDocument
[14 September 2002]

THOMAS EAKINS

Images

The Gross Clinic, oil on canvas, 1875, approximately 8' x 6½'. Philadelphia: Jefferson Medical College.

Web Addresses

Artcyclopedia. *Thomas Eakins.*
http://www.artcyclopedia.com/artists/eakins_thomas.html
[14 September 2002]
Directory to links of information and image galleries.

Gerten-Jackson, Carol. *CGFA: A Virtual Art Museum: Eakins.*
http://sunsite.dk/cgfa/eakins/index.html (images)
http://sunsite.dk/cgfa/eakins/eakins_bio.htm *Thomas Eakins* (biography)
[14 September 2002]
Image gallery and biography link.

Oxford Dictionary of Art (1997). From *Xrefer, The Web's Reference Engine: Thomas Eakins.*
http://xrefer.com/entry.jsp?xrefid=143628&secid=
[26 September 2002]
Short biography from the *Oxford Dictionary of Art* (1997).

Thomas Jefferson University, Philadelphia, PA. *Thomas Jefferson University: The Eakins Gallery: The Gross Clinic.*
http://www.tju.edu/eakins/grossclinic.cfm
[14 September 2002]
Eakins Gallery. Philadelphia: Jefferson Medical College.

Site Summary

At the end of the eighteenth century, many artists turned away from the order and rationalism of the Neoclassic and Enlightenment era. They wanted to be more romantic, mystical, expressive, and melodramatic. This changing attitude reflected human fragility within nature itself, as well as in the human spirit. Thus, the era of Romanticism evolved in several countries in Europe and the United States. In England, by about 1804, William Blake (1757–1827) was expressing his spirituality through engravings, temperas, and watercolors. He illustrated Milton's and Dante's famous texts as well as the *Book of Job* in a manner that was as mystical as the texts themselves.

The expressive scenic paintings by Joseph Mallard Turner (1775–1851) of London exploited the effects of light when depicting natural elements such as fire, wind, water, and rain. French artists Eugène Delacroix (1798–1863) and Théodore Géricault (1791–1924) used color and controversial subjects to convey their romantic attitudes. The German philosopher G. W. F. Hegel inspired artists to be violently emotional and melodramatic (termed "Storm and Stress") in their art. Thus, several German landscape artists, such as Caspar David Friedrich (1774–1840), painted a sense of spirituality that was contained in the context of nature.

Other French artists preferred a more naturalistic approach to landscape painting and were known as the Barbizon School (1830–1870). The group was led by Théodore Rousseau (1812–1867) and Jean François Millet (1814–1875), who chose the theme of the noble peasant worker set within the landscape. Although Jean-Auguste-Dominique Ingres (1780–1867) remained Neoclassic in style through the nineteenth century, he uniquely captured the realistic character of his subjects in their portraitures.

In the United States, artists who were inspired by the beauty of their rugged homeland of the Hudson River Valley and the Catskill Mountains of New York were known as the Hudson River School. The three major painters, Thomas Cole (1801–1848), Thomas Doughty (1793–1856), and Asher B. Durand (1796–1886), acquired a sense of spirituality in their landscapes by studying in Europe and were acquainted with the works of Turner and Friedrich. Later in the century, Thomas Eakins (1844–1916) of Philadelphia used his knowledge of anatomy and science to create penetrating scenes of realism. Eventually, others preferred to return to a closer observation of nature and genre with a realistic eye.

Gustave Courbet (1819–1877) was the first major Realist painter and became known for two of his paintings, *The Stone Breakers* (done in 1849, destroyed) and *Burial at Ornans* (1848). Courbet chose to depict everyday life scenes of work and death, a subject of controversy in the salons of France. In England, the Pre-Raphaelites (circa 1848–1852) developed an interpretation of Realism that combined the influence of both Florentine and Sienese painters who predated Raphael of the Renaissance. Édouard Manet (1832–1883) used Realism to paint directly from the subjects he observed, as did the Impressionists. Manet's paintings were blatant and bold because of their controversial subject matter and technique. His style of painting utilized clean lines, loose brushwork, flattened volumes, and a contrast of light and dark for dramatic effects. These elements opened the door for the development of Impressionism in the late nineteenth century as well as the foundation for modern art of the twentieth century.

Discussion Questions and Activities

1. Read some background information about Romanticism at http://www.ibiblio.org/wm/paint/glo
/romanticism/ and http://artcyclopedia.com/history/romanticism.html from the Artcyclopedia. What
are some of the aesthetic characteristics of Romanticism? What was Romanticism a reaction against?
Read the biography of William Blake and view the images at http://sunsite.dk/cgfa/blake/index.html.
What German mystic did Blake admire? How did Blake support himself? What was the title of the
popular poem that he wrote and illustrated? Describe the technique he used to illustrate his poetry.
What famous Renaissance artist inspired Blake when he was working on *The Ancient of Days*? What
aspects of Blake's art make him a Romantic artist?

2. Two popular schools of landscape painting were the Barbizon School in France and the Hudson River
School in the United States. Read information at http://xrefer.com/entry.jsp?xrefid=650323&secid= and at
http://www.xrefer.com/entry.jsp?xrefid=144146&secid= from the Xrefer web site. What type of
landscape did the Barbizons paint? Who led the Barbizon School? View some of Millet's paintings at
http://www.wetcanvas.com/Museum/Artists/m/Jean_Francois_Millet/index.html. How did Millet's
landscapes differ from those of other Barbizon artists? What aspect of painting did the Impressionists
acquire from the Barbizons? Who were the Hudson River School painters? What area in the United
States inspired these painters? What type of inspiration did these American painters rely on? View
some of the image galleries of Barbizon and Hudson River School landscapes at http://artcyclopedia
.com/history/barbizon-school.html and at http://artcyclopedia.com/history/hudson-river-school.html.
Describe some of the similarities and differences between the two styles.

3. Eugène Delacroix and Caspar David Friedrich exemplify Romantic artists. But each had a unique way
of depicting romantic themes. Refer to the biographical web sites about Delacroix at http://www
.abcgallery.com/D/delacroix/delacroix.html and http://sunsite.dk/cgfa/delacroi/index.html. What
made his paintings unique among those of the Romantic painters? What was the title of the painting
that portrayed a heroic Greek uprising? Why is the painting *Liberty Leading the People* (1830) considered a romantic theme? View this painting at http://sunsite.dk/cgfa/delacroi/p-delacroix5.htm.
How does this painting depict the concept of liberty? Read the biography of Friedrich at
http://sunsite.dk/cgfa/friedric/friedrich_bio.htm and view the image gallery. How do Friedrich's
paintings differ from Delacroix's? How do his landscapes differ from those of other landscape painters?
Look at the painting of *The Cross in the Mountains* (1811) at http://www.ibiblio.org/wm/paint
/auth/friedrich/. What do the fir trees and mountains symbolize? In viewing his landscapes, what do
you think his philosophy of the human element in nature was?

4. Jean François Millet and Gustave Courbet created innovations that were important to the development of painting in the late nineteenth century. Refer to http://www.oir.ucf.edu/wm/paint/auth/millet/
and http://www.wetcanvas.com/Museum/Artists/m/Jean_Francois_Millet/index.html for information
about Millet. Read about Courbet at http://www.wetcanvas.com/Museum/Artists/c/Gustave_Courbet
/index.html and http://sunsite.dk/cgfa/courbet/index.html and view the images. In what kind of social
background did Millet grow up? How did this affect the themes of his paintings? What school of art
did he help to establish? This school was a group of Romantic painters, but Millet belonged more to
the Realist school—why? Why were some of the Impressionist painters interested in Millet's work?
Did Courbet have strong political opinions? If so, how did they affect his painting in the 1840s? Why
was his painting style characterized as in the style of Realism? What are the titles of the paintings that
provoked furor among art critics because they depicted laborers and peasants? View the painting of
The Artist's Studio (1855) at http://www.musee-orsay.fr:8081/ORSAY/orsaygb/HTML.NSF/By
+Filename/mosimple+collect+courbet+index?OpenDocument. Why was this painting so controversial?

5. Édouard Manet inspired the work of many Impressionist painters, both in subject matter and technique. Read his biography at http://www.wetcanvas.com/Museum/Artists/m/Edouard_Manet/index.html and at http://sunsite.dk/cgfa/manet/index.html and view the image gallery. Why was the painting *Luncheon on the Grass (Le Déjeuner sur l'Herbe)* not accepted in the traditional salons of Paris? Why is this painting unusually striking? Who was the Impressionist artist who was impressed by this painting, and what technique did he teach Manet? Who was the Spanish artist whose work Manet emulated, and what were the titles of these paintings? How and why did Manet have such an influence upon the Impressionist painters?

6. Thomas Eakins is an accomplished American Realist painter. Read his biographies and view the image gallery at http://sunsite.dk/cgfa/eakins/index.html and http://www.xrefer.com/entry/143628. Where did Eakins study anatomy? How did the coursework in anatomy affect his painting style? Who were the Dutch artists who influenced his work and why? What was his contribution to American art education as we know it today? Refer to the information about his studies at http://www.tju.edu/eakins/grossclinic .cfm and view the image. Who was Dr. Gross? Why was it important for Eakins to paint a portrait of Dr. Gross situated in a surgical amphitheater? What is particularly striking about the painting *The Gross Clinic* (1875)?

Related Internet Sites

William Blake

Library of Congress. *William Blake Archive.*
- http://www.blakearchive.org/
  [14 September 2002]
  Blake hypermedia archive.

Pioch, Nicolas. *WebMuseum, Paris: Blake, William.*
- http://www.oir.ucf.edu/wm/paint/auth/blake/
  [14 September 2002]
  Blake biography and image gallery.

Romanticism and Realism

Oxford Dictionary of Art (1997). From *Xrefer, The Web's Reference Engine: Romanticism.*
- http://www.xrefer.com/entry.jsp?xrefid=145286&secid=
  [26 September 2002]
  Definition of Romanticism from the *Oxford Dictionary of Art* (1997).

Thames and Hudson Dictionary of Art Terms (1984). From *Xrefer, The Web's Reference Engine: Romanticism.*
- http://www.xrefer.com/entry.jsp?xrefid=649674&secid=
  [26 September 2002]
  Definition of Romanticism from *The Thames and Hudson Dictionary of Art Terms* (1984).

Barbizon and Hudson River Schools

Delahunt, Michael. *ArtLex: Barbizon School.*
- http://www.artlex.com/ArtLex/b/barbizon.html
  [1996–2002]
  Barbizon School background information and images.

Harden, Mark. *Artchive: The Hudson River School: From Arthur Danto, "Encounters & Reflections: Art in the Historical Present."*
- http://www.artchive.com/artchive/hudsonriver.html
  [14 September 2002]
  Hudson River School excerpt from Arthur Danto's "Encounters and Reflections: Art in the Historical Present."

Eugène Delacroix, Caspar David Friedrich

Fisher, Glenn. *Caspar David Friedrich Gallery.*
- http://www.geocities.com/Area51/2229/Friedrich.html
  [14 September 2002]
  Delacroix background information.

Pioch, Nicolas. *WebMuseum, Paris: Delacroix, Eugène.*
- http://www.oir.ucf.edu/wm/paint/auth/delacroix/
  [14 September 2002]

Jean François Millet, Gustave Courbet

Tigertail Associates. *Tigertail Virtual Art Museum: Impressionism 1850 to 1875: Gustav Courbet.*
- http://tigtail.org/L_View/TVM/X2/b.Impressionism/courbet/courbet.html
  [14 September 2002]

Édouard Manet, Thomas Eakins

ARC Art Renewal Center. *ARC Art Renewal Center: Thomas Eakins.*
- http://www.artrenewal.org/museum/e/Eakins_Thomas/page1.html
  [14 September 2002]
  Eakins image gallery.

Cleveland Museum of Art. *Sister Wendy at the Cleveland Museum of Art: Thomas Eakins: The Biglin Brothers Turning the Stake, 1873.*
- http://www.clemusart.com/museum/collect/sisterwendy/html/4833885.html
  [14 September 2002]
  Eakins painting and description by Sister Wendy.

Harden, Mark. *Artchive: Édouard Manet.*
- http://www.artchive.com/artchive/ftptoc/manet_ext.html
  [14 September 2002]

Olga's Gallery. *Édouard Manet.*
- http://www.abcgallery.com/M/manet/manet.html (images)
  http://www.abcgallery.com/M/manet/manetbio.html (biography)
  [14 September 2002]

Other Nineteenth-Century Artists

Artcyclopedia. *Jean-Auguste-Dominique Ingres.*
- http://www.artcyclopedia.com/artists/ingres_jean-auguste-dominique.html
  [14 September 2002]
  Jean-Auguste-Dominique Ingres directory of links to information and image galleries.

Artcyclopedia. *Théodore Rousseau.*
- http://www.artcyclopedia.com/artists/rousseau_theodore.html
  [14 September 2002]
  Théodore Rousseau directory of links to information and image galleries.

Russ, Wendy and Carrie Carolin. *Women Artists in History: Nineteenth Century.*
- http://www.wendy.com/women/artists.html#19
  [14 September 2002]
  A list of nineteenth-century women artists.

CHAPTER 19

Impressionism

(Circa 1860–1900)

Claude Monet (1840–1926), Edgar Degas (1834–1917), and Mary Cassatt (1844–1926)

IMPRESSIONISM

Web Addresses

Artcyclopedia. *Artists by Movement: Impressionism: Centered in France, 1860's to 1880's.*
http://www.artcyclopedia.com/history/impressionism.html
[16 September 2002]
Background information about and links to Impressionist images.

Fleischer Museum of American and Russian Impressionism, Scottsdale, Arizona. *Characteristics of Impressionism: Genres in Impressionism.*
http://www.fleischer.org/impchar.html
[16 September 2002}

National Gallery, Washington, D.C. *National Gallery of Art: Tour: Impressionism.*
http://www.nga.gov/collection/gallery/gg86/gg86-main1.html
[16 September 2002]

Pioch, Nicolas. *WebMuseum, Paris: Impressionism.*
http://www.ibiblio.org/wm/paint/glo/impressionism/
[16 September 2002]
General information about Impressionism.

Site Summary

Impressionism refers to a French movement in art that began with a group of artists who were considered antiacademic. It is characterized by its innovative use of color, attention to atmospheric handling of light, and loose brushstrokes. Édouard Manet helped to establish the Impressionist movement by introducing a new subject: depictions of scenes of everyday life and recreation. By participating in the 1863 Salon des Refusés and exhibiting his painting titled *Luncheon on the Grass (Le Déjeuner sur l'Herbe),* Manet not only presented a leisurely theme but also shocked the establishment by depicting a nude figure in a genre scene.

Two art critics helped to coin the name of the movement as "Impressionism." The first use of the term was in an 1874 art review by Louis Leroy, who commented negatively about Monet's *Impression: Sunrise,* painted in 1873. In the same year, a review by Jules-Antoine Castagnary stated that these artists "are impressionists in the sense that they render not the landscape but the sensation produced by the landscape," thus officially bestowing the name. A core of French artists instituted the movement that spread to several countries and developed a variation in artistic style, specifically Post-Impressionism. Most of these artists (Claude Monet, Edgar Degas, Camille Pissarro, Pierre Auguste Renoir, Alfred Sisley, Paul Cézanne, Berthe Morisot) met in Paris around 1860. But as each artist reached artistic maturity, they ventured forward on their own but maintained the Impressionist tenets of theme, use of light, and naturalistic rendering.

Discussion Questions and Activities

1. Compare the art of French Impressionists to that of the American Impressionists from the "Artists by Movement: Impressionism" list from the Artcyclopedia at http://artcyclopedia.com/history/impressionism .html. Do the two groups have different themes? Is there a difference between the handling of paint (type of color, brushstrokes, and composition)? Who is the well-known American artist associated with many of the French Impressionists?

2. Usually male French artists are featured in the literature about Impressionism. Try to find more information about other nationalities (e.g., Canadian, Italian, Austrian) and women who are associated with the Impressionists. Use the artists featured in the "Artists by Movement: Impressionism" list from the Artcyclopedia at http://artcyclopedia.com/history/impressionism.html and then log onto a search engine such as Google or an online encyclopedia to find more information about them. What is a common theme among all of these artists? Other than the French, do other nationalities follow the style of Impressionism?

3. Read the excerpt about Impressionism at http://www.ibiblio.org/wm/paint/glo/impressionism/ from the WebMuseum, Paris. Impressionist artists liked to paint outdoors while viewing the landscape and would use photographs to capture the natural look of the composition. First, try to paint or draw a landscape scene from memory; then try to paint or draw the same scene from a photograph; then try to paint or draw the same scene outdoors (at the site). Compare the different compositions. Does the one from memory look much different from the composition copied from the photograph? If so, how? Did you notice more of your surroundings when you painted or drew outside? Did you notice that you saw things differently at different times of the day? What were these differences? Another technique of the Impressionists was to apply paint directly to the canvas rather than mix colors on the palette. Try both techniques using the same colors. What results do you get?

CLAUDE MONET
(1840–1926)

Images

Gare St. Lazare, Paris, oil on canvas, 1877, approximately 33" x 40". Harvard: Fogg Art Museum.

Impression: Sunrise, oil on canvas, 1873. Paris: Musée Marmottan.

Rouen Cathedral, oil on canvas, circa 1890s, approximately 39.5" x 26", Boston: Museum of Fine Arts, Boston; New York: Metropolitan Museum of Art (other paintings of the series are located at various museums).

Rue Montargueil with Flags, oil on canvas, 1878. Paris: Musée des Beaux Arts.

Water Lilies, oil on canvas, 1919–1920. 200.6 cm. x 425.3 cm. Cleveland: Cleveland Museum of Art (other paintings of the series are located at various museums).

Women in the Garden, oil on canvas, 1866–1867. Paris: Musée d'Orsay.

Web Addresses

Artcyclopedia. *Claude Monet.*
http://www.artcyclopedia.com/artists/monet_claude.html
[16 September 2002]
Directory of links to information and image galleries.

Cleveland Museum of Art. *Cleveland Museum of Art: Explore Our Collections: Painting: Monet: Water Lilies (Agapanthus).*
http://www.clevelandart.org/explore/artistwork.asp?searchText=Claude+Monet&display=list&tab=1&recNo=0&workRecNo=5
[16 September 2002]
Water Lilies (1915–1926).

Gerten-Jackson, Carol. *CGFA: A Virtual Art Museum: Monet.*
http://sunsite.dk/cgfa/monet/index.html (images)
http://sunsite.dk/cgfa/monet/monet_bio.htm (biography)
[16 September 2002]
Image gallery and biography link.

Gerten-Jackson, Carol. *CGFA: A Virtual Art Museum: Monet: Rue Montargueil with Flags, 1878.*
http://sunsite.dk/cgfa/monet/monet2.htm
[16 September 2002]

GiVerNet Organization. *Claude Monet's Garden at Giverny.*
http://giverny.org/gardens/fcm/visitgb.htm
[16 September 2002]
Photographic tour of Monet's home and garden at Giverny.

Harden, Mark. *Artchive: Claude Monet.*
http://www.artchive.com/artchive/ftptoc/monet_ext.html
[16 September 2002]
Background information and links to images.

Olga's Gallery. *Claude Monet.*
http://www.abcgallery.com/M/monet/monet.html (images)
http://www.abcgallery.com/M/monet/monetbio.html (biography)
[16 September 2002]
Image gallery and biography link.

Pioch, Nicolas. *WebMuseum, Paris: Monet, Claude.*
http://www.ibiblio.org/wm/paint/auth/monet/
[16 September 2002]
Information and image gallery.

Site Summary

Claude Monet is one of the major artists of the Impressionist era. His painting *Impression: Sunrise* (1873), which was shown at an independent exhibit in 1874, helped to coin the name of the movement as Impressionism. Monet was particularly interested in landscape painting and in capturing its natural elements by painting outdoors, which is known as plein-air painting. During the 1860s, he became acquainted with other Impressionist artists in Paris (Auguste Renoir, Alfred Sisley, and Frédéric Bazille) and continued to paint landscape themes that contained figures.

During the 1870s, Monet began to abandon or minimize figures in his landscapes and Paris cityscapes. His paintings continued to capture the freshness of the outdoors and emphasize the effects of light, especially at different times of the day. His brushwork was small and varied as well as soft, free, and loose. He experimented with a range of colors that varied from warm to cool pastels as well as the scale of grays. Monet also varied the tone of his primed canvas (sometimes white, tan, or a light gray) to achieve different color effects of the paint.

While in Paris during this time, he began working with other Impressionist painters, painting not only landscapes but cityscapes as well. Monet depicted street scenes and over a dozen views of the St-Lazare railway station, which became the focus of the Third Impressionist Exhibition in 1876. In 1883, Monet rented a house in Giverny, which eventually became his home for the rest of his life and a major theme of his paintings. The Giverny home now stands as a museum dedicated to his artistic career.

Discussion Questions and Activities

1. Log onto an image search engine, such as Google (http://www.google.com/imghp?hl=en&ie=ISO -8859-1&q). Type in the words "Monet and sunrise" and view the image gallery. Why do you think that the title *Impression: Sunrise* relates to the idea of the Impressionist movement? How do you think the painting would look if it were painted at different times of the day? How does Monet use the effects of light as it shines upon the water?

2. Read Monet's biography and view the image galleries at http://sunsite.dk/cgfa/monet/ and at http://www.abcgallery.com/M/monet/monet.html. Look at the images from the 1860s and 1870s. Who are the women in the painting *Women in the Garden*? Describe the different poses of the figures. At what point in his career did Monet begin to eliminate figures from these paintings?

3. View the image galleries at http://www.abcgallery.com/M/monet/monet.html. Are there any paintings that are *not* landscapes or cityscapes? If so, what kind of subject did Monet paint? At what point in his career do you see that he painted only landscapes? Did Monet concentrate on the effects of light in nature at different times of the day? Is this a characteristic of Impressionist painting?

4. While in Paris during the 1870s, Monet painted several cityscapes. View the image galleries at http://www.abcgallery.com/M/monet/monet.html and at http://sunsite.dk/cgfa/monet/html. Name some of the titles of paintings from this decade. What kinds of scenes did he depict? What is the name of the famous train station that is seen in several of Monet's paintings? Look at the painting of a train station dated 1877 and *Rue Montargueil with Flags* (1878). What did Monet paint into these scenes to create the effect of movement?

5. Monet moved into his home in Giverny in 1883 and created more than one version of his famous *Water Lilies* painting. View some of the image galleries at http://www.artcyclopedia.com/artists/monet _claude.html from the Artcyclopedia. What other museums own panels of the *Water Lilies* series? Describe some of the differences between the panels. Log onto the web site http://giverny.org/gardens /fcm/visitgb.htm for a photographic tour of Monet's home and garden at Giverny. Do you see any similarities between the photographs and the paintings?

6. View image galleries of paintings dated after 1890 at http://www.abcgallery.com/M/monet/monet.html and at http://sunsite.dk/cgfa/monet/html. Other than the Giverny garden paintings, do any other paintings repeat the same scene? If so, what makes them different? What was Monet concentrating on when he painted these? What is the name of the famous cathedral he painted, and how many views did he create of it?

EDGAR (Hilaire Germain Edgar) DEGAS (1834–1917)

Images

Frieze of Dancers, oil on canvas, circa 1895, 70 cm. x 22.5 cm. Cleveland: Cleveland Museum of Art.

The Little Fourteen-Year-Old Dancer, bronze, partially tinted with cotton skirt and satin hair ribbon on a wood base; the original wax figure was executed circa 1881; bronze cast done in 1922 by A. A. Hébrard. 39" (99.1 cm.) (without the base). New York: Metropolitan Museum of Art.

The Rehearsal, oil on canvas, circa 1878–1879, 47.6 cm. x 60.9 cm. New York: Frick Collection.

Web Addresses

About.com. *Photography with Peter Marshall: Edweard Muybridge — The Conquest of Motion.*
http://photography.about.com/library/weekly/aa121399.htm
[16 September 2002]

Artcyclopedia. *Edgar Degas.*
http://www.artcyclopedia.com/artists/degas_edgar.html
[16 September 2002]
Directory of links to information and image galleries.

Cleveland Museum of Art. *Cleveland Museum of Art: Explore Our Collections: Painting: Degas: Frieze of Dancers.*
http://www.clevelandart.org/explore/artistwork.asp?searchText=Edgar+Degas&display=list&tab=1
&recNo=0&workRecNo=11
[16 September 2002]
Image and brief information about the painting *Frieze of Dancers,* oil on canvas, circa 1895. 70 cm. x 22.5 cm.

Frick Collection, New York, NY. *Collection: Paintings: Hilaire-Germain, Edgar Degas: The Rehearsal.*
http://www.frick.org/html/pntg3f.htm
[16 September 2002]
Image and information about the painting *The Rehearsal,* oil on canvas, circa 1878–1879, 18¾" x 24" (47.6 cm. x 60.9 cm.).

Gerten-Jackson, Carol. *CGFA: A Virtual Art Museum: Degas.*
http://sunsite.dk/cgfa/degas/index.html (images)
http://sunsite.dk/cgfa/degas/degas_bio.htm *Edgar Degas* (biography)
[16 September 2002]
Image gallery and biography link.

Metropolitan Museum of Art, New York. *Metropolitan Museum of Art: The Collection: European Sculpture and Decorative Arts: The Little Fourteen-Year-Old Dancer, by Edgar Degas.*
http://www.metmuseum.org/collections/view1.asp?dep=12&full=0&item=29%2E100%2E370
[16 September 2002]
The Little Fourteen-Year-Old Dancer image with several views.

Pioch, Nicolas. *WebMuseum, Paris: Degas (Hilaire-Germain-) Edgar.*
http://www.ibiblio.org/louvre/paint/auth/degas/
[16 September 2002]
Biography and image gallery.

Site Summary

Edgar Degas's artwork is more realistic than that of his contemporary Impressionist friends. While studying at the École des Beaux Arts in the mid 1850s, he often went to the Louvre and sketched the works of the Italian masters. His mentor, Louis Lamothe, was a pupil of Ingres, who was known for the clarity of line in his masterpieces. Between 1853 and 1860, Degas studied extensively throughout Italy. He became aware of the importance of line while examining Italian fourteenth- and fifteenth-century painting and printmaking, thus developing a fine sense of draftsmanship.

His first encounter with the Impressionist spirit happened around 1862, when he met Manet in the Louvre, who then introduced him to other Impressionist artists. Degas's work consists of portraits, scenes of recreation, and illustrations of horse racing up until 1870. He then became interested in themes of the opera, theater, and dance (often of ballerinas). During this time Degas experimented with printmaking and incorporating various types of media in his sculpture pieces. Most of his sculptures were small wax figures of dancers, women, and horses.

The best-known of his sculptures is *The Little Fourteen-Year-Old Dancer,* which he exhibited in 1881 at the Sixth Impressionist Exhibition. This particular piece is made of wax and stands on a wooden base but wears a wig with a real satin ribbon and an actual ballerina tutu. The sculpture received much criticism for its starkness and realism, yet the critics overlooked the way Degas captured the natural position of the little dancer. He observed a dancer and focused on her gestures and body movements. When he observed someone that he wanted to feature, he then sketched the person's pose and later painted or sculpted the figure from memory. He did not want to distract his subjects from moving naturally, thus capturing an intimate moment. The result is a composition of realistic gestures and poses of dancers or women working at their chores.

Over the course of his career, Degas constantly worked with the theme of dancers and produced more than 600 versions of ballerinas during his lifetime. In 1919, Adrien Hébrard made twenty-two bronze-cast copies of Degas's *Little Fourteen-Year-Old Dancer* using the lost wax technique of casting.

By the 1880s, Degas's eyesight was failing, so he began drawing in pastels and gouache, which required less detail of line. After meeting Gauguin, Degas's work of the 1890s began to move away from naturalism; his use of line became more expressive and colors were bolder. Characteristics of Degas's Impressionism consist of his technique of painting or drawing scenes of everyday activities with the strokes of his brush, using the effects of light, and manipulating line with pastels. But his overarching achievement is his keen ability to visually record the spontaneity of a simple moment or gesture of his subjects.

Discussion Questions and Activities

1. Review the image gallery of paintings at http://sunsite.dk/cgfa/degas/index.html and identify the themes of the paintings dated before 1870. What themes did Degas paint after 1870? Which paintings make you feel as if you are in the audience observing? Which ones make you feel as though you are onstage or backstage? Does Degas use the effect of illuminated light in his compositions? If so, how?

2. Read some of the biographies at http://sunsite.dk/cgfa/degas/index.html and from the WebMuseum, Paris, at http://www.ibiblio.org/louvre/paint/auth/degas/. Why is Degas's art considered Impressionist? What type of brushstrokes did he use to create a sense of movement? How did he manipulate light in his paintings?

3. When did Degas begin to lose his eyesight? How did his artwork then change? What kinds of things did he begin to experiment with and why? What medium did he prefer after 1880?

4. When did the dancer (ballerina) theme become popular in Degas's work? View some of the image galleries from the Artcyclopedia at http://www.artcyclopedia.com/artists/degas_edgar.html. Which artworks have the dancer theme? What kinds of media did Degas use to depict dancers? What is the difference between the dancers Degas painted and those that Toulouse-Lautrec painted? Use a search engine and the phrases "Degas and dancers" and "Toulouse-Lautrec and dancers" to compare their themes.

5. View the image of *The Little Fourteen-Year-Old Dancer* sculpture from the Metropolitan Museum of Art, New York, at http://www.metmuseum.org/collections/view1.asp?dep=12&full=0&item=29%2E100 %2E370 and describe what the piece is made of. What was the original figure made of in 1881? What year was the sculpture cast in bronze? Use a search engine and the phrase "lost wax method" to find a web site that describes the technique for casting bronze. Is this technique still used today?

6. View the paintings of dancers at http://www.clevelandart.org/explore/artistwork.asp?searchText =Edgar+Degas&display=list&tab=1&recNo=0&workRecNo=11 from the Cleveland Museum of Art and from the Frick Collection, New York, at http://www.frick.org/html/pntg3f.htm. Describe what the dancers are doing. Are they posing in the same way in the paintings? What makes the Cleveland Museum of Art piece ambitious? What makes it "photographic" in style? Who is Eadweard Muybridge? Read the article at http://photography.about.com/library/weekly/aa121399.htm about him. What is the contribution he made to photography that might have affected Degas's artwork?

MARY CASSATT
(1844–1926)

Images

The Letter, drypoint and aquatint on cream laid paper, 1890–1891. Massachusetts: Worcester Art Museum.

Web Addresses

Gerten-Jackson, Carol. *CGFA: A Virtual Art Museum: Cassatt.*
http://sunsite.dk/cgfa/cassatt/index.html (images)
http://sunsite.dk/cgfa/cassatt/cassatt_bio.htm *Mary Cassatt* (biography)
[17 September 2002]
Image gallery and biography link.

National Gallery, Washington, D.C. *National Gallery of Art: Collection: Mary Cassatt American, 1844–1926: The Letter, 1890–1891.*
http://www.nga.gov/collection/gallery/cassatt/cassatt-46444.0.html
[17 September 2002]
Information about *The Letter* (1890–1891).

National Gallery, Washington, D.C. *National Gallery of Art: Tour: Mary Cassat: Selected Color Prints.*
http://www.nga.gov/collection/gallery/cassatt/cassatt-main1.html
[17 September 2002]
Information about prints and an image gallery.

Olga's Gallery. *Mary Cassatt.*
http://www.abcgallery.com/C/cassatt/cassatt.html
[17 September 2002]
Image gallery and biography link.

Oxford Paperback Encyclopedia (1998). From *Xrefer, The Web's Reference Engine: Drypoint.*
http://www.xrefer.com/entry.jsp?xrefid=214463&secid=
[17 September 2002]

PageWise. *Different Techniques in the Art of Pastel Drawing: Written by Gary Smith.*
http://nd.essortment.com/artofpasteldr_rjqa.htm
[17 September 2002]
Read the article titled "Different Techniques in the Art of Pastel Drawing."

Pioch, Nicolas. *WebMuseum, Paris: Cassatt, Mary.*
http://www.ibiblio.org/wm/paint/auth/cassatt/
[17 September 2002]
Biography and image gallery.

Worcester Art Museum, Worcester, MA. *Worcester Art Museum: Collection: Mary Cassatt: The Letter.*
http://www.worcesterart.org/Collection/American/1926.205.html
[17 September 2002]
Image of *The Letter* (1890–1891).

Site Summary

Mary Cassatt was an American artist who studied in Europe in 1866 and later settled in Paris. In the United States, she attended the Pennsylvania Academy of Fine Arts in 1860 and then studied in Paris at the studio of Jean-Léon Gérôme in 1866. Scenes of Parisian women, portraiture, and other typical genre activities characterize her work. She accepted an invitation to participate in the Fourth Annual Impressionist Exhibition of 1879. At this particular time Cassatt focused on her printmaking and developed her draftsmanship using pastels. She manipulated the pastels to emphasize their rich color and created strokes using line in her compositions.

Because line was important to her artwork, Cassatt studied Japanese printmaking techniques. She developed an original use of line and color using drypoint, etchings, and aquatints. By the 1880s, her artwork had become very popular in Europe and the United States. She concentrated on women—especially mothers and children— as a theme. Her paintings and prints depict women engaged in daily activities or as mothers attending to their children. Cassatt was able to capture the intimate essence of a moment in the activity.

Cassatt's most ambitious printmaking attempt was a series of eighteen color prints produced in the 1890s. She hand-inked and wiped the plate of each print in the series. One of the best-known prints of the series is *The Letter,* a drypoint and aquatint that was printed on cream laid paper. The composition has an oriental flavor because of its line, design, and opaque colors, which are reminiscent of Japanese prints. In 1904, Cassatt was awarded the Légion d'Honneur and was considered one of the most prominent American artists of her time. In 1915, Cassatt lost her eyesight to cataracts and was no longer able to paint. One of her final contributions was to help her American friends establish major art collections in the United States that consisted of the Old Masters, contemporary European art, and work of the French Impressionists.

Discussion Questions and Activities

1. Read the biographies and view the image galleries at http://sunsite.dk/cgfa/cassatt/index.html, at http://www.ibiblio.org/wm/paint/auth/cassatt/, and at http://www.abcgallery.com/C/cassatt/cassatt .html. Who was the Impressionist artist that Cassatt first met and greatly admired? What do you think attracted Cassatt to the artwork of the Impressionists? Who was the popular model Cassatt depicted in several of her works?

2. View an image gallery and look at the paintings dated before 1879. What are some of their themes? Which paintings show a Spanish influence? Who were the Spanish painters that Cassatt respected and emulated in theme? Why was Cassatt interested in depicting Spanish themes?

3. What important exhibition did Cassatt participate in that established her affiliation with the Impressionists? Besides Degas, what other Impressionist artist did Cassatt admire and why? How did Cassatt promote the art of the Impressionists in the United States? Were any other women artists mentioned that were considered Impressionists?

4. What culture influenced Cassatt's printmaking technique? Read about drypoint at http://www.xrefer .com/entry.jsp?xrefid=214463&secid= and view the image of *The Letter* at http://www.worcesterart .org/Collection/American/1926.205.html or from the National Gallery of Art at http://www.nga.gov /collection/gallery/cassatt/cassatt-46444.0.html. What are some of the oriental qualities of this print? Describe the use of line and colors. What is the theme?

5. What other medium did Cassatt master besides printmaking and painting? In what decade did she exploit the use of this medium? Log onto the web site at http://nd.essortment.com/artofpasteldr_rjqa.htm to answer the following questions: What is this medium made of and how it is used in drawing? Who was another Impressionist artist that Cassatt knew also liked to use this medium? Look at some of Cassatt's drawings at http://www.abcgallery.com/C/cassatt/cassatt.html and at http://sunsite.dk/cgfa /cassatt/index.html to see how she applied these techniques.

6. The mother and child theme dominates Cassatt's artwork. Refer to http://sunsite.dk/cgfa/cassatt/index .html and http://www.abcgallery.com/C/cassatt/cassatt.html to view this theme. What are some of the activities a mother and her children participate in? Are the scenes of daily activities considered a characteristic of Impressionism? Did Cassatt have any children of her own? Did any other Impressionist artists popularize this theme?

Related Internet Sites

Impressionism

Cleveland Museum of Art. *Cleveland Museum of Art: Explore: Education and Research: For Schools and Teachers: Teachers Resource Center: Slide Packets: Sample Slide Packet: Impressionist and Post-Impressionist Art.*
- http://www.clemusart.com/educatn/trc-news/slidepac/sample.html
  [17 September 2002]
  Brief overview of Impressionism and Post-Impressionism.

Harden, Mark. *Artchive: Impressionism: (listed first by influences, then Impressionists proper, then influenced by:)*
- http://www.artchive.com/artchive/impressionism.html
  [17 September 2002]
  List of Impressionist artists.

Harden, Mark. *Artchive: Post-Impressionism.*
- http://www.artchive.com/artchive/post_impressionism.html
  [17 September 2002]
  List of Post-Impressionist artists.

Tigertail Associates. *Tigertail Virtual Art Museum: Modern Art 1750–1900.*
- http://www.tigtail.org/M_View/TVM/X2/X2fp.html
  Image gallery of Impressionist and Post-Impressionist art.

Witcombe, Chris. *Art History Resources on the Web: 19th-Century Art.*
- http://witcombe.sbc.edu/ARTHLinks5.html
  [17 September 2002]
  Links to numerous web sites on late-nineteenth-century art.

Claude Monet

Seanet Consulting Services. *Claude Monet: Impression: Sunrise.*
- http://www.seanet.com/users/mfost/mon/mon00.html
  [17 September 2002]
  Brief general information about the painting *Impression: Sunrise.*

Tigertail Associates. *Tigertail Virtual Art Museum: Impressionism: Monet.*
- http://tvm.tigtail.org/TVM/L_View/X2/b.Impressionism/monet/monet.html
  [17 September 2002]
  Image gallery.

Edgar Degas

Centaro, Orazio. *Orazio Centaro's Art Images on the Web: Galerie Degas.*
- http://www.ocaiw.com/degaleri.htm
  [17 September 2002]
  Biography and image gallery.

MacDonald, Lisa. *Halaire-Germain-Edgar Degas (1834–1917).*
■ http://www.cafeguerbois.com/degasbio.html
[17 September 2002]
Biography and image gallery.

Olga's Gallery. *Edgar Degas.*
■ http://www.abcgallery.com/D/degas/degas.html
[17 September 2002]
Image gallery and biography link.

Sterling and Francine Clark Art Institute, Williamstown, MA. *Sterling and Francine Clark Art Institute: Collections: Impressionist & Post-Impressionist Painting & Sculpture: Hilaire Germain Edgar Degas: The Dancing Lesson.*
■ http://www.clarkart.edu/museum_programs/collections/impressionist/content.cfm?ID=30&marker=3&start=3
[17 September 2002]
Image and brief information about the painting *The Dancing Lesson,* oil on canvas, circa 1880, 39.4 cm. x 88.4 cm.

World Wide Arts Resources Corp. *World Wide Arts Resources: Artists: Masters: Impressionism: Degas, Edgar.*
■ http://wwar.com/categories/Artists/Masters/Impressionism/Degas_Edgar/index.html
[17 September 2002]
Links to art museums and arts information.

Mary Cassatt

Artcyclopedia. *Mary Cassatt.*
■ http://www.artcyclopedia.com/artists/cassatt_mary.html
[17 September 2002]
Directory of links to information and image galleries.

Harden, Mark. *Artchive: Mary Cassatt: From "Mary Cassatt: Modern Woman," by Judith A. Barter.*
■ http://artchive.com/artchive/C/cassatt.html#images
[17 September 2002]
Background information and links to images.

Pioch, Nicolas. *WebMuseum, Paris: Impressionism.*
■ http://www.ibiblio.org/wm/paint/glo/impressionism/
[17 September 2002]
Information about the Impressionists.

Tigertail Associates. *Tigertail Virtual Art Museum: Impressionism: Mary Cassatt.*
■ http://tvm.tigtail.org/TVM/L_View/X2/b.Impressionism/cassatt/cassatt.html
[9 June 2001]
Image gallery of paintings and pastels.

CHAPTER 20

Post-Impressionism
(Circa 1886–1905)

Vincent van Gogh (1853–1890), Paul Gauguin (1848–1903), and Georges Seurat (1859–1891)

Post-Impressionism Web Addresses

Art Institute of Chicago. *Art Institute of Chicago: Student and Teacher Programs: ArtAccess: Impressionism and Post-Impressionism.*
http://www.artic.edu/artaccess/AA_Impressionist/
[18 September 2002]

Alacritude. *Encyclopedia.com: Nabis.*
http://www.encyclopedia.com/html/n/nabis.asp
[18 September 2002]
Encyclopedia article about the "Nabis."

Artcyclopedia. *Artists by Movement: Impressionism: Centered in France, 1860's to 1880's.*
http://www.artcyclopedia.com/history/impressionism.html
[18 September 2002]

Artcyclopedia. *Artists by Movement: Les Nabis: 1891–1899.*
http://www.artcyclopedia.com/history/les-nabis.html
[18 September 2002]

Artcyclopedia. *Artists by Movement: Pointillism: France, 1880's.*
http://www.artcyclopedia.com/history/pointillism.html
[18 September 2002]

Artcyclopedia. *Artists by Movement: Post-Impressionism: France, 1880's to 1900.*
http://www.artcyclopedia.com/history/post-impressionism.html
[18 September 2002]
Background information and links to Post-Impressionist images (links to the Pointillists and "Les Nabis").

Artcyclopedia. *Artists by Movement: Symbolism: Late 19th Century.*
http://www.artcyclopedia.com/history/symbolism.html
[18 September 2002]
List of Symbolist artists.

Cleveland Museum of Art. *Cleveland Museum of Art: Explore: Education and Research: For Schools and Teachers: Teachers Resource Center: Slide Packets: Sample Slide Packet: Impressionist and Post-Impressionist Art.*
http://www.clemusart.com/educatn/trc-news/slidepac/sample.html
[18 September 2002]

Delahunt. Michael. *ArtLex: Post-Impressionism.*
http://www.artlex.com/ArtLex/p/postimp.html
[18 September 2002]

Oxford Dictionary of Art (1997). From *Xrefer, The Web's Reference Engine: Nabis.*
http://www.xrefer.com/entry.jsp?xrefid=144799&secid=
[18 September 2002]

Pioch, Nicolas. *WebMuseum, Paris: Redon, Odilon.*
http://www.oir.ucf.edu/wm/paint/auth/redon/
[18 September 2002]
Biography and image gallery of Odilon Redon (Symbolist artist).

Site Summary

About the time of Manet's death in 1883, a major shift from the Impressionist style began to occur. Artists such as Paul Gauguin, Vincent van Gogh, and Georges Seurat introduced a more spiritual, emotional, and scientific approach to Impressionist art. Their art was more abstract and symbolic in form and interpretation—a reaction to the naturalism of Impressionism. Post-Impressionism had an effect upon artists around the world. Abstraction, spirituality, and symbolic content could be adapted by various cultures, societies, politics, and religions. Post-Impressionist movements branched out into factions such as the Nabis and the Symbolists. The impact of Post-Impressionist art gave way to the twentieth-century artistic developments of Expressionism, Fauvism, and Futurism.

Discussion Questions and Activities

1. Log onto the Artcyclopedia and minimize the files for "Artists by Movement" under Impressionism at http://artcyclopedia.com/history/impressionism.html and Post-Impressionism at http://artcyclopedia .com/history/post-impressionism.html. View the artworks under several of the artists of each movement. Name some of the natural elements of the Impressionists and some of the abstractions of the Post-Impressionists. How did Impressionist artists paint in order to capture the naturalism of the outdoors? Why did Post-Impressionist artists react against the Impressionists' naturalism?

2. Read about Impressionism and Post-Impressionism at http://www.artic.edu/artaccess/AA_Impressionist/ and at http://www.clemusart.com/educatn/trc-news/slidepac/sample.html from the Cleveland Museum of Art. Who coined the term "Post-Impressionism"? Who are some of the artists associated with this movement? What did Post-Impressionist art influence and why?

3. Refer to http://www.artcyclopedia.com/history/pointillism.html about Pointillism and http://www .artcyclopedia.com/history/les-nabis.html about the Nabis. Why are the Nabis and the Pointillists considered Post-Impressionists? What is the difference between divisionism and Pointillism? Who were "les Nabis" (the Nabis)? What medium did they excel in? Read http://www.xrefer.com/entry .jsp?xrefid=144799&secid= about the Nabis. What does the term "Nabis" refer to? What other aspects of the arts did artists engage in? Where and when was the first Nabis exhibit held?

4. Another Post-Impressionist movement was called Symbolism. Refer to http://www.artcyclopedia .com/history/symbolism.html, read the biography, and view the images by Odilon Redon at http://www.oir.ucf.edu/wm/paint/auth/redon/. What theme did Symbolist artists paint? What are some of the subjects Redon painted? Describe the way he used color and applied it to canvas.

VINCENT VAN GOGH
(1853–1890)

Images

Portraits (various portraits), circa 1885–1890. From various museums.

The Potato-Eaters, oil on canvas, 1885, 44 cm. x 27 cm. Amsterdam: Rijksmuseum.

Self-Portraits (various self-portraits), circa 1885–1890. From various museums.

Web Addresses

Brooks, David. *Vincent van Gogh Gallery.*
http://www.vangoghgallery.com/
[18 September 2002]
Extensive web site of information about van Gogh.

Brooks, David. *Vincent van Gogh Gallery: The Portraits.*
http://www.vangoghgallery.com/painting/main_po.htm
[18 September 2002]
Various *Portraits* (circa 1885–1890).

Gerten-Jackson, Carol. *CGFA: A Virtual Art Museum: van Gogh.*
http://sunsite.dk/cgfa/gogh/index.html (images)
http://sunsite.dk/cgfa/gogh/gogh_bio.htm *Vincent van Gogh* (biography)
[18 September 2002]
Image gallery and biography link.

Harden, Mark. *Artchive: Vincent van Gogh.*
http://www.artchive.com/artchive/V/vangogh.html
[18 September 2002]
Biography and link to "View Image List."

Incursio, Inc. *WetCanvas: Vincent van Gogh.*
http://www.wetcanvas.com/Museum/Artists/v/Vincent_van_Gogh/index.html
[18 September 2002]
Extensive biography and some images.

Olga's Gallery. *Vincent van Gogh.*
http://www.abcgallery.com/V/vangogh/vangogh.html (images)
http://www.abcgallery.com/V/vangogh/vangoghbio.html (biography)
[18 September 2002]
Image gallery and biography link.

Olga's Gallery. *Vincent van Gogh: The Potato-Eaters.*
http://www.abcgallery.com/V/vangogh/vangogh8.html
[18 September 2002]
The Potato-Eaters (1885) image.

Pioch, Nicolas. *WebMuseum, Paris: Gogh, Vincent van.*
http://www.oir.ucf.edu/wm/paint/auth/gogh/
[18 September 2002]
Biography and image gallery.

Pioch, Nicolas. *WebMuseum, Paris: Gogh, Vincent van: Self-Portraits.*
http://www.oir.ucf.edu/wm/paint/auth/gogh/self/
[18 September 2002]
Various *Self-Portraits* gallery (circa 1885–1890).

Site Summary

Vincent van Gogh's work is Post-Impressionist. Post-Impressionism is a term that denotes the work of artists associated with the French modernists of the late nineteenth and early twentieth centuries. Van Gogh was a Dutch painter who was strongly influenced by French Post-Impressionist artists such as Jules Breton, Paul Gauguin, Georges Seurat, and Émile Bernard. He began his professional career as an apprentice art dealer, working for his uncle in London and Paris between 1869 and 1873. He was surrounded by works of art by the Old Masters as well as contemporary artists. Returning to the Netherlands between 1877 and 1880, he trained to be a minister and was assigned to work with peasants in rural Belgium. This became a turning point in van Gogh's life when he decided to become somewhat of a peasant painter instead. His paintings at this time are reminiscent of those by Jean François Millet. Millet popularized the genre of the peasant lifestyle.

To develop his artistic talents, in 1880 van Gogh went to Brussels to study drawing, anatomy, and physiognomy at the Académie Royale des Beaux Arts. He became financially dependent upon his younger brother, Theo, who supported him throughout his life. Much biographical and artistic information about van Gogh is revealed through his letters to Theo and his personal diaries.

Van Gogh's earliest paintings (1880–1885) are dark in color, much like the traditional Dutch style of Rembrandt. They depict the theme of simple peasant life and show an influence of strong line, which is sometimes seen in Dutch prints. An example is van Gogh's painting *The Potato-Eaters,* done in 1885. He used dark, earthy colors and heavy outlines to shape the figures. After an unfavorable reception of *The Potato-Eaters* by the critics, van Gogh went to Paris in 1886 to work with other French avant-garde artists.

In Paris, he attempted to use the technique of Pointillism, developed by Georges Seurat. Pointillist painting utilizes the placement of small dots of color, which visually blend into one solid color. But its complicated execution was too restrictive and rigorous for van Gogh. Instead, he created an aspect of rhythm and pattern by applying thick paint to the canvas with sweeping brushstrokes. Another influence came from Japanese prints, from which van Gogh learned to flatten color on the surface of the picture plane. Artists such as Émile Bernard and Paul Gauguin also used this technique.

While painting in this new style, van Gogh conceived the idea of creating an artists' colony in Arles that would bring the avant-garde artists together. By 1888, Theo had convinced Gauguin to join Vincent in Arles to establish the colony. The two artists disagreed bitterly, and the partnership came to an end when van Gogh became distraught and severed a piece of his own earlobe. Gauguin was appalled at this rash act and quickly left Arles. Under the watchful care of his friend, the postman Roulin, van Gogh recuperated and continued to paint. These paintings consisted of portraits of Roulin and his family and other people in the village, as well as his self-portraits.

In 1889, van Gogh created some of his most famous paintings such as *Starry Night* and a series of sunflower paintings. His brushstrokes were wild, torrent, and heavy—much like his mental state. But by 1890, his failing mental health caused him to be institutionalized in Auvers under the care of a homeopathic practitioner, Dr. Gachet. The town of Auvers seemed to settle van Gogh, who again painted portraits and scenes of fields and crows. Quietly one afternoon in July 1890, van Gogh, apparently depressed, went out to the field to paint but instead shot himself. His brother Theo was at his side when he died two days later. Van Gogh did not enjoy financial or artistic success during his lifetime; in fact, he sold only one painting while he was alive. Ironically, his paintings have sold at record prices at auction in the twentieth century.

Discussion Questions and Activities

1. Read some of the biographical information from http://www.vangoghgallery.com/ and from http://wwar
    .com/artchive/vangogh.html. At what point did van Gogh become serious about becoming an artist?
    What happened early in his life that nurtured his pursuit of art?

2. View the image of *The Potato-Eaters* at http://www.abcgallery.com/V/vangogh/vangogh8.html
    from Olga's Gallery. Describe the light and colors in this painting. Does *Potato-Eaters* look like a
    typical Impressionist painting? What elements are unlike the paintings of Impressionists such as
    Monet? What is this painting's theme? Is it in keeping with those the Impressionists depicted?

3. Vincent van Gogh decided to live in Paris with his brother, Theo, in 1886. Besides meeting other
    French Post-Impressionists, what other aspect of art influenced him? What is the technique that he
    incorporated in his paintings? View the image gallery at http://www.abcgallery.com/V/vangogh
    /vangogh.html. Do the paintings appear to have a thick, rough surface? How do you think van Gogh
    applied paint to the canvas? Do you think he always used a brush? How do the brushstrokes look on
    some of the surfaces of the paintings?

4. Why did van Gogh decide to live in Arles from 1888 to 1889? What artist did he want to work with?
    What happened between these two artists? View some of the image galleries and paintings of 1889,
    such as Olga's Gallery at http://www.abcgallery.com/V/vangogh/vangogh.html or http://sunsite.dk
    /cgfa/gogh/index.html. What theme did van Gogh paint in 1889? Describe some of the scenes. How
    are the compositions arranged in the landscapes?

5. Vincent van Gogh painted many portraits of people that he was acquainted with. Refer to the David
    Brooks web site at http://www.vangoghgallery.com/painting/main_po.htm, which contains lists of
    people's portraits by their name. Who was Roulin? Looking at Roulin's portraits, how do we know
    that he was a postman? View the portraits of Dr. Gachet. What happened to van Gogh when he became
    acquainted with Dr. Gachet? In what kind of pose is Dr. Gachet positioned? What kind of plant is on
    the table, and what does it represent? Describe the poses of some of the people in the portraits.

6. Van Gogh reveals much about his mental state through his self-portraits. View the self-portraits from
    the WebMuseum, Paris, at http://www.oir.ucf.edu/wm/paint/auth/gogh/self/. During what time span
    were most of the self-portraits created? What is the title of the painting van Gogh did after cutting his
    earlobe? As you view these paintings, what mental state do you think van Gogh was in? Does he look
    physically stressed out? How old does he look in these paintings? What is his real age at the date of
    each of the self-portraits? How many paintings did he create of himself?

PAUL GAUGUIN
(1848–1903)

Images

Vision After the Sermon: Jacob Wrestling with the Angel, oil on canvas, 1888, 73 cm. x 92 cm. Edinburgh: National Gallery of Scotland.

Where Do We Come From? Who Are We? Where Are We Going?, oil on hessian sacking, 1897. 54¾ x 147½. Boston: Museum of Fine Arts, Boston.

Web Addresses

Artcyclopedia. *Artists by Movement: Symbolism: Late 19th Century.*
http://www.artcyclopedia.com/history/symbolism.html
[18 September 2002]

Carpenter, Douglas. *Art and Artist Links: Paul Eugène Henri Gauguin (1848–1903).*
http://www.van-gogh-art.co.uk/artist/gauguin.htm
[18 September 2002]
Biography and images.

Gerten-Jackson, Carol. *CGFA: A Virtual Art Museum: Gauguin.*
http://sunsite.dk/cgfa/gauguin/index.html (images)
http://sunsite.dk/cgfa/gauguin/gauguin_bio.htm (biography)
[18 September 2002]
Image gallery and biography link.

Gerten-Jackson, Carol. *CGFA: A Virtual Art Museum: Gauguin: Where Do We Come From? Who Are We? Where Are We Going?*
http://sunsite.dk/cgfa/gauguin/p-gauguin23.htm
[18 September 2002]
Where Do We Come From? Who Are We? Where Are We Going? (1897) image.

Harden, Mark. *Artchive: Gauguin, Paul: Where Do We Come From? Who Are We? Where Are We Going?: Text from "Sister Wendy's American Masterpieces."*
http://www.artchive.com/artchive/G/gauguin/where.jpg.html
[18 September 2002]
Image of and information about the painting *Where Do We Come From? Who Are We? Where Are We Going?*

Howe, Jeffery. Boston College. *19th Century Painting: Paul Gauguin: French Symbolist: Early Works.*
http://www.bc.edu/bc_org/avp/cas/fnart/art/gauguin_ptg.html
[18 September 2002]
Images of sculptures and paintings by Paul Gauguin.

Howe, Jeffery. Boston College. *The Sculpture of Paul Gauguin.*
http://www.bc.edu/bc_org/avp/cas/fnart/art/gauguin_sculp.html
[18 September 2002]

Museum of Fine Arts, Boston. *Museum of Fine Arts, Boston: Guide to the Collection: European Art to 1900: Paul Gauguin: Where Do We Come From? Who Are We? Where Are We Going?*
http://www.mfa.org/handbook/portrait.asp?id=272&s=6
[18 September 2002]
Image of and information about the painting *Where Do We Come From? Who Are We? Where Are We Going?*

National Gallery of Art, Washington, D.C. *National Gallery of Art: Collection: Paul Gauguin.*
http://www.nga.gov/cgi-bin/psearch?Request=S&imageset=1&Person=11750 (images)
http://www.nga.gov/cgi-bin/pbio?11750 (biography)
[18 September 2002]
Brief biography and image gallery.

Olga's Gallery. *Paul Gauguin.*
http://www.abcgallery.com/G/gauguin/gauguin.html
[18 September 2002]
Image gallery and biography link.

Olga's Gallery. *Paul Gauguin. Vision After the Sermon; Jacob Wrestling with the Angel.*
http://www.abcgallery.com/G/gauguin/gauguin17.html
[18 September 2002]
Vision After the Sermon: Jacob Wrestling with the Angel (1888) image.

Oxford Dictionary of Art (1997). From *Xrefer, The Web's Reference Engine: Primitive.*
http://www.xrefer.com/entry.jsp?xrefid=145129&secid=.-
[18 September 2002]
Definition of *primitive.*

Pioch, Nicolas. *WebMuseum, Paris: Gauguin (Eugène-Henri-) Paul.*
http://www.ibiblio.org/wm/paint/auth/gauguin/
[18 September 2002]
Biography and image gallery.

Site Summary

Because Paul Gauguin's early artworks resemble Impressionist landscapes dated circa 1878 and because of his social acquaintance with Camille Pissarro and other Impressionist artists, Gauguin's career is loosely linked with the Impressionist movement. His father was a liberal French journalist, and his mother's family background indicates a Peruvian ancestry. Her Peruvian background inspired Gauguin later in life to apply aspects of primitivism, mysticism, and exoticism to his art. As a child, he lived in Lima, Peru, with his great-uncle on an estate; at age seventeen, he joined the navy and traveled to Rio de Janeiro.

Gauguin enjoyed a financially secure life, due to the estate left him by his parents and overseen by his savvy guardian, Gustave Arosa. Arosa was responsible for appointing Gauguin as a successful stockbroker in 1871. In 1873, Gauguin married, and in 1874 he began to paint seriously after he viewed the First Impressionist Exhibition in Paris. After meeting Pissarro, Gauguin associated himself with other Impressionists and joined them in the Salon Exhibition of 1876 as well as other exhibitions up until 1880. Pissarro is said to have encouraged Gauguin to loosen his use of color. Gauguin enjoyed painting with Pissarro and Paul Cézanne without financial worries until the stock crash of 1882.

In July 1886, Gauguin moved to the Breton village of Pont-Aven. There he developed the style of first sketching his subject, making different studies and various copies of the sketch, and then producing a final version. This approach was unlike the method the Impressionists used. Gauguin documented this technique through his writings, titled *Notes Synthétiques*. After various trips to Martinique, he returned to Pont-Aven and reacquainted himself with Émile Bernard. Stylistically, Bernard inspired Gauguin to paint using large patches of color that were heavily outlined—similar to a stained glass effect. An example of this is depicted in the painting *Vision After the Sermon: Jacob Wrestling with the Angel,* done in 1888.

But Gauguin's use of space and color went beyond Bernard's abstraction technique. Gauguin wanted to create a psychological and spiritual concept of the scene that shows Breton women contemplating a sermon about Jacob that they just listened to. Gauguin simultaneously shows the vision in thought and reality on the same canvas surface. This is a complete juxtaposition of what Impressionist painters depicted.

Gauguin had a brief encounter with Vincent van Gogh later in 1888. He decided to join van Gogh in Arles, where they wished to establish an artists' colony. Their relationship was evidently strained due to their opposite personalities and different artistic styles. After van Gogh severed his own earlobe following an argument with Gauguin, Gauguin quickly left Arles and returned to Paris, where he worked with several of the French Symbolist artists between 1889 and 1891. Gauguin despised the sophisticated life in Paris, so he left for Pont-Aven and then decided in 1891 to try a simpler life in Tahiti.

Gauguin's artwork in Tahiti consists of small, somewhat crude sculptures and woodcuts. His painting utilizes patches of color intertwined with a new theme—mystical spirituality. He documented his artistic revelations in a text called *Noa-Noa*. After an unsuccessful trip to Paris, Gauguin returned to Tahiti in 1895. He was sick and financially broken. In 1897, he learned that his favorite daughter, Aline, had died. This personal tragedy moved him to paint a visual document that represents his last will. The painting *Where Do We Come From? Who Are We? Where Are We Going?* depicts the phases of life. After the painting was completed, Gauguin unsuccessfully attempted suicide. He then left Tahiti and went to the Marquesas Islands, where he produced his last sculptures, wooden reliefs, and images of Tahitian women. Gauguin's color legacy continued throughout the twentieth century, as seen in the art of the French Fauvists, the expressive paintings of Edvard Munch of Norway, and the works of the German Expressionists.

Discussion Questions and Activities

1. Refer to the biographies and view the images at http://www.abcgallery.com/G/gauguin/gauguin.html and at http://www.ibiblio.org/wm/paint/auth/gauguin/. What events in Gauguin's early childhood and young adulthood affected his art later in life? Why did he decide to go to Tahiti? View some of the works he painted after this date at http://www.abcgallery.com/G/gauguin/gauguin.html. How do they differ from the ones he painted while living in France around 1880? Are the colors different in the Tahitian paintings? How does Gauguin handle space in these compositions?

2. Which two French artists influenced Gauguin around 1884? Which of them encouraged Gauguin to loosen up his use of color and line? What theme did Gauguin depict during this period?

3. Gauguin became acquainted with the Symbolists while living periodically in Pont-Aven from 1886 to 1888. Refer to http://www.artcyclopedia.com/history/symbolism.html and then view Gauguin's image gallery at http://sunsite.dk/cgfa/gauguin/. Look at the paintings he created during this time. How did they change? What new technique did he develop and document? What artist inspired Gauguin during this period?

4. The painting *Vision After the Sermon: Jacob Wrestling with the Angel* was created in 1888 while Gauguin was working in Pont-Aven. Refer to the image at http://www.abcgallery.com/G/gauguin /gauguin17.html and describe the composition of the foreground and background. What color adds intensity to the scene? What image separates the space, thereby creating a visual, spiritual, and psychological space? How is Gauguin's use of the surface space different from that of the Impressionists?

5. Gauguin's art became dominated by themes of mysticism and spirituality after 1886. Gauguin felt that the Western European lifestyle stifled these concepts, so he left for Tahiti in 1891. View the image of and information about the painting *Where Do We Come From? Who Are We? Where Are We Going?* at http://www.artchive.com/artchive/G/gauguin/where.jpg.html or from the Boston Museum web site at http://www.mfa.org/handbook/portrait.asp?id=272&s=6. From which direction is the painting supposed to be viewed? What three phases of life does it depict? How does Gauguin group the figures across the surface of the canvas? What event happened in Gauguin's life before and after he completed this painting?

6. The concept of primitivism dominates Gauguin's late work. He especially liked to work with wood to create small sculptures, reliefs, and woodcuts. Refer to the following web site for a definition of primitive at http://www.xrefer.com/entry.jsp?xrefid=145129&secid=.-. View the wooden pieces from Boston College at http://www.bc.edu/bc_org/avp/cas/fnart/art/gauguin_sculp.html. Why do you think Gauguin preferred to work with wood? What qualities does it have that enhances primitivism? What kinds of effects are created when a print is made from a woodcut?

GEORGES SEURAT
(1859–1891)

Images

The Circus, oil on canvas, 1890–1891, 73" x 59". Paris: Musée d'Orsay.

A *Sunday Afternoon on the Island of La Grande Jatte*, oil on canvas, 1884–1886, 207.6 cm. x 308 cm. Chicago: Art Institute of Chicago.

Web Addresses

About.com. *Art History with Andrea Mulder-Slater: Georges Seurat.*
http://arthistory.about.com/library/blartist_seurat.htm?terms=Seurat+Pointillism
[18 September 2002]
Technique of Pointillism described.

Art Institute of Chicago. *Art Institute of Chicago: Student and Teacher Programs: ArtAccess: Georges Seurat's A Sunday on La Grande Jatte.*
http://www.artic.edu/artaccess/AA_Impressionist/pages/IMP_7.shtml
[18 September 2002]
A *Sunday Afternoon on the Island of La Grande Jatte* (1884–1886) image and information.

Gerten-Jackson, Carol. *CGFA: A Virtual Art Museum: Seurat.*
http://sunsite.dk/cgfa/seurat/index.html (images)
http://sunsite.dk/cgfa/seurat/seurat_bio.htm *Georges Seurat* (biography)
[18 September 2002]
Image gallery and biography link.

Gerten-Jackson, Carol. *CGFA: A Virtual Art Museum: Seurat. The Circus.*
http://sunsite.dk/cgfa/seurat/p-seurat2.htm
[18 September 2002]
The Circus (1890–1891) image.

Harden, Mark. *Artchive: Seurat, Georges: A Sunday Afternoon on the Island of La Grande Jatte.*
http://www.artchive.com/artchive/S/seurat/jatte.jpg.html
[18 September 2002]
Information about and image of *A Sunday Afternoon on the Island of La Grande Jatte* (1884–1886).

Howe, Jeffery. *Boston College. Notes on Color Theory.*
http://www.bc.edu/bc_org/avp/cas/fnart/fa257/color_notes.html
[18 September 2002]
Notes on color theory.

Incursio, Inc. *WetCanvas: Georges Seurat.*
http://www.wetcanvas.com/Museum/Artists/s/Georges_Seurat/index.html
[18 September 2002]
Biography and directory of links to information and image galleries.

Incursio, Inc. *WetCanvas: Impressionism: Color and Composition Systematized.*
http://www.wetcanvas.com/Museum/Artists/s/Georges_Seurat/index.html
[18 September 2002]

Information about Seurat's theory of "color and composition systematized," which focuses on the painting *The Circus* (1890–1891).

Musée d'Orsay, Paris. *Musée d'Orsay: Georges Seurat: The Circus.*
http://www.musee-orsay.fr:8081/ORSAY/orsaygb/HTML.NSF/By+Filename/mosimple+collect+seurat +index?OpenDocument
[18 September 2002]
Information about and image of the painting *The Circus* (1890–1891).

Pioch, Nicolas. *WebMuseum, Paris: Seurat, Georges: The Circus.*
http://www.oir.ucf.edu/wm/paint/auth/seurat/circus/
[18 September 2002]
Information about and image of the painting *The Circus* (1890–1891).

Pioch, Nicolas. *WebMuseum, Paris: Seurat, Georges: Un dimanche après-midi à l'Ile de la Grande Jatte (A Sunday Afternoon on the Island of La Grande Jatte).*
http://www.oir.ucf.edu/wm/paint/auth/seurat/grande-jatte/
[18 September 2002]
Information about the painting *A Sunday Afternoon on the Island of La Grande Jatte* (1884–1886).

Site Summary

Georges Seurat approached Post-Impressionist painting more scientifically than his contemporaries did. He began his early training in 1878 at the École des Beaux Arts, where he concentrated on drawing and studied the works of Ingres and Piero della Francesca. He then studied briefly with Pierre Puvis de Chavannes and became more interested in aspects of proportion, harmony, and composition. Seurat also began to read various treatises on color theory written by Charles Blanc, Michel-Eugène Chevreul, Ogden Rood, and others. Because color became a focus of his work, he keenly examined paintings by Delacroix, Rubens, and Murillo, who were strong colorist artists. Between 1881 and 1883, Seurat began to consciously apply his color theories to his paintings. After he viewed the Fourth Impressionist Exhibition (1879), his early paintings reflect his technique of sweeping brushstrokes and texture created with paint.

Later Seurat developed a more focused use of paint, in which he applied color directly to the canvas (see his first major painting, *The Bathers,* done in 1883). Seurat's style, now known as pointillism (divisionism), is evident in the companion painting, *A Sunday Afternoon on the Island of La Grande Jatte.* He worked on this large painting for about two years and created a number of small studies. *La Grande Jatte* depicts a mixed urban society enjoying a day of leisure at a park. The painting comments on contemporary society and suggests the Post-Impressionist style of abandoning the representation of naturalism. The Post-Impressionists felt that naturalism reflects society's lust for materialism.

The formal, stylized figures in *La Grande Jatte* illustrate this viewpoint, yet Seurat shows several levels of society enjoying the same surroundings on the same picture plane. Seurat used these juxtapositions in theme and combined them with his color theory of Pointillism. Pointillist painting applies pure color to the canvas in the form of dots. It creates an optical mixture of colors that appear to blend. Seurat perfected this technique and caught the attention of some of the Symbolist artists. By 1885, Seurat's association with Symbolist theory inspired him to create emotion and rhythm with color and line. From 1887 to 1891, he created three major paintings that master this technique. These works are known as his "entertainment" paintings and depict a sideshow *(The Parade),* a dance act *(La Chahut),* and an animal act *(The Circus).* Seurat's use of color, line, and composition impart a musical rhythm and emotion to the scenes. Seurat worked intensely on these paintings; the technique alone consumed him socially and physically, and he ignored his own health and the welfare of his family. *The Circus* was never finished, and in 1891 Seurat died of ill health while preparing for an exhibition.

Discussion Questions and Activities

1. View the image galleries and read the biographies at http://sunsite.dk/cgfa/seurat/index.html and http://www.wetcanvas.com/Museum/Artists/s/Georges_Seurat/index.html. Then answer the following questions: What is the title of Seurat's first major Pointillist painting? How many major paintings did Seurat create during his short lifetime? What is the title of the companion piece?

2. Read the information on Pointillism at http://arthistory.about.com/library/blartist_seurat.htm?terms=Seurat+Pointillism. Which artists inspired Seurat to paint brighter? Who introduced him to theories about color? What color theorists did he read? Which theorist was a chemist, not an artist? What is Pointillism?

3. What colors did Seurat use to create Pointillism? What is another term for Pointillism? What is the scientific term that Seurat preferred? Try the technique by placing dots of color according to the theory (with paint or magic marker) together on a sheet of paper. Tape the sheet of paper to a wall and stand back several feet; then squint and look at the color. Do the dots blend into other colors? Do you notice that certain colors create different tones?

4. Read the *Notes on Color Theory* at http://www.bc.edu/bc_org/avp/cas/fnart/fa257/color_notes.html. What are primary colors? What are secondary colors? Use crayons, markers, or paint to answer the following questions: What colors do you get when you mix all three primary colors? What color do you get when you mix yellow and blue? Try mixing other primary or secondary colors, and create a chart of your results.

5. View the painting and read information about *A Sunday Afternoon on the Island of La Grande Jatte* (1884–1886) at http://www.oir.ucf.edu/wm/paint/auth/seurat/grande-jatte/ and http://www.artchive.com/artchive/S/seurat/jatte.jpg.html and from the Art Institute of Chicago at http://www.artic.edu/artaccess/AA_Impressionist/pages/IMP_7.shtml. How does Seurat express social views in *La Grande Jatte*? How long did it take him to create this work? Did he paint outdoors like some of the other Impressionist artists did? Why would this painting be of interest to twentieth-century Surrealist artists? What is unusual about the frame? Look at the composition and how the light is directed across the canvas. Can you tell the time of day from the shadows? Stand outside on a sunny day and notice how the shadows fall at different hours in the afternoon.

6. Refer to the following web sites and read the information and view the painting of *The Circus* (1890–1891) at http://www.oir.ucf.edu/wm/paint/auth/seurat/circus/ and from the Musée d'Orsay at http://www.musee-orsay.fr:8081/ORSAY/orsaygb/HTML.NSF/By+Filename/mosimple+collect+seurat+index?OpenDocument and from http://www.wetcanvas.com/Museum/Impressionists/History/colorcomp.html. Whose color theory did Seurat apply to his painting? What changed in his painting style because of the influence of this theorist? Why was the painting never finished? What is its theme? Name the titles of other paintings done about the same time period. What elements in the composition make your eye "swirl" upward? What image did Seurat copy from a poster? What makes this painting look like a poster?

Related Internet Sites

Impressionism and Post-Impressionism

Harden, Mark. *Artchive: Post-Impressionism.*
- http://www.artchive.com/artchive/post_impressionism.html
  [18 September 2002]
  List of Post-Impressionist artists.

Harden, Mark. *Artchive: Impressionism: (listed first by influences, then Impressionists proper, then influenced by:)*
- http://www.artchive.com/artchive/impressionism.html
  [18 September 2002]
  List of Impressionist artists.

Tigertail Associates. *Tigertail Virtual Art Museum: Impressionism.*
- http://tvm.tigtail.org/M_View/TVM/X2/b.Impressionism/impressionism.html
  [18 September 2002]

Tigertail Associates. *Tigertail Virtual Art Museum: Post-Impressionism.*
- http://tvm.tigtail.org/M_View/TVM/X2/c.PImpressionism/post-impressionism.html
  [18 September 2002]
  Image gallery of Impressionist and Post-Impressionist art.

Witcombe, Chris. *Art History Resources on the Web: 19th-Century Art.*
- http://witcombe.sbc.edu/ARTHLinks5.html
  [18 September 2002]
  Resource directory that links to information and images about nineteenth-century art.

Vincent van Gogh

Artcyclopedia. *Vincent van Gogh.*
- http://www.artcyclopedia.com/artists/van_gogh_vincent.html
  [18 September 2002]
  Directory of links to information and image galleries.

Brooks, David. *Vincent van Gogh Gallery: Starry Night.*
- http://www.vangoghgallery.com
  [18 September 2002]
  Refer to the sections on van Gogh's letters to his brother Theo and information about the painting *Starry Night.*

Center for Faith and Art. *Vincent van Gogh's Portraits by James Romaine from Re:Generation Quarterly, Fall 2000.*
- http://www.faithandart.org/vangogh2.htm
  [18 September 2002]
  Article about portraits.

Pioch, Nicolas. *WebMuseum, Paris: Gogh, Vincent van: Dr Paul Gachet.*
http://www.oir.ucf.edu/wm/paint/auth/gogh/portraits/gachet/
[18 September 2002]
Background information about Dr. Gachet.

Tigertail Associates. *Tigertail Virtual Art Museum: Post-Impressionism: Vincent van Gogh.*
- http://tvm.tigtail.org/TVM/L_View/X2/c.PImpressionism/van-gogh/van-gogh.html
  [18 September 2002]
  Image gallery.

Paul Gauguin

Artcyclopedia. *Paul Gauguin.*
- http://www.artcyclopedia.com/artists/gauguin_paul.html
  [18 September 2002]
  Directory of links to information and image galleries.

Delahunt, Michael. *ArtLex Art Dictionary: Paul Gauguin.*
- http://www.artlex.com/ArtLex/p/postimp.gauguin.html
  [18 September 2002]
  Brief background information about Gauguin and links to images.

Harden, Mark. *Artchive: Paul Gauguin: "Notes Synthetiques," by Paul Gauguin from the manuscript, c. 1888 Excerpted from "Theories of Modern Art," by Herschel B. Chipp.*
- http://www.artchive.com/artchive/G/gauguin.html
  [18 September 2002]
  An excerpt about synthetism by Gauguin from "Theories of Modern Art" by Herschel B. Chipp. Links to images.

Tigertail Associates. *Tigertail Virtual Art Museum: Post-Impressionism: Paul Gauguin.*
- http://tvm.tigtail.org/TVM/L_View/X2/c.PImpressionism/gauguin/gauguin.html
  [18 September 2002]
  Image gallery.

Georges Seurat

All About Artists. *All About Artists: Biographies: Georges Seurat.*
- http://www.allaboutartists.com/bios/seurat.html
  [18 September 2002]
  Biography.

Artcyclopedia. *Georges Seurat.*
- http://www.artcyclopedia.com/artists/seurat_georges.html
  [18 September 2002]
  Directory of links to information and image galleries.

Harden, Mark. *Artchive: Georges Seurat: From Meyer Shapiro, "Modern Art."*
- http://www.artchive.com/artchive/S/seurat.html
  [18 September 2002]
  Essay from *Modern Art* by Meyer Shapiro.

Howe, Jeffery. Boston College. *Charles Blanc, The Grammar of Painting and Engraving, translated by Kate N. Doggett, Chicago, 1889.*
- http://www.bc.edu/bc_org/avp/cas/fnart/fa257/blanc_ch1.html
  [18 September 2002]
  The Grammar of Painting and Engraving, an essay by Charles Blanc.

Incursio, Inc. *WetCanvas: Impressionism: The Circus Influence: Georges Seurat.*
■ http://www.wetcanvas.com/Museum/Impressionists/Cirque/seurat.html
   [18 September 2002]
   Information about and image of the painting *The Circus.*

Pioch, Nicolas. *WebMuseum, Paris: Seurat, Georges.*
■ http://www.oir.ucf.edu/wm/paint/auth/seurat
   [18 September 2002]
   Biography and image gallery.

Oxford Dictionary of Art (1997). From *Xrefer, The Web's Reference Engine: Pointillism.*
■ http://www.xrefer.com/entry.jsp?xrefid=145076&secid=
   [18 September 2002]
   Definition of Pointillism from the *Oxford Dictionary of Art* (1997).

CHAPTER 21

Early Modern Art and Cubism

(Circa 1895–1914)

Paul Cézanne (1839–1906), Pablo Picasso (1881–1973), Cubism (Circa 1907–1914), Georges Braque (1882–1963), Fernand Léger (1881–1955), Raymond Duchamp-Villon (1876–1918), Marcel Duchamp (1887–1968), and Diego Rivera (1886–1957)

EARLY MODERN ART

Web Addresses

Artcyclopedia. *Artists by Movement: Modernism.*
http://www.artcyclopedia.com/history/index.html
[18 September 2002]
Twentieth-century artists grouped by movement. Directory of links to information and image galleries.

Artifice. *Great Buildings Online: Architect: Frank Lloyd Wright.*
http://www.greatbuildings.com/architects/Frank_Lloyd_Wright.html
[18 September 2002]
Directory of buildings by Frank Lloyd Wright.

Artifice. *Great Buildings Online: Architect: I. M. Pei.*
http://www.greatbuildings.com/architects/I._M._Pei.html
[18 September 2002]
Directory of buildings by I. M. Pei.

Artifice. *Great Buildings Online: Architect: Le Corbusier.*
http://www.greatbuildings.com/architects/Le_Corbusier.html
[18 September 2002]
Directory of buildings by Charles Le Corbusier.

Macmillan Encyclopedia (2001). From *Xrefer, The Web's Reference Engine: Modern Art.*
http://www.xrefer.com/entry.jsp?xrefid=510271&secid=.-
[18 September 2002]
Definition of modern art from *The Macmillan Encyclopedia* (2001).

Pioch, Nicolas. *WebMuseum, Paris: The 20th century.*
http://www.ibiblio.org/wm/paint/tl/20th/
[18 September 2002]
General background information about twentieth-century modern art with links to different art movements and artists.

Witcombe, Chris. *Art History Resources on the Web: 20th-Century Art.*
http://witcombe.sbc.edu/ARTH20thcentury.html
[18 September 2002]
Resource directory that links to information about twentieth-century modern art and artists.

PAUL CÉZANNE
(1839–1906)

Images

Large Bathers, oil on canvas, 1899–1906, 208 cm. x 249 cm. Philadelphia: Philadelphia Museum of Art.

Mont Sainte-Victoire, oil on canvas, circa 1894–1900, 71.5 cm. x 92.1 cm. Cleveland: Cleveland Museum of Art.

Web Addresses

Artcyclopedia. *Paul Cézanne.*
http://www.artcyclopedia.com/artists/cezanne_paul.html
[18 September 2002]
Resource directory that links to information and image galleries about Paul Cézanne.

Cleveland Museum of Art. *Cleveland Museum of Art: Explore: Education and Research: For Schools and Teachers: Teachers Resource Center: Slide Packets: Sample Slide Packet: Impressionist and Post-Impressionist Art: Paul Cézanne: Mount Sainte-Victoire, c. 1894–1900.*
http://www.clemusart.org/educatn/trc-news/slidepac/11.html
[18 September 2002]
Mount Sainte-Victoire (circa 1894–1900) image and information.

Gerten-Jackson, Carol. *CGFA: A Virtual Art Museum: Cezanne.*
http://sunsite.dk/cgfa/cezanne/index.html (images)
http://sunsite.dk/cgfa/cezanne/cezanne_bio.htm *Paul Cézanne* (biography)
[18 September 2002]
Image gallery and biography link.

Harden, Mark. *Artchive: Cezanne, Paul: Large Bathers 1899–1906.*
http://www.artchive.com/artchive/C/cezanne/bathers.jpg.html
[18 September 2002]
Large Bathers (1899–1906) image.

Olga's Gallery. *Paul Cézanne.*
http://www.abcgallery.com/C/cezanne/cezanne.html
[18 September 2002]
Image gallery and biography link.

Philadelphia Museum of Art, Philadelphia, PA. *Philadelphia Museum of Art: Collections: European Painting and Sculpture: The Large Bathers: Paul Cézanne.*
http://www.philamuseum.org/collections/euro-painting/W1937-1-1.shtml
[18 September 2002]
Large Bathers (1899–1906) image and information.

PABLO PICASSO
(1881–1973)

Images

Les Demoiselles d'Avignon, oil on canvas, 1907, 8' x 7'8" (243.9 cm. x 233.7 cm.). New York: The Museum of Modern Art.

Web Addresses

Artcyclopedia. *Pablo Picasso.*
http://www.artcyclopedia.com/artists/picasso_pablo.html
[18 September 2002]
Resource directory that links to information and image galleries of Pablo Picasso's works.

Gerten-Jackson, Carol. *CGFA: A Virtual Art Museum: Picasso.*
http://sunsite.dk/cgfa/picasso/index.html (images)
http://sunsite.dk/cgfa/picasso/picasso_bio.htm *Pablo Picasso* (biography)
[18 September 2002]
Image gallery and biography link.

Museum of Modern Art, New York, NY. *Museum of Modern Art: Collection: Painting and Sculpture: Pablo Picasso. Les Demoiselles d'Avignon. 1907.*
http://www.moma.org/collection/paintsculpt/picasso.demoiselles.html
[18 September 2002]
Les Demoiselles d'Avignon (1907) image.

Olga's Gallery. *Pablo Picasso.*
http://www.abcgallery.com/P/picasso/picasso.html
[18 September 2002]
Image gallery and biography link.

Site Summary

The term early-twentieth-century modern art encompasses an amalgamation of the arts, cultures, philosophies, religions, social issues, ethics, and technology. Church and state are no longer the dominant patrons; because of this, artists began to enjoy more freedom to express themselves. They experimented with ideas of abstraction, themes of psychological and social issues, and mixed culturalism in a single society. Technology and the advent of the Industrial Revolution at the turn of the century complemented these experimentations in the visual arts. Photography not only was a technological innovation but also expanded into its own art form.

The work of Paul Cézanne launched ideas of modernism in the early twentieth century. His work featured a use of color, shape, and volume that inspired the art of the Fauves, Expressionists, Cubists, Surrealists, and Abstractionists. Cézanne viewed nature as forms that can be transformed into combinations of the shapes of cylinders, spheres, and cones. The structures of modern architecture have also incorporated this philosophy, as seen in the designs of Walter Gropius, Charles Le Corbusier, Frank Lloyd Wright, and I. M. Pei. Pablo Picasso is an artistic icon whose work spans more than three-quarters of the century and continues to influence others. Public sculpture expanded its presence to be more than just commissioned pieces; several have become known for the controversy they stirred up as well as their aesthetics. Social issues such as AIDS, sexuality, conceptualism, advertisement, and multiculturalism made their own visual statements during the second half of the twentieth century. The age-old question "What is next?" remains for the twenty-first century. The dawn of the Internet and computer-generated images has already affected the arts. But what remains a constant is the ability to create art by using one's imagination, emotion, intellect, skill, and a medium for expression.

Discussion Questions and Activities

1. Read the biographies and view the image galleries of Paul Cézanne at http://sunsite.dk/cgfa/cezanne /index.html and at http://www.abcgallery.com/C/cezanne/cezanne.html. Who are some of the Impressionist artists that Cézanne knew? Which artist had a major influence upon the development of his painting technique using color and planar compositions? What major art movement developed from this type of painting? Compare Cézanne's *Large Bathers* at http://www.artchive.com/artchive/C /cezanne/bathers.jpg.html to Picasso's *Les Demoiselles d'Avignon* at http://www.moma.org/collection /paintsculpt/picasso.demoiselles.html (minimize each image on the toolbar in order to view both). What is the shape of the composition created by the positions of the figures in both paintings? How do both artists use their brushstrokes in these paintings? Do you see much detail in these paintings? If not, why?

2. View the image of Cézanne's *Mont Sainte-Victoire* (circa 1894–1900) and read the information at http://www.clemusart.com/educatn/trc-news/slidepac/11.html. What was unique about this series of mountain scenes? What made Cézanne's paintings different from those of the Impressionists? View the image and identify the elements of the scene that appear flat and geometric. How do you think he used his paintbrush to paint this scene?

3. Refer to the following web sites that give background information about early-twentieth-century modern art at http://www.ibiblio.org/wm/paint/tl/20th/ and at http://www.xrefer.com/entry.jsp?xrefid =510271&secid=. What art movements of the early twentieth century were popular in Italy, England, Russia, Germany, and France? When did the center of modern art shift to New York? Which American artist was a known leader of abstraction after World War II?

4. Read about "The Age of Machinery" at http://www.ibiblio.org/wm/paint/tl/20th/machinery.html from the WebMuseum, Paris. What group of artists was interested in aspects of machinery and what country did they come from? How does their name relate to their artwork? Read the article "Towards Abstraction" at http://www.ibiblio.org/wm/aint/tl/20/abstract.html. What is the name of the group who began to paint abstract forms? What does its name mean? Is color important in their artwork? If so, why? Who was the artist credited to paint the first abstract picture? Name the three artists of this group. What happened to some of these artists because of World War I?

5. Refer to the structures by Le Corbusier at http://www.greatbuildings.com/architects/Le_Corbusier.html, by Frank Lloyd Wright at http://www.greatbuildings.com/architects/Frank_Lloyd_Wright.html, and by I. M. Pei at http://www.greatbuildings.com/architects/I._M._Pei.html. What buildings have the shape of a triangle? What are the geometric shapes in Wright's buildings? Did Le Corbusier use the shape of a cylinder in any of his buildings? If so, which one? Name some of the famous museum buildings that I. M. Pei designed. What is unique about them?

6. Read about Fauvism from the Artcyclopedia at http://www.artcyclopedia.com/history/index.html and from http://witcombe.sbc.edu/ARTH20thcentury.html. Who originated this art movement? What does the word "fauve" mean, and how does it relate to this type of art? What was the focus of the paintings by the Fauves? How did Fauvist art affect other art movements throughout the century?

CUBISM
(Circa 1907–1914)

Web Addresses

Artcyclopedia. *Artists by Movement: Cubism: Europe, 1908–1920.*
http://www.artcyclopedia.com/history/cubism.html
[18 September 2002]
Resource directory that links to information and image galleries on cubism and a list of artists.

Asakawa, Sachiyo. *Cubism, Cubists: Picasso and Braque, and Their Great Influences.*
http://sachiyoasakawa.tripod.com/
[18 September 2002]
Article on cubism, cubists (Picasso and Braque), and their influences.

Delahunt, Michael. *ArtLex: Analytic Cubism.*
http://www.artlex.com/ArtLex/a/analyticcubism.html
[18 September 2002]

Delahunt, Michael. *ArtLex: Cubism.*
http://www.artlex.com/ArtLex/c/cubism.html
[18 September 2002]
Background information and image gallery.

Oxford Dictionary of Art (1997). From *Xrefer, The Web's Reference Engine: Cubism.*
http://www.xrefer.com/entry.jsp?xrefid=143452&secid=
[18 September 2002]
Definition of cubism from the *Oxford Dictionary of Art* (1997).

Oxford Dictionary of Art (1997). From *Xrefer, The Web's Reference Engine: Papier Collé (French: "Pasted Paper").*
http://www.xrefer.com/entry.jsp?xrefid=144942&secid=
[18 September 2002]
Definition of papier collé from the *Oxford Dictionary of Art* (1997).

Thames and Hudson Dictionary of Art Terms (1984). From *Xrefer, The Web's Reference Engine: Collage.*
http://www.xrefer.com/entry.jsp?xrefid=648402&secid=
[18 September 2002]
Definition of collage from *The Thames and Hudson Dictionary of Art Terms* (1984).

PABLO PICASSO
(1881–1973) (Cubism)

Images

Les Demoiselles d'Avignon, 1907, oil on canvas, 8' x 7'8". New York: Museum of Modern Art.

Still-Life with Chair Caning, 1911–1912, collage of oil, oilcloth, and pasted paper simulating chair caning on canvas, 10½" x 13¾". Paris: Musée Picasso.

Web Addresses

Artcyclopedia. *Picasso.*
http://www.artcyclopedia.com/artists/picasso_pablo.html
[18 September 2002]
Directory of links to information and image galleries about Pablo Picasso.

Harden, Mark. *Artchive: Pablo Picasso.*
http://www.artchive.com/artchive/P/picasso.html
[18 September 2002]
Biography with link to "View Image List."

Museum of Modern Art, New York, NY. *Museum of Modern Art: Collection: Painting and Sculpture: Pablo Picasso. Les Demoiselles d'Avignon. 1907.*
http://www.moma.org/collection/paintsculpt/picasso.demoiselles.html
[18 September 2002]
Les Demoiselles d'Avignon (1907) image.

Olga's Gallery. *Pablo Picasso.*
http://www.abcgallery.com/P/picasso/picasso.html
[18 September 2002]
Image gallery and biography link.

Olga's Gallery. *Pablo Picasso. Still-Life with Chair Caning.*
http://www.abcgallery.com/P/picasso/picasso78.html
[18 September 2002]
Still-Life with Chair Caning (circa 1911–1912) image.

Tigertail Associates. *Tigertail Virtual Art Museum: European Art Before World War I: Picasso Cubism and Abstraction.*
http://tigtail.org/L_View/TVM/B/European/a.%20pre%20WW%20I/picasso/picasso-cubism.html
[18 September 2002]
Image gallery of Picasso cubism and abstraction.

GEORGES BRAQUE
(1882–1963)

Images

Fruitdish and Glass, 1912, pasted papers and charcoal on paper, 62 cm. x 44.5 cm. (24⅜" x 17½"). Private collection.

Houses at L'Éstaque, 1908, oil on canvas, 73 cm. x 60 cm. (28¾" x 23½"). Bern: Kunstmuseum Bern.

Web Addresses

Artcyclopedia. *Georges Braque.*
http://www.artcyclopedia.com/artists/braque_georges.html
[19 September 2002]
Directory of links to information about and image galleries of Georges Braque.

Harden, Mark. *Artchive: Georges Braque: From "The A–Z of Art: The World's Greatest and Most Popular Artists and Their Works," by Nicola Hodge and Libby Anson.*
http://www.artchive.com/artchive/B/braque.html
[19 September 2002]
Biography and image gallery.

Harden, Mark. *Artchive: Braque, Georges: Fruitdish and Glass: September 1912.*
http://www.artchive.com/artchive/B/braque/papcol1.jpg.html
[19 September 2002]
Fruitdish and Glass (1912) image.

Pioch, Nicolas. *WebMuseum, Paris: Braque, Georges: Houses at L'Estaque.*
http://www.hipernet.ufsc.br/wm/paint/auth/braque/houses-estaque/
[19 September 2002]
Houses at L'Éstaque (1908) image.

Tigertail Associates. *Tigertail Virtual Art Museum: European Art Before World War I: Georges Braque.*
http://www.tigtail.org/L_View/TVM/B/European/a.%20pre%20WW%20I/braque/braque.html
[19 September 2002]
Image gallery.

FERNAND LÉGER
(1881–1955)

Images

The City, 1919, oil on canvas, 7'7" x 9'½". Philadelphia: Philadelphia Museum of Art.

Web Addresses

Artcyclopedia. *Fernand Léger.*
http://www.artcyclopedia.com/artists/leger_fernand.html
[19 September 2002]
Directory of links to information and image galleries about Fernand Léger.

Harden, Mark. *Artchive: Fernand Léger: The following review of the Leger retrospective held at the Museum of Modern Art in 1998 was written by Dr. Francis V. O'Connor.*
www.artchive.com/artchive/L/leger.html#images
[19 September 2002]
A review of the 1998 Léger exhibition.

Horsley, Carter B. *The City Review: Fernand Léger: The Museum of Modern Art, February 15 to May 12, 1998: "La Ville" ("The City"), oil on canvas, 1910.*
http://www.thecityreview.com/leger.html
[19 September 2002]

Philadelphia Museum of Art, Philadelphia, PA. *Philadelphia Museum of Art: Collections: Modern and Contemporary Art: The City: Fernand Léger.*
http://www.philamuseum.org/collections/modern_contemporary/1952-61-58.shtml
[19 September 2002]
The City (1919) image.

RAYMOND DUCHAMP-VILLON
(1876–1918)

Images

Large Horse, original 1914, then cast (1961), bronze, 1000 mm. x 987 mm. x 660 mm. London: Tate Gallery.

Web Addresses

Artcyclopedia. *Raymond Duchamp-Villon.*
http://www.artcyclopedia.com/artists/duchamp-villon_raymond.html
[19 September 2002]
Directory of links to information about and image galleries of Raymond Duchamp-Villon.

Oxford Dictionary of Art (1997). From *Xrefer, The Web's Reference Engine: Duchamp-Villon, Raymond.*
http://www.xrefer.com/entry.jsp?xrefid=143601&secid=
[19 September 2002]
Brief background information about Raymond Duchamp-Villon.

Tate Gallery, London. *Tate Gallery: General Collection: Duchamp-Villon, Raymond: Large Horse.*
http://www.tate.org.uk/servlet/AText?id=4031&sid=842511084&group=general&name=&start=1&end=2&type=fc
[19 September 2002]
Large Horse (original 1914; then cast, 1961, bronze).

MARCEL DUCHAMP
(1887–1968)

Images

Nude Descending a Staircase (No. 2), oil on canvas, 1912, 57" x 35". Philadelphia: Philadelphia Museum of Art.

Web Addresses

Artcyclopedia. *Marcel Duchamp.*
http://www.artcyclopedia.com/artists/duchamp_marcel.html
[19 September 2002]
Directory of links to information and image galleries of Marcel Duchamp.

Harden, Mark. *Artchive: Marcel Duchamp.*
http://www.artchive.com/artchive/D/duchamp.html
[19 September 2002]
Biography and image gallery.

Philadelphia Museum of Art, Philadelphia, PA. *Philadelphia Art Museum: Collections: Modern and Contemporary Art: Nude Descending a Staircase (No. 2): Marcel Duchamp.*
http://www.philamuseum.org/collections/modern_contemporary/1950-134-59.shtml
[19 September 2002]
Nude Descending a Staircase (No. 2), oil on canvas, 1912, 57" x 35".

DIEGO RIVERA
(1886–1957)

Images

Portrait of Jacques Lípchitz, oil on canvas, 1914. Private collection.

Web Addresses

Gerten-Jackson, Carol. *CGFA: A Virtual Art Museum: Diego Rivera.*
http://sunsite.dk/cgfa/rivera/index.html (images)
http://sunsite.dk/cgfa/rivera/rivera_bio.htm *Diego Rivera* (biography)
[19 September 2002]
Image gallery and biography link.

Buch, Fred. *Cubism: Diego Rivera: Master Cubist: Portrait of Jacques Lipschitz, 1914.*
http://www.fbuch.com/cubism.htm
[19 September 2002]
Portrait of Jacques Lipschitz (1914).

ArtSceneCal. *ArtScene: The Guide to Art Galleries and Museums in Southern California:*
    Articles: July/August, 1999: Diego Rivera by Margarita Nieto.
http://artscenecal.com/ArticlesFile/Archive/Articles1999/Articles0799/DRiveraB.html
[19 September 2002]
Biography of Deigo Rivera.

Artcyclopedia. *Diego Rivera.*
http://www.artcyclopedia.com/artists/rivera_diego.html
[19 September 2002]
Directory of links to information and image galleries of Diego Rivera's works.

Rivera, Javier A. *Virtual Diego Rivera Web Museum.*
http://www.diegorivera.com/index.html
[19 September 2002]
Home page of the Diego Rivera Web Museum.

Site Summary

Paul Cézanne's paintings at the turn of the century utilized color and planar compositions to create landscapes and still lifes. Cubist artists, such as Pablo Picasso and Georges Braque, were intrigued with Cézanne's theories and ways of depicting objects using planes to create volume and mass. But they took Cézanne's method one step further. They created multiple views of figures and objects and placed them on the same picture plane—all of which were to be viewed simultaneously. Color no longer dominated the composition; the object became the focus of the painting. The first hint of the Cubist style was Picasso's painting titled *Les Demoiselles d'Avignon* (1907) and Braque's landscape series of the *Houses at L'Éstaque* (1908). Art critic Louis Vauxcelles helped to coin the term Cubist in a 1908 review of Braque's paintings, describing them as "geometric schemas and cubes." This early phase of Cubism (1907–1909) is often referred to as the "Cézanne phase."

The second phase of Cubism is referred to as "analytic" and shows a breakdown of form by viewing the same object from different angles. Picasso and Braque began to experiment with this by applying other pieces of matter on their paintings, thus developing the collage and papier collé technique of the Cubists. After 1913, the object became extremely distorted and often unrecognizable; this period is known as the "synthetic phase." Juan Gris and Fernand Léger expanded other Cubist techniques of composition.

Another core of artists, known as the Puteaux group (Francis Picabia, Jacques Villon, Raymond Duchamp-Villon, and Marcel Duchamp), created alternative interpretations of Cubism. Duchamp-Villon depicts strength and power by building up volume and planes in his three-dimensional sculptures. Marcel Duchamp was more conceptual and wanted the viewer to look at things that already existed in a different context. By taking an already-made object and either placing it in a particular space or giving it a different name, he believed he would give the item a different interpretation. Thus, the "readymade" was created along with the controversy surrounding the idea as well as establishing the Dada movement.

Marcel Duchamp helped bring concepts of Cubism and other avant-garde art to the United States through the 1913 Armory Show of the International Exhibition of Modern Art in New York. Other Cubist followers were Alexander Archipenko, Ossip Zadkine, Jacques Lipchitz, Marc Chagall, and Diego Rivera. The outbreak of World War I in 1914 dispersed many of the Cubist artists, although some of them adhered to the structure of Cubism in their later work. Others sought to develop new ideas that were influenced by Cubism. The progressiveness of the Futurists, the nonsensible art of Dada, and the bizarre imaginative art of the Surrealists are a few of Cubism's offspring.

Discussion Questions and Activities

1. Refer to the Artcyclopedia article on Cubism at http://artcyclopedia.com/history/cubism.html and ArtLex at http://www.artlex.com/ArtLex/c/cubism.html. What non-European art inspired the Cubists? View Picasso's painting of *Les Demoiselles d'Avignon* (1907) at http://www.moma.org/collection /paintsculpt/picasso.demoiselles.html. What elements in this painting reflect this non-European influence? How many different poses does it depict? Is there any type of background? How did Picasso model the shape of the figures? View other work by Cubist artists at http://artcyclopedia.com/history /cubism.html. Are there any other artists that depict non-European imagery? If so, who are they? Describe the images.

2. Refer to the definition of Cubism at the Xrefer web site at http://www.xrefer.com/entry.jsp?xrefid =143452&secid= and an essay at http://sachiyoasakawa.tripod.com/. What traditional aspects of painting did Braque abandon? What types of colors were used in the analytical style? What is the difference between analytical and synthetic Cubism? Who else utilized the collage technique? A collage is more than merely cutting out images and pasting them together on the same surface. As an activity, cut out images of the same type of object seen from different views. An example might be various images of a car: These might consist of its interior, exterior, wheels, muffler, radio, and so on. Arrange the images together on card-stock paper—add objects such as a car freshener, pieces of a car model, a piece of tire, and so forth. Did you find that the object you chose had a number of images that you could cut out and apply?

3. Picasso created a collage titled *Still-Life with Chair Caning* (1912), and Braque created a papier collé titled *Fruitdish and Glass* (1912). Read the definitions of collage and papier collé from the Xrefer web site at http://xrefer.com/entry.jsp?xrefid=648402&secid=.- and http://xrefer.com/entry.jsp?xrefid =144942. Also read background information at http://www.artchive.com/artchive/B/braque.html and an article titled "Cubism 1907–1917" at http://www.abcgallery.com/P/picasso/picassobio.html. What is the difference between a collage and a papier collé? What phase of Cubism do these pieces belong to? What objects were used in Picasso's piece? What was unique to Braque's piece? Identify the actual pieces used in both artworks.

4. Read the review of the 1998 retrospective of Fernand Léger's exhibition and view the images at http://www.artchive.com/archive/L/leger.html#images. What is the theme of many of his paintings? What kinds of colors did he use? Describe the figures that he paints and compare them to those of other Cubist artists such as Picasso. Describe his interpretation of *The City* at http://www.philamuseum .org/collections/modern_contemporary/1952-61-58.shtml.

5. Raymond Duchamp-Villon and Marcel Duchamp were brothers who were part of the Puteaux group of Cubists. Read background information about Duchamp-Villon at http://www.xrefer.com/entry.jsp ?xrefid=143601&secid= and view the image of the *Large Horse* (1914) at http://www.tate.org.uk /servlet/AText?id=4031&sid=842511084&group=general&name=&start=1&end=2&type=fc from the Tate Gallery. How does the sculpture depict the power of a horse? How does the title "Horse" relate to the power of an engine? Describe the surface of the sculpture. Does the composition give you the sense of turning, like an engine? If so, what elements create this feeling? Did you realize that you would have to move around this sculpture in order to view it from all angles?

6. Marcel Duchamp created quite a controversy by exhibiting his 1912 painting *Nude Descending a Staircase (No.2)* at the 1913 Armory Show in New York. View the image and read the background information from the Philadelphia Museum of Art at http://www.philamuseum.org/collections/modern _contemporary/1950-134-59.shtml. Why were Americans upset by this exhibit? Why was this painting considered outrageous? Do the colors and composition adhere to the Cubists' techniques?

7. As a young man, Mexican artist Diego Rivera studied in Europe and worked with several of the Cubists in Paris. View some of his paintings at http://www.fbuch.com/cubism.htm and read the information at http://artscenecal.com/ArticlesFile/Archive/Articles1999/Articles0799/DRiveraB.html from Arts Central.com. What are the colors used during this period? Can you distinguish the analytical paintings from the synthetic Cubist ones? Which artistic influences did Rivera introduce to other Mexican artists after he came back from Europe?

Related Internet Sites

Early Modern Art

Artcyclopedia. *Artists by Movement: Abstract Expressionism Centered in New York City, 1946 to 1960's.*
- http://www.artcyclopedia.com/history/abstract-expressionism.html
  [19 September 2002]
  Background information and a list of artists of the abstract Expressionist movement that was centered in New York City from 1946 to the 1960s.

Artcyclopedia. *Artists by Movement: Expressionism Centered in Germany, c. 1905 to 1940's.*
- http://www.artcyclopedia.com/history/expressionism.html
  [19 September 2002]
  List of Expressionist artists including Die Brücke, Der Blaue Reiter, Die Neue Sachlichkeit, and the Bauhaus School of Germany.

Artcyclopedia. *Artists by Movement: Fauvism 1898–1908.*
- http://www.artcyclopedia.com/history/fauvism.html
  [19 September 2002]
  List of Fauve artists of the early twentieth century.

Delahunt, Michael. *ArtLex Art Dictionary: Abstraction.*
- http://www.artlex.com/ArtLex/a/abstraction.html
  [19 September 2002]
  Definition and images related to abstraction.

Perl, Jed. *New Republic Online (April 26–May 3, 1999 Issue): What "W" Stands For: On Art: What is Modern Art, Anyway?*
- http://www.tnr.com/archive/0499/042699/perl042699.html
  [19 September 2002]
  Article titled "On Art: What Is Modern Art, Anyway?" by Jed Perl.

Pioch, Nicolas. *WebMuseum, Paris: Cézanne, Paul: Bathers.*
- http://www.ibiblio.org/wm/paint/auth/cezanne/bath/
  [19 September 2002]
  Information and image gallery about Cézanne's bathers series.

Pioch, Nicolas. *WebMuseum, Paris: Pre-War American Painting.*
- http://www.ibiblio.org/wm/paint/tl/20th/pre-war.html
  [19 September 2002]
  Background information about prewar American paintings and links to artists.

Tigertail Associates. *Tigertail Virtual Art Museum: European Art Before World War I (part 1 of 3).*
- http://tvm.tigtail.org/TVM/B/European/a.%20pre%20WW%20I/european-a.html
  [19 September 2002]
  Image gallery of European art before World War I.

Tigertail Associates. *Tigertail Virtual Art Museum: European Art Between the World Wars.*
- http://tvm.tigtail.org/TVM/M_View/B/European/b.%20between%20wars/european-b.html
  [20 September 2002]
  Image gallery of European art between the world wars.

Cubism

About.com. *Art History 101 with Andrea Mulder-Slater: Cubism 1905–1939.*
- http://arthistory.about.com/library/bl101_cubism.htm
  [19 September 2002]
  General information and links to specific artists related to Cubism.

Trachtman, Paul. *Smithsonian Magazine (July 1996): When Cubism Met the Decorative Arts in France.*
- http://www.smithsonianmag.si.edu/smithsonian/issues96/jul96/cubism.html
  [20 September 2002]
  Information about Sonia Delaunay and the way Cubism affected the decorative arts.

CHAPTER 22

Dada and Surrealism

(Circa 1916–1922 and Circa 1924–1930s)

Marcel Duchamp (1887–1968), Francis Picabia (1879–1953), Man Ray (1890–1976), Max Ernst (1891–1976), Joan Miró (1893–1983), René Magritte (1898–1967), and Salvador Dalí (1904–1989)

DADA

Web Addresses

Andrade, Mary Anne. Collin County Community College, Decatur, GA. *Dada.*
http://jade.ccccd.edu/Andrade/WorldLitII2333/dada.htm
[19 September 2002]
Background information and links to images about Dada.

Hermus Fine Arts. *Dada.*
http://www.hermus.com/dada.htm
[19 September 2002]
Information about Dada.

Kortum, Richard. East Tennessee State University, Johnson City, TN. *Dada Gallery.*
http://www.etsu.edu/philos/classes/rk/modernzenith/htmdescriptionpages/dadagallery.htm
[19 September 2002]
Information and image gallery of Dada art.

Oxford Dictionary of Art (1997). From *Xrefer, The Web's Reference Engine: Ready-Made.*
http://www.xrefer.com/entry.jsp?xrefid=145190&secid=
[19 September 2002]
Definition of ready-made.

MARCEL DUCHAMP
(1887–1968)

Images

Fountain, glazed ceramic with black paint, original 1917, then replicated in 1964, 14" x 19$\frac{5}{16}$" x 24$\frac{5}{8}$". San Francisco: San Francisco Museum of Modern Art.

L.H.O.O.Q. (Mona Lisa with a moustache and goatee), perfected readymade, pencil on reproduction, 1919, 7¾" x 4". France: Musée Maillol.

Web Addresses

Artcyclopedia. *Marcel Duchamp.*
http://www.artcyclopedia.com/artists/duchamp_marcel.html
[19 September 2002]
Directory of links to information and image galleries of Marcel Duchamp.

Beat Museum. *Marcel Duchamp 1887–1968: Selected Works.*
http://www.beatmuseum.org/duchamp/marcelduchamp.html
[19 September 2002]
Biography and links to images.

Beniger, James R. University of Southern California, Los Angeles, CA. *Comm 544: Image Library: L.H.O.O.Q., Duchamp, 1919.*
http://www.usc.edu/schools/annenberg/asc/projects/comm544/library/images/116.html
[22 September 2002]

Harden, Mark. *Artchive: Marcel Duchamp: Text from Janis Mink, "Marcel Duchamp, 1887–1968: Art as Anti-Art."*
http://www.artchive.com/artchive/D/duchamp.html
[19 September 2002]
Biography with a link to "View Image List."

Kortum, Richard. East Tennessee State University, Johnson City, TN. *Dada Gallery: Marcel Duchamp. L.H.O.O.Q. 1919.*
http://www.etsu.edu/philos/classes/rk/modernzenith/htmdescriptionpages/lhooq.htm
[19 September 2002]
L.H.O.O.Q. (Mona Lisa with a moustache and goatee) (1919) information and image.

San Francisco Museum of Modern Art, CA. *San Francisco Museum of Modern Art: Collections: Recent Acquisitions: Marcel Duchamp: Fountain 1917/1964 (this Arturo Schwarz edition of Fountain is the fourth full-scale version).*
http://www.sfmoma.org/collections/recent_acquisitions/ma_coll_duchamp.html
[19 September 2002]
Fountain (original 1917, then replicated in 1964) information and image.

Succession Marcel Duchamp. *Marchel Duchamp: Porte-bouteilles (Bottle Rack).*
http://www.zumbacombo.com/duchamp/rack.html
[13 October 2002]

University Honors Program, University of South Dakota, Vermillion, SD. *Marcel Duchamp's L.H.O.O.Q.*
http://www.usd.edu/honors/HWB/hwb_a/robin2.htm
[19 September 2002]
L.H.O.O.Q, (Mona Lisa with a moustache and goatee) (1919) background information only (no image).

FRANCIS PICABIA
(1879–1953)

Images

The Cacodylic Eye, oil on canvas with collage of photographs, postcards, and cut papers, 1921, 148.6 cm. x 117.4 cm. Paris: Pompidou Center.

Web Addresses

Andrade, Mary Anne. Collin County Community College, Decatur, GA. *Dada: Picabia, Cacodylic Eye.*
http://jade.ccccd.edu/Andrade/WorldLitII2333/dada.htm
[21 September 2002]
Background information and links to images about Dada (includes an image of *The Cacodylic Eye* [1921]).

Artcyclopedia. *Francis Picabia.*
http://www.artcyclopedia.com/artists/picabia_francis.html
[22 September 2002]
Directory of links to information and image galleries.

Centre Georges Pompidou, Paris, France. *Centre Georges Pompidou: Museum: Modern Art: Francis Picabia: L'Oeil Cacodylate (The Cacodylic Eye).*
http://www2.centrepompidou.fr/cgi-bin/collection_e-96&work&zoom+AM_4408_P.htm
[21 September 2002]
The Cacodylic Eye (1921) image.

Solomon R. Guggenheim Museum, New York, NY. *Guggenheim Museum: The Collection: Francis Picabia Biography.*
http://www.guggenheimcollection.org/site/artist_bio_125.html
[19 September 2002]
Biography.

MAN RAY
(1890–1976)

Images

Untitled (Self-Portrait Cast in Plaster with Mannequin Hands, Angular Ball, and Light Bulb), gelatin silver print photograph, 1933, 29.3 cm. x 23 cm. San Francisco: San Francisco Museum of Modern Art.

Web Addresses

Artcyclopedia. *Man Ray.*
http://www.artcyclopedia.com/artists/man_ray.html
[22 September 2002]
Directory of links to information and image galleries.

Harden, Mark. *Artchive: Man Ray: Text from The Encyclopedia of Photography (1986).*
http://www.artchive.com/artchive/M/man_ray.html
[22 September 2002]
Background information and links to images.

San Francisco Museum of Modern Art, CA. *San Francisco Museum of Modern Art: Collections: Photography: Man Ray: Untitled (Self-Portrait cast in plaster with mannequin hands, angular ball and light bulb 1933).*
http://www.sfmoma.org/collections/photography/ma_coll_manray.html
[22 September 2002]
Untitled (Self-Portrait Cast in Plaster with Mannequin Hands, Angular Ball, and Light Bulb) (1933) image.

Site Summary

Early twentieth-century modern art evolved into many factions. The arts were affected by changes in industry, psychology, politics, and war on a worldwide scale. Artists felt that, through their art, they had a voice with which to communicate their ideas and philosophies. Literary, performing, and visual artists banned together and united their ideas through writings, music, theater, and artworks. Dada was a movement that spread throughout Europe and the United States (especially New York).

Dadaists created outrageous and nonsense pieces of art as a reaction to the irrationalities of war and current society. Their goal was to provoke an intellectual dialogue so that people would begin questioning their values. The original group of Dada artists (Hugo Ball, Emmy Hennings, Tristan Tzara, Richard Huelsenbeck, Hans Arp, Marcel Janco, and Hans Richter) came together in Zurich in 1916. The name "dada" was randomly chosen from a French dictionary definition meaning "hobbyhorse." The name made no sense, and that was the foundation of the Dadaist ideology.

Marcel Duchamp, Francis Picabia, Marius de Zayas, and photographer Man Ray formed a New York group of Dada artists. This group introduced the concept of "ready-mades." A ready-made was an ordinary mass-produced object that, once placed in a different context, would be transformed into a work of art. The object was not altered from its original state. Marcel Duchamp shocked the conventional American museum audience by placing a common bottle rack and a urinal on a museum pedestal. Francis Picabia eventually left the New York group and returned to Europe in 1917. He began to publish the review *391* and contributed to the Zurich publication known as *Dada*. Artists Richard Huelsenbeck, John Heartfield, Raoul Hausmann, Hannah Hoch, and George Grosz formed the German faction of Dada. Eventually the Dada groups disintegrated because of conflicting opinions. Some of these artists went on to become the Surrealists of the 1920s and 1930s.

Discussion Questions and Activities

1. Read background information about Dada at http://jade.ccccd.edu/Andrade/WorldLitII2333/dada.htm and at http://www.etsu.edu/philos/classes/rk/modernzenith/htmdescriptionpages/dadagallery.htm. Where was the original group formed? How was Dada introduced in the United States? How did this group choose their name, and what does it mean? Why was Dada art so outrageous? What was happening in Europe at the time the Dada artists formed their group?

2. Read the biographical information and view the image galleries of Marcel Duchamp's works at http://www.beatmuseum.org/duchamp/marcelduchamp.html and from http://www.artchive.com/artchive /D/duchamp.html. Why did Duchamp come to New York? What was the name of the 1913 New York exhibition he participated in? What is important about this exhibition? What artists did he meet with whom he eventually formed the New York version of Dada? View the list of Duchamp images on the Web at http://www.artchive.com/artchive/D/duchamp.html and name some of the titles of Dada artworks. Describe some of the compositions. Do any of the artworks make sense to you?

3. Duchamp's ready-mades sparked controversy in the traditional art world. Read the definition of a ready-made at http://www.xrefer.com/entry.jsp?xrefid=145190&secid= and refer to the web site at http://www.sfmoma.org/collections/recent_acquisitions/ma_coll_duchamp.html. How does the term ready-made relate to these pieces? What is Duchamp's *Fountain*? Where did he get the piece, and what is it made of? What is the significance of the signature "R. Mutt 1917"? Do you have one of these in your home? Is it positioned the same way as Duchamp's piece? What makes this piece so ridiculous? What happened to the original piece? Duchamp challenged the museum's audience by asking them what they considered as "art." With a friend, view the image at http://www.zumbacombo.com /duchamp/rack.html and describe what you see to each other. Did you find that each of you saw something different even though you looked at the same piece? Do you understand why Duchamp took already-made items and placed them in exhibits so that people would have multiple interpretations of them? Was the controversy over the fact that the piece was a commonly used item or the fact that people had different interpretations of the item because it was placed in a museum exhibit?

4. View the image of Duchamp's *L.H.O.O.Q. (Mona Lisa with a moustache and goatee)* at http://www .usc.edu/schools/annenberg/asc/projects/comm544/library/images/116.html and read the background information at http://www.usd.edu/honors/HWB/hwb_a/robin2.htm. What is the title of the original painting? What did Duchamp do to this piece to alter its appearance? Does this make sense to you? What was his intention?

5. Read information about Francis Picabia at http://www.guggenheimcollection.org/site/artist_bio_125.html and view the image of *The Cacodylic Eye* (1921) at http://jade.ccccd.edu/Andrade/WorldLitII2333 /dada.htm. What style did he paint in before 1913? What 1913 New York exhibition did he participate in? Who was the Dada artist he became good friends with? What does *The Cacodylic Eye* look like to you? Does it remind you of graffiti? Does the writing on the painting make any kind of sense? Did Picabia stay with the Dada group?

6. Read about Man Ray at http://www.artchive.com/artchive/M/man_ray.html and view his photograph *Untitled (Self-Portrait Cast in Plaster with Mannequin Hands, Angular Ball, and Light Bulb)* (1933) at http://www.sfmoma.org/collections/photography/ma_coll_manray.html. What different groups of artists did he work with? What kind of photographs did he create? When did he meet Marcel Duchamp? Why do you think *Untitled* is a self-portrait? Man Ray moved on from the Dada group to the Surrealists. Why do you think this photograph is more surreal than Dada?

SURREALISM
(Circa 1924–1930s)

Web Addresses

Artcyclopedia. *Artists by Movement: Surrealism: Europe, 1924 to 1950s.*
http://www.artcyclopedia.com/history/surrealism.html
[22 September 2002]
Directory of links to information and image galleries.

Banjo Ruthless Creations. Washington University Medical School, St. Louis, MO. *Automatic Writing.*
http://www.madsci.org/~lynn/juju/surr/zamaton/auto.html
[22 September 2002]
Definition of automatic writing.

Delahunt, Michael. *ArtLex: Surrealism.*
http://www.artlex.com/ArtLex/s/surrealism.html
[22 September 2002]
Definition of surrealism.

OnFineArt.com. *On Fine Art.com: Surrealism.*
http://www.onfineart.com/surrealism.htm
[22 September 2002]

Pioch, Nicolas. *WebMuseum, Paris: Surrealism.*
http://www.ibiblio.org/wm/paint/glo/surrealism/
[22 September 2002]
Background information about surrealism.

MAX ERNST
(1891–1976)

Images

The Eye of Silence, oil on canvas, circa 1946, 42½" x 55½". Missouri: Washington University Gallery of Art.

Two Children Are Threatened by a Nightingale, oil on wood with wood construction, 1924. New York: Museum of Modern Art.

Web Addresses

Beniger, James R. University of Southern California, Los Angeles, CA. *Comm 544: Image Library: Two Children Are Threatened by a Nightingale: Max Ernst.*
http://www.usc.edu/schools/annenberg/asc/projects/comm544/library/images/343.html
[22 September 2002]

OnFineArt.com. *On Fine Art.com: Surrealism: Max Ernst, Two Children Are Threatened by a Nightingale.*
http://www.onfineart.com/surrealism.htm
[22 September 2002]

Surrealist.com. *Surrealist.com: Ernst, Max.*
http://www.surrealist.com/new/selectedinfo.asp?artistid=11
[22 September 2002]
Ernst biography.

Washington University in St. Louis, St. Louis, MO. *Washington University in St. Louis Gallery of Art: Permanent Collection: Eye of Silence: Max Ernst.*
http://galleryofart.wustl.edu/art/imgLarge/51lg.html
[22 September 2002]
The Eye of Silence (circa 1946) image and background information.

JOAN MIRÓ
(1893–1983)

Images

The Policeman, oil on canvas, 1925, 248 cm. x 194.9 cm. Chicago: Art Institute of Chicago.

Web Addresses

Art Institute of Chicago. *Art Institute of Chicago: Collections: Joan Miró: The Policeman.*
http://www.artic.edu/aic/collections/modern/71pc_miro.html
[22 September 2002]
The Policeman (1925) image and background information.

Gerten-Jackson, Carol. *CGFA: A Virtual Art Museum: Miró.*
http://sunsite.dk/cgfa/miro/index.html (images)
http://sunsite.dk/cgfa/miro/miro_bio.htm *Joan Miró* (biography)
[22 September 2002]
Image gallery and biography link.

Malek, Massoud. California State University at Hayward. *Joan Miró.*
http://www.mcs.csuhayward.edu/~malek/Miro.html
[22 September 2002]
Biography information.

RENÉ MAGRITTE
(1898–1967)

Images

Treachery of Images (Ceci n'est pas une pipe), oil on canvas, circa 1928–1929, 25$\frac{7}{16}$" x 37$\frac{1}{16}$". Los Angeles: Los Angeles County Museum of Art.

Web Addresses

Gerten-Jackson, Carol. *CGFA: A Virtual Art Museum: Magritte.*
http://sunsite.dk/cgfa/magritte/index.html (images)
http://sunsite.dk/cgfa/magritte/magritte_bio.htm (biography)
[22 September 2002]
Image gallery and biography link.

Matsumoto, Tetsuya. Nagoya University, Nagoya, Japan. *René Magritte: The Betrayal of Images (Ceci n'est pas une pipe).*
http://www.ohnishi.nuie.nagoya-u.ac.jp/~matumoto/art/images/pipe.jpg
[22 September 2002]
Treachery of Images (Ceci n'est pas une pipe) (circa 1928–1929) image.

XS4ALL. *René Magritte: 10 Genius Paintings.*
http://www.xs4all.nl/~renebos/magritte.html
[22 September 2002]
Treachery of Images (Ceci n'est pas une pipe) (circa 1928–1929) image.

SALVADOR DALÍ
(1904–1989)

Images

The Persistence of Memory, oil on canvas, 1931, 24.2 cm. x 33 cm. New York: Museum of Modern Art.

Web Addresses

British Broadcasting Corporation. *BBC Four: Voices from the Archive: Salvador Dali.*
http://www.bbc.co.uk/bbcfour/voices/profilepages/dalis2.shtml
[13 October 2002]
Biography.

Salvador Dalí Museum, Inc. *Dali Museum: Collection: Brief Biography.*
Http://www.salvadordalimuseum.org/cgi-bin/SoftCart.exe/collection
/bio.html?L+dali+sqqa2130+1032650326
Biography.

Salvador Dalí Museum, Inc. *Dali Museum: Collection: Surrealism Period (1929–40).*
http://www.salvadordalimuseum.org/cgi-bin/SoftCart.exe/collection/surreal/index
.html?L+dali+sqqa2130+1032652398
[22 September 2002]

Sarphy Production. *The ArtFile: Salvador Dali: Dali Gallery: The Persistence of Memory.*
http://www.the-artfile.com/uk/artists/dali/persmemory.htm
[22 September 2002]

Tigertail Associates. *Tigertail Virtual Art Museum: European Art Before the First World War: Salvador Dalí.*
http://tvm.tigtail.org/TVM/M_View/B/European/b.%20between%20wars/Spanish/dali/dali-1.html#dali_2
[22 September 2002]
Gallery of images.

Site Summary

Surrealism was an intellectual movement that had its origin in Paris and grew out of the Dada movement after World War I. Surrealists were influenced by the psychological theories of Freud and Jung, as well as the political writings of Karl Marx. Its founder, André Breton, made an official declaration in his publication, *Manifeste du Surrealisme* (1924), in which he criticized ideas of coherence and reason in a time of chaos. But Breton did not pursue the Dada approach of expressing destruction and negativity. He was more interested in an unrealistic idealism and extreme ultrarealism—thus a surreal approach to human thoughts and behavior. Artists, poets, writers, and filmmakers who were attracted to this group embraced the concept of expressing themselves through thoughts and images of the subconscious. The practice of "automatic writing" inspired images that seemed nonfunctional, irrational, dreamlike, and suspended in time.

Max Ernst and Joan Miró were two of the first painters to join the Surrealists. The first major exhibition of Surrealist art took place at the Galerie Pierre in Paris in 1925. Works by Max Ernst, Joan Miró, Giorgio De Chirico, Paul Klee, Man Ray, and Pablo Picasso were exhibited. By 1928, the emerging group of Belgian Surrealists was being led by René Magritte. The publication of Breton's second manifesto (1929) caught the attention of Salvador Dalí. Dalí's art manifested hallucinatory images linked to his fascination with psycho-analysis and his right-wing politics.

Other Surrealist groups flourished around the world throughout the 1930s. On a trip to Mexico in 1938, Breton allied himself with Leon Trotsky and Diego Rivera to form the International Federation of Independent Revolutionary Artists. Breton continued his journey to the United States and Cuba in the early 1940s and met artists such as Alexander Calder, David Hare, and Wilfredo Lam. After World War II, artists were still intrigued by Breton's ideas of Surrealism, but their artistic approach took on a different tone reflecting the spirit of the times. The last two major exhibitions of Surrealist art appeared in 1959 at the Galerie Daniel Cordier in Paris and in 1965 at the International Exhibition of Surrealism at the Galerie de l'Oeil in Paris. The year 1966 marked not only the death of Surrealism as a movement but also that of André Breton himself.

Discussion Questions and Activities

1. Refer to the background information about Surrealism at http://www.ibiblio.org/wm/paint/glo/surrealism/ and the Artcyclopedia at http://www.artcyclopedia.com/history/surrealism.html. Which major artists were involved with the Surrealist movement? Who was the founder, and what important Surrealist publication did he write? What types of imagery are depicted in Surrealist art? What movement did it develop from? What is the difference between Surrealism and Dada?

2. "Automatic writing" is a technique of writing down any thought that comes to mind. Surrealist paintings seem to give the impression that the artist would paint anything that would come to mind, as if they were dreaming. View images by different Surrealist artists from the Artcyclopedia directory listing at http://www.artcyclopedia.com/history/surrealism.html. What images remind you of dreams? Why do you think the idea of "flowing" relates to dreams? Refer to the article at http://www.madsci .org/~lynn/juju/sur/zamaton/auto.html about automatic writing to understand the concept of letting our thoughts flow. Are some of your dreams like images that go through your mind that may not have anything to do with one another? Is automatic writing a way to jot down ideas that come to mind like our dreams? Do you think the artists used the idea of automatic writing, but rather than writing the ideas they had, they painted them as dreams?

3. Refer to information about Max Ernst at http://www.surrealist.com/new/selectedinfo.asp?artistid=11 and at http://galleryofart.wustl.edu/art/imgLarge/511g.html and view the image of *The Eye of Silence* (circa 1946). What technique did he develop in 1925? Describe this painting technique. How did Ernst create the landscape in *The Eye of Silence*? What colors are used in the landscape? Are they natural or do they look surreal? Try the technique by using paints (acrylic, watercolor, or oil) dripped onto a piece of wax paper. Transfer this onto a sheet of paper and create a landscape. Describe what you see there.

4. View Ernst's painting *Two Children Are Threatened by a Nightingale* (1924) at http://www.usc.edu /schools/annenberg/asc/projects/comm544/library/images/343.html or at http://www.onfineart.com /surrealism.htm. What do you see? What is surreal-looking about this painting? Do you think it illustrates a childhood fear? How does Ernst depict fear?

5. Refer to Joan Miró's biography at http://sunsite.dk/cgfa/miro/miro_bio.htm and images at http:// sunsite.dk/cgfa/magritte/index.html and the painting *The Policeman* (1925) at http://www.artic.edu /aic/collections/modern/71pc_miro.html. What style did his early work look like, and what types of colors did he use? How did he get involved with Surrealism? What kinds of imagery does he depict in these Surrealist paintings (view the image gallery)? What are the shapes in the painting *The Policeman* (1925)? What technique did he use for this painting, and what later art movement did it influence?

6. Read Magritte's biography at http://sunsite.dk/cgfa/magritte/magritte_bio.htm and view images at http://sunsite.dk/cgfa/magritte/index.html and the painting of *Treachery of Images (Ceci n'est pas une pipe)* (circa 1928–1929) at http://www.ohnishi.nuie.nagoya-u.ac.jp/~matumoto/art/images/pipe.jpg. Do the themes of Magritte's paintings follow the concepts of Surrealism? What are some of the strange images from his paintings? Describe what you see in this painting. What are the conflicting elements of his painting *Treachery of Images (Ceci n'est pas une pipe)*? Is this a pipe or is it a painting of a pipe?

7. Read the biography of Salvador Dalí at http://www.salvadordalimuseum.org/cgi-bin/SoftCart.exe /collection/bio.html?L+dali+sqqa2130+1032650326 and view the image gallery at http://tvm.tigtail .org/TVM/M_View/B/European/b.%20between%20wars/Spanish/dali/dali-1.html#dali_2. Where did Dalí grow up, and why was it an important place to him? When did Dalí join the Surrealists? Why did the Surrealists expel him from their group? View the image gallery and identify the surreal images. Which paintings have landscapes in the background? Would you consider these paintings dreamlike or nightmares?

8. View Dalí's *The Persistence of Memory* (1931) at http://www.the-artfile.com/uk/artists/dali /persmemory.htm. Is this a landscape or a still-life with watches? What makes each watch in the painting seem illogical? What hour do the watches show, or do they show different times? Does the landscape indicate any elements that may specify the time of day, a certain place, or a season? Are the colors natural? Does this painting follow the concepts of Surrealism?

Related Internet Sites

Dada

Beniger, James R. University of Southern California, Los Angeles, CA. *Comm 544: Image Library: L.H.O.O.Q., Duchamp, 1919.*
■ http://www.usc.edu/schools/annenberg/asc/projects/comm544/library/images/116.html
[22 September 2002]
Marcel Duchamp's *L.H.O.O.Q. (Mona Lisa with a moustache and goatee)* (1919) image.

Pioch, Nicolas. *WebMuseum, Paris: Dada.*
■ http://www.ibiblio.org/wm/paint/glo/dada
[22 September 2002]
Background information about Dada.

Tal, Ehud. *Focus on Art: Marcel Duchamp: Fountain 1964 (replica of 1917 original).*
■ http://www.geocities.com/Paris/8111/fountain.htm
[22 September 2002]
Marcel Duchamp's *Fountain* (original 1917, then replicated in 1964) image.

Surrealism

Nakazato LaFreniere, Maren. *Hungry Flower Photography, Surrealists, Books.*
■ http://hungryflower.com/leonreme.html
[22 September 2002]
Directory of resources about Surrealist women.

Surrealist.com. *Surrealist.com: André Breton, What is Surrealism?*
■ http://www.surrealist.com/new/what_is_surrealism.asp
[22 September 2002]
Surrealism according to Breton.

Surrealist.com. *Surrealist.com: Surrealism.*
■ http://www.surrealist.com/new/default.asp
[22 September 2002]
Surrealism article.

Max Ernst

Artcyclopedia. *Max Ernst.*
■ http://www.artcyclopedia.com/artists/ernst_max.html
[22 September 2002]

Buell, John. *DaDa Online: Max Ernst.*
■ http://www.peak.org/~dadaist/English/Graphics/ernst.html
[22 September 2002]
Ernst biography.

Joan Miró

Artcyclopedia. *Joan Miró.*
- http://www.artcyclopedia.com/artists/miro_joan.html
  [22 September 2002]

Surrealist.com. *Surrealist.com: Miró, Joan.*
- http://www.surrealist.com/new/selectedinfo.asp?artistid=21
  [22 September 2002]
  Biography information.

René Magritte

Artcyclopedia. *René Magritte.*
- http://www.artcyclopedia.com/artists/magritte_rene.html
  [22 September 2002]
  Directory of links to information and image galleries.

Malek, Massoud. California State University at Hayward. *René Francois Ghislain Magritte.*
- http://www.mcs.csuhayward.edu/~malek/Magrit.html
  [22 September 2002]
  Brief biographical information and some images.

Surrealist.com. *Surrealist.com: Magritte, René.*
- http://www.surrealist.com/new/selectedinfo.asp?artistid=17
  [22 September 2002]
  Biographical information.

Virtuo. *Magritte: Biography.*
- http://www.magritte.com/2.cfm
  [22 September 2002]
  Time line.

Salvador Dalí

Artcyclopedia. *Salvador Dali.*
- http://www.artcyclopedia.com/artists/dali_salvador.html
  [22 September 2002]
  Directory of links to information and image galleries.

MicroVision. *WebCoast: Salvador Dali.*
- http://www.daliweb.tampa.fl.us/
  [22 September 2002]
  List of various resources on Dalí. Includes images.

Mishka. *Salvador Dali Art Gallery.*
- http://wwww.dali-gallery.com/dali.htm
  [22 September 2002]
  Various links to information about Dalí and Surrealism.

Salvador Dalí Museum, Inc. *Dali Museum: Education: Teacher Resources: Destination Dalí: Lesson Plans from the Salvador Dalí Museum.*

■ http://www.salvadordalimuseum.org/cgi-bin/SoftCart.exe/edu/teacher/guide/index.html?L+dali +sqqa2130+1034560412
[13 October 2002]

CHAPTER 23

Art Since the 1930s

(Social Realism and WPA/FAP Art)

Ben Shahn (1898–1969), Dorothea Lange (1895–1965), Diego Rivera (1886–1957), Wassily Kandinsky (1866–1944), Arshile Gorky (1904–1948), Jackson Pollock (1912–1956), Bridget Riley (1931–   ), Andy Warhol (1928–1987), Robert Rauschenberg (1925–   ), Laurie Anderson (1947–   ), Cindy Sherman (1954–   ), Maya Lin (1959–   )

BEN SHAHN
(1898–1969)

Image

The Passion of Sacco and Vanzetti, mosaic tile mural, installed in 1967, 60' x 12'. New York: Syracuse University.

Web Addresses

Anreus, Alejandro. *NY Arts Magazine (Vol.6 No.10 October 2001): Ben Shahn and The Passion of Sacco and Vanzetti.*
http://nyartsmagazine.com/58/shahn.htm
[23 September 2002]

Myhashiro, Todd. Tower Hill School, Wilmington, DE. *Ben Shahn: As It Is: The Passion of Sacco and Vanzetti.*
http://www-2.towerhill.org/SJhtml/Todd/shahn.html
[23 September 2002]
Background information and image of *The Passion of Sacco and Vanzetti* (installed in 1967).

Spartacus Educational. *Education on the Internet & Teaching History Online: Ben Shahn.*
http://www.spartacus.schoolnet.co.uk/ARTshahn.htm
[23 September 2002]
Biography of Ben Shahn.

DOROTHEA LANGE
(1895–1965)

Image

Farm Security Administration Collection Series, photographs, circa 1940. Washington, D.C.: National Archives and Records Administration, Records of the Bureau of Agricultural Economics.

Web Addresses

Library of Congress. *Prints and Photographs Division. Dorothea Lange's "Migrant Mother." Photographs in the Farm Security Administration Collection: An Overview.*
http://www.loc.gov/rr/print/128_migm.html
[23 September 2002]
Background information and images of Dorothea Lange's *Migrant Mother* photographs.

Oakland Museum of California. *Oakland Museum of California: Art: Dorothea Lange Archive.*
http://www.museumca.org/global/art/collections_dorothea_lange.html
[23 September 2002]
Background information and images of the "Dorothea Lange Collection."

DIEGO RIVERA
(1886–1957),
JOSÉ CLEMENTE OROZCO
(1883–1949),
and
DAVID ALFARO SIQUEIROS
(1896–1975)

Images

Detroit Industry, mural by Diego Rivera, circa 1932–1933. Detroit: Detroit Institute of Arts.

Echo of a Scream, enamel on wood painting by David Alfaro Siqueiros, 1937, 121.9 cm. x 91.4 cm. New York: Museum of Modern Art.

The Epic of American Civilization, mural by José Clemente Orozco, circa 1932. Hanover, NH: Baker Library at Dartmouth College.

Web Addresses

Detroit Institute of Arts, Detroit, MI. *Detroit Institute of Arts: Education: Lesson Plans: Diego Rivera: Detroit Industry Murals Lesson Plans for Teachers: Detroit Industry Information and Images—Index.*
http://www.dia.org/rivera/infoidx.htm
[23 September 2002]
Background information and images of Diego Rivera's *Detroit Industry* (circa 1932–1933).

Hood Museum of Art. Dartmouth College, Hanover, NH. *The Epic of American Civilization.*
http://www.dartmouth.edu/~hood/collections/orozco-murals.html
[23 September 2002]
Images of the painting *The Epic of American Civilization,* a mural by José Clemente Orozco (circa 1932).

PBS. *Rings of Passion: Anguish: David Alfaro Siqueiros: Echo of a Scream.*
http://www.pbs.org/ringsofpassion/anguish/siqueiros.html
[23 September 2002]
Image and background information about *Echo of a Scream* (1937) by David Alfaro Siqueiros.

___

Abstraction

___

WASSILY KANDINKSY (1866–1944)

___

Image

Study for Improvisation V, oil on cardboard pulp, 1910, approximately 28" x 28½". Minneapolis: Minneapolis Institute of Arts.

___

Web Addresses

Delahunt, Michael. *ArtLex: Abstraction.*
http://www.artlex.com/ArtLex/a/abstraction.html
[23 September 2002]
Definition of abstraction with a list of artists.

Minneapolis Institute of Arts, MN. *Minneapolis Institute of Arts: The Collection: Wassily Kandinsky: Study for Improvisation V.*
http://www.artsmia.org/uia-bin/uia_doc.cgi/query/2?uf=uia_jNttUV
[23 September 2002]
Image and information about *Study for Improvisation V.*

ARSHILE GORKY
(1904–1948)

Image

Painter and Model, lithograph on cream wove paper, 1931. Worcester, MA: Worcester Art Museum.

Web Addresses

Solomon R. Guggenheim Museum, New York, NY. *Guggenheim Museum: The Collection: Artists: Arshile Gorky: Biography.*
http://www.guggenheimcollection.org/site/artist_bio_57.html
[23 September 2002]
Biography.

University of Michigan School of Information and Library Studies. *Painter and Model.*
http://www.si.umich.edu/Art_History/demoarea/details/1948_1.353.html
[23 September 2002]

JACKSON POLLOCK
(1912–1956)

Image

Number 10, oil, enamel, and aluminum paint on canvas mounted on panel, 1949, approximately 46.1 cm. x 272.4 cm. Boston: Museum of Fine Arts, Boston.

Web Addresses

Museum of Fine Arts, Boston. *Museum of Fine Arts, Boston: Guide to the Collection: Modern World: Jackson Pollock: Number 10.*
http://www.mfa.org/handbook/portrait.asp?id=375&s=9
[23 September 2002]
Image and information about the painting *Number 10* (1949).

Op, Pop, and Assemblage

BRIDGET RILEY
(1931–)

Image

Balm, oil on canvas, 1964, approximately 6½' x 6½'. Washington, D.C.: National Gallery of Art.

Web Addresses

Artcyclopedia. *Artists by Movement: Optical Art: 1950s to 1960s.*
http://www.artcyclopedia.com/history/optical.html
[23 September 2002]
Information on optical art from the 1950s to the 1960s.

Beniger, James R. University of Southern California, Los Angeles, CA. *Comm 544: Image Library: Balm: Bridget Riley.*
http://www.usc.edu/schools/annenberg/asc/projects/comm544/library/images/785.html
[23 September 2002]
Image of the painting *Balm* (1964).

ANDY WARHOL
(1928–1987)

Image

Last Self-Portrait, acrylic and silkscreen on canvas, 1986, 203.2 cm. x 203.2 cm. New York: Metropolitan Museum of Art.

Web Addresses

Harden, Mark. *Artchive: Andy Warhol: From "American Visions," by Robert Hughes.*
http://www.artchive.com/artchive/W/warhol.html
[23 September 2002]
Biography and link to "View Images List."

Metropolitan Museum of Art, New York. *Metropolitan Museum of Art: The Collection: Modern Art: Last Self-Portrait: Andy Warhol.*
http://www.metmuseum.org/collections/view1.asp?dep=21&full=0&item=1987%2E88
[23 September 2002]
Background information and image of the *Last Self-Portrait* (1986).

ROBERT RAUSCHENBERG
(1925–)

Image

Trophy II (for Teeny and Marcel Duchamp), oil, charcoal, paper, fabric, metal on canvas, drinking glass (not original), metal chain, spoon, 1960, 90" x 118". Minneapolis: Walker Art Center.

Web Addresses

ArtsConnectEd. *ArtsConnectEd: Walker Art Center: Minneapolis Institute of Arts: Robert Rauschenberg Trophy II (for Teeny and Marcel Duchamp).*
http://www.artsconnected.org/artsnetmn/whatsart/rausch.html
[26 September 2002]
Image and information about *Trophy II (for Teeny and Marcel Duchamp)* (1960).

Performance Art, Photography, and Public Monuments

LAURIE ANDERSON
(1947–   )

Image

Night in Baghdad, performance, circa 1990.

Web Addresses

Art21, Inc. *PBS: Art: 21—Art in the Twenty-First Century: Laurie Anderson.*
http://www.pbs.org/art21/artists/anderson/
[26 September 2002]
Biography.

Clemovich, Robert A. Rochester Institute of Technology, Rochester, NY. *Laurie Anderson: Night in Baghdad.*
http://www.rit.edu/~rac2112/anderson.html/html
[28 September 2002]
Biography and sound plug-in of the performance of *Night in Baghdad.*

CINDY SHERMAN
(1954–   )

Image

Untitled Film Still #30, gelatin silver print, 1979, 76.2 cm. x 101.6 cm. San Francisco: San Francisco Museum of Modern Art.

Web Addresses

Museum of Modern Art, New York, NY. *Museum of Modern Art: Collection: Photography: Cindy Sherman. Untitled Film Still #21. 1978.*
http://www.moma.org/docs/collection/photography/c96.htm
[26 September 2002]

Museum of Modern Art, New York, NY. *Museum of Modern Art: What's On Now: Online Projects: Index of Artists: Solo Exhibitions and Artist Projects: Cindy Sherman: The Complete Untitled Film Stills.*
http://www.moma.org/exhibitions/sherman/
[23 September 2002]

San Francisco Museum of Modern Art, CA. *San Francisco Museum of Modern Art: Collections: Photography: Cindy Sherman: Untitled Film Still #30, 1979.*
http://www.sfmoma.org/collections/photography/ma_coll_sherman.html
[26 September 2002]
Image of the photograph print *Untitled Film Still #30* (1979).

Williams College Museum of Art. Williamstown, MA. *Artnet Speak Out! Sherman: Cindy Sherman: Untitled, 1991.*
http://www.williams.edu/WCMA/artnet/kids/sherman.html
[26 September 2002]
Biography.

MAYA LIN
(1959–   )

Image

Vietnam Veterans Memorial, black granite panels, etched with the names of dead and missing soldiers of the Vietnam War, dedicated on Veterans Day, November 13, 1982. Washington, D.C.: National Mall.

Web Addresses

Art21, Inc. *PBS: Art: 21—Art in the Twenty-First Century: Maya Lin.*
http://www.pbs.org/art21/artists/lin/
[26 September 2002]
Biography.

Artifice, Inc. *Great Buildings Online: Architect: Maya Lin.*
http://www.greatbuildings.com/architects/Maya_Lin.html
[26 September 2002]
Background information and a list of structures.

Sullivan, Mary Ann. Bluffton College, Bluffton, OH. *Digital Imaging Project: Vietnam Veterans Memorial: Maya Lin.*
http://www.bluffton.edu/~sullivanm/vietnam/vietnamlin.html
[26 September 2002]
Information about and images of the *Vietnam Veterans Memorial* (dedicated on November 13, 1982).

Site Summary

Since the 1930s, the world has changed in many ways. The Industrial Revolution had a major impact on technology, transportation, and communication. People have become more aware of events around the world as they happen. Artists are communicating their ideas and opinions through their artwork, which is often recognized internationally. Visual artists have addressed issues such as revolutions, world wars, the Depression, civil wars, the development of nuclear warheads, medical advances, and philanthropy. Social Realism of the 1930s documented social injustices, questioned the reasons for war, and addressed the plight of the poor and the division of society into classes.

Artists such as Ben Shahn and the Mexican muralists, Diego Rivera, José Clemente Orozco, and David Alfaro Siqueiros, painted their feelings about these issues on public walls for all to see. The photographs of Dorothea Lange documented the struggles of society during the Great Depression. Her photographs were commissioned by the federal government under the Farm Security Administration.

Other federal art programs were the Works Progress Administration (WPA) and the Federal Art Project (FAP). These programs (1935–1943) hired thousands of artists to create photographs, murals, and sculptures for public buildings throughout the country. The programs created jobs for artists and promoted an awareness of art and culture throughout the United States.

Abstract art of the twentieth century encompasses a wide range of interpretations. Artists used the basic elements of shape, form, color, light, and line to create an expression of their ideas. Abstraction is not limited to twentieth-century art, however. Abstract imagery has always been utilized in other cultures and eras. Wassily Kandinsky and Arshile Gorky used abstraction to simulate rhythm, speed, and symbolic iconography. Jackson Pollock's version of abstraction was considered an attitude. He wanted to be spontaneous, free, and unconventional, so his images are wild, loose, and sporadic. Abstraction will continue to change over time.

The art of the 1960s and 1970s evolved into the visual impact associated with the Op (optical) and Pop (popular) era. Optical effects made things look visually provocative. The paintings of artists such as Bridget Riley and Richard Anuszkiewicz were intriguing and mind altering. The media popularized certain images commonly seen in the art of Andy Warhol. Warhol took those images and turned them into popular icons of art. Experimentation combining a variety of materials is evident in the assemblages of Robert Rauschenberg. Live "performance art" is another way artists express their conceptual ideas. The performance is the art, and the artists often use their own bodies as the vehicle. Laurie Anderson, Bruce Nauman, and Vito Acconci performed their conceptual ideas in an artistic presentation before audiences.

Early photography documented events and visually recorded personal memories. Eventually artists began to experiment with photography on an aesthetic level. For Cindy Sherman, documentation has become more than just a frozen moment in time. She uses photography as a way to deliver a message of observation behind and in front of the camera lens.

Public monuments often glorify or honor brave people. Monuments that address social issues and promote healing and resolution are that by Maya Lin. Art will continue to evolve and revolve around human factors. Life events, physical surroundings, and conceptual ideas will always be an impetus for artists to express themselves.

Discussion Questions and Activities

1. Ben Shahn helped to introduce the concept of social realism to art. Read his biographies and view the image of *The Passion of Sacco and Vanzetti* (installed 1967) at http://www-2.towerhill.org/SJhtml /Todd/shahn.html and at http://www.spartacus.schoolnet.co.uk/ARTshahn.htm. What initially inspired his artwork? Who were Nicola Sacco and Bartolomeo Vanzetti? Why was Shahn so interested in their story? What does this mural look like? Where was it installed? Who do you think sees the mural? Why did Shahn feel that he had to create this mural? What organization did he work for after 1934? What were the themes of these murals?

2. Dorothea Lange's photographs of the late 1920s and 1930s were part of the Works Progress Admin-istration and the Federal Art Project. Refer to http://www.loc.gov/rr/print/128_migm.html and http://www.museumca.org/global/art/collections_dorothea_lange.html for images and biographical information. What is the title of the series she produced for the FAP? What was the theme of these photographs? Do you consider this a documentary? Describe some of the images. Why did Lange want to photograph these people? What are some other themes of her photographs? Why are these photographs considered an aspect of Social Realism?

3. The murals and paintings by Mexican artists Diego Rivera, José Clemente Orozco, and David Alfaro Siqueiros were an important aspect of Social Realism. View images at http://www.dia.org/rivera /infoidx.htm, at http://web.dartmouth.edu/~hood/collections/orozco-murals.html, and at http://www .pbs.org/ringsofpassion/anguish/siqueiros.html. What are the themes of these paintings? In which ones do you find social issues represented? Do you think that the paintings document certain events? Are these artists capturing the ideas of Social Realism?

4. Abstract art varies among artists. Read the definition of abstraction from ArtLex at http://www .artlex.com/ArtLex/a/abstraction.html and view the images of Kandinsky, Gorky, and Pollock at the following web sites: http://www.si.umich.edu/Art_History/demoarea/details/1948_1.353.html; http:// www.mfa.org/handbook/portrait.asp?id=375&s=9; and http://www.artsmia.org/uia-bin/uia_doc.cgi /list/218?uf=mia_collection.ldb&key=paintings&noframes=x&page_len=10&hr=http%3A%2F%2Fwww .artsmia.org%2Fpermanent%2Fintro.html&nd=355. Does the definition of abstraction apply to all of these artworks? How does each artist render shapes and forms? In which artwork can you deter-mine a figure? Describe Pollock's technique of painting.

5. Read about Op art at http://www.artcyclopedia.com/history/optical.html and view the painting *Balm* (1964) by Bridget Riley at http://www.usc.edu/schools/annenberg/asc/projects/comm544/library /images/785.html. How does an artist create optical illusions using abstract forms? When was the term Op art coined? Is math important to optical art? Which early-twentieth-century artists experimented with optical illusions? What elements does Riley use to create optical movement in this painting? How does she manipulate the shapes and colors in it?

6. Andy Warhol and the term Pop art are almost synonymous. View Warhol's image of himself at http://www.metmuseum.org/collections/view1.asp?dep=21&full=0&item=1987%2E88 and read the background information. What kind of artistic background did he have? What did he introduce to the contemporary art scene? What kinds of images did he use? What is unusual about this self-portrait? What painting technique did he use to create this image? Why do you think he chose camouflage colors for his self-portrait?

7. Another technique that artists experimented with during the late 1950s and early 1960s was assemblage. Refer to http://www.artsconnected.org/artsnetmn/whatsart/rausch.html and view the image and the vocabulary terms that apply to Robert Rauschenberg's *Trophy II (for Teeny and Marcel Duchamp)* (1960). What is an assemblage? What is *Trophy II* made of? Who was Rauschenberg honoring by creating this piece? How are the objects in the composition arranged? Does he use lettering? What is it supposed to signify?

8. You can explore the performance art of Laurie Anderson at http://www.rit.edu/~rac2112/anderson.html. Read her biography at http://www.pbs.org/art21/artists/anderson/. Where did she first begin to perform? What kind of instrument does she play? What other types of media does she include? What does she do in her performance of *Night in Baghdad* (circa 1990)? What is she poking fun at?

9. Cindy Sherman uses herself as the subject of her photographs. Refer to http://www.williams.edu /WCMA/artnet/kids/sherman_info.html and view the photograph print at http://www.sfmoma .org/collections/photography/ma_coll_sherman.html of *Untitled Film Still #30* (1979). Who does Sherman often photograph? Are these prints self-portraits? What does she do to herself for the photograph? What is the theme of *Untitled Film Still #30* (1979)? How does she place herself in the composition?

10. Maya Lin has produced some of the most powerful American monuments of the last quarter of the twentieth century. Read her biography at http://www.pbs.org/art21/artists/lin/ and view the images of the *Vietnam Veterans Memorial* at http://www.bluffton.edu/~sullivanm/vietnam/vietnamlin.html. Name some of the things that inspired Lin's artwork. What was she trying to accomplish with her design of the *Vietnam Veterans Memorial*? How is this memorial situated on the National Mall? What are the visitors to the memorial doing in many of the photographs? Do you feel that this memorial is an area where people are solemn and reflective? What do you think about the color of the granite panels?

Related Internet Sites

Ben Shahn

Artcyclopedia. *Ben Shahn.*
- http://www.artcyclopedia.com/artists/shahn_ben.html
  [26 September 2002]

Williams College Museum of Art. Williamstown, MA. *American Collections: Ben Shahn: Portrait of Walker Evans.*
- http://www.williams.edu/WCMA/collections/american/bshahn_wevans.html
  Image of *Portrait of Walker Evans* (1931).

President and Fellows of Harvard College. *Harvard University Art Museums: Fogg Art Museum: Ben Shahn: Untitled (Houston Street Playground, New York City).*
- http://www.artmuseums.harvard.edu/fogg/shahnpic.html
  [26 September 2002]
  Image of the photograph *Untitled (Houston Street Playground, New York)* (circa 1932–1936).

Dorothea Lange

Artcyclopedia. *Dorothea Lange.*
- http://www.artcyclopedia.com/artists/lange_dorothea.html
  [26 September 2002]

Library of Congress. *America's Story from America's Library!: Dorothea Lange.*
- http://www.americaslibrary.gov/cgi-bin/page.cgi/aa/lange
  [26 September 2002]
  Biography and images.

NARA: U.S. National Archives and Records Administration. *Picturing the Century: One Hundred Years of Photography from the National Archives: Portfolios: Dorothea Lange.*
- http://www.archives.gov/exhibit_hall/picturing_the_century/portfolios/port_lange.html
  [26 September 2002]
  Background information and images.

Diego Rivera

Artcyclopedia. *Diego Rivera.*
- http://www.artcyclopedia.com/artists/rivera_diego.html
  [26 September 2002]

Detroit Institute of Arts, Detroit, MI. *Detroit Institute of Arts: Education: Lesson Plans: Diego Rivera: Detroit Industry Murals Lesson Plans for Teachers: Site Map: Lesson Plans.*
- http://www.dia.org/rivera/sitemap.htm
  [13 October 2002]

Rivera, Javier A. *Virtual Diego Rivera Web Museum: Detroit Industry or Man and Machine, South Wall.*
- http://www.diegorivera.com/murals/detroit3.html
  [26 September 2002]
  Image of *Detroit Industry* (circa 1932–1933) (in Spanish).

José Clemente Orozco

Art Institute of Chicago. *Art Institute of Chicago: Student and Teacher Programs: ArtAccess: José Clemente Orozco.*
- http://www.artic.edu/artaccess/AA_Modern/pages/MOD_10.shtml
  [26 September 2002]
  Background information and image of *Zapata* (1930).

Artcyclopedia. *José Clemente Orozco.*
- http://www.artcyclopedia.com/artists/orozco_jose_clemente.html
  [26 September 2002]

David Alfaro Siqueiros

Artcyclopedia. *David Alfaro Siqueiros.*
- http://www.artcyclopedia.com/artists/siqueiros_david_alfaro.html
  [26 September 2002]

Wassily Kandinsky

Minneapolis Institute of Arts, MN. *Minneapolis Institute of Arts: The Collection: Wassily Kandinsky: Am Stande.*
- http://www.artsmia.org/uia-bin/uia_doc.cgi/query/1?uf=uia_NADjvN
  [27 September 2002]
  Image and information about the painting *Am Stande* (1903).

Museum of Fine Arts, Boston. *Museum of Fine Arts, Boston: Guide to the Collection: Modern World: Wassily Kandinsky: Poster for the first Phalanx exhibition, 1901.*
- http://www.mfa.org/handbook/portrait.asp?id=357.5&s=9
  [27 September 2002]
  Image of a poster for the First Phalanx Exhibition (1901).

State Hermitage Museum, St. Petersburg, Russia. *State Hermitage Museum: Digital Collections: Wassily Kandinsky.*
- http://www.hermitagemuseum.org/fcgi-bin/db2www/quickSearch.mac/gallery?selLang=English&tmCond=kandinsky
  [27 September 2002]
  Extensive Kandinsky collection.

Arshile Gorky

Artcyclopedia. *Arshile Gorky.*
■ http://www.artcyclopedia.com/artists/gorky_arshile.html
[30 July 2002]
Directory of links to information and image galleries.

Brain-Juice.Com, Inc. *Arshile Gorky.*
■ http://www.brain-juice.com/cgi-bin/show_bio.cgi?p_id=82
[27 September 2002]

Jackson Pollock

Artcyclopedia. *Artists by Movement: Abstract Expressionism Centered in New York City, 1946 to 1960s.*
■ http://www.artcyclopedia.com/history/abstract-expressionism.html
[27 September 2002]

Artcyclopedia. *Jackson Pollock.*
■ http://www.artcyclopedia.com/artists/pollock_jackson.html
[27 September 2002]

Metropolitan Museum of Art, New York. *Metropolitan Museum of Art: The Collection: Modern Art: Autumn Rhythm (Number 30), 1950: Jackson Pollock.*
■ http://metmuseum.org/collections/view1.asp?dep=21&full=0&item=57%2E92
[27 September 2002]
Image of the painting *Autumn Rhythm* (1950).

Pioch, Nicolas. *WebMuseum, Paris: Lavender Mist: Number 1, 1950: Action Painting.*
■ http://www.ibiblio.org/wm/paint/auth/pollock/lavender-mist/
[27 September 2002]

Pioch, Nicolas. *WebMuseum, Paris: Pollock, Jackson.*
■ http://www.ibiblio.org/wm/paint/auth/pollock
[27 September 2002]
Biography and images.

Bridget Riley

About.com. *Art History 101 with Andrea Mulder-Slater: Op Art 1960s.*
■ http://arthistory.about.com/library/bl101_opart.htm
[27 September 2002]

Artcyclopedia. *Bridget Riley.*
■ http://www.artcyclopedia.com/artists/riley_bridget.html
[27 September 2002]
Directory of links to information and image galleries.

Har'El, Nadav. *Bridget Riley's optical art (Op Art).*
■ http://harel.org.il/nadav/Bridget_Riley/
[27 September 2002]
Image gallery.

Andy Warhol

Andy Warhol Museum, Pittsburgh, PA. *The Warhol.*
- http://www.warhol.org/
  [27 September 2002]
  Information and resources.

Artcyclopedia. *Andy Warhol.*
- http://www.artcyclopedia.com/artists/warhol_andy.html
  [27 September 2002]
  Directory of links and image galleries.

PBS. *American Masters: Andy Warhol.*
- http://www.pbs.org/wnet/americanmasters/database/warhol_a.html
  [27 September 2002]
  Biography.

Pioch, Nicolas. *WebMuseum, Paris: Pop Art.*
- http://www.ibiblio.org/wm/paint/tl/20th/pop-art.html
  [27 September 2002]

Robert Rauschenberg

Artcyclopedia. *Robert Rauschenberg.*
- http://www.artcyclopedia.com/artists/rauschenberg_robert.html
  [27 September 2002]

Oxford Dictionary of Art (1997). From *Xrefer, The Web's Reference Engine: Assemblage.*
- http://xrefer.com/entry.jsp?xrefid=142795&secid=
  [27 September 2002]

Smithsonian Institution. *Smithsonian American Art Museum: Collections: Robert Rauschenberg: Reservoir.*
- http://nmaa-ryder.si.edu/cgi-bin/search/isearch.pl?DB=pcdb&FPASS=N&FORMAT=one&FHIT=22&ESET=RECORD&QUERY=creator@id/004064
  [13 October 2002]
  Image of *Reservoir* (1961).

Laurie Anderson

Anderson, Laurie. *LaurieAnderson.com.*
- http://www.laurieanderson.com/
  [27 September 2002]

Cindy Sherman

Artcyclopedia. *Cindy Sherman.*
- http://www.artcyclopedia.com/artists/sherman_cindy.html
  [27 September 2002]
  Directory of links to information and image galleries.

Maya Lin

International Alliance for Women In Music. Abilene Christian University, Abilene, TX. *Women's Early Music, Art, Poetry. Maya Lin: Ancient and Modern.*
- http://womensearlyart.net/lin/lin.html
  [27 September 2002]
  Directory of resources to information and images.

Artcyclopedia. *Maya Lin.*
- http://www.artcyclopedia.com/artists/lin_maya.html
  [30 July 2002]
  Directory of links to information and image galleries.

Yale Bulletin & Calendar (June 7, 2002, Volume 30, Number 31). *Renowned architect Maya Lin elected to Yale Corporation.*
- http://www.yale.edu/opa/v30.n31/story3.html
  [27 September 2002]

CHAPTER 24

Women Artists of the Twentieth Century

*Käthe Kollwitz (1867–1945), Frida Kahlo (1907–1954),
Georgia O'Keeffe (1887–1986), Judy Chicago (1939–   ),
Betye Saar (1926–   ), Jenny Holzer (1950–   )*

KÄTHE KOLLWITZ
(1867–1945)

Web Addresses

MyStudios. *Women in Art: Käthe Kollwitz.*
http://mystudios.com/women/klmno/kollwitz.html
[28 September 2002]
Biography and image gallery.

National Museum of Women in the Arts, Washington, DC. *National Museum of Women
in the Arts: Collection: Käthe Kollwitz: Artist Profile.*
http://www.nmwa.org/collection/profile.asp?LinkID=511
Collection: Käthe Kollwitz: Artist Portfolio.
http://www.nmwa.org/collection/portfolio.asp?LinkID=511
[28 September 2002]
Biography.

Spartacus Educational. *Education on the Internet & Teaching History Online: Käthe
Kollwitz.*
http://www.spartacus.schoolnet.co.uk/ARTkollwitz.htm
[28 September 2002]
Biography and images.

Vallen, Mark. *Art for A Change: Käthe Kollwitz.*
http://www.art-for-a-change.com/Express/ex8.htm
[28 September 2002]
Biography.

FRIDA KAHLO
(1907–1954)

Web Addresses

Artcyclopedia. *Frida Kahlo.*
http://www.artcyclopedia.com/artists/kahlo_frida.html
[28 September 2002]
Directory of links to information and image galleries.

Buch, Fred. *Frida Kahlo.*
http://www.fbuch.com/fridakahlo.htm
[28 September 2002]
Biography and image gallery of self-portraits.

Falini, Daniela. *Frida Kahlo: Contemporary Thoughts.*
http://www.fridakahlo.it/
[28 September 2002]
Comprehensive web site about Frida Kahlo.

Harden, Mark. *Artchive: Frida Kahlo.*
http://www.artchive.com/artchive/ftptoc/kahlo_ext.html
[28 September 2002]
Text from Edward Lucie-Smith's "Lives of the Great Twentieth-Century Artists" and image gallery.

National Museum of Women in the Arts, Washington, DC. *National Museum of Women in the Arts: Collection: Frida Kahlo: Artist Profile.*
http://www.nmwa.org/collection/profile.asp?LinkID=471
Collection: Frida Kahlo: Artist Portfolio.
http://www.nmwa.org/collection/portfolio.asp?LinkID=471
[28 September 2002]
Biography.

PhotoAssist, Inc. *Masters of Photography: Manuel Alvarez Bravo: Frida Kahlo in Manuel Alvarez Bravo's Studio 1930s.*
http://www.masters-of-photography.com/A/alvarez_bravo/alvarez_bravo_frida_kahlo_full.html
[28 September 2002]
Photograph of Frida Kahlo by Manuel Alvarez Bravo (circa 1930).

GEORGIA O'KEEFFE
(1887–1986)

Web Addresses

Artcyclopedia. *Georgia O'Keeffe.*
http://www.artcyclopedia.com/artists/okeeffe_georgia.html
[28 September 2002]
Directory of links to information and image galleries.

Ellen's Place. *Georgia O'Keeffe.*
http://ellensplace.net/okeeffe1.html
[28 September 2002]
Images and biography of Georgia O'Keeffe.

Georgia O'Keeffe Museum, Santa Fe, NM. *Georgia O'Keeffe Museum Home Page.*
http://www.okeeffemuseum.org/indexflash.html
[28 September 2002]
Home page of the Georgia O'Keeffe Museum; includes a biography and an image gallery.

Gerten-Jackson, Carol. *CGFA: A Virtual Art Museum: O'Keeffe.*
http://sunsite.dk/cgfa/okeeffe/index.html (images)
http://sunsite.dk/cgfa/okeeffe/okeeffe_bio.htm *Georgia O'Keeffe* (biography)
[28 September 2002]
Biography and image gallery.

JUDY CHICAGO
(1939-   )

Web Addresses

Artcyclopedia. *Judy Chicago.*
http://www.artcyclopedia.com/artists/chicago_judy.html
[28 September 2002]
Directory of links to information and image galleries.

Chicago, Judy and Donald Woodman. *Judy Chicago: Through the Flower Home Page.*
http://www.judychicago.com/
[28 September 2002]

Chicago, Judy and Donald Woodman. *Judy Chicago: Through the Flower: Judy Chicago's Biography.*
http://www.judychicago.com/scripts/shopplus.cgi?DN=judychicago.com&CARTID=244189278277&ACTION=add&FILE=biography/bio.html
[28 September 2002]
Biography and links to exhibition projects by Judy Chicago.

Florida State University Museum of Fine Arts, Tallahassee, FL. *Judy Chicago: Trials and Tributes.*
http://www.fsus.fsu.edu/EducationCurriculum/tetac/chicago99/index.html
[28 September 2002]
Resource page.

Malaspina Great Books. *Judy Chicago (1939-): Library of Congress Citations.*
http://www.mala.bc.ca/~mcneil/cit/citlcchicago.htm
[28 September 2002]
A list of books by Judy Chicago.

BETYE SAAR
(1926–   )

Web Addresses

Artcyclopedia. *Betye Saar.*
http://www.artcyclopedia.com/artists/saar_betye.html
[28 September 2002]
Directory of links to information and image galleries.

Elliot Sherman, Ann. *MetroActive (February 8–14, 1996): Soaring Saar.*
http://www.metroactive.com/papers/metro/02.08.96/saar-9606.html
[28 September 2002]
An exhibition review.

Michael Rosenfeld Gallery. *Betye Saar: Personal Icons.*
http://www.bisaar.com/gal/gallery.html
[28 September 2002]
Image gallery.

Michael Rosenfeld Gallery. *Betye Saar Main Page.*
http://www.netropolitan.org/saar/saarmain.html
[16 January 2003]
Resource page about Betye Saar.

Public Art in Los Angeles, University of Southern California. *Betye Saar and Sheila Levrant de Bretteville Biographical Information.*
http://www.usc.edu/isd/archives/la/pubart/Downtown/Broadway/Biddy_Mason/saar_bio.html
[28 September 2002]
Brief biography.

JENNY HOLZER
(1950–   )

Web Addresses

Artcyclopedia. *Jenny Holzer.*
http://www.artcyclopedia.com/artists/holzer_jenny.html
[28 September 2002]
Background information and link to an Internet piece of art.

Leijenaar, Matthijs W. *the-artists.org: Artists: Jenny Holzer.*
http://www.the-artists.org/ArtistView.cfm?id=8A01F62E%2DBBCF%2D11D4%2DA93500D0B7069B40
[13 October 2002]
Directory of links to information and image galleries.

Oxford Paperback Encyclopedia (1998). From *Xrefer, The Web's Reference Engine: Conceptual Art.*
http://xrefer.com/entry.jsp?xrefid=213247&secid=
[28 September 2002]

Solomon R. Guggenheim Museum, New York, NY. *Guggenheim Museum: The Collection: Artists: Jenny Holzer: Biography.*
http://204.168.68.231/site/artist_bio_65.html
[28 September 2002]
Installation piece of *Untitled (Selections from Truisms, Inflammatory Essays, the Living Series, the Survival Series, Under a Rock, Laments, and Child Text),* 1989, extended helical tricolor LED electronic display signboard in two sections, site-specific dimensions.

Solomon R. Guggenheim Museum, New York, NY. *Guggenheim Museum: The Collection: Artists: Jenny Holzer: Untitled (Selections from Truisms, Inflammatory Essays, The Living Series, The Survival Series, Under a Rock, Laments, and Child Text).*
http://204.168.68.231/site/artist_works_65_0.html
[28 September 2002]
Resume of Jenny Holzer.

Thames & Hudson Dictionary of Art and Artists (1994). From *Xrefer, The Web's Reference Engine: Holzer, Jenny (1950).*
http://xrefer.com/entry.jsp?xrefid=651328&secid=
[28 September 2002]
Brief biography.

WOMEN ARTISTS
(In General)

Web Addresses

National Museum of Women in the Arts, Washington, DC. *National Museum of Women in the Arts Home Page.*
http://www.nmwa.org/
[28 September 2002]
Home page of the National Museum of Women in the Arts, Washington, D.C.

Russ, Wendy and Carrie Carolin. *Women Artists in History.*
http://www.wendy.com/women/artists.html
[28 September 2002]
Extensive historical directory of resources.

Sullivan, Mary Ann. Bluffton College, Bluffton, OH. *Digital Imaging Project: Women Architects.*
http://www.bluffton.edu/~sullivanm/women/contents.html
[28 September 2002]
Web site about and for women architects.

University Art Museum, University at Albany, New York. *Crossing the Threshold.*
http://www.albany.edu/museum/wwwmuseum/crossing/crossing.htm
[28 September 2002]
Exhibition of *Crossing the Threshold,* held at the University Art Museum at Albany, SUNY. It celebrates "the strength and resolve of thirty-two women artists, ranging in age from 70 to 95 years, who have persevered throughout the twentieth century and created a visual legacy for the future millennia."

Site Summary

For the first time in history, the twentieth century gave women artists an opportunity to be prolific and gain recognition from their male peers. Certainly women have always participated in the arts, but only a few names have been documented historically. Most of the well-known women artists in the past either were associated with a family of artists or had a relationship with a male artist. Prior to the twentieth century, it was socially unacceptable for a woman to belong to a guild or attend a prestigious art academy. If a woman did attend an art school in the early nineteenth century, they were not allowed to participate in the nude drawing classes.

The turn of the nineteenth century provided a breeding ground for the suffrage movement and the sexual revolution, including within the arts. Never before the twentieth century have so many women artists been publicly acknowledged and appreciated. Feminist art of the 1960s and 1970s helped to create more opportunities for women in different facets of the visual arts. More women began to receive scholarships to art schools and a new network of support groups had emerged. Galleries and museums finally recognized the impact women had on the arts and began to sponsor more of their exhibitions. By the 1980s, many major universities began incorporating women's studies programs and offering courses focusing on women's art.

Women have taken their place as individual artists in art education, arts management, and architecture as curators, museum directors, and authors of theory. Many women have participated in different camps of the arts ranging from traditional crafts to computer-generated images. Their contributions are a reflection of and legacy to culture and society as well as its future in the new millennium. The following questions address only a small fraction of the aesthetic contributions of women artists of the twentieth century.

Discussion Questions and Activities

1. Käthe Kollwitz was not only an artist but also a mother who believed in social justice. Her work depicts the ravages of war and death. Refer to biographies and image galleries at http://www.nmwa.org /collection/profile.asp?LinkID=511, at http://www.nmwa.org/collection/portfolio.asp?LinkID=511, and http://mystudios.com/women/klmno/kollwitz.html. What medium did Kollwitz prefer to work in and why? What kind of formal training did she receive and where? What is the theme of most of her artwork? What academy was she elected to, and what title did she receive? Her personal losses as a result of wars are reflected in her art; describe what happened to her.

2. Frida Kahlo was literally a suffering artist, physically and emotionally. Her paintings are a personal reflection of her life and loves. Some of the most intriguing pieces are her self-portraits. Read the essay *Frida and Her Obsession of Self-Portraits* at http://www.fridakahlo.it/, and view the image gallery at http://www.artchive.com/artchive/ftptoc/kahlo_ext.html. What is unique about Frida's hair, face, and clothes? Do you think she painted herself realistically? Can you identify the paintings that reveal Frida's physical pain? Which paintings show her psychological side and her love for Diego Rivera? Who was Leon Trotsky, and why is he important to Frida's art?

3. Georgia O'Keeffe's image has been immortalized through photographic portraits done by her husband, Alfred Stieglitz. O'Keeffe has immortalized her artistic achievements through her paintings of landscapes and flowers. Read her biography and view an image gallery at http://www.okeeffemuseum.org /indexflash.html and at http://sunsite.dk/cgfa/okeeffe/index.html. Who was the art teacher who had an early influence on O'Keeffe's work? What were the art theories that O'Keeffe applied to her own work? Look at some of her paintings and decide which ones reflect some of these theories. Name them. What kinds of images that reflect the time she lived in New Mexico did she like to paint? What kinds of colors do you see in these paintings? What are some of the abstract qualities of her paintings?

4. Judy Chicago is an artist who pioneered feminist art and, with artist Miriam Schapiro, established the first feminist art program at the California Institute of the Arts in the 1970s. Read her biography at http://www.judychicago.com/scripts/shopplus.cgi?DN=judychicago.com&CARTID=2441892782 77&ACTION=add&FILE=biography/bio.html. Which installation is a symbolic history of women in western civilization? View the installation at http://www.judychicago.com/ and look at some of the details. What kinds of pieces were created for this project? What does each piece symbolize? What is the symbolic meaning of the inscription on the floor?

5. Betye Saar is an African American assemblage artist who was born and raised in Los Angeles. As she watched Simon Rodia's *Watts Towers* being built, she became aware of how discarded items could be used to create art pieces. Read the exhibition review at http://metroactive.com/papers/metro/02.08 .96/saar-9606.html from *MetroActive* and view some of her pieces at http://www.bisaar.com/gal /gallery.html. What kinds of objects did Saar use in her art? Do the items represent something? Did she ever use photographs in her assemblages? Who is Alison Saar? Use a search engine and type in *Watts Towers* and read some of the information from the various web sites. What aspects of the *Watts Towers* inspired Betye Saar?

6. Jenny Holzer is an American conceptual artist. Her work utilizes words and multimedia such as neon lights, moving LED digital signs, theater marquis, and the Internet. View the installation piece from the Guggenheim at http://204.168.68.231/site/artist_works_65_0.html and read the biography at http://www.xrefer.com/entry.jsp?xrefid=651328&secid= from the Xrefer web site. What do you think you see from the image? What phrase is lit up on the moving electronic display board? Would you be uncomfortable reading the message as it swirls around the spiral walls of the Guggenheim? Do you think Holzer designed the message so that you would feel uncomfortable reading it in that particular space? Read the definition of conceptual art from the Xrefer web site at http://xrefer.com /entry.jsp?xrefid=213247&secid= to explain the conceptual meaning of this piece.

Related Internet Sites

Artcyclopedia. *Käthe Kollwitz.*
- http://www.artcyclopedia.com/artists/kollwitz_kathe.html
  [28 September 2002]

Artcyclopedia. *Women Artists.*
- http://www.artcyclopedia.com/artists/women.html
  [5 October 2002]

Bois, Danuta. *Distinguished Women of Past and Present.*
- http://www.distinguishedwomen.com/
  [28 September 2002]
  Directory of historical resources.

Buschen, John. University of Wisconsin, River Falls. *300 Important Women Artists Medieval to Modern.*
- http://www.uwrf.edu/history/women.html
  [28 September 2002]
  A comprehensive image gallery of works by women artists (medieval to modern).

Entitled: Black Women Artists. *Artists Profiles.*
- http://www.entitled-bwartists.com/artistprofiles.html
  [28 September 2002]
  Home page of the "Entitled: Black Women Artists" web site, which is a "network for women visual artists of African descent in the Americas."

Georgia O'Keeffe Museum, Santa Fe, NM. *Georgia O'Keeffe Museum Home Page.*
- http://www.okeeffemuseum.org/indexflash.html
  Georgia O'Keeffe Museum, Santa Fe, NM. *Georgia O'Keeffe Museum: Education and Programs.*
  http://www.okeeffemuseum.org/programs/index.html
  [5 October 2002]

Guerrilla Girls. *Guerrilla Girls Official Web Site.*
- http://www.guerrillagirls.com/
  [1995–2002]
  Home page of Guerrilla Girls, a group of women artists who fight discrimination.

Harden, Mark. *Artchive: Women Artists.*
- http://www.artchive.com/artchive/women.html
  [28 September 2002]
  A short list of women artists and photographers.

Nakazato LaFreniere, Maren. *Hungry Flower Photography, Surrealists, Books.*
- www.hungryflower.com/leonreme.html
  [28 September 2002]
  Directory of resources about Surrealist women of the twentieth century.

National Museum of Women in the Arts, Washington, DC. *National Museum of Women in the Arts Home Page.*
- http://www.nmwa.org/
  National Museum of Women in the Art: Resources for Educators.
  http://www.nmwa.org/resources/edu_workshop.asp
  [28 September 2002]

National Women's Caucus for Art. *National Women's Caucus for Art Home Page.*
- www.nationalwca.com/
  [15 October 2002]

Oxford Dictionary of Art (1997). From *Xrefer, The Web's Reference Engine: Conceptual art.*
- http://xrefer.com/entry.jsp?xrefid=143371&secid=
  [28 September 2002]
  Definition of conceptual art from the *Oxford Dictionary of Art* (1997).

Russ, Wendy and Carrie Carolin. *Women Artists in History.*
- http://www.wendy.com/women/artists.html
  [15 October 2002]

Sullivan, Mary Ann. Bluffton College, Bluffton, OH. *Digital Imaging Project: Catalog of links to Whitney Chadwick's "Women, Art and Society."*
- http://bluffton.edu/womenartists/contents.html
  [28 September 2002]
  Catalog of links to Whitney Chadwick's *Women, Art and Society.*

Varo Registry. *Our Favorite Art Links: Here are some Web sites that focus on the visual arts and women.*
- http://www.varoregistry.com/links.html
  [28 September 2002]
  Directory of resources pertaining to women artists.

Yale-New Haven Teachers Institute, CT. *Women of Color as Artists by Val-Jean Belton.*
- http://www.yale.edu/ynhti/curriculum/units/1996/3/96.03.09.x.html
  [15 October 2002]

CHAPTER 25

Introduction to Diversity

(Art of the Americas; Asian, African, African American Art)

ART OF THE AMERICAS

Images and Web Addresses

Aleut

Hunting Helmet, Aleut from Alaska, painted bentwood, decorated with sea-lion whiskers, glass beads wound with wire, and ivory carvings, nineteenth century A.D., Length: 94 cm., London, England: British Museum.

British Museum, London, England. *The British Museum: Compass: Explore the Collections On-line: Hunting Helmet, Aleut.*
http://www.thebritishmuseum.ac.uk/compass/ixbin/hixclient.exe?%7BUPPER%7D%3Av2_free_text
_tindex=aleut+hunting+helmet&_IXDB_=compass&_IXSPFX_=graphical%2Fsummary%2F&_IXFPFX
_=graphical%2Ffull%2F&_IXNOMATCHES_=graphical%2Fno_matches.html&%24+%28with+v2
_searchable_index%29+sort=.&_IXsearchterm=aleut%2520hunting%2520helmet&_IXspage=search
&submit-button=summary
[14 October 2002]
    Or try the following link and search:

British Museum, London, England. *The British Museum: Compass: Explore the Collections On-line: Search (Do a Quick Search for Hunting helmet Aleut).*
http://www.thebritishmuseum.ac.uk/compass/
[14 October 2002]

Aztec

Mosaic Mask of Tezcatlipoca, Aztec/Mixtec from Mexico, human skull with turquoise and lignite mosaic work, iron pyrite discs for eyes set in rings of shell, fifteenth–sixteenth century A.D., height: 19.5 cm., width: 12.5 cm., London, England: British Museum.

British Museum, London, England. *The British Museum: Compass: Explore the Collections On-line: Mosaic Mask of Tezcatlipoca, Aztec/Mixtec, 15th–16th Century* A.D., *from Mexico.*
http://www.thebritishmuseum.ac.uk/compass/ixbin/hixclient.exe?_IXDB_=compass&_IXFIRST_=1&_IXMAXHITS_=1&_IXSPFX_=graphical/full/&$+with+all_unique_id_index+is+$=OBJ2669&submit-button=summary
[14 October 2002]
    Or try the following link and search:

British Museum, London, England. *The British Museum: Compass: Explore the Collections On-line: Search (Do a Quick Search for Mosaic Mask of Tezcatlipoca).*
http://www.thebritishmuseum.ac.uk/compass/
[14 October 2002]

Maya

Ball-Court Panel, Central American, Mexico or Guatemala, Usumacinta River area, limestone, late eighth century, 25.1 cm. x 43.2 cm., Chicago, IL: Art Institute of Chicago.

Art Institute of Chicago. *Art Institute of Chicago: Collections: African and Amerindian Art: Late Classic Maya Culture: Ball-Court Panel.*
http://www.artic.edu/aic/collections/afr/83pc_panel.html
[14 October 2002]

Mimbres

Ceramic Bowl with Composite Zoomorphic Creature (left), Mimbres from southwestern New Mexico, earthenware, white slip, black mineral paint, A.D. 1000–1200, diameter 7.5", Miami, FL: Lowe Art Museum, University of Miami.

Ceramic Bowl with Rabbits (right), Mimbres from southwestern New Mexico, earthenware, white slip, black mineral paint, A.D. 1000–1200, diameter 6.5", Miami, FL: Lowe Art Museum, University of Miami.

Lowe Art Museum, University of Miami, Miami, FL. *Lowe Art Museum: Collections: Native American Art: Ceramic Bowls, (left) Bowl with Composite Zoomorphic Creature: (right) Bowl with Rabbits.*
http://www.lowemuseum.org/90.0031.html
[14 October 2002]

Navajo

Wearing Blanket, Navajo peoples, Arizona, wool, 1860–1870, 69" x 48" (175.3 cm. x 121.9 cm.), New York: Metropolitan Museum of Art.

Metropolitan Museum of Art, New York. *Metropolitan Museum of Art: The Collection: Antonio Ratti Textile Center: Wearing Blanket, 1860–1870, Navajo Peoples; Arizona.*
http://metmuseum.org/collections/result.asp?collection=entire&Artist=&Title=wearing+blanket&Country=&Date1=&Era1=AD&Date2=&Era2=AD&Keyword=&image.x=10&image.y=3
[14 October 2002]

Olmec

Mask, Olmec culture, Mexico, jadeite with black inclusions, 1150–550 B.C., height: 8½" (21.6 cm.), Boston: Museum of Fine Arts, Boston.

Museum of Fine Arts, Boston. *Museum of Fine Arts, Boston: Guide to the Collection: Native Art of the Americas: Mask, Olmec Culture.*
http://www.mfa.org/handbook/portrait.asp?id=278&s=7
[14 October 2002]

Tsimshian

Bent-Corner Chief's Chest, probably Tsimshian culture Canada (coastal British Columbia), yellow cedar and red cedar with black, red, and blue pigment, circa 1860, 26¾" x 41⅜" x 24¼" (67.7 cm. x 105.1 cm. x 61.8 cm.), Boston: Museum of Fine Arts, Boston.

Museum of Fine Arts, Boston. *Museum of Fine Arts, Boston: Guide to the Collection: Native Art of the Americas: Bent-Corner Chief's Chest.*
http://www.mfa.org/handbook/portrait.asp?id=288&s=7
[14 October 2002]

ASIAN ART

Images and Web Addresses

Chinese Jin (Ch'in) Dynasty

Guanyin, Buddhist China, lacquered wood with painting and gilding, Jin Dynasty twelfth century, Boston: Museum of Fine Arts, Boston.

Museum of Fine Arts, Boston. *Museum of Fine Arts, Boston: Collections: A One-Hour Tour, 14 Highlights: Guanyin.*
http://www.mfa.org/collections/one_hour/14.htm
[14 October 2002]

Chinese Ming Dynasty

Lotus Bowl, China, porcelain with cobalt oxide pigment under transparent glaze, Xuande period and reign mark (1426–1435) of the Ming Dynasty (1368–1644), 4¼" x 8¼" diameter (10.6 cm. x 20.8 cm. diameter), Fort Worth, TX: Kimbell Art Museum.

Kimbell Art Museum, Fort Worth, TX. *Kimbell Art Museum: Collections: Asian Art: Ming Dynasty: Lotus Bowl.*
http://www.kimbellart.org/database/index.cfm?detail=yes&ID=AP%201970.14
[14 October 2002]

Chinese Southern Song Dynasty

Returning Sails off a Distant Shore (from Eight Views of the Xiao and Xiang Rivers) Attributed to Mu Xi, Hunan Province of China, hanging scroll, ink on paper, thirteenth century, height: 32.3 cm., width: 103.6 cm., Kyoto, Japan: Kyoto National Museum.

Kyoto National Museum, Kyoto, Japan. *Kyoto National Museum: The Collection: Masterworks: Painting: Chinese Paintings: Returning Sails off a Distant Shore (from Eight Views of the Xiao and Xiang Rivers), Attributed to Mu Xi.*
http://www.kyohaku.go.jp/meihin/kaiga/chugoku/mh503e.htm
[14 October 2002]

Japanese Edo Period

Netsuke, Japan, wood and ivory, Edo period late eighteenth to early nineteenth centuries, height about 1⅜" (3.4 cm.), Boston: Museum of Fine Arts, Boston.

Museum of Fine Arts, Boston. *Museum of Fine Arts, Boston: Guide to the Collection: Art of Asia: Netsuke.*
http://www.mfa.org/handbook/portrait.asp?id=148.5&s=3
[14 October 2002]

Japanese Kamakura Period

Standing Shaka Buddha by Kaikei (Japanese, active circa 1185–1225), Japan, gilt and lacquered wood, circa 1210 (Kamakura period 1185–1333), 54⅜" x 19¼" x 13½" (138.2 cm. x 48.9cm. x 34.3 cm.), Fort Worth, TX: Kimbell Art Museum.

Kimbell Art Museum, Fort Worth, TX. *Kimbell Art Museum: Collections: Asian Art: Kamakura Period: Kaikei (Japanese, active circa 1185-1225), Standing Shaka Buddha.*
http://www.kimbellart.org/database/index.cfm?detail=yes&ID=AP%201984.01%20a,b,c
[14 October 2002]

Japanese Muromachi Period

Illustrated Fan of Wang Xizhi by Josetsu, Japan, hanging scroll, light color on paper, circa 1403 (Muromachi Period, first half of fifteenth century), proportions: 83.1 cm. x 32.6 cm., Kyoto, Japan: Kyoto National Museum.

Kyoto National Museum, Kyoto, Japan. *Kyoto National Museum: The Collection: Masterworks: Painting: Muromachi Ink Paintings: Illustrated Fan of Wang Xizhi by Josetsu.*
http://www.kyohaku.go.jp/meihin/kaiga/suiboku/mh45e.htm
[14 October 2002]

AFRICAN ART

Images and Web Addresses

Benin (Edo)

Leopard Hip Pendant, Nigeria, Kingdom of Benin, Edo, cast brass with copper inlay, height 9½" (24.1 cm.), Raleigh, NC: North Carolina Museum of Art.

North Carolina Museum of Art Foundation, Raleigh, NC. *North Carolina Museum of Art: Collections: Highlights: African: Nigeria, Kingdom of Benin, Edo, Leopard Hip Pendant.*
http://ncartmuseum.org/collections/highlights/african/nigeria_lrg.shtml
[14 October 2002]

Benin (Edo)

Head of a King, Nigeria, Edo, Benin City, bronze, seventeenth century, 29.9 cm. x 21.6 cm. x 20.4 cm., Cleveland, OH: Cleveland Museum of Art.

Cleveland Museum of Art. *Cleveland Museum of Art: Explore Our Collections: Africa: Head of a King: Africa, Nigeria, Edo, Benin City, Seventeenth Century: Bronze, Measurements: Overall: 29.9 cm. x 21.6 cm. x 20.4 cm., Date: 1600s.*
http://www.clevelandart.org/Explore/departmentWork.asp?level=2&deptgroup=1&recNo=3&display=
[14 October 2002]

Yoruba

Beaded Crown, Nigeria, Yoruba, glass beads and grass cloth, twentieth century, height 20⅜" (51.7 cm.), Raleigh, NC: North Carolina Museum of Art.

North Carolina Museum of Art Foundation, Raleigh, NC. *North Carolina Museum of Art: Collections: Highlights: African: Nigeria, Yoruba, Beaded Crown.*
http://ncartmuseum.org/collections/highlights/african/beaded_lrg.shtml
[14 October 2002]

Yoruba

Door, Yoruba from the Kwara state in western Nigeria, wood, metal fittings, nails, early twentieth century, height 89½" x width 43½" x diameter 1¼", Minneapolis, MN: Minneapolis Institute of Arts.

Minneapolis Institute of Arts, MN. *Minneapolis Institute of Arts: The Collection: Africa, Oceania, and the Americas: Yoruba, Door, Early Twentieth Century, Wood, Metal Fittings, Nails, H.89½ x W.43½ x D.1¼ in.*
http://www.artsmia.org/uia-bin/uia_doc.cgi/query/1?uf=uia_hjbBaV
[14 October 2002]

AFRICAN AMERICAN

Images and Web Addresses

Romare Bearden (1914–1988)

Jazz, hand-colored photo etching, 1979, 22¼" by 30⅛", Lincoln, NE: Sheldon Memorial Art Gallery and Sculpture Garden, University of Nebraska-Lincoln.

Sheldon Memorial Art Gallery and Sculpture Garden, University of Nebraska-Lincoln, Lincoln, NE. *Sheldon Selections II: Nebraska's Ethnic Heritages: Romare Bearden (1914–1988), Jazz.*
http://sheldon.unl.edu/HTML/ARTIST/Bearden_R/SSII.html
[5 October 2002]

Jacob Lawrence (1917–2000)

Free Clinic–Harlem Hospital's Free Clinic Is Crowded with Patients Every Morning and Evening, from the *Harlem Series*, 1943, gouache on paper, 14⅛" x 21¼" (38.1 cm. x 55.2 cm.), Portland, OR: Portland Museum of Art.

Portland Museum of Art, Portland, OR. *Portland Museum of Art: American Collection: Jacob Lawrence (1917–2000): Free Clinic–Harlem Hospital's Free Clinic Is Crowded with Patients Every Morning and Evening, from the Harlem Series.*
http://www.pam.org/museum%20plaza/collections/listing/american/catalog/1943.9.4.html
[14 October 2002]

Horace Pippin (1888–1946)

Zachariah, oil on canvas, 1943, 11" x 14" (2 7.94 cm. x 35.56 cm.), Youngstown, OH: Butler Institute of American Art.

Butler Institute of American Art, Youngstown, OH. *Butler Institute of American Art: America's Museum: The Butler Youngstown: Horace Pippin 1888–1946, Zachariah.*
http://www.butlerart.com/pc_book/pages/horace_pippin_1888.htm
[14 October 2002]

Site Summary

The artworks of different cultures, past and present, offer a variety of perspectives on life and societies. Cultural respect broadens our perspective about the world around us. We may not fully understand different traditions, politics, religions, and ethnicity, but learning to respect and appreciate diversity enhances personal growth. Iconography, imagery, and design basics enable us to view the artworks of different cultures aesthetically. The following questions deal with societies of the past and present.

Discussion Questions and Activities

1. View the image of the Olmec mask at http://www.mfa.org/handbook/portrait.asp?id=278&s=7 and compare it to the Aztec *Mosaic Mask of Tezcatlipoca* at http://www.thebritishmuseum.ac.uk/compass /ixbin/hixclient.exe?_IXDB_=compass&_IXFIRST_=1&_IXMAXHITS_=1&_IXSPFX_=graphical /full/&$+with+all_unique_id_index+is+$=OBJ2669&submit-button=summary. What country do both of these masks come from? When was each piece created? Who were the Olmecs? What is the Olmec mask made of, and what is special about this material? What was the purpose of the Olmec mask? Describe its features. What is the Aztec mask made of? What special feature of this mask is different from the Olmec mask? Who does the Aztec mask represent?

2. The Mayans lived in various regions of Central America. The culture still exists today in Belize and areas of Mexico. Its ancient traditions date as far back as the eighth century. View the *Ball-Court Panel* at http://www.artic.edu/aic/collections/afr/83pc_panel.html. What is this panel made of? What type of scene does it depict? Describe the positions of the figures in the composition. Is this a ritual piece? What is the writing on the panel called? Where do you think this panel came from?

3. Native American art reveals long-standing traditions in the techniques of ceramics, painting, sculpture, weaving, drawing, beadwork, and so on. View the Mimbres *Ceramic Bowl*s at http://www.lowemuseum .org/90.0031.html and the Navajo *Wearing Blanket* at http://metmuseum.org/collections/result.asp ?collection=entire&Artist=&Title=wearing+blanket&Country=&Date1=&Era1=AD&Date2= &Era2=AD&Keyword=&image.x=10&image.y=3. Where and when did the Mimbres culture live? What type of pottery did they create? Describe the designs of both bowls. What do the creatures represent? What was the function of these bowls? Why are some bowls cracked in the center? What is the Navajo *Wearing Blanket* made of? What is special about this material? What were the Navajos known for? Describe the design and color of the *Wearing Blanket*. Does the blanket's design indicate where it might have been made?

4. North American Indians include those who live in Alaska and in British Columbia, Canada. View the images of the Aleut *Hunting Helmet* at http://www.thebritishmuseum.ac.uk/compass/ixbin/hixclient .exe?%7BUPPER%7D%3Av2_free_text_tindex=aleut+hunting+helmet&_IXDB_=compass&_IXSPFX _=graphical%2Fsummary%2F&_IXFPFX_=graphical%2Ffull%2F&_IXNOMATCHES_=graphical %2Fno_matches.html&%24+%28with+v2_searchable_index%29+sort=.&_IXsearchterm=aleut %2520hunting%2520helmet&_IXspage=search&submit-button=summary and the Tsimshian *Bent-Corner Chief's Chest* at http://www.mfa.org/handbook/portrait.asp?id=288&s=7. What is the helmet made of? Who wore the helmets? What was the significance of the materials used to make the helmet? Describe the design on the Tsimshian *Bent-Corner Chief's Chest*. Do you see any special features? What is special about the construction of this chest? What was the chest used for? Do you find that many of these pieces were created for or used in rituals?

5. Eastern Asian philosophy and religions are very different from those of Western cultures. The beauty of the objects created for religious use can be appreciated at any level. Compare the Japanese wood sculpture of the *Standing Shaka Buddha* at http://www.kimbellart.org/database/index.cfm?detail =yes&ID=AP%201984.01%20a,b,c to the Chinese wood sculpture of *Guanyin* at http://www.mfa .org/collections/one_hour/14.htm. What type of religion do both of these sculptures represent? What are the hand gestures of the *Standing Shaka Buddha,* and why are they significant? Where was this piece to be placed? What is a Chinese "Guanyin"? What is a "bodhisattva"? What is the pose of the Guanyin? How is the figure clothed? Compare the drapery of the two figures.

6. Japanese and Chinese scroll painting incorporates calligraphy and scenery. View the Japanese *Illustrated Fan of Wang Xizhi by Josetsu* at http://www.kyohaku.go.jp/meihin/kaiga/suiboku/mh45e.htm and the Chinese *Returning Sails off a Distant Shore Attributed to Mu Xi* at http://www.kyohaku.go.jp/meihin/kaiga/chugoku/mh503e.htm. What element dominates the Japanese scroll? What was the scroll originally used for? Do you consider the calligraphy as part of the composition? How does one view the Japanese scroll compared to the Chinese scroll? What medium is used to paint the Chinese scroll? What brush technique did the artist use? How did the artist create depth in the landscape?

7. Objects of beauty are status symbols in any culture. View the Japanese *Netsuke* figurines at http://www.mfa.org/handbook/portrait.asp?id=148.5&s=3 and the Chinese Ming Dynasty *Lotus Bowl* at http://www.kimbellart.org/database/index.cfm?detail=yes&ID=AP%201970.14. What are *Netsuke* figurines, and who used them? What are *Netsuke* usually made of? What were the popular subjects? What eventually happened to the netsuke after Western dress was introduced? What is a significant characteristic of Ming porcelain? What does the exterior decoration look like compared to the interior design? How does the artist render a lotus flower on the Chinese bowl?

8. The African culture of the Yoruba often depicts the royal figure of the oba (ruler) and creates ritual items. Look at the images of the *Beaded Crown* at http://ncartmuseum.org/collections/highlights/african/beaded_lrg.shtml and the *Door* at http://www.artsmia.org/uia-bin/uia_doc.cgi/query/1?uf=uia_hjbBaV. What does the oba rule over? When does the oba wear the beaded crown? What is the shape of this beaded crown? Why is this shape important in Yoruba culture? Why are there faces on the crown? What is the significance of the patterns? Where does the oba live? What is the design of the carved wood door? What do the crossed hands of the figures represent? Where are the crocodile designs on the door, and what do they signify?

9. The royal art of the Benin reinforces the idea of glorifying the oba. View the *Leopard Hip Pendant* at http://ncartmuseum.org/collections/highlights/african/nigeria_lrg.shtml and the *Head of a King* at http://www.clevelandart.org/Explore/departmentWork.asp?level=2&deptgroup=1&recNo=3&display=. What is the *Leopard Hip Pendant* made of? Who wears these ornaments? What is the function of a hip pendant? What is unusual about its features? How does the artist represent the leopard's spots on the hip pendant? What does the leopard symbolize in Benin culture? What technique created the *Head of a King*? How do you know that this piece represents royalty? Where is this particular piece supposed to be placed, and what is its function?

10. African American art encompasses a variety of traditions and innovations. Color, pattern, technique, medium, and subject matter might reflect African customs or address contemporary issues. View the *Free Clinic–Harlem Hospital's Free Clinic Is Crowded with Patients Every Morning and Evening* (from the *Harlem Series*) by Jacob Lawrence at http://www.pam.org/museum%20plaza/collections/listing/american/catalog/1943.9.4.html and Horace Pippin's painting of *Zachariah* at http://www.butlerart.com/pc_book/pages/horace_pippin_1888.htm. How are the figures depicted in both compositions? Where does the viewer stand to observe the scene at the *Free Clinic*? What is this series about, especially to the artist? By painting in a series, do you think the artist has a story to tell? What does the painting of *Zachariah* depict? What can we learn from such a theme?

11. Romare Bearden loved jazz music and art. Look at his photo etching of *Jazz* at http://sheldon.unl.edu/HTML/ARTIST/Bearden_R/SSII.html. What are the figures doing in the scene? What is the relationship that Bearden created between jazz music and painting? How does he use space in his compositions? Describe how color is represented.

Related Internet Sites

British Museum, London, England. *The British Museum: Illuminating World Cultures.*
- http://www.thebritishmuseum.ac.uk/
  [15 October 2002]

Exploring Ancient World Cultures. University of Evansville, Evansville, IN. *Exploring Ancient World Cultures: An Introduction to Ancient World Cultures on the World Wide Web.*
- http://eawc.evansville.edu/
  [5 October 2002]

Graffiti Art

@149st. *@149st New York City Cyber Bench.*
- http://www.at149st.com/women.html
  [15 October 2002]

B-Boys.com. *International Graffiti Gallery.*
- http://www.b-boys.com/graffitigallery.html
  [15 October 2002]

Farrell, Susan and Art Crimes. *Art Crimes: The Writing on the Wall.*
- http://www.graffiti.org/
  [15 October 2002]
  A web site that covers different types of graffiti from all over the world. It lists various shows and events.

Pacific News Service. *Jinn: Movements of the Dispossessed: Why Graffiti Artists Aim to Keep the City Seedy by A. Clay Thompson.*
- http://www.pacificnews.org/jinn/stories/3.24/971125-graffiti.html
  [15 October 2002]
  Thompson, A. Clay. 11-25-97. Pacific News Service.

UC Berkeley Academic Talent Development Program of the University of California at Berkeley and the Regents of the University of California. *Graffiti: Art and Crime by Daniel Oliver Tucker: History, Introduction.*
- http://www-atdp.berkeley.edu/Studentpages/cflores/historygraffiti.html
  [15 October 2002]
  Brief history of graffiti.

Hispanic Art

Artasma. *Artasma.com! Welcome to Artasma.com: The Premier Virtual Latin American Art Gallery.*
- http://www.artasma.com/index.htm
  [15 October 2002]

California Ethnic and Multicultural Archives, University Library, University of California, Santa Barbara, CA. *California Ethnic and Multicultural Archives: Chicano Art: A Resource Guide.*
- http://cemaweb.library.ucsb.edu/chicanoArt.html
  [15 October 2002]
  "Chicano Art: A Resource Guide" includes background information, a bibliography, teachers' kits, and additional resources.

El Museo del Barrio, New York, NY. *El Museo del Barrio Home Page.*
- http://www.elmuseo.org/
  El Museo del Barrio, New York, NY. *El Museo del Barrio: Educational Programs.*
  http://www.elmuseo.org/edu.html
  [15 October 2002]

The Mexican Museum, San Francisco, CA. *The Mexican Museum: Collection.*
- http://www.mexicanmuseum.org/collection/collection.asp?key=233&language=english
  [15 October 2002]

Museum of Spanish Colonial Arts, Santa Fe, NM. *Museum of Spanish Colonial Art Home Page.*
- http://www.spanishcolonial.org/
  Museum of Spanish Colonial Arts, Santa Fe, NM. *Museum of Spanish Colonial Art: Education Programs of the Museum of Spanish Colonial Art.*
  http://www.spanishcolonial.org/schedule.shtml
  [15 October 2002]

Rice University Art Gallery, Houston, TX. *The Shame Man and El Mexican't Meet the CyberVato Performed by Guillermo Gómez-Peña, James Luna, and Roberto Sifuentes.*
- http://www.rice.edu/projects/CyberVato/cybervato-new.html
  [15 October 2002]
  "CyberVato" is a performance artist who challenges stereotypes of Mexicans and Native Americans. Along with his two friends, "The Shame Man" and "El Mexican't," he makes people see the biases they have against Mexicans with humor and cutting wit. The site provides thought-provoking quizzes throughout.

African and African American Art

African Art Museum. *African Art Museum: On-line reference to the artistic styles of Africa Curated by Dr. Ilya Raskin and Yuri Raskin.*
- http://www.zyama.com/
  [15 October 2002]

Art Institute of Chicago. *Art Institute of Chicago: Student and Teacher Programs: ArtAccess: African American Art.*
- http://www.artic.edu/artaccess/AA_AfAm/index.html
  [15 October 2002]

Artcyclopedia. *Artists by Nationality: African-American Artists.*
- http://www.artcyclopedia.com/nationalities/African-American.html
  [15 October 2002]

B. Davis Schwartz Memorial Library, Long Island University. *African American Art on the Internet.*
- http://www.brooklyn.liunet.edu/cwis/cwp/library/aavawww.htm
  [15 October 2002]

British Museum, London, England. *The British Museum: Compass: Illuminating World Cultures: Africa.*
- http://www.thebritishmuseum.ac.uk/world/africa/africa.html
  [15 October 2002]

Butler Institute of American Art, Youngstown, OH. *Butler Institute of American Art: America's Museum: The Butler Youngstown: Masters of African American Art: Selections from the Permanent Collection.*
- http://www.butlerart.com/Web_Shows/Black_Artist/artists.htm
  [14 October 2002]

Emory University, Atlanta, GA. *Michael C. Carlos Museum of Emory University: Permanent Collection: Sub-Saharan African Art.*
- http://carlos.emory.edu/COLLECTION/AFRICA/
  [15 October 2002]
  Directory of links to major resources for African American art on the Internet.

National Gallery of Art, Washington, D.C. *National Gallery of Art: Tour: Selected African American Artists at the National Gallery of Art.*
- http://www.nga.gov/collection/gallery/ggafamer/ggafamer-main1.html
  [15 October 2002]

Rector and Visitors of the University of Virginia, Charlottesville, VA. *African Art: Aesthetics and Meaning: An Electronic Exhibition Catalog by Benjamin C. Ray.*
- http://www.lib.virginia.edu/clemons/RMC/exhib/93.ray.aa/African.html
  [15 October 2002]

Smithsonian Institution. *National Museum of African Art Home Page.*
- http://www.nmafa.si.edu/
  Smithsonian Institution. *National Museum of African Art: Education Programs.*
  http://www.nmafa.si.edu/educ/educprog.htm
  [15 October 2002]

Solomon R. Guggenheim Museum, New York, NY. *Africa: The Art of a Continent.*
- http://artnetweb.com/guggenheim/africa/
  [15 October 2002]

Gay and Lesbian Art

Keith Haring Foundation. *Haring Kids.*
- http://www.haringkids.com/index.html
  Keith Haring Foundation. *Haring Kids: Lesson Plans for Parents, Teachers, Institutions.*
  http://www.haringkids.com/lessons/envs/live/htdocs/
  [15 October 2002]

Queer Arts Resource. *Queer Arts Resource: QUR Is Opening Minds Online. Museum and Gallery Links.*
- http://www.queer-arts.org/links/links_museums.html
  [15 October 2002]

Yerba Buena Center for the Arts, San Francisco, CA. *Yerba Buena Center for the Arts: Education and Community Programs.*
- http://www.yerbabuenaarts.org/education/index.htm
  [15 October 2002]

Asian and Asian American Art

Asian American Women Artists Association. *Asian American Women Artists Association Home Page.*
■ http://www.aawaaart.com/
[15 October 2002]

Cleveland Museum of Art. *Cleveland Museum of Art: Explore Our Collections: Asian Art.*
■ http://www.clevelandart.org/Explore/department.asp?level=1&deptgroup=4
[15 October 2002]

Kimbell Art Museum, Fort Worth, TX. *Kimbell Art Museum: Collections: Asian Art.*
■ http://www.kimbellart.org/database/index.cfm?region=yes&mainregion=3
[14 October 2002]

Kyoto National Museum, Kyoto, Japan. *Kyoto National Museum (in English).*
■ http://www.kyohaku.go.jp/indexe.htm
[5 October 2002]

Museum of Fine Arts, Boston. *Museum of Fine Arts, Boston: Guide to the Collection: Art of Asia.*
■ http://www.mfa.org/handbook/section.asp?s=3&p=1
[14 October 2002]

Smithsonian Institution. *Archives of American Art Museum: Preliminary Guide to Resources on Asian Pacific American Artists at the Archives of American Art.*
■ http://artarchives.si.edu/guides/asianam/asianam.htm
[15 October 2002]

Witcombe, Chris. *Art History Resources on the Web: Asian Art.*
■ http://witcombe.sbc.edu/ARTHLinks3.html#general
[15 October 2002]

Bibliography

Alexander, Mary S. The Art of Teaching Students to Think Critically. *The Chronicle of Higher Education* (6 August 1999): B9.

American Library Association. Filters and Filtering. [Online]. http://www.ala.org/alaorg/oif/filtersandfiltering.html [17 November 2001]

Arnheim, Rudolf. *Art and Visual Perception: A Psychology of the Creative Eye.* Berkeley: University of California Press, 1954.

Arts, Education, and Americans Panel. *Coming to Our Senses: The Significance of the Arts for American Education.* New York: McGraw-Hill, 1977.

Association for the Advancement of Arts Education. How the Arts Contribute to Education. [Online]. http://www.aaae.org/artsbro/arts_bro.htm [17 November 2001]

Baca, Murtha, ed. *Introduction to Metadata: Pathways to Digital Information.* Los Angeles: Getty Information Institute, 1998.

Baldwin, Gordon. *Looking at Photographs.* Malibu, CA: J. Paul Getty Museum in association with the British Museum Press, 1991.

Bancroft Library, University of California, Berkeley. California Heritage Collection: K–12 Lessons: Using Primary Sources—Overview. [Online]. http://sunsite.berkeley.edu/calheritage/k12/primary_lesson.htm#what [17 November 2001]

Bassett, Jane. *Looking at European Sculpture.* Los Angeles: J. Paul Getty Museum in association with the Victoria and Albert Museum, 1997.

Berenson, Bernard. *Aesthetics and History.* New York: Pantheon Books, 1948.

Berinstein, Paula. The Big Picture: Turning Visual: Image Search Engines on the Web. (January 1998). [Online]. http://www.onlineinc.com/onlinemag/OL1998/berinstein5.html [26 November 2001]

Besser, Howard. *Introduction to Imaging.* Santa Monica: Getty Art History Information Program, 1995.

Carr, Dawson, W. *Looking at Paintings.* Malibu, CA: J. Paul Getty Museum in association with the British Museum Press, 1992.

Center for Critical Thinking. Foundations for Critical Thinking Home Page. [Online]. http://www.criticalthinking.org [17 November 2001]

Cohen, Davis Harris. *Looking at European Ceramics.* Malibu, CA: J. Paul Getty Museum in association with the British Museum Press, 1993.

Colyer, Anita F. A Copyright Guide for Librarians: A Subject Guide to Copyright Information on the Internet. [Online]. http://slis.cua.edu/ihy/SP/GG.htm [17 November 2001]

Copyright Act of 1976. [Online]. http://www.law.cornell.edu/copyright/copyright.table.html [17 November 2001]

Corwin, Sylvia K., ed. *Exploring the Legends: Guideposts to the Future.* Reston, VA: National Art Education Association, 2001.

Dobbs, Stephen M. *The DBAE Handbook: An Overview of Discipline-Based Art Education.* Santa Monica: J. Paul Getty Trust, 1992.

Dobbs, Stephen M. *Learning in and Through Art: A Guide to Discipline-Based Art Education.* Los Angeles: Getty Education Institute for the Arts, 1998.

Dorn, Charles M. Art as Intelligent Activity. *Arts Education Policy Review* (November/December 1993): 2–9.

Education World. Picture This: Art Every Day, Enrich Learning with Discipline-Based Art Education. [Online]. http://www.education-world.com/a_lesson/lesson002.shtml [17 November 2001]

Edwards, Betty. *Drawing on the Right Side of the Brain: A Course in Enhancing Creativity and Artistic Confidence.* Los Angeles: St. Martin's Press, 1989.

Eisner, Elliot. Curriculum Ideas in a Time of Crisis. *Art Education* 18 (1965): 10.

Elsen, Albert Edward. *Purposes of Art: An Introduction to the History and Appreciation of Art.* New York: Rinehart and Winston, 1971.

Feldman, Edmund Burke. *Varieties of Visual Experience.* New York: Harry N. Abrams, 1992.

Fiedler, Conrad. *On Judging Works of Visual Art.* Berkeley: University of California Press, 1949.

Finn, David. *How to Look at Everything.* New York: Harry N. Abrams, 2000.

Foundation for Critical Thinking Home Page. [Online]. http://www.criticalthinking.org [5 November 2001]

Gage, John. *Color and Meaning: Art, Science, and Symbolism.* Berkeley: University of California Press, 1999.

Gardner, Louise. *Gardner's Art Through the Ages.* New York: Harcourt Brace Jovanovich, 1996.

Getty ArtsEdNet. ArtsEdNet: The Getty Art Education Web Site Home Page. [Online]. http://www.getty.edu/artsednet/ [17 November 2001]

Getty ArtsEdNet. Learning and Teaching for Teachers. [Online]. http://www.getty.edu/visit/learning/teachers.html [17 November 2001]

Getty Center for Education in the Arts. *Beyond Creating: The Place for Art in America's Schools.* Santa Monica: J. Paul Getty Trust, 1985.

Goldman, Paul. *Looking at Prints, Drawings, and Watercolors.* London: British Museum Publications, 1988.

Goldstein, Kurt. Some Experimental Observations Concerning the Influence of Colors on the Function of the Organism. *Occupational Therapy and Rehabilitation* 21 (1942): 147–51.

Google Image Search. [Online]. http://images.google.com/help.faq_images.html [19 November 2001]

Green, Gaye Leigh. Imagery as Ethical Inquiry. *Art Education* (November 2000): 19–24.

Greer, W. Dwaine. *Art as a Basic: The Reformation in Art Education.* Bloomington, IN: Phi Delta Kappa Education Foundation, 1997.

Greer, W. Dwaine. A Structure of Discipline Concepts for DBAE. *Studies in Art Education* 28 (Summer 1987): 227–33.

Grove Dictionary of Art Online. [Online]. http://www.groveart.com/macmillan-owned/art/private.htm [5 November 2001]

Harnack, Andrew. *Online: A Reference Guide to Using Internet Sources.* New York: St. Martin's Press, 2000.

Harris, Robert. *A Guidebook to the Web.* Guilford, CT: Dushkin, McGraw-Hill, 2000.

Hatcher, Colin Gabriel. Internet Content Filtering: Issues Facing Parents, Schools, and Libraries. [Online]. http://www.safetyed.org/help/filtering.html [8 November 2001]

Hock, Randolph. *The Extreme Searcher's Guide to Web Search Engines: A Handbook for the Serious Searcher.* Medford, NJ: CyberAge Books, 1999.

Hoffa, Harlan. *Revisitations: Ten Little Pieces on Art Education.* Reston, VA: National Art Education Association, 1994.

Horowitz, Frederick A. *More than You See: A Guide to Art.* San Diego: Harcourt Brace Jovanovich, 1992.

Houghton, Barbara. *The Internet and Art: A Guidebook for Artists.* Upper Saddle River, NJ: Prentice-Hall, 2002.

Improving Visual Arts Education: Final Report on the Los Angeles Getty Institute for Education on the Visual Arts. Santa Monica: J. Paul Getty Trust, 1993.

Janson, H. W. *History of Art for Young People.* New York: Harry N. Abrams, 1997.

Jones, Lois Swan. *Art Information and the Internet: How to Find It, How to Use It.* Phoenix: Oryx Press, 1999.

Jones, Lois Swan. *Art Information: Research Methods and Resources.* Dubuque: Kéndall/Hunt Publishing Co., 1990.

Joseph, Linda C. *Net Curriculum: An Educator's Guide to Using the Internet.* Medford, NJ: CyberAge Books, 1999.

Junion-Metz, Gail. The Art of Evaluation. *School Library Journal* (May 1998): 57.

Kennedy Center. ArtsEdge Curriculum WebLinks Visual Arts. [Online]. http://artsedge.kennedy-center.org/teaching _materials/weblinks/weblinks.cfm?subject_id=VIA [17 November 2001]

Kennedy Center. ArtsEdge Home Page. [Online]. Washington, DC: Kennedy Center. http://artsedge.kennedy-center .org/ [15 November 2001]

Kennedy Center. ArtsEdge: Standards and Exemplars: National Standards for Arts Education. [Online]. http://artsedge .kennedy-center.org/professional_resources/standards/nat_standards_main.html [17 November 2001]

Kirk, Elizabeth. Evaluating Information Found on the Internet. [Online]. (1996). http://milton.mse.jhu.edu:8001/research /education/net.html [29 November 2001]

Kranz, Cindy. Filtering Software Varies: Here's 4 of the Best. [Online]. http://enquirer.com/editions/1999/11/04/loc _filtering_software.html [17 November 2001]

Krebs, Brian. Web Filters at Schools, Libraries by July 2002-FCC. [Online]. (6 April 2001). http://www.newsbytes.com /news/01/j164204.html [17 November 2001]

Learning Page of the Library of Congress. Using Primary Sources in the Classroom. [Online]. http://memory.loc.gov /ammem/ndlpedu/lessons/primary.html [8 November 2001]

Leshnoff, Susan K. Art, Ambiguity, and Critical Thinking. *Art Education* (September 1995): 51–56.

Liu, Jian. Guide to Meta-Search Engines. [Online]. (June 1999). http://www.indiana.edu/~librcsd/search/meta.html [24 November 2001]

Longview Community College. Critical Thinking Across the Curriculum Project: Are You Thinking Yet? [Online]. http://www.kcmetro.cc.mo.us/longview/ctac/toc.htm [17 November 2001]

Metropolitan Museum of Art. Timeline of Art History. [Online]. http://www.metmuseum.org/toah/splash.htm [20 November 2001]

Michael, J. A. *The Lowenfeld Lectures.* University Park: Pennsylvania State University Press, 1982.

Morton, J. L. Color Matters. [Online]. http://www.colormatters.com/bio.html [20 November 2001]

National Art Education Association. *The Essentials of a Quality School Art Program.* Washington, DC: The Association, 1968.

National Art Education Association. NAEA Home Page. [Online]. http://www.naea-reston.org/ [17 November 2001]

National Association of Secondary Principals. *Art Education in the Secondary School.* Washington, DC: The Association, 1961.

National Endowment for the Arts. *Towards Civilization: A Report on Arts Education.* Washington, DC: Government Printing Office, 1988.

National PTA. Arts in Education Resource Libraries. [Online]. http://www.pta.org/programs/arts/keeping/artdaily.htm [17 November 2001]

National School Boards Association. *The Arts in Education.* Washington, DC: National School Boards Association, 1978.

North Carolina Public Schools. Arts Education Curriculum: Visual Arts. [Online]. http://www.ncpublicschools.org /curriculum/ArtsEd/visual.htm [17 November 2001]

O'Harrow Jr., Robert. Curbs on Web Access Face Attack: Content Filters for Children Also Restrict Adults, Groups Say. *Washington Post* (20 March 2001): A4.

Olson, Ivan. *The Arts and Critical Thinking in American Education.* Westport, CT: Greenwood, 2000.

Olson, Ivan. The Arts and Educational Reform: More Critical Thinking in the Classroom of the Future. *Journal of Aesthetic Education* (Fall 1997): 107–17.

Olson, Ivan. The Arts, Critical Thinking, and Reform: Classrooms of the Future. [Online]. http://horizon.unc.edu /projects/HSJ/Olson.asp [17 November 2001]

Parks, Michael E. *The Art Teacher's Desktop Reference.* Englewood Cliffs, NJ: Prentice-Hall, 1994.

Perspectives on Education Reform: Arts Education as Catalyst. Santa Monica: Getty Center for Education in the Arts, 1993.

Raish, Martin, ed. *Key Guide to Electronic Resources: Art and Art History.* Medford, NJ: Information Today, 1996.

Read, Herbert. *Education Through Art.* New York: Pantheon Books, 1945.

Read, Herbert. *The Meaning of Art.* London: Penguin Books, 1949.

Roukes, Nicholas. *Art Synthetics.* Worchester, MA: Davis Publications, 1982.

Sargent, Walter. *The Enjoyment and Use of Color.* New York: Dover Publications, 1964.

Shipps, Stephen W. About Thinking, About Art. *Journal of Aesthetic Education* (Spring 1996): 73–83.

Slatkin, Wendy. *Women Artists in History: From Antiquity to the Present.* Upper Saddle River, NJ: Prentice-Hall, 2001.

Stout, Candace Jesse. The Dialogue Journal: A Forum for Critical Consideration. *Studies in Art Education* (Fall 1993): 34–44.

Stout, Candace Jesse. Multicultural Reasoning and the Appreciation of Art. *Studies in Art Education* (Winter 1997): 96–111.

Taylor, Joshua C. *Learning to Look: A Handbook for the Visual Arts.* Chicago: University of Chicago Press, 1981.

Trochim, William. Evaluating Web Sites. [Online]. (1996). http://trochim.human.cornell.edu/webeval/webintro /webintro.htm [20 November 2001]

Turner, Jane, ed. *Grove Dictionary of Art*. New York: Grove's Dictionaries, 1996.

United States. President Bill Clinton. *Proposed Legislation: Goals 2000: Educate America Act: Message from the President of the United States*. Washington, DC: Government Printing Office, 1993.

University of California, Berkeley. Library Research Using Primary Sources. [Online]. (2001). http://www.lib.berkeley.edu/TeachingLib/Guides/PrimarySources.html [20 November 2001]

University of California, Berkeley. Library Research Using Primary Sources. [Online]. (2001). http://www.lib.berkeley.edu/TeachingLib/Guides/PrimarySourcesOnTheWeb.html [20 November 2001]

University of California, Los Angeles. Hoax? Scholarly Research? Personal Opinion? You Decide! [Online]. (1996). http://www.library.ucla.edu/libraries/college/help/hoax/ [20 November 2001]

University of California, Los Angeles. Thinking Critically About World Wide Web Resources. [Online]. (June 1995). http://www.library.ucla.edu/libraries/college/help/critical/index.htm [20 November 2001]

University of California, Santa Barbara. How Do I Know What's Good on the Web? [Online]. (April 2001). http://www.library.ucsb.edu/libinst/lib101/webfaq08.html [20 November 2001]

University of Connecticut History Online. How to Use Primary Sources. [Online]. http://lib.uconn.eduj/cho/classrm_primsource.html [5 November 2001]

University of Idaho. Repositories of Primary Sources. [Online]. http://www.uidaho.edu/special-collections/Other.Repositiories.html [5 November 2001]

Walker, Sydney R. Thinking Strategies for Interpreting Artworks. *Studies in Art Education* (Winter 1996): 80–91.

White, David A. Critical Thinking and Artistic Creation. *Journal of Aesthetic Education* (Summer 2001): 77–85.

Willard, Christopher. A Dystopia of Color Education in a Utopia of Color Experience. [Online]. (1998). http://www.colormatters.com/willard.html [17 November 2001]

Yale University Library. Visual Materials as Primary Sources. [Online]. http://www.library.yale.edu/ref/err/vismats.htm [5 November 2001]

Yale University Library. Yale University Library Primary Sources Research. [Online]. http://www.library.yale.edu/ref/err/primsrcs.htm [5 November 2001]

Zelanski, Paul, and Mary Pat Fisher. *The Art of Seeing*. Englewood Cliffs, NJ: Prentice-Hall, 1991.

Index